Pragmatism and Religion

Pragmatism and Religion

Classical Sources and Original Essays

EDITED BY

STUART ROSENBAUM

University of Illinois

URBANA AND CHICAGO

Publication of this book was supported
by a grant from Baylor University.
© 2003 by the Board of Trustees
of the University of Illinois
All rights reserved
Manufactured in the United States of America
1 2 3 4 5 C P 5 4 3 2 1

Library of Congress Cataloging-in-Publication Data
Pragmatism and religion : classical sources and original essays /
edited by Stuart Rosenbaum.
p.   cm.
Includes bibliographical references and index.
ISBN 0-252-02838-4 (cloth : alk. paper)
ISBN 0-252-07122-0 (pbk. : alk. paper)
1. Philosophy and religion. 2. Pragmatism. I. Rosenbaum, Stuart E.
BL51.P725   2003
291.1'75—dc21   2002015350

Contents

Introduction

STUART ROSENBAUM

Pragmatism is once again a growing influence in American intellectual life. Why this is so is a matter of speculation, although there is no shortage of reputable work on American cultural and intellectual history both endorsing the renewal and suggesting plausible explanations for it. The general intellectual effort recently invested in the American pragmatic tradition has manifested itself in works by philosophers such as Hilary Putnam, Richard Rorty, John E. Smith, and Richard Bernstein; by historians such as Robert Westbrook, David Hollinger, and Bruce Kuklick; and by theologians such as William Dean and Robert C. Neville.

This renewal is not without its critics, however, and many intellectuals continue to see the American pragmatic tradition as mired in unproductive commitments to relativism, skepticism, scientism, or extreme individualism. For these critics, pragmatism seems in effect, if not in intent, an intellectual invitation to cultural disorder. These individuals range across a continuum with respect to their attitudes toward American pragmatism, from those, such as Alasdair MacIntyre, who do not engage the classical American pragmatists and appear indifferent to their thought to those, such as Greg Bahnsen, who are overtly inimical. Bahnsen, for example, says that "Dewey's pragmatism . . . is unclear, circular, subject to self-delusion, shortsighted, self-defeating . . . and incoherently dialectical."[1] Another critic of pragmatism is R. Albert Mohler, president of the Southern Baptist Seminary; Mohler sees pragmatism, along with postmodernism, as undermining standards of moral behavior and as being exactly the sort of intellectual perspective that must be resisted by all who care about the integrity of family, religion, and country.[2] Each of these thinkers has a relatively distinctive religious perspective: MacIntyre is Catholic, Bahnsen is Reformed, and Mohler is Baptist.

Perhaps it is no accident that these representatives of traditional religious perspectives all reject the American pragmatic tradition. This tradition is, after all, adamant in rejecting prominent traditional philosophical and theological perspectives. Throughout the nineteenth and twentieth centuries, pragmatists have rejected orthodoxies of all kinds, whether of religion, morality, or epistemology. Thus, it is understandable that pragmatists appear deeply heretical when they are viewed from the perspective of any traditional philosophical or theological position.

The heresy in question is not heresy simply about one or another disputed item of doctrine but heresy "wholesale." In epistemology, for example, pragmatists reject not only rationalism but also empiricism, and in metaphysics they reject not only idealism but also realism. In moral theory pragmatists reject not only deontological and utilitarian theories but also virtue ethics theories. In the area of religion, pragmatists reject competing theological perspectives from the Catholic to the Reformed to the Baptist. The heresy of the pragmatists is complete in that it sees the glory of our human situation not in our separateness from nature but in our unity with it. The theme of human unity with nature is a common thread that runs unbroken throughout the American tradition of thought; it runs from Emerson, Thoreau, and Whitman to Dewey, James, and Rorty. This commitment to human unity with nature embodies in embryonic form the many dimensions of pragmatism's heresy.

In their embrace of wholesale heresy, pragmatists join Continental thinkers who, following Nietzsche, also affirm the continuity of humanity with the natural world. To put the general point baldly, pragmatists, existentialists, and postmodernists all conceive humans as animals. Existentialists and postmodernists join pragmatists in rejecting all intellectual traditions that seek to separate humanity from nature. Theology, moral theory, metaphysics, and epistemology, along with other areas of traditional philosophical interest, have borne the burden of rationalizing humanity's uniqueness and separateness from nature. In an extensive critique of these areas of traditional philosophical interest, pragmatists, along with their postmodernist siblings, have turned their backs on the idea that humans are ontologically special in the natural world. For pragmatists, humans have no natural telos, no natural eternal destiny, no special faculty of cognition that when properly exercised enables them to know independent reality, and they have no moral law within. Humans are animals—clever animals to be sure, but animals nonetheless.

To say that humans are animals, however, answers no interesting questions. We humans do have religious communities, we do have moral values, we do know our world, and we do reason either well or poorly. These facts about humans are tied up in myriad and subtle ways with every human enterprise, from educating our children to carrying on political relations with other countries. These facts about humans magnify differences among different human communities. Being pervasive and magnifying differences, these facts thus frequently generate temptations to conquest or to conversation, invitations to love or to hate, and motivations to hope or to fear. Christians must figure out how to interact with Jews and Muslims, Western scientists must figure out how to interact with practitioners of acupuncture, capitalists must figure out how to deal with communists, and Western logicians must figure out how to interact with those who listen to the sound of one hand clapping. For pragmatists who believe that humans are animals, this many-sided task of dealing with others may no longer include the strategy of intellectual conquest by techniques of rational coercion. The idea of such pure rational strategies is a remnant of the traditional philosophy and theology that pragmatists reject.

The institutions of religion, morality, knowledge, and thought, however, inevitably remain significant for humanity. Furthermore, critical questions concerning how to live among these institutions and how to shape them remain to be answered. What may we think about our religious communities, our moral values, and our cognitive and rational abilities? What may we hope about our religious communities, our moral values, and our cognitive and rational abilities? And how may we approach those whose religious, moral, and cognitive values and communities differ from our own? All these questions remain, along with many others of more specific content.

The questions that remain when traditional philosophy succumbs to critique are the questions pragmatists seek to address. They are foremost among what John Dewey called "the problems of men." As the leading pragmatist thinker of the twentieth century, Dewey spent his life seeking to turn intellectuals toward these problems and away from the problems of epistemology and moral theory that had dominated seventeenth- through nineteenth-century thought. Perhaps only now, at the beginning of a new millennium, are intellectuals beginning to be able to hear and heed Dewey's advice.

Just as humans continue to have institutions of knowledge, morality, and reason, they also continue to have institutions of religion. Needless to say, these institutions remain profoundly significant for humanity in spite of, or perhaps especially because of, the pragmatists' conception of humans as animals who are thoroughly part of the natural world. Accordingly, pragmatists face the significant intellectual tasks of constructing accounts of knowledge, morality, reason, and religion that cohere with this understanding of who and what humans are and that retain the vitality of these essential human institutions.

The focal point of this collection is the pragmatists' intellectual task of constructing accounts of religion, religious experience, and religious institutions that cohere with their dominant understanding of humanity. That the focal point presupposes this constructive task to be incomplete may appear to downplay the extent to which this task has been an ongoing project of pragmatists for more than a century and a half. Certainly one must acknowledge that central thinkers in the pragmatic lineage have contributed strongly to the project of constructing understandings of religion that acknowledge humanity's reintegration into the fabric of nature. For writers from Jonathan Edwards and Ralph Waldo Emerson to Charles Sanders Peirce, John Dewey, and William James, the need to understand religious phenomena in a way coherent with humanity's place in the natural world has been a pressing one. From Emerson's insistently individualistic transcendental mysticism to Dewey's egalitarian democratic common faith, central figures in the pragmatic tradition have sought religious perspectives appropriate to their larger intellectual commitments.

Two large problems have limited acceptance of these pragmatic religious perspectives. First, both philosophy and theology have maintained an intransigent commitment to traditional otherworldliness. Traditional otherworldly religious thinkers abound in the contemporary world, and many have never taken seriously pragmatism's central idea, that humans are integral parts of their natural world. Most religious perspectives still encompass supernaturalism, largely ignoring pragmatism's critique of and alternatives to it. In the words of Emerson, "We grizzle every day."[3] Second, some thinkers in the pragmatic tradition doubt that pragmatism may legitimately embrace any religious perspectives whatsoever. Prominent thinkers with deep roots in the pragmatic tradition aggressively deny that their tradition has any properly religious dimensions. Steven Rockefeller and Michael Eldridge constitute two examples. Eldridge in particular, in his recent and influential book *Transforming Experience: John Dewey's Cultural Instrumentalism,* insists on the thorough secularity of Dewey's pragmatism.[4] For those aligned with Rockefeller and Eldridge, the idea that pragmatism might have something interesting or useful to offer religious thinkers is at best naïve and at worst misguided.

These two problems set the context within which the contemporary contributors to this volume design their efforts to move beyond the conventional traditions of supernaturalism still prominent in contemporary religious culture. How to move beyond those supernatural traditions is a matter of dispute even among those who agree about pragmatism's central tenet, that humans are, in every detail of their constitutions, parts of the natural world. The contributors to this volume include Catholics, Protestants, and Jews; philosophers, theologians, and historians; and religious as well as secular thinkers. All agree, however, in seeing the pragmatic tradition as an essential tool for reorienting religious and intellectual culture toward the natural world.

An oddity of American intellectual culture is its relative ignorance of its own past and traditions. American education at all levels frequently looks beyond, behind, or around American intellectual culture to European or Eastern sources and traditions. The contemporary contributors to this collection appreciate the ways some intellectual developments have been unique to the American context of cultural development, and they believe that these particular developments can become globally useful in ways not yet fully appreciated. They share a hope that the American context of intellectual development may enable a convergence of diverse intellectual contexts, whether of European or Eastern origin, into moral and spiritual coherence. This exciting possibility expresses the more ambitious dreams of prominent historical representatives of American intellectual culture and significantly motivates several of the contemporary contributions to this volume.

* * *

The American intellectual tradition, however, is neither unitary nor monolithic; instead, it is built up from diverse strands of interest and emphasis. Even a cursory look at the American past reveals ardent disagreement about fundamental concerns. Implicit in the disagreement, however, is a common commitment to the idea that disagreement, no matter how ardent, may be overcome or accommodated in constructive social and political arrangements. The diversity of the American intellectual tradition sustains hope for a coherent outcome beyond disagreement. Just mentioning some prominent names from this tradition reinforces the idea of diversity of interest and focus, as well as change or progress. John Winthrop and Jonathan Edwards appear to have been committed supernaturalists, while Emerson, James, and Dewey appear to have been committed naturalists. Contemporary thinkers in this same tradition, including those who appear in this collection, are distinctively different from the earlier thinkers as well. All agree, however, in seeing this tradition to exhibit a unity and a promise unparalleled in Western intellectual history.

The unity of the tradition is a common value among these diverse thinkers. Even John Winthrop and John Dewey, separated by three centuries and massive shifts in intellectual context, share basic communitarian values and a vital respect for the religious dimensions of life, and these are core aspects of their thought. Even Richard Rorty, widely considered a committed secularist, shares these basic values, which continue to be prominent in the American intellectual tradition.[5] Because both these values are inadequately appreciated by most Americans, and because the contemporary contributors to this volume depend on and sustain these values, part 1 of this book contains representative selections from prominent intellectual forebears in this tradition.

Part 1 contains classical sources of American religious thought, each of which expresses values central to the American intellectual tradition. In spite of their obvious diversity, these selections express central values that molded and inspired the thinking of their successors. John Winthrop's 1630 sermon aboard the *Arbella,* "A Model of Christian Charity," for example, is noteworthy because it voices a deep commitment to community solidarity and service to others that echoes profoundly in the thought of many later purveyors of the American tradition who have not shared Winthrop's early-seventeenth-century Christian views, including John Dewey and Richard Rorty. Jonathan Edwards's 1741 sermon "Sinners in the Hands of an Angry God," delivered more than a century later during the Great Awakening, stands in stark contrast to Winthrop's earlier address. Edwards's theme is individual responsibility for one's own destiny, which becomes a continuing value in the American tradition. (Notice especially in these two sermons the different use of personal pronouns: Winthrop's *we* is pervasive in his sermon, while Edwards's *you* is pervasive in his; this difference of pronoun use is symptomatic of the largest religious difference between the two thinkers.) Winthrop's "communitarianism" and Edwards's "individualism" are in the moral and religious tradition following them symbiotic values that approach full coherence only in the thought of John Dewey.[6]

Henry David Thoreau's 1862 "Walking" amply expresses what Dewey later calls "natural piety," a sense appropriate to individual humans that they are parts—intelligent parts—of a larger world not of their making in which they are, or should seek to be, at home. The natural world, in Thoreau's vision, is a richness of experience to be embraced; not embracing it brings increasing spiritual impoverishment. Ralph Waldo Emerson's 1883 "Circles" is a symphony of thought and passion woven together in a way all contemporary philosophers should recognize as distinctively philosophical; the earlier selections by Winthrop, Edwards, and Thoreau may not qualify as philosophical in so specific a way. Emerson's commitment to individualism is obvious in this essay, but so also is his deliberate rejection of more traditional Western philosophical modes of thought. Here Emerson fully looks his part as Nietzsche's mentor while still embodying the hope and optimism of his own American traditions.[7] Definitive perspectives of the tradition later identified as pragmatism emerge with great vigor in Emerson's essay; these include the rejection of fixity and cognitive passivity as well as the embrace of activity, experience, experiment, life, nature, and the future.

Charles Sanders Pierce, the first "official" pragmatist in this lineage, is frequently identified as the most scientistic of pragmatists, the one who most definitively embraces science as the tool for significant problem solving and as the measure of what is and what is not. In his 1893 essay "Evolutionary Love" Pierce makes evident his own pragmatic understanding of science; he suggests without equivocation that he regards science as primarily a tool of human cognitive needs rather than a way of getting to the ultimate reality of things. Pierce acknowledges that ideas of science are no less subject to cultural influences than are ideas of art or literature. Pierce argues that Darwinian evolution imports into scientific understandings of biology a way of thinking about industrial economy during the nineteenth century and suggests an alternative account of biological evolution. In this dimension of his thought about science, Pierce is solidly in the distinctive American lineage of thought.

William James's well-known 1896 essay "The Will to Believe" has long been widely read and is sometimes admired and sometimes detested. Included here instead is "Philosophy," chapter 18 of the published version of his 1902 Gifford Lectures, entitled *The Varieties of Religious Experience*. This chapter appears near the end of the book and serves as a kind of summary of James's attitude toward philosophy as conventionally conceived. James's concern in these lectures, to honor the content of religious experience and to refrain from intellectually funded discrimination against it, becomes the "radical empiricism" that is now a hallmark of pragmatism. Philosophy, in James's account of it, may no longer pretend to adjudicate legitimacy among the alleged contents of experience. Rather, it must accept subordination to science or at least parity with other parts of intellectual culture; in any case, it may no longer disingenuously posture as the final arbiter of claims to truth, knowledge, goodness, or beauty. In his respect for experience, and in his subordination of philosophy, James exhibits his solidarity with the intellectual tradition now known as pragmatism.

John Dewey, perhaps the greatest in this lineage, lived ninety-three years, and his productive philosophical work spanned more than half a century. The changes of intellectual culture that appeared during his lifetime (1859–1952), and of which he took account in his voluminous works, were the most extensive and momentous of human history. He saw emerge and incorporated into his thought the work of Darwin, Einstein, and Heisenberg, and fortunately he found great affinity between the intellectual threads of his own American philosophical heritage and the work of these towering figures of nineteenth- and twentieth-century science. The two selections from Dewey that appear in this volume strongly (and properly) suggest the unity of his thought about value. Dewey's thought about morality and society cannot be segregated from his thought about religion. This collection offers two selections. The first is "Creative Democracy: The Task before Us," Dewey's address on the occasion of his eightieth birthday in 1939. The ideal of democracy was always central to his thought; it was always something for which to strive, something always awaiting us and never quite achieved. Furthermore, his commitment to the democratic ideal definitively shaped Dewey's religious thought; consequently, a second selection included here is a part of the second lecture in his Yale University Terry Lectures, known as *A Common Faith* and published in 1934. In this selection Dewey speaks distinctively and creatively about God, and he does so in a way that has always occasioned much controversy among scholars and religious persons.

W. E. B. Du Bois was a contemporary of Dewey, born in 1868. Like Dewey, he lived into his nineties and saw almost a century of wrenching social change. Du Bois devoted his life to realizing the democratic ideal as captured in the best of American political culture. He believed the American democratic ideal should transcend and help people overcome the social and cultural barriers separating black people from full participation in the potential goods of American society, and he spent his life trying to realize their fuller participation in that democratic ideal. Like Dewey, Du Bois was initially attracted to philosophy, and especially to the pragmatism of William James, with whom he studied at Harvard. Although Du Bois ended up taking his Ph.D. in a field other than philosophy, the pragmatic tradition left a permanent mark on all his work. DuBois greatest work, by customary acclaim, is *The Souls of Black Folk*, published in 1903. The selection included here is from chapter 9, "Of Beauty and Death," from Du Bois's 1920 work *Darkwater: Voices from within the Veil.* This selection expresses themes that recur continuously throughout the American tradition of thought: natural piety, human continuity with nature, the poignancy of unrealized yet compelling ideals, and the place of religious traditions in human thought about all these issues.

John J. McDermott is a contemporary philosopher who has experienced fully both the densely eastern and urban dimension of American life and the intensity of American westward-leaning hopes. His work is a projection into the end of the twentieth century and the beginning of the twenty-first century of the dynamic hope deeply embedded in the American intellectual tradition. His essay in this volume is "The Aesthetic Drama of the Ordinary," a reflection of the texture, structure, and value of American life in both its various urban and its spacious western settings.

Richard Rorty is a contemporary philosopher intimately familiar with the varieties of intellectual and cultural traditions that move humanity in all its settings. The final essay in part 1 comes from his essay "Pragmatism as Romantic Polytheism." Rorty's effort to express and defend a version of this American tradition sustains the common themes of its earlier expressions and points toward a future in which those themes may come to greater fruition.

Part 2 of this collection comprises a series of original contemporary essays that express, reflect about, and seek to defend the same American tradition of values found in the selections of part 1. The first essay in part 2 is Richard J. Bernstein's "Pragmatism's Common Faith." Bernstein begins by defeating the idea that the classical pragmatists were hostile to religion. He follows by giving an account of the classical pragmatists' intellectual values. These values include hostility to dogmatism of all kinds, religious or secular; opposition to epistemological foundationalism; and commitment to "natural piety." Bernstein concludes by cautiously embracing Dewey's religious views while noting that, in his view, Dewey does not do full justice to supernaturalist perspectives about religion.

Douglas R. Anderson, in "Awakening in the Everyday: Experiencing the Religious in the American Philosophical Tradition," focuses on specific commitments that he believes unite individuals throughout the entire American pragmatic tradition, including specifically Henry David Thoreau, Jonathan Edwards, and John Dewey. In Anderson's account, Dewey's location of the divine within experience unites him not only with Thoreau but also with Edwards. In focusing on the religious as being located within experience for all three of these thinkers, Anderson provides "the ongoing career of an account of experience that is religious," a hallmark of the American tradition.

William Dean's "Pragmatism, History, and Theology" suggests that the American pragmatic tradition moves away from "speech orientation" of Greek intellectual culture and back to the "act orientation" of Hebrew intellectual culture. In Dean's view, Western intellectual culture has been something of a "wilderness" in which Western humanity has wandered, whereas the American pragmatic tradition offers the hope of rescue from that "wilderness" through its offer to make experience, history, and action once again central to human culture, as they were central to the Jewish and the Christian scriptural traditions. For Dean, only a pragmatic historicism can fully appreciate the mystery at the heart of traditional biblical Christianity; not seeking to transcend history but embracing it is what enables the mystery that is the heart of genuine faith.

In "Morality and Religion: Why Not Pragmatism?" I defend pragmatism against standard charges leveled by opponents, especially the charge that pragmatists are committed to a self-defeating relativism, and suggest a concrete way to develop pragmatism's promise for morality and religion. Robert Westbrook's essay "An Uncommon Faith: Pragmatism and Religious Experience" focuses on the marked individualism of large segments of the pragmatic religious heritage. Westbrook is troubled about pragmatism's apparent indifference to the communal aspects of religious experience; as he puts it, pragmatism's religious faith is "uncommonly un-common."

Part 3 consists of original, contemporary essays concerned about the continuing tension between the more intellectual or "supernaturalist" concepts of religion and the more experience-oriented ideas of religion that flourish within pragmatism. Each of the authors in this section seeks a way of thinking about religion that supersedes the supernaturalism of traditional theology. A word of caution is in order here because of the natural-seeming contrast between "supernaturalistic" and "naturalistic" ideas of religion and morality. Western intellectual traditions tend toward an "either-or" mentality; either one embraces supernaturalism, or one must embrace naturalism, with the two options being exhaustive. Pragmatic thinkers typically reject this contrast as derived from, and dependent on, the very traditions of thought they reject. Pragmatists think of this distinction as a false dichotomy, one that can be detected only from beyond the boundaries of the more conventional Western intellectual traditions they reject. This issue is a concern of all the selections in part 3 and some in part 2.

Raymond D. Boisvert's essay "What Is Religion? A Pragmatist Response" recasts traditional understandings of the secular and the religious in terms of community practices. His emphasis on community practices is faithful to pragmatism's insistence on natural piety, on bringing humanity into a more harmonious and more direct relationship with the natural world and with the larger encompassing cosmos. Sandra B. Rosenthal, in her "Spirituality and the Spirit of American Pragmatism: Beyond the Theism-Atheism Split," confirms Boisvert's suggestion by saying that pragmatists celebrate "the relational, qualitative, value-laden richness of human existence and the universe in which it is embedded." Rosenthal emphasizes pragmatism's commitment to the concrete dimensions of lived experience rather than the abstractions of traditional theology. She sees that those abstractions presume what Dewey derided as a "spectator theory of knowledge" and of necessity mire humanity in the outworn and outdated projects of Western philosophical theology.

Nancy K. Frankenberry's essay "Pragmatism, Truth, and the Disenchantment of Subjectivity" explicates alternatives to the idea of religious truth in terms of contemporary debates about truth and meaning, making use especially of Tarski's and Davidson's accounts of truth. As she develops it, this pragmatic view about truth and meaning shows that religious perspectives may no longer privilege themselves as superior to alternative religious perspectives, nor may they any longer present themselves as vying with science for cognitive legitimacy. Frankenberry's development of this perspective is especially useful because it seeks to bring contemporary developments of pragmatic traditions together with issues central to contemporary concerns of analytic philosophy, those of truth and meaning.

Carl G. Vaught's essay "John Dewey's Conception of the Religious Dimension of Experience" is a close reading of Dewey's book *A Common Faith* intending to highlight Dewey's perspective on the religious with the goal of bringing his thought about it into harmony with the thought of some phenomenologists of religion, particularly Rudolf Otto and Paul Tillich. Vaught's treatment is sensitive both to Dewey's rejection of the central supernatural traditions of Western religious thought and to Dewey's desire to preserve the vitality of the religious in experience and in community. Whereas Vaught's essay focuses on Dewey's religious views, Robert Cumming Neville's essay focuses on Peirce's usefulness for understanding how a religious perspective can convey religious truth. Neville makes use of Peirce's semiotics to show how religious symbols, despite their lack of iconic reference, nevertheless convey indexically the truths of religion. In Neville's view the indexical dimension of meaning and practice, as Peirce understood it, can express and bring individuals into causal contact with religious reality.

In the final essay in the collection, "Faith and Ethics in an Interdependent World," Steven C. Rockefeller points toward constructive pragmatist possibilities for developing a moral faith common to all humanity. The moral and spiritual commitments of pragmatism, in Rockefeller's view, cannot survive apart from the values of American democracy and those of the experimental sciences; neither, however, can those commitments survive or flourish without cooperative engagement on the part of the world's religions toward common human goals. Rockefeller's essay concludes this collection on a note of idealistic optimism that is one of the hallmarks of the thought of John Dewey, the central figure in the pragmatic tradition of thought.

Each selection in part 1 represents a prominent dimension of the American pragmatic heritage of thought about religion and morality. Each of the nine essays included in parts 2 and 3 is an original essay by a prominent scholar who takes the American pragmatic tradition seriously. Each of these authors seeks to bring distinctive focus to the effort to restore American pragmatism to its rightful place at the center of religious, moral, and intellectual culture.

Notes

1. This attack by Bahnsen appears in *The Foundations of Christian Scholarship,* ed. Gary North, (Vallicito, Calif.: Ross House Books, 1976), 258. Alasdair MacIntyre avoids the American tradition entirely in all his published work except his early volume *A Short History of Ethics* (New York: Macmillan, 1966), 253, wherein he gives less than one page to the moral perspective of John Dewey. (MacIntyre's failure to engage the pragmatists likely suggests an intellectual judgment about the relative worth of that tradition, although he is not a critic, as are the others mentioned here.)

2. Mohler explicitly mentions Richard Rorty as a pragmatist and postmodernist who supports extreme relativism and individualism. See R. Albert Mohler's essay "Ministry Is Stranger Than It Used to Be: The Challenge of Postmodernism," *The Southern Seminary Magazine* 65, no. 2 (Spring 1997): 4.

3. Emerson rails against tradition-bound thinkers in his "Circles," reprinted in part 1 of this volume.

4. Michael Eldridge, *Transforming Experience: John Dewey's Cultural Instrumentalism* (Nashville, Tenn.: Vanderbilt University Press, 1998); see especially chapters 5 and 6. Rockefeller, too (though perhaps less aggressively), embraces the secularism in Dewey's pragmatism. See Steven Rockefeller's *John Dewey: Religious Faith and Democratic Humanism* (New York: Columbia University Press, 1991) and his more recent essay "Dewey's Philosophy of Religious Experience," in *Reading Dewey,* ed. Larry Hickman (Bloomington: Indiana University Press, 1998).

5. This claim about Rorty is controversial precisely because he is adamant in his rejection of traditional, supernatural religion. Nonetheless, Rorty shares with John Winthrop and John Dewey their commitments to communitarian values as well as their respect for the religious dimensions of life; Rorty, like the prominent pragmatists before him, hopes to see these values become more vigorous and widely extended. See, for example, Rorty's "Human Rights, Rationality, and Sentimentality," *Truth and Progress: Philosophical Papers,* vol. 3, (Cambridge: Cambridge University Press, 1998); and also Rorty's "Pragmatism as Romantic Polytheism," reprinted in part 1 of this volume.

6. Readers should know that Jonathan Edwards's sermon, reprinted here, is powerful, impressive, and typical of the religious culture of the Great Awakening, for which Edwards's sermon was a model often emulated. However, the sermon gives little indication of the depth, profundity, or sophistication of Edwards's philosophical and theological thought. Edwards was probably the most influential thinker in America during the second half of the eighteenth century and the first half of the nineteenth century. Many works of secondary scholarship provide appropriate introductions to Edwards's significance. One provocative such work is Perry Miller's *Jonathan Edwards* (Amherst: University of Massachusetts Press, 1981).

7. See George Stack, *Nietzsche and Emerson: An Elective Affinity* (Athens: Ohio University Press, 1992).

PART 1

Classical Sources

Notes on Authors

JOHN WINTHROP (1588–1649) was the first governor of the Massachusetts Bay Colony. In order to lead the 1630 expedition to New England, Winthrop sold his entire estate in England and put all his resources into the adventure into the wilderness. Winthrop served as the colony's governor intermittently until his death in 1649. His autocratic personality was both a blessing and a curse; he was a good leader, but his strong convictions occasionally led him to overstep his political authority and thus bring political difficulties on himself. The freemen of his colony, however, recognizing his strong leadership qualities, elected him to govern the colony on four separate occasions. The selection here, "A Model of Christian Charity," is a sermon he delivered to his companions on his 1630 voyage; the sermon exhorts them to hold fast to the Christian ideals that united them in their common search for new opportunities in the New World. Most noteworthy in Winthrop's address is his strong commitment to the value of Christian community, a value he believed should dominate the settlers' lives in America. Winthrop urges his companions to be "knit together" as one individual, to "entertain each other in brotherly affection," and to be "willing to abridge [themselves] of . . . superfluities for the supply of others' necessities." One source for further information is Perry Miller, *Orthodoxy in Massachusetts, 1630–1650* (Cambridge, Mass.: Harvard University Press, 1933).

JONATHAN EDWARDS (1703–58) was one of the greatest preachers and the greatest theologian of the American colonies during the eighteenth century. A precocious youth, he began his studies at Yale when he was not quite thirteen and graduated first in his class. At the age of twenty-one Edwards took over the ministry of his grandfather's church at Northampton, and he continued to preach and write until 1750. He was called on late in life to take up the presidency of the College of New Jersey, now Princeton University, but died within a few months of accepting this position. His death interrupted not only his academic career but also his intellectual work, and he left unfinished what was to be his greatest work, to be titled *A History of the Work of Redemption*. Apart from his sermons, Edwards's works include *A Treatise Concerning the Religious Affections*, *The Freedom of the Will*, and *Original Sin*. Edwards became one of the most influential thinkers of the Great Awakening and indeed one of the greatest of American thinkers; he sounded themes that reverberate throughout the intellectual culture of America in the centuries following his life. The selection here, his "Sinners in the Hands of an Angry God," is undoubtedly his best-known work; as a sermon it gave form and substance to the religious culture of the Great Awakening. Many of his fellow preachers admired and sought to emulate the intensity of Edwards's sermon. The individualism in Edward's thought about religion is undoubtedly evident in this sermon. What is not so evident, but of equal if not greater importance to an assessment of his influence on his American intellectual progeny, is the central place his thought gives to the role beauty and affection play in human religious life. The beauty of life and the natural world, affection for and relationship to the natural world, and affection within human communities are central to Edwards's philosophy and theology. These latter themes, as much as the individual responsibility before God evident in this sermon, are important for the American pragmatic tradition. A source for further information about Edwards is Roland A. Delattre, *Beauty and Sensibility in the Thought of Jonathan Edwards* (New Haven, Conn.: Yale University Press, 1968).

HENRY DAVID THOREAU (1817–62) was an iconoclast in the middle of a burgeoning commercial culture. He was deliberate in choosing how to live, and he viewed his freedom and connection with nature as more important than his social standing. After studying at Harvard, he continued to educate himself by reading widely. His connection to Ralph Waldo Emerson was important to him, and during his life he was best known as a disciple of Emerson. He was an avid abolitionist and advocate of individual responsibility. His most famous work is *Walden.* Themes in the work reprinted here include the need to transcend our European past in thought, word, and deed; the bright hope of a "westward turn" toward a more promising future sought independently of the staid, sluggish "East" of our past; the vigor of "wildness" in this new land, along with its prospects for a new kind of poetry and philosophy; and the prospect of distinguishing among different kinds of truth that may be important to humanity in very different ways. These themes echo in subsequent thinkers in the American tradition. One source for further information is Walter Harding, *The Days of Henry Thoreau: A Biography* (New York: Dover, 1982).

RALPH WALDO EMERSON (1803–82) was, during much of his life, America's premier intellectual. He began his career as a Unitarian minister but resigned that calling when he found he could not in good conscience participate in the life of the church. He found his proper niche in nineteenth-century American culture as a lecturer; his lectures around the country in different venues earned him a reputation as an original and creative thinker of a uniquely American turn of mind. Emerson had his finger on the pulse of the new and vital in the burgeoning American culture, and he saw that this new development needed an intellectual gulf between the American and European continents that was comparable to the geographical gulf of the Atlantic Ocean. He devoted much of his life to building such an intellectual gulf. His well-known essay "The American Scholar," delivered in 1837, argues that Americans need not bow to the wisdom of European thought, nor need they seek to model their own intellectual lives on those of prominent European exemplars; instead, they should transcend their European heritage and strike out on their own. Americans will find themselves, according to Emerson, in seeking their own original relation to the universe. The essay here, "Circles," exhibits deep familiarity with, and a biting critical assessment of, the European philosophical heritage Emerson believed American thinkers should transcend. The essay also seeks a romantic reorientation of American intellectual and spiritual life toward this life, this world, and this time rather than an accommodation of the reasoned coldness of European Platonic or Aristotelian traditions of intellect and religion. A source for further information is Robert D. Richardson, *Emerson: The Mind on Fire* (Berkeley: University of California Press, 1995).

CHARLES SANDERS PEIRCE (1839–1914) is generally considered to have been one of America's greatest philosophers. He came to maturity in the intense intellectual culture of Harvard University, where his father, Benjamin Peirce, was widely respected as a professor of mathematics and astronomy. His father nourished the highest hopes for Charles's intellectual development and tended to his education with scrupulous care. His early experiences in his father's laboratory and his early careful readings of philosophical classics—in particular, Kant's *Critique of Pure Reason*—gave Charles himself very high expectations of his own intellectual potential. Although he was an unusually creative and original thinker, his personal life hindered his recognition as such during his own lifetime. He served only five years in an official academic position, and this at Johns Hopkins University rather than at his own and his father's institution of choice, Harvard. His mathematical and scientific background made him the most scientifically sophisticated of the classical pragmatists; indeed, he is often regarded as the most scientific, sometimes almost even positivistic, thinker among them. In his well-known essay "The Fixation of Belief," Peirce contrasts various methods of arriving at and maintaining belief, concluding with a decided preference for the alternative he called the scientific method over those he called the method of tenacity, the method of authority, and the a priori method (which he found ubiquitous in traditional, particularly Cartesian, philosophy). In the essay included here, "Evolutionary Love," however, Peirce moves away from his extreme preference for scientific method, at least to the extent of arguing that it is as likely as any other institution of culture to be infused with a particular and local zeitgeist, or spirit of its age, to which Peirce argues there are equally reputable alternatives. A source for further information is Christopher Hookaway, *Peirce* (London: Routledge and Kegan Paul, 1985).

WILLIAM JAMES (1842–1910) met grand success in the world of academic philosophy, but his success came only after three decades of searching not only for a vocation but also for an avocation. Convinced he should become a scientist, James pursued that goal with vigor and conviction until he found a central part of science, laboratory work, dull and boring. Since he loved art and was frequently exposed to European classics of art in the great museums of Europe, he also for a time sought to develop his skills toward a career in painting; he became convinced, however, that he lacked the requisite talent for success in this direction. He did, however, finally persevere in the study of medicine to the point of earning his medical degree, his only professional degree, from the Harvard College of Medicine. He never practiced medicine, however, but he did secure an academic position at Harvard in 1872, teaching anatomy and physiology. From this position he built a life of international academic success. His first widely recognized work was his *Principles of Psychology*, published in 1890 after an extraordinarily long time—more than twelve years—in preparation. From this time until the end of his life, James traveled and lectured widely, both in America and abroad. Unlike his famous brother, the novelist Henry James, William always had a distinct preference for the American cultural scene over the European. James's most famous work, *The Varieties of Religious Experience*, was the Gifford Lectures he delivered in Scotland during the years 1901 and 1902. The selection from his works included here is the part of those lectures in which James explains his uneasiness with the philosophy that seeks purely intellectual solutions to the multifaceted dimensions of human religious aspiration.

W. E. B. DU BOIS (1868–1963) was born in Massachusetts. Although his parents were descended from slaves, Du Bois's own social situation was relatively tolerable. He was well though modestly educated, and although he could not attend Harvard, as he had wished, he did attend Fisk University, in Nashville, Tennessee, where he first experienced the conditions under which most African Americans lived. After graduating from Fisk, Du Bois did attend Harvard College, where he was admitted with junior standing because of his previous B.A. degree from Fisk. At Harvard he fell under the influence of William James. Although he loved philosophy, he felt a need to address the problems of society and culture that were, he believed, of greater personal and social significance than the usually abstract intellectual problems of Western philosophy. Having a strong undergraduate background in philosophy after taking a second B.A. degree at Harvard, Du Bois became the first African American to earn a doctoral degree from Harvard. His dissertation, *The Suppression of the African Slave Trade to the United States of America, 1638–1870,* was published in 1896.

Du Bois was an internationally recognized figure who traveled widely and conversed with leading intellectuals throughout the world. His career was multifaceted, including scholarship, journalism, and leadership in social and labor organizations. His best-known work is *The Souls of Black Folk,* published in 1903. He published widely in popular magazines and journals. In 1910 he became a cofounder of the NAACP and edited its magazine, *Crisis,* which came to have 100,000 subscribers by the end of World War I.

During the 1940s, Du Bois's inclinations toward Marxism grew stronger, and in 1951 he was indicted for refusing to register as an agent of the Soviet Union. Although the charges were finally dismissed, the experiences of being indicted and appearing as a criminal in an American courtroom left him profoundly discouraged about the prospects for his own hopes and for America's historical democratic ideals. He joined the Communist Party in 1961. Du Bois died in 1963, the day before Martin Luther King Jr. led the now famous march on Washington.

The selection included here is from Du Bois's *Darkwater: Voices from within the Veil* and captures his depth of character, hope, and feeling. The selection also expresses Du Bois's roots in the pragmatic, and ideally American, tradition of thought that goes back to his love for, and inspiration by, William James. For more information about Du Bois, as well as more of Du Bois's own writings, readers may consult Eric J. Sundquist, ed., *The Oxford W. E. B. Du Bois Reader* (Oxford: Oxford University Press, 1996).

JOHN DEWEY (1859–1952) is America's greatest philosopher. Born and raised in Burlington, Vermont, in a devout Congregationalist home, Dewey never lost the earnestness and idealism of his youth. His experiences of New England religion and democracy vitally shaped his moral and intellectual character. Dewey had some firsthand experience of the Civil War; his mother took him and his brothers to the battlefields where his father served as a quartermaster to Northern troops. The University of Vermont was the site of Dewey's undergraduate education and provided his first taste of philosophy. After graduation Dewey spent two years teaching high school in Oil City, Pennsylvania; while teaching high school he continued his study of philosophy and decided to pursue the discipline professionally, taking up Ph.D. studies at Johns Hopkins University.

Dewey spent the first ten years of his university teaching career (1884–94) at the University of Michigan. In 1894 he moved to the University of Chicago, where he met Jane Addams and became involved in addressing the myriad social problems generated by the rapid industrializing of America. He spent the bulk of his professional career, however, at Columbia University, where he became America's most prominent intellectual figure of the time. Dewey wrote and published copiously during his lifetime; his books and essays fill thirty-seven volumes in the Southern Illinois University edition of his collected works.

Dewey managed to address incisively every significant philosophical problem of the Western intellectual tradition. In addition, he wrote on virtually every pressing social and political issue America faced during his mature years. Known as the philosopher of democracy, Dewey brought his commitments to the fundamental positive values of American life into intimate contact with every issue he addressed.

The two selections included in this volume are his "Creative Democracy: The Task before Us," an address written for his eightieth birthday celebration in 1939, and a portion of the second of his Terry Lectures at Yale University in 1934. The first expresses Dewey's fundamental commitments to the values of democracy; the second suggests how these values might come into play in the vigorous religious culture he believed might support those democratic values.

Readers interested in further information about John Dewey may consult Robert B. Westbrook, *John Dewey and American Democracy,* (Ithaca, N.Y.: Cornell University Press, 1991).

JOHN J. MCDERMOTT is a Distinguished Professor of Philosophy and Humanities, the Abell Professor of Liberal Arts, and a professor of humanities in medicine at Texas A&M University. McDermott has edited and published editions of the writings of William James, Josiah Royce, and John Dewey; he is the project director and general editor of a multivolume critical edition of the correspondence of William James to be published by the University Press of Virginia. In addition, McDermott has published numerous articles in American philosophy, philosophy of medicine, and environmental aesthetics. Two collections of his essays, *The Culture of Experience: Philosophical Essays in the American Grain* (New York: New York University Press, 1976) and *Streams of Experience: Reflections on the History and Philosophy of American Culture* (Amherst: University of Massachusetts Press, 1986), are readily available, as is his *Cultural Introduction to Philosophy, from Antiquity to Descartes* (New York: Knopf, 1985).

McDermott is a classical American thinker in many respects. Notably, his academic career has literally exemplified the "westward yearning" of the American tradition; it has moved across North America from the New York City of his youth and early maturity to the College Station of central Texas, where he currently teaches. The essay included here, "The Aesthetic Drama of the Ordinary," is a meditation on the texture and meaning of contemporary American life that has deep roots in classical American traditions of thought.

RICHARD RORTY is the most prominent of American thinkers now working in the American tradition of pragmatism. Rorty grew up in New York City and received his Ph.D. from the University of Chicago. Currently at Stanford University, Rorty taught for many years at Princeton and then at the University of Virginia before his move to California.

Rorty's book *Philosophy and the Mirror of Nature* (Princeton, N.J.: Princeton University Press, 1979) caused a furor within mainstream academic philosophy. In that book Rorty employed strategies of argument normally associated with analytic philosophy to point toward a possible philosophical culture beyond analytic philosophy; he argued in favor of a "philosophy without mirrors." Rorty's books and articles since 1979 have flooded across American culture in an increasingly bountiful stream of incisive commentary not only about issues of philosophy but also about issues central to America's social and political life. His *Achieving Our Country* (Cambridge, Mass.: Harvard University Press, 1998), for example, has engendered widespread commentary and irritated social and political thinkers on both left and right. Further information about Rorty is available at his own Web site or in Herman J. Saatkamp Jr., *Rorty and Pragmatism: The Philosopher Responds to His Critics* (Nashville, Tenn.: Vanderbilt University Press, 1995). Rorty's autobiographical essay "Trotsky and the Wild Orchids" appears in his collection of essays *Philosophy and Social Hope* (London: Penguin Books, 1999).

1. A Model of Christian Charity (1630)

JOHN WINTHROP

This law of the Gospel propounds likewise a difference of seasons and occasions. There is a time when a Christian must sell all and give to the poor as they did in the apostles' times; there is a time also when a Christian, though they give not all yet, must give beyond their ability, as they of Macedonia (II Cor. 8). Likewise, community of perils calls for extraordinary liberality, and so doth community in some special service for the church. Lastly, when there is no other means whereby our Christian brother may be relieved in this distress, we must help him beyond our ability, rather than tempt God in putting him upon help by miraculous or extraordinary means.

1. For the persons, we are a company professing ourselves fellow members of Christ, in which respect only, though we were absent from each other many miles, and had our employments as far distant, yet we ought to account ourselves knit together by this bond of love, and live in the exercise of it, if we would have comfort of our being in Christ.

2. For the work we have in hand, it is by mutual consent, through a special overruling providence and a more than an ordinary approbation of the churches of Christ, to seek out a place of cohabitation and consortship, under a due form of government both civil and ecclesiastical. In such cases as this, the care of the public must oversway all private respects by which not only conscience but mere civil policy doth bind us; for it is a true rule that particular estates cannot subsist in the ruin of the public.

3. The end is to improve our lives to do more service to the Lord, the comfort and increase of the body of Christ whereof we are members, that ourselves and posterity may be the better preserved from the common corrup-

tions of this evil world, to serve the Lord and work out our salvation under the power and purity of His holy ordinances.

4. For the means whereby this must be effected, they are twofold: a conformity with the work and the end we aim at; these we seek are extraordinary, therefore we must not content ourselves with usual ordinary means. Whatsoever we did or ought to have done when we lived in England, the same must we do, and more also where we go. That which the most in their churches maintain as a truth in profession only, we must bring into familiar and constant practice: as in this duty of love we must love brotherly without dissimulation; we must love one another with a pure heart fervently, we must bear one another's burdens, we must not look only on our own things but also on the things of our brethren. Neither must we think that the Lord will bear with such failings at our hands as He doth from those among whom we have lived. [. . .]

Thus stands the cause between God and us; we are entered into covenant with Him for this work; we have taken out a commission, the Lord hath given us leave to draw our own articles. We have professed to enterprise these actions upon these and these ends; we have hereupon besought Him of favor and blessing. Now if the Lord shall please to hear us and bring us in peace to the place we desire, then hath He ratified this covenant and sealed our Commission, [and] will expect a strict performance of the articles contained in it. But if we shall neglect the observation of these articles which are the ends we have propounded, and dissembling with our God, shall fall to embrace this present world and prosecute our carnal intentions, seeking great things for ourselves and our posterity, the Lord will surely break out in wrath against us, be revenged of such a perjured people, and make us know the price of the breach of such a covenant.

Now the only way to avoid this shipwreck and to provide for our posterity is to follow the counsel of Micah: to do justly, to love mercy, to walk humbly with our God. For this end, we must be knit together in this work as one man. We must entertain each other in brotherly affection; we must be willing to abridge ourselves of our superfluities for the supply of others' necessities; we must uphold a familiar commerce together in all meekness, gentleness, patience and liberality. We must delight in each other, make others' condition our own, rejoice together, mourn together, labor and suffer together always having before our eyes our commission and community in the work, our community as members of the same body. So shall we keep the unity of the spirit in the bond of peace, the Lord will be our God and delight to dwell among us, as His own people, and will command a blessing upon us in all our ways, so that we shall see much more of His wisdom, power, goodness, and truth than formerly we have been acquainted with. We shall find that the God of Israel is among us, when ten of us shall be able to resist a thousand of our enemies, when He shall make us a praise and glory, that men shall say of succeeding plantations: "The Lord make it like that of New England." For we must consider that we shall be as a city upon a hill, the eyes of all people are upon us. So that if we shall deal falsely with our God in this work we have under-taken, and so cause Him to withdraw His present help from us, we shall be made a story and a by-word through the world: we shall open the mouths of enemies to speak evil of the ways of God and all professors for God's sake; we shall shame the faces of many of God's worthy servants, and cause their prayers to be turned into curses upon us, till we be consumed out of the good land whither we are going.

And to shut up this discourse with that exhortation of Moses, that faithful servant of the Lord, in his last farewell to Israel (Deut. 30): Beloved, there is now set before us life and good, death and evil, in that we are commanded this day to love the Lord our God, and to love one another, to walk in His ways and to keep His commandments and His ordinance and His laws and the articles of our covenant with Him, that we may live and be multiplied, and that the Lord our God may bless us in the land whither we go to possess it: but if our hearts shall turn away so that we will not obey, but shall be seduced and worship [. . .] other gods, our pleasures and profits, and serve them, it is propounded unto us this day, we shall surely perish out of the good land whither we pass over this vast sea to possess it.

> Therefore, let us choose life,
> that we, and our seed,
> may live: by obeying His
> voice and cleaving to Him,
> for He is our life
> and our prosperity.

2. Sinners in the Hands of an Angry God (1741)

JONATHAN EDWARDS

This that you have heard is the case of every one of you that are out of Christ. That world of misery, that lake of burning brimstone, is extended abroad under you. There is the dreadful pit of the glowing flames of the wrath of God; there is hell's wide gaping mouth open; and you have nothing to stand upon, nor any thing to take hold of; there is nothing between you and hell but the air; 'tis only the power and mere pleasure of God that holds you up.

You probably are not sensible of this; you find you are kept out of hell, but don't see the hand of God in it, but look at other things, as the good state of your bodily constitution, your care of your own life, and the means you use for your own preservation. But indeed these things are nothing; if God should withdraw his hand, they would avail no more to keep you from falling, than the thin air to hold up a person that is suspended in it.

Your wickedness makes you as it were heavy as lead, and to tend downwards with great weight and pressure towards hell; and, if God should let you go, you would immediately sink, and swiftly descend and plunge into the bottomless gulf; and your healthy constitution, and your own care and prudence, and best contrivance, and all your righteousness, would have no more influence to uphold you and keep you out of hell, than a spider's web would have to stop a falling rock. Were it not that so is the sovereign pleasure of God, the earth would not bear you one moment; for you are a burden to it; the creation groans with you; the creation is made subject to the bondage of your corruption, not willingly; the sun don't willingly shine upon you, to give you light to serve sin and Satan; the earth don't willingly yield her increase to satisfy your lusts, nor is it willingly a stage for your wickedness to be acted upon; the air don't willingly serve you for breath to maintain the flame of life in your vitals, while you spend your life in the service of God's enemies. God's creatures are good, and were made for men to serve God with, and don't willingly subserve to any other purpose, and groan when they are abused to purposes so directly contrary to their nature and end. And the world would spue you out, were it not for the sovereign hand of him who hath subjected it in hope. There are the black clouds of God's wrath now hanging directly over your heads, full of the dreadful storm, and big with thunder; and, were it not for the restraining hand of God, it would immediately burst forth upon you. The sovereign pleasure of God for the present stays his rough wind; otherwise it would come like a whirlwind, and you would be like the chaff of the summer threshing-floor.

The wrath of God is like great waters that are dammed for the present; they increase more and more, and rise higher and higher, till an outlet is given; and the longer the stream is stopt, the more rapid and mighty is its course when once it is let loose. 'Tis true, that judgment against your evil works has not been executed hitherto; the floods of God's vengeance have been withheld; but your guilt in the mean time is constantly increasing, and you are every day treasuring up more wrath; the waters are continually rising, and waxing more and more mighty; and there is nothing but the mere pleasure of God that holds the waters back that are unwilling to be stopt, and press hard to go forward. If God should only withdraw his hand from the floodgate, it would immediately fly open, and the fiery floods of the fierceness and wrath of God would rush forth with inconceivable fury, and would come upon you with omnipotent power; and if your strength were ten thousand times greater than it is, yea ten thousand times greater than the strength of the stoutest, sturdiest devil in hell, it would be nothing to withstand or endure it.

The bow of God's wrath is bent, and the arrow made ready on the string, and justice bends the arrow at your heart, and strains the bow; and it is nothing but the mere pleasure of God, and that of an angry God, without any promise or obligation at all, that keeps the arrow one moment from being made drunk with your blood.

Thus are all you that never passed under a great change of heart, by the mighty power of the spirit of God upon your souls; all that were never born again, and made new creatures, and raised from being dead in sin, to a state of new, and before altogether unexperienced light and life. However you may have reformed your life in many things, and may have had religious affections, and may keep up a form of religion in your families and closets, and in the house of God, and may be strict in it, you are thus in the hands of an angry God; 'tis nothing but his mere pleasure that keeps you from being this moment swallowed up in everlasting destruction.

However unconvinced you may now be of the truth of what you hear, by and by you will be fully convinced of it. Those that are gone from being in the like circumstances with you, see that it was so with them; for destruction came suddenly upon most of them, when they expected nothing of it, and while they were saying, peace and safety. Now they see, that those things that they depended on for peace and safety, were nothing but thin air and empty shadows.

The God that holds you over the pit of hell, much as one holds a spider or some loathesome insect over the fire, abhors you, and is dreadfully provoked; his wrath towards you burns like fire; he looks upon you as worthy of nothing else but to be cast into the fire; he is of purer eyes than to bear to have you in his sight; you are ten thousand times so abominable in his eyes as the most hateful venomous serpent is in ours. You have offended him infinitely more than ever a stubborn rebel did his prince; and yet 'tis nothing but his hand that holds you from falling into the fire every moment. 'Tis to be ascribed to nothing else, that you did not go to hell the last night; that you was suffered to awake again in this world, after you closed your eyes to sleep. And there is no other reason to be given why you have not dropt into hell since you arose in the morning, but that God's hand has held you up. There is no other reason to be given why you haven't gone to hell since you have sat here in the House of God, provoking his pure eyes by your sinful wicked manner of attending his solemn worship; yea, there is nothing else that is to be given as a reason why you don't this very moment drop down into hell.

O Sinner! Consider the fearful danger you are in. 'Tis a great furnace of wrath, a wide and bottomless pit, full of the fire of wrath, that you are held over in the hand of that God, whose wrath is provoked and incensed as much against you as against many of the damned in hell. You hang by a slender thread, with the flames of divine wrath flashing about it, and ready every moment to singe it, and burn it asunder; and you have no interest in any mediator, and nothing to lay hold of to save yourself, nothing to keep off the flames of wrath, nothing of your own, nothing that you ever have done, nothing that you can do, to induce God to spare you one moment. [...]

How dreadful is the state of those that are daily and hourly in danger of this great wrath, and infinite misery! But this is the dismal case of every soul in this congregation that has not been born again, however moral and strict, sober and religious they may otherwise be. Oh that you would consider it, whether you be young or old! There is reason to think, that there are many in this congregation, now hearing this discourse, that will actually be the subjects of this very misery to all eternity. We know not who they are, or in what seats they sit, or what thoughts they now have. It may be they are now at ease, and hear all these things without much disturbance, and are now flattering themselves that they shall escape. If we knew that there was one person, and but one, in the whole congregation, that was to be the subject of this misery, what an awful thing would it be to think of! If we knew who it was, what an awful sight would it be to see such a person! How might all the rest of the congregation lift up a lamentable and bitter cry over him! But alas! Instead of one, how many is it likely will remember this discourse in hell? And it would be a wonder if some that are now present should not be in hell in a very short time before this year is out; and it would be no wonder if some person that now sits here in some seat of this meetinghouse, in health, and quiet and secure, should be there before tomorrow morning.

3. Walking (Part 2)

HENRY DAVID THOREAU

What is it that makes it so hard sometimes to determine whither we will walk? I believe that there is a subtle magnetism in Nature, which, if we unconsciously yield to it, will direct us aright. It is not indifferent to us which way we walk. There is a right way; but we are very liable from heedlessness and stupidity to take the wrong one. We would fain take that walk, never yet taken by us through this actual world, which is perfectly symbolical of the path which we love to travel in the interior and ideal world; and sometimes, no doubt, we find it difficult to choose our direction, because it does not yet exist distinctly in our idea.

When I go out of the house for a walk, uncertain as yet whither I will bend my steps, and submit myself to my instinct to decide for me, I find, strange and whimsical as it may seem, that I finally and inevitably settle south-west, toward some particular wood or meadow or deserted pasture or hill in that direction. My needle is slow to settle, varies a few degrees, and does not always point due south-west, it is true, and it has good authority for this variation, but it always settles between west and south-southwest. The future lies that way to me, and the earth seems more unexhausted and richer on that side. The outline which would bound my walks, would be, not a circle, but a parabola, or rather like one of those cometary orbits, which have been thought to be non-returning curves, in this case opening westward, in which my house occupies the place of the sun. I turn round and round irresolute sometimes for a quarter of an hour, until I decide for the thousandth time, that I will walk into the southwest or west. Eastward I go only by force; but westward I go free. Thither no business leads me. It is hard for me to believe that I shall find fair landscapes, or sufficient Wildness and Freedom behind the eastern horizon. I am not excited by the prospect of a walk thither; but I believe that the forest which I see in the western horizon stretches uninterruptedly towards the setting sun, and that there are no towns nor cities in it of enough consequence to disturb me. Let me live where I will, on this side is the city, on that the wilderness, and ever I am leaving the city more and more, and withdrawing into the wilderness. I should not lay so much stress on this fact, if I did not believe that something like this is the prevailing tendency of my countrymen. I must walk toward Oregon, and not toward Europe. And that way the nation is moving, and I may say that mankind progress from east to west. Within a few years we have witnessed the phenomenon of a south-eastward migration, in the settlement of Australia; but this affects us as a retrograde movement, and, judging from the moral and physical character of the first generation of Australians, has not yet proved a successful experiment. The eastern Tartars think that there is nothing west beyond Tibet. "The World ends there," say they, "beyond there is nothing but a shoreless sea." It is unmitigated East where they live.

We go eastward to realize history, and study the works of art and literature, retracing the steps of the race; we go westward as into the future, with a spirit of enterprise and adventure. The Atlantic is a Lethean stream, in our passage over which we have had an opportunity to forget the old world and its institutions. If we do not succeed this time, there is perhaps one more chance for the race left before it arrives on the banks of the Styx; and that is in the Lethe of the Pacific, which is three times as wide.

I know not how significant it is, or how far it is an evidence of singularity, that an individual should thus consent in his pettiest walk, with the general movement of the race; but I know that something akin to the migratory instinct in birds and quadrupeds, which, in some instances, is known to have affected the squirrel tribe, impelling them to a general and mysterious movement, in which they were seen, say some, crossing the broadest rivers, each on its particular chip, with its tail raised for a sail, and bridging narrower streams with their dead,—that something like *the furor* which affects the domestic cattle in the spring, and which is referred to a worm in their tails— affects both nations and individuals, either perennially or from time to time. Not a flock of wild geese cackles over our town but it to some extent unsettles the value of real estate here, and if I were a broker I should probably take that disturbance into account. [. . .]

Every sunset which I witness inspires me with the desire to go to a west as distant and as fair as that into which the Sun goes down. He appears to migrate westward daily and tempt us to follow him. He is the Great Western Pioneer whom the nations follow. We dream all night of those mountain ridges in the horizon, though they may be of vapor only, which were last gilded by his rays. The island of Atlantis, and the islands and gardens of the Hesperides, a sort of terrestrial paradise, appear to have been the Great West of the ancients, enveloped in mystery and poetry. Who has not seen in imagination, when looking into the sunset sky, the gardens of the Hesperides, and the foundation of all those fables?

Columbus felt the westward tendency more strongly than any before. He obeyed it, and found a New World for Castile and Leon. The herd of men in those days scented fresh pastures from afar.

> "And now the sun had stretched out all the hills,
> And now was dropt into the western bay;
> At last *he* rose, and twitch'd his mantle blue;
> To-morrow to fresh woods and pastures new."

Where on the Globe can there be found an area of equal extent with that occupied by the bulk of our states, so fertile and so rich and varied in its productions, and at the same time so habitable by the European, as this is? Michaux who knew but part of them, says that "the species of large trees are much more numerous in North America than in Europe: in the United States there are more than 140 species that exceed thirty feet in height; in France there are but thirty that attain this size." Later botanists more than confirm his observations. Humboldt came to America to realize his youthful dreams of a tropical vegetation, and he beheld it in its greatest perfection in the primitive forests of the Amazon, the most gigantic wilderness on the earth, which he has so eloquently described. The geographer Guyot, himself a European, goes farther—farther than I am ready to follow him, yet not when he says, "As the plant is made for the animal, as the vegetable world is made for the animal world, America is made for the man of the Old World. The man of the Old World sets out upon his way. Leaving the highlands of Asia, he descends from station to station, towards Europe. Each of his steps is marked by a new civilization superior to the preceding, by a greater power of development. Arrived at the Atlantic, he pauses on the shore of this unknown Ocean, the bounds of which he knows not, and turns upon his foot prints for an instant." When he has exhausted the rich soil of Europe and reinvigorated himself—"Then recommences his adventurous career westward as in the earliest ages." So far Guyot.

From this western impulse coming in contact with the barrier of the Atlantic sprang the commerce and enterprise of modern times. The younger Michaux, in his "Travels West of the Alleghanies in 1802," says that the common inquiry in the newly settled West was "From what part of the world have you come?" As if these vast and fertile regions would naturally be the place of meeting and common country of all the inhabitants of the globe.

To use an obsolete Latin word, I might say *Ex oriente lux; ex occidente frux.* From the East light; from the West fruit.

Sir Francis Head, an English traveler, and a Governor-General of Canada, tells us that "in both the northern and southern hemispheres of the new world, Nature has not only outlined her works on a larger scale, but has painted the whole picture with brighter and more costly colors than she used in delineating and in beautifying the old world." "The heavens of America appear infinitely higher, the sky is bluer, the air is fresher, the cold is intenser, the moon looks larger, the stars are brighter, the thunder is louder, the lightning is vivider, the wind is stronger, the rain is heavier, the mountains are higher, the rivers larger, the forests bigger, the plains broader." This statement will do at least to set against Buffon's account of this part of the world and its productions.

Linnaeus said long ago *Nescio quae facies laeta, glabra plantis Americanis.* I know not what there is of joyous and smooth in the aspect of American plants; and I think that in this country there are no, or at most, very few, *Africanae bestiae,* African beasts, as the Romans called them, and that in this respect also it is peculiarly fitted for the habitation of man. We are told that within three miles of the center of the East Indian city of Singapore some of the inhabitants are annually carried off by tigers; but the traveler can lie down in the woods at night almost anywhere in North America without fear of wild beasts.

These are encouraging testimonies. If the moon looks larger here than in Europe, probably the sun looks larger also. If the heavens of America appear infinitely higher, the stars brighter, I trust that these facts are symbolical of the height to which the philosophy and poetry and religion of her inhabitants may one day soar. At length perchance the immaterial heaven will appear as much higher to the American mind, and the intimations that star it as much brighter. For I believe that climate does thus react on man—as there is something in the mountain air that feeds the spirit and inspires. Will not man grow to greater perfection intellectually as well as physically under these influences? Or is it unimportant how many foggy days there are in his life? I trust that we shall be more imaginative; that our thoughts will be clearer, fresher and more ethereal, as our sky—our understanding more comprehensive and broader, like our plains—our intellect generally on a grander scale, like our thunder and lightning, our rivers and mountains and forests. And our hearts shall even correspond in breadth and depth and grandeur to our inland seas. Perchance there will appear to the traveler something, he knows not what, of *laeta* and *glabra*—of joyous and serene, in our very faces. Else, to what end does the world go on, and why was America discovered?

To Americans I hardly need to say—

"Westward the star of empire takes its way."

As a true patriot I should be ashamed to think that Adam in paradise was more favorably situated on the whole than the backwoodsman in this country.

Our sympathies in Massachusetts are not confined to New England, though we may be estranged from the south, we sympathize with the west. There is the home of the younger sons, as among the Scandinavians they took to the sea for their inheritance. It is too late to be studying Hebrew; it is more important to understand even the slang of today.

Some months ago I went to see a panorama of the Rhine. It was like a dream of the Middle Ages. I floated down its historic stream in something more than imagination, under bridges built by the Romans, and repaired by later heroes, past cities and castles whose very names were music to my ears, and each of which was the subject of a legend. There were Ehrenbreitstein and Rolandseck and Coblentz, which I knew only in history. They were ruins that interested me chiefly. There seemed to come up from its waters and its vine-clad hills and valleys a hushed music as of crusaders departing for the Holy Land. I floated along under the spell of enchantment, as if I had been transported to a heroic age, and breathed an atmosphere of chivalry.

Soon after I went to see a panorama of the Mississippi, and as I worked my way up the stream in the light of today, and saw the steam-boats wooding up, counted the rising cities, gazed on the fresh ruins of Nauvoo, beheld the Indians moving west across the stream, and, as before I had looked up the Moselle, now looked up the Ohio and the Missouri, and heard the legends of Dubuque and of Wenona's Cliff, still thinking more of the future than of the past or present, I saw that this was a Rhine stream of a different kind; that the foundations of castles were yet to be laid, and the famous bridges were yet to be thrown over the stream; and I felt that *this was the Heroic Age itself* though we know it not, for the hero is commonly the simplest and obscurest of men.

The West of which I speak is but another name for the Wild; and what I have been preparing to say is, that in Wildness is the preservation of the world. Every tree sends its fibres forth in search of the Wild. The cities import it at any price. Men plow and sail for it. From the forest and wilderness come the tonics and barks which brace mankind. Our ancestors were savages. The story of Romulus and Remus being suckled by a wolf is not a meaningless fable. The founders of every state which has risen to eminence have drawn their nourishment and vigor from a similar wild source. It is because the children of the empire were not suckled by the wolf that they were conquered and displaced by the children of the northern forests who were.

I believe in the forest, and in the meadow, and in the night in which the corn grows. We require an infusion of hemlock spruce or Arbor vitae in our tea. There is a difference between eating and drinking for strength and from mere gluttony. The Hottentots eagerly devour the marrow of the Koodoo and other antelopes raw, as a matter of course. Some of our northern Indians eat raw the marrow of the Arctic reindeer, as well as various other parts, including the summits of the antlers as long as they are soft. And herein perchance they have stolen a march on the cooks of Paris. They get what usually goes to feed the fire. This is probably better than stall-fed beef and slaughterhouse pork to make a man of. Give me a Wildness whose glance no civilization can endure, as if we lived on the marrow of koodoos devoured raw.

There are some intervals which border the strain of the woodthrush, to which I would migrate, wild lands where no settler has squatted; to which, methinks, I am already acclimated.

The African hunter Gordon-Cumming tells us that the skin of the Eland, as well as that of most other antelopes just killed, emits the most delicious perfume of trees and grass. I would have every man so much a wild antelope, so much a part and parcel of Nature, that his very person should thus sweetly advertise our senses of his presence, and remind us of those parts of nature which he most haunts. I feel no disposition to be satirical when the trapper's coat emits the odor of musquash even; it is a sweeter scent to me than that which commonly exhales from the merchant's or the scholar's garments. When I go into their wardrobes and handle their vestments, I am reminded of no grassy plains and flowery meads which they have frequented, but of dusty merchants' exchanges and libraries rather.

A tanned skin is something more than respectable, and perhaps olive is a fitter color than white for a man, a denizen of the woods. "The pale white man!" I do not wonder that the African pitied him. Darwin the naturalist says "A white man bathing by the side of a Tahitian was like a plant bleached by the gardener's art compared with a fine, dark green one growing vigorously in the open fields. "

Ben Jonson exclaims—

"How near to good is what is fair!"

So I would say—

How near to good is what is wild!

Life consists with Wildness. The most alive is the wildest. Not yet subdued to man, its presence refreshes him. One who pressed forward incessantly and never rested from his labors, who grew fast and made infinite demands on life, would always find himself in a new country or wilderness, and surrounded by the raw material of life. He would be climbing over the prostrate stems of primitive forest trees.

Hope and the future for me are not in lawns and cultivated fields, not in towns and cities, but in the impervious and quaking swamps. When, formerly, I have analysed my partiality for some farm which I had contemplated purchasing, I have frequently found that I was attracted solely by a few square rods of impermeable and unfathomable bog, a natural sink in one corner of it. That was the jewel which dazzled me. I derive more of my subsistence from the swamps which surround my native town than from the cultivated gardens in the village. There are no richer parterres to my eyes than the dense beds of dwarf andromeda (*Cassandra calyculata*) which cover these tender places on the earth's surface. Botany cannot go further than tell me the names of the shrubs which grow there—the high-blueberry, panicled andromeda, lamb-kill, azalea and rhodora—all standing in the quaking sphagnum. I often think that I would like to have my house front on this mass of dull red bushes, omitting other flower plots and borders, transplanted spruce and trim box, even graveled walks, to have this fertile spot under my windows, not a few imported barrow-fuls of soil only, to cover the sand which was thrown out in digging the cellar. Why not put my house, my parlor, behind this plot instead of behind that meagre assemblage of curiosities, that poor apology for a Nature and art, which I call my front yard? It is an effort to clear up and make a decent appearance when the carpenter and mason have departed, though done as much for the passer by as the dweller within. The most tasteful front-yard fence was never an agreeable object of study to me; the most elaborate ornaments, acorn tops, or what not, soon wearied and disgusted me. Bring your sills up to the very edge of the swamp then (though it may not be the best place for a dry cellar) so that there be no access on that side to citizens. Front-yards are not made to walk in, but at most, through, and you could go in the back way.

Yes; though you may think me perverse, if it were proposed to me to dwell in the neighborhood of the most beautiful garden that ever human art contrived, or else of a dismal swamp, I should certainly decide for the swamp. How vain then have been all your labors, citizens, for me!

My spirits infallibly rise in proportion to the outward dreariness. Give me the Ocean, the desert, or the wilderness. In the desert a pure air and solitude compensate for want of moisture and fertility. The traveler Burton says of it

"Your *morale* improves: you become frank and cordial, hospitable and single-minded. [. . .] In the desert spirituous liquors excite only disgust. There is a keen enjoyment in a mere animal existence." They who have been traveling long on the steppes of Tartary, say "On reentering cultivated lands, the agitation, perplexity and turmoil of civilization oppressed and suffocated us; the air seemed to fail us, and we felt every moment as if about to die of asphyxia." When I would recreate myself, I seek the darkest wood, the thickest and most interminable, and, to the citizen, most dismal swamp. I enter a swamp as a sacred place, a *sanctum sanctorum*. There is the strength, the marrow of Nature. The wild wood covers the virgin mould, and the same soil is good for men and for trees. A man's health requires as many acres of meadow to his prospect as his farm does loads of muck. There are the strong meats on which he feeds. A town is saved, not more by the righteous men in it, than by the woods and swamps that surround it. A township where one primitive forest waves above, while another primitive forest rots below—such a town is fitted to raise not only corn and potatoes, but poets and philosophers for the coming ages. In such a soil grew Homer and Confucius and the rest, and out of such a wilderness comes the reformer eating locusts and wild honey.

To preserve wild animals implies generally the creation of a forest for them to dwell in or resort to. So is it with man. A hundred years ago they sold bark in our streets peeled from our own woods. In the very aspect of those primitive and rugged trees, there was methinks a taming principle which hardened and consolidated the fibres of men's thoughts. Ah! Already I shudder for these comparatively degenerate days of my native village, when you cannot collect a load of bark of good thickness, and we no longer produce tar and turpentine.

The civilized nations—Greece, Rome, England—have been sustained by the primitive forests which anciently rotted where they stand. They survive as long as the soil is not exhausted. Alas for human culture! Little is to be expected of a nation when the vegetable mould is exhausted, and it is compelled to make manure of the bones of its fathers. There the poet sustains himself merely by his own superfluous fat, and the philosopher comes down on to his marrow bones.

It is said to be the task of the American, "to work the virgin soil," and that "Agriculture here already assumes proportions unknown everywhere else." I think that the farmer displaces the Indian even because he redeems the meadow, and so makes himself stronger and in some respects more natural. I was surveying for a man the other day a single straight line one hundred and thirty-two rods long through a swamp, at whose entrance might have been written the words which Dante read over the entrance to the Infernal regions—Leave all hope ye that enter—that is of ever getting out again; where at one time I saw my employer actually up to his neck and swimming for his life in his property, though it was still winter. He had another similar swamp which I could not survey at all because it was completely under water, and nevertheless, with regard to a third swamp which I did *survey* from a distance, he remarked to me, true to his instincts, that he would not part with it for any consideration, on account of the mud which it contained. And that man intends to put a girdling ditch round the whole in the course of forty months, and so redeem it by the magic of his spade. I refer to him only as the type of a class.

The weapons with which we have gained our most important victories, which should be handed down as heirlooms from father to son, are not the sword and the lance, but the bush-whack, the turf-cutter, the spade, and the bog-hoe, rusted with the blood of many a meadow, and begrimed with the dust of many a hard-fought field. The very winds blew the Indian's cornfield into the meadow, and pointed out the way which he had not the skill to follow. He had no better implement with which to entrench himself in the land than a clamshell. But the farmer is armed with plow and spade.

In Literature, it is only the wild that attracts us. Dullness is but another name for tameness. It is the uncivilized free and wild thinking in Hamlet and the Iliad, in all the scriptures and mythologies, not learned in the Schools, that delights us. As the wild duck is more swift and beautiful than the tame, so is the wild, the mallard thought, which, 'mid falling dews wings its way above the fens. A truly good book is something as natural, and as unexpectedly and unaccountably fair and perfect, as a wild flower discovered on the prairies of the west, or in the jungles of the east. Genius is a light which makes the darkness visible, like the lightning's flash, which perchance shatters the temple of knowledge itself, and not a taper lighted at the hearth-stone of the race which pales before the light of common day.

English literature from the days of the minstrels to the Lake Poets, Chaucer and Spenser and Milton, and even Shakespeare included, breathes no quite fresh and in this sense wild strain. It is an essentially tame and civilized literature reflecting Greece and Rome. Her wilderness is a green wood, her wild man a Robinhood. There is plenty of genial love of nature, but not so much of Nature herself. Her chronicles inform us when her wild animals, but not when the wild man in her, became extinct. The science of Humboldt is one thing; poetry is another thing. The poet today, notwithstanding all the discoveries of science, and the accumulated learning of mankind, enjoys no advantage over Homer.

Where is the literature which gives expression to Nature? He would be a poet who could impress the winds and streams into his service, to speak for him; who nailed words to their primitive senses, as farmers drive down stakes in the spring which the frost has heaved; who derived his words as often as he used them, transplanted them to his page with earth adhering to their roots; whose words were so true, and fresh, and natural that they would appear to expand like the buds at the approach of spring, though they lay half smothered between two musty leaves in a library, aye, to bloom and bear fruit there after their kind annually for the faithful reader, in sympathy with surrounding Nature.

I do not know of any poetry to quote which adequately expresses this yearning for the Wild. Approached from this side the best poetry is tame. I do not know where to find in any literature, ancient or modern, any account which contents me, of that Nature with which even I am acquainted. You will perceive that I demand something which no Augustan nor Elizabethan age, which no *culture,* in short, can give. Mythology comes nearer to it than anything. How much more fertile a nature at least has Grecian mythology its root in than English Literature! Mythology is the crop which the old world bore before its soil was exhausted, before the fancy and imagination were affected with blight, and which it still bears wherever its pristine vigor is unabated. All other literatures endure only as the elms which overshadow our houses, but this is like the great Dragon tree of the Western isles, as old as mankind, and whether that does or not, will endure as long; for the decay of other literatures makes the soil in which it thrives.

The West is preparing to add its fables to those of the east. The valleys of the Ganges, the Nile, and the Rhine, having yielded their crop, it remains to be seen what the valleys of the Amazon, the Plate, the Orinoco, the St. Lawrence and the Mississippi will produce. Perchance, when in the course of ages, American Liberty has become a fiction of the past—as it is to some extent a fiction of the present—the poets of the world will be inspired by American Mythology.

The wildest dreams of wild men, even, are not the less true, though they may not recommend themselves to the sense which is most common among Englishmen and Americans today. It is not every truth that recommends itself to the common sense. Nature has a place for the wild clematis as well as for the cabbage. Some expressions of truth are reminiscent, others merely *sensible,* as the phrase is, others prophetic. Some forms of disease even may prophesy forms of health. The geologist has discovered that the figures of serpents, griffins, flying dragons, and other fanciful embellishments of heraldry, have their prototypes in the forms of fossil species which were extinct before man was created, and hence "indicate a faint and shadowy knowledge of a previous state of organic existence." The Hindus dreamed that the earth rested on an elephant, and the elephant on a tortoise, and the tortoise on a serpent; and though it may be an unimportant coincidence, it will not be out of place here to state, that a fossil tortoise has lately been discovered in Asia large enough to support an elephant. I confess that I am partial to these wild fancies, which transcend the order of time and development. They are the sublimest recreation of the intellect. The partridge loves peas, but not those that go with her into the pot.

In short, all good things are wild and free. There is something in a strain of music, whether produced by an instrument or by the human voice—take the sound of a bugle in a summer night, for instance—which by its wildness, to speak without satire, reminds me of the cries emitted by wild beasts in their native forests. It is so much of their wildness as I can understand. Give me for my friends and neighbors wild men, not tame ones. The wildness of the savage is but a faint symbol of the awful ferity with which good men and lovers meet.

I love even to see the domestic animals reassert their native rights, any evidence that they have not wholly lost their original wild habits and vigor; as when my neighbor's cow breaks out of her pasture early in the Spring and boldly swims the river, a cold grey tide, twenty-five or thirty rods wide, swollen by the melted snow. It is the Buffalo crossing the Mississippi. This exploit confers some dignity on the herd in my eyes, already dignified. The seeds of instinct are preserved under the thick hides of cattle and horses, like seeds in the bowels of the earth, an indefinite period.

Any sportiveness in cattle is unexpected. I saw one day a herd of a dozen bullocks and cows running about and frisking in unwieldly sport, like huge rats, even like kittens. They shook their heads, raised their tails, and rushed up and down a hill, and I perceived by their horns, as well as by their activity, their relation to the deer tribe. But, alas! a sudden loud whoa! would have damped their ardor at once, reduced them from venison to beef, and stiffened their sides and sinews like the locomotive. Who but the Evil One has cried "Whoa!" to mankind? Indeed, the life of cattle, like that of many men, is but a sort of locomotiveness, they move a side at a time, and Man by his machinery is meeting the horse and ox half way. Whatever part the whip has touched is thenceforth palsied. Who would ever think of a *side* of any of the supple cat tribe, as we speak of a *side* of beef?

I rejoice that horses and steers have to be broken before they can be made the slaves of men, and that men themselves have some wild oats still left to sow before they become submissive members of society. Undoubtedly, all men are not equally fit subjects for civilization, and because the majority, like dogs and sheep are tame by inherited disposition, is no reason why the others should have their natures broken that they may be reduced to the same level. Men are in the main alike, but they were made several in order that they might be various. If a low use is to be served, one man will do nearly or quite as well as another; if a high one, individual excellence is to be regarded. Any man can stop a hole to keep the wind away, but no other man could serve so rare a use as the author of this illustration did. Confucius says "The skins of the tiger and the leopard when they are tanned, are as the skins of the dog and the sheep tanned." But it is not the part of a true culture to tame tigers, any more than it is to make sheep ferocious, and tanning their skins for shoes is not the best use to which they can be put.

4. Circles

RALPH WALDO EMERSON

Nature centres into balls,
And her proud ephemerals,
Fast to surface and outside,
Scan the profile of the sphere;
Knew they what that signified
A new genesis were here.

The eye is the first circle; the horizon which it forms is the second; and throughout nature this primary figure is repeated without end. It is the highest emblem in the cipher of the world. St. Augustine described the nature of God as a circle whose centre was everywhere and its circumference nowhere. We are all our lifetime reading the copious sense of this first of forms. One moral we have already deduced in considering the circular or compensatory character of every human action. Another analogy we shall now trace, that every action admits of being outdone. Our life is an apprenticeship to the truth that around every circle another can be drawn; that there is no end in nature, but every end is a beginning; that there is always another dawn risen on mid-noon, and under every deep a lower deep opens.

This fact, as far as it symbolizes the moral fact of the Unattainable, the flying Perfect, around which the hands of man can never meet, at once the inspirer and the condemner of every success, may conveniently serve us to connect many illustrations of human power in every department.

There are no fixtures in nature. The universe is fluid and volatile. Permanence is but a word of degrees. Our globe seen by God is a transparent law, not a mass of facts. The law dissolves the fact and holds it fluid. Our culture is the predominance of an idea which draws after it this train of cities and institutions. Let us rise into another idea; they will disappear. The Greek sculpture is all melted away, as if it had been statues of ice; here and there a solitary figure or fragment remaining, as we see flecks and scraps of snow left in cold dells and mountain clefts in June and July. For the genius that created it creates now somewhat else. The Greek letters last a little longer, but are already passing under the same sentence and tumbling into the inevitable pit which the creation of new thought opens for all that is old. The new continents are built out of the ruins of an old planet; the new races fed out of the decomposition of the foregoing. New arts destroy the old. See the investment of capital in aqueducts, made useless by hydraulics; fortifications, by gunpowder; roads and canals, by railways; sails, by steam; steam by electricity.

You admire this tower of granite, weathering the hurts of so many ages. Yet a little waving hand built this huge wall, and that which builds is better than that which is built. The hand that built can topple it down much faster. Better than the hand and nimbler was the invisible thought which wrought through it; and thus ever, behind the coarse effect, is a fine cause, which, being narrowly seen, is itself the effect of a finer cause. Everything looks permanent until its secret is known. A rich estate appears to women a firm and lasting fact; to a merchant, one easily created out of any materials, and easily lost. An orchard, good tillage, good grounds, seem a fixture, like a gold mine, or a river, to a citizen; but to a large farmer, not much more fixed than the state of the crop. Nature looks provokingly stable and secular, but it has a cause like all the rest; and when once I comprehend that, will these fields stretch so immovably wide, these leaves hang so individually considerable? Permanence is a word of degrees. Every thing is medial. Moons are no more bounds to spiritual power than bat-balls.

The key to every man is his thought. Sturdy and defying though he look, he has a helm which he obeys, which is the idea after which all his facts are classified. He can only be reformed by showing him a new idea which commands his own. The life of man is a self-evolving circle, which, from a ring imperceptibly small, rushes on all sides outwards to new and larger circles, and that without end. The extent to which this generation of circles, wheel without wheel, will go, depends on the force or truth of the individual soul. For it is the inert effort of each thought, having formed itself into a circular wave of circumstance—as for instance an empire, rules of an art, a local usage, a religious rite—to heap itself on that ridge and to solidify and hem in the life. But if the soul is quick and strong it bursts over that boundary on all sides and expands another orbit on the great deep, which also runs up into a high wave, with attempt again to stop and to bind. But the heart refuses to be imprisoned: in its first and narrowest pulses it already tends outward with a vast force and to immense and innumerable expansions.

Every ultimate fact is only the first of a new series. Every general law only a particular fact of some more general law presently to disclose itself. There is no outside, no enclosing wall, no circumference to us. The man finishes his story—how good! how final! how it puts a new face on all things! He fills the sky. Lo! on the other side rises also a man and draws a circle around the circle we had just pronounced the outline of the sphere. Then already is our first speaker not man, but only a first speaker. His only redress is forthwith to draw a circle outside of his antagonist. And so men do by themselves. The result of to-day, which haunts the mind and cannot be escaped, will presently be abridged into a word, and the principle that seemed to explain nature will itself be included as one example of a bolder generalization. In the thought of to-morrow there is power to upheave all thy creed, all the creeds, all the literatures of the nations, and marshal thee to a heaven which no epic dream has yet depicted. Every man is not so much a workman in the world as he is a suggestion of that he should be. Men walk as prophecies of the next age.

Step by step we scale this mysterious ladder; the steps are actions, the new prospect is power. Every several result is threatened and judged by that which follows. Every one seems to be contradicted by the new: it is only limited by the new. The new statement is always hated by the old, and, to those dwelling in the old, comes like an abyss of skepticism. But the eye soon gets wonted to it, for the eye and it are effects of one cause: then its innocency and benefit appear, and presently, all its energy spent, it pales and dwindles before the revelation of the new hour.

Fear not the new generalization. Does the fact look crass and material, threatening to degrade thy theory of spirit? Resist it not; it goes to refine and raise thy theory of matter just as much.

There are no fixtures to men, if we appeal to consciousness. Every man supposes himself not to be fully understood; and if there is any truth in him, if he rests at last on the divine soul, I see not how it can be otherwise. The last chamber, the last closet, he must feel was never opened; there is always a residuum unknown, unanalyzable. That is, every man believes that he has a greater possibility.

Our moods do not believe in each other. Today I am full of thoughts and can write what I please. I see no reason why I should not have the same thought, the same power of expression, tomorrow. What I write, whilst I write it, seems the most natural thing in the world: but yesterday I saw a dreary vacuity in this direction in which now I see so much; and a month hence, I doubt not, I shall wonder who he was that wrote so many continuous pages. Alas for this infirm faith, this will not strenuous, this vast ebb of a vast flow! I am God in nature: I am a weed by the wall.

The continual effort to raise himself above himself, to work a pitch above his last height, betrays itself in a man's relations. We thirst for approbation, yet cannot forgive the approver. The sweet of nature is love; yet if I have a friend I am tormented by my imperfections. The love of me accuses the other party. If he were high enough to slight me, then could I love him, and rise by my affection to new heights. A man's growth is seen in the successive choirs of his friends. For every friend whom he loses for truth, he gains a better. I thought as I walked in the woods and mused on my friends, why should I play with them this game of idolatry? I know and see too well, when not voluntarily blind, the speedy limits of persons called high and worthy. Rich, noble and great they are by the liberality of our speech, but truth is sad. O blessed Spirit, whom I forsake for these. They are not thou! Every personal consideration that we allow costs us heavenly state. We sell the thrones of angels for a short and turbulent pleasure.

How often must we learn this lesson? Men cease to interest us when we find their limitations. The only sin is limitation. As soon as you once come up with a man's limitations, it is all over with him. Has he talents? Has he enterprise? Has he knowledge? It boots not. Infinitely alluring and attractive was he to you yesterday, a great hope, a sea to swim in; now, you have found his shores, found it a pond, and you care not if you never see it again.

Each new step we take in thought reconciles twenty seemingly discordant facts, as expressions of one law. Aristotle and Plato are reckoned the respective heads of two schools. A wise man will see that Aristotle platonizes. By going one step farther back in thought, discordant opinions are reconciled by being seen to be two extremes of one principle, and we can never go so far back as to preclude a still higher vision.

Beware when the great God lets loose a thinker on this planet. Then all things are at risk. It is as when a conflagration has broken out in a great city, and no man knows what is safe, or where it will end. There is not a piece of science but its flank may be turned to-morrow; there is not any literary reputation, not the so-called eternal names of fame, that may not be revised and condemned. The very hopes of man, the thoughts of his heart, the religion of nations, the manners and morals of mankind are all at the mercy of a new generalization. Generalization is always a new influx of the divinity into the mind. Hence the thrill that attends it.

Valor consists in the power of self-recovery, so that a man cannot have his flank turned, cannot be out-generalled, but put him where you will, he stands. This can only be by his preferring truth to his past apprehension of truth, and his alert acceptance of it from whatever quarter; the intrepid conviction that his laws, his relations to society, his Christianity, his world, may at any time be superseded and decease.

There are degrees in idealism. We learn first to play with it academically, as the magnet was once a toy. Then we see in the heyday of youth and poetry that it may be true, that it is true in gleams and fragments. Then its countenance waxes stern and grand, and we see that it must be true. It now shows itself ethical and practical. We learn that God IS; that he is in me; and that all things are shadows of him. The idealism of Berkeley is only a crude statement of the idealism of Jesus, and that again is a crude statement of the fact that all nature is the rapid efflux of goodness executing and organizing itself. Much more obviously is history and the state of the world at any one time directly dependent on the intellectual classification then existing in the minds of men. The things which are dear to men at this hour are so on account of the ideas which have emerged on their mental horizon, and which cause the present order of things, as a tree bears its apples. A new degree of culture would instantly revolutionize the entire system of human pursuits.

Conversation is a game of circles. In conversation we pluck up the *termini* which bound the common of silence on every side. The parties are not to be judged by the spirit they partake and even express under this Pentecost. To-morrow they will have receded from this high-water mark. Tomorrow you shall find them stooping under the old pack-saddles. Yet let us enjoy the cloven flame whilst it glows on our walls. When each new speaker strikes a new light, emancipates us from the oppression of the last speaker to oppress us with the greatness and exclusiveness of his own thought, then yields us to another redeemer, we seem to recover our rights, to become men. O, what truths profound and executable only in ages and orbs, are supposed in the announcement of every truth! In common hours, society sits cold and statuesque. We all stand waiting, empty—knowing, possibly, that we can be full, surrounded by mighty symbols which are not symbols to us, but prose and trivial toys. Then cometh the god and converts the statues into fiery men, and by a flash of his eye burns up the veil which shrouded all things, and the meaning of the very furniture, of cup and saucer, of chair and clock and tester, is manifest. The facts which loomed so large in the fogs of yesterday—property, climate, breeding, personal beauty and the like, have strangely changed their proportions. All that we reckoned settled shakes and rattles; and literatures, cities, climates, religions, leave their foundations and dance before our eyes. And yet here again see the swift circumscription! Good as is discourse, silence is better, and shames it. The length of the discourse indicates the distance of thought betwixt the speaker and the hearer. If they were at a perfect understanding in any part, no words would be necessary thereon. If at one in all parts, no words would be suffered.

Literature is a point outside of our hodiernal circle through which a new one may be described. The use of literature is to afford us a platform whence we may command a view of our present life, a purchase by which we may move it. We fill ourselves with ancient learning, install ourselves the best we can in Greek, in Punic, in Roman houses, only that we may wiselier see French, English and American houses and modes of living. In like manner we see literature best from the midst of wild nature, or from the din of affairs, or from a high religion. The field cannot be well seen from within the field. The astronomer must have his diameter of the earth's orbit as a base to find the parallax of any star.

Therefore we value the poet. All the argument and all the wisdom is not in the encyclopedia, or the treatise on metaphysics, or the Body of Divinity, but in the sonnet or the play. In my daily work I incline to repeat my old steps, and do not believe in remedial force, in the power of change and reform. But some Petrarch or Ariosto, filled with the new wine of his imagination, writes me an ode or a brisk romance, full of daring thought and action. He smites and arouses me with his shrill tones, breaks up my whole chain of habits, and I open my eye on my own possibilities. He claps wings to the sides of all the solid old lumber of the world, and I am capable once more of choosing a straight path in theory and practice.

We have the same need to command a view of the religion of the world. We can never see Christianity from the catechism—from the pastures, from a boat in the pond, from amidst the songs of wood-birds we possibly may. Cleansed by the elemental light and wind, steeped in the sea of beautiful terms which the field offers us, we may chance to cast a right glance back upon biography. Christianity is rightly dear to the best of mankind, yet was there never a young philosopher whose breeding had fallen into the Christian church by whom that brave text of Paul's was not specially prized: "Then shall also the Son be subject unto Him who put all things under him, that God may be all in all." Let the claims and virtues of persons be never so great and welcome, the instinct of man presses eagerly onward to the impersonal and illimitable, and gladly arms itself against the dogmatism of bigots with this generous word out of the book itself.

The natural world may be conceived of as a system of concentric circles, and we now and then detect in nature slight dislocations which apprise us that this surface on which we now stand is not fixed, but sliding. These manifold tenacious qualities, this chemistry and vegetation, these metals and animals, which seem to stand there for their own sake, are means and methods only, are words of God, and as fugitive as other words. Has the naturalist or chemist learned his craft, who has explored the gravity of atoms and the elective affinities, who has not yet discerned the deeper law whereof this is only a partial or approximate statement, namely that like draws to like, and that the goods which belong to you gravitate to you and need not be pursued with pains and cost? Yet is that statement approximate also, and not final. Omnipresence is a higher fact. Not through subtle subterranean channels need friend and fact be drawn to their counterpart, but rightly considered, these things proceed from the eternal generation of the soul. Cause and effect are two sides of one fact.

The same law of eternal procession ranges all that we call the virtues, and extinguishes each in the light of a better. The great man will not be prudent in the popular sense: all his prudence will be so much deduction from his grandeur.

But it behooves each to see, when he sacrifices prudence, to what god he devotes it; if to ease and pleasure, he had better be prudent still; if to a great trust, he can well spare his mule and panniers who has a winged chariot instead. Geoffrey draws on his boots to go through the woods, that his feet may be safer from the bite of snakes; Aaron never thinks of such a peril. In many years neither is harmed by such an accident. Yet it seems to me that with every precaution you take against such an evil you put yourself into the power of the evil. I suppose that the highest prudence is the lowest prudence. Is this too sudden a rushing from the centre to the verge of our orbit? Think how many times we shall fall back into pitiful calculations before we take up our rest in the great sentiment, or make the verge of today the new centre. Besides, your bravest sentiment is familiar to the humblest men. The poor and the low have their way of expressing the last facts of philosophy as well as you. "Blessed be nothing" and "The worse things are, the better they are" are proverbs which express the transcendentalism of common life.

One man's justice is another's injustice; one man's beauty another's ugliness; one man's wisdom another's folly: as one beholds the same objects from a higher point. One man thinks justice consists in paying debts, and has no measure in his abhorrence of another who is very remiss in this duty and makes the creditor wait tediously. But that second man has his own way of looking at things; asks himself which debt must I pay first, the debt to the rich, or the debt to the poor? the debt of money, or the debt of thought to mankind, of genius to nature? For you, O broker, there is no other principle but arithmetic. For me, commerce is of trivial import: love, faith, truth of character, the aspiration of man, these are sacred: nor can I detach one duty, like you, from all other duties, and concentrate my forces mechanically on the payment of moneys. Let me live onward; you shall find that, though slower, the progress of my character will liquidate all these debts without injustice to higher claims. If a man should dedicate himself to the payment of notes, would not this be injustice? Does he owe no debt but money? And are all claims on him to be postponed to a landlord's or a banker's?

There is no virtue which is final; all are initial. The virtues of society are vices of the saint. The terror of reform is the discovery that we must cast away our virtues, or what we have always esteemed such, into the same pit that has consumed our grosser vices:

> Forgive his crimes, forgive his virtues too,
> Those smaller faults, half converts to the right.

It is the highest power of divine moments that they abolish our contritions also. I accuse myself of sloth and unprofitableness day by day; but when these waves of God flow into me I no longer reckon lost time. I no longer poorly compute my possible achievement by what remains to me of the month or the year; for these moments confer a sort of omnipresence and omnipotence which asks nothing of duration, but sees that the energy of the mind is commensurate with the work to be done, without time.

And thus, O circular philosopher, I hear some reader exclaim, you have arrived at a fine Pyrrhonism, at an equivalence and indifferency of all actions, and would fain teach us that *if we are true,* forsooth, our crimes may be lively stones out of which we shall construct the temple of the true God!

I am not careful to justify myself. I own I am gladdened by seeing the predominance of the saccharine principle throughout vegetable nature, and not less by beholding in morals that unrestrained inundation of the principle of good into every chink and hole that selfishness has left open, yea into selfishness and sin itself; so that no evil is pure. Nor hell itself without its extreme satisfactions. But lest I should mislead any when I have my own head and obey my whims, let me remind the reader that I am only an experimenter. Do not set the least value on what I do, or the least discredit on what I do not, as if I pretended to settle any thing as true or false. I unsettle all things. No facts are to me sacred; none are profane; I simply experiment, an endless seeker with no Past at my back.

Yet this incessant movement and progression which all things partake could never become sensible to us but by contrast to some principle of fixture or stability in the soul. Whilst the eternal generation of circles proceeds, the eternal generator abides. That central life is somewhat superior to creation, superior to knowledge and thought, and contains all its circles. Forever it labors to create a life and thought as large and excellent as itself, but in vain, for that which is made instructs how to make a better.

Thus there is no sleep, no pause, no preservation, but all things renew, germinate and spring. Why should we import rags and relics into the new hour? Nature abhors the old, and old age seems the only disease: all others run into this one. We call it by many names—fever, intemperance, insanity, stupidity and crime; they are all forms of old age; they are rest, conservatism, appropriation, inertia; not newness, not the way onward. We grizzle every day. I see no need of it. Whilst we converse with what is above us, we do not grow old, but grow young. Infancy, youth, receptive, aspiring, with religious eye looking upward, counts itself nothing and abandons itself to the instruction flowing from all sides. But the man and woman of seventy assume to know all. They have outlived their hope, they renounce aspiration, accept the actual for the necessary and talk down to the young. Let them then become organs of the Holy Ghost; let them be lovers; let them behold truth; and their eyes are uplifted, their wrinkles smoothed, they are perfumed again with hope and power. This old age ought not to creep on a human mind. In nature every moment is new; the past is always swallowed and forgotten; the coming only is sacred. Nothing is secure but life, transition, the energizing spirit. No love can be bound by oath or covenant to secure it against a higher love. No truth so sublime but it may be trivial to-morrow in the light of new thoughts. People wish to be settled; only as far as they are unsettled is there any hope for them.

Life is a series of surprises. We do not guess today the mood, the pleasure, the power of tomorrow, when we are building up our being. Of lower states, of acts of routine and sense, we can tell somewhat; but the masterpieces of God, the total growths and universal movements of the soul, he hideth; they are incalculable. I can know that truth is divine and helpful; but how it shall help me I can have no guess, for *so to be* is the sole inlet of *so to know.* The new position of the advancing man has all the powers of the old, yet has them all new. It carries in its bosom all the energies of the past, yet is itself an exhalation of the morning. I cast away in this new moment all my once hoarded knowledge, as vacant and vain. Now for the first time seem I to know any thing rightly. The simplest words—we do not know what they mean except when we love and aspire.

The difference between talents and character is adroitness to keep the old and trodden round, and power and courage to make a new road to new and better goals. Character makes an overpowering present; a cheerful, determined hour, which fortifies all the company by making them see that much is possible and excellent that was not thought of. Character dulls the impression of particular events. When we see the conqueror we do not think much of any one battle or success. We see that we had exaggerated the difficulty. It was easy to him. The great man is not convulsible or tormentable; events pass over him without much impression. People say sometimes, "See what I have overcome; see how cheerful I am; see how completely I have triumphed over these black events." Not if they still remind me of the black event. True conquest is the causing the calamity to fade and disappear as an early cloud of insignificant result in a history so large and advancing.

The one thing which we seek with insatiable desire is to forget ourselves, to be surprised out of our propriety, to lose our sempiternal memory and to do something without knowing how or why; in short to draw a new circle. Nothing great was ever achieved without enthusiasm. The way of life is wonderful; it is by abandonment. The great moments of history are the facilities of performance through the strength of ideas, as the works of genius and religion. "A man," said Oliver Cromwell, "never rises so high as when he knows not whither he is going." Dreams and drunkenness, the use of opium and alcohol are the semblance and counterfeit of this oracular genius, and hence their dangerous attraction for men. For the like reason they ask the aid of wild passions, as in gaming and war, to ape in some manner these flames and generosities of the heart.

5. Evolutionary Love

CHARLES SANDERS PEIRCE

At First Blush. Counter Gospels.

Philosophy, when just escaping from its golden pupa-skin, mythology, proclaimed the great evolutionary agency of the universe to be Love. Or, since this pirate-lingo, English, is poor in such-like words, let us say Eros, the exuberance-love. Afterwards, Empedocles set up passionate love and hate as the two coordinate powers of the universe. In some passages, kindness is the word. But certainly, in any sense in which it has an opposite, to be senior partner of that opposite, is the highest position that love can attain. Nevertheless, the ontological gospeller, in whose days those views were familiar topics, made the One Supreme Being, by whom all things have been made out of nothing, to be cherishing-love. What, then, can he say to hate? Never mind, at this time, what the scribe of the Apocalypse, if he were John, stung at length by persecution into a rage, unable to distinguish suggestions of evil from visions of heaven, and so become the Slanderer of God to men, may have dreamed. The question is rather what the sane John thought, or ought to have thought, in order to carry out his idea consistently. His statement that God is love seems aimed at that saying of Ecclesiastes that we cannot tell whether God bears us love or hatred. "Nay," says John, "we can tell, and very simply! We know and have trusted the love which God hath in us. God is love." There is no logic in this, unless it means that God loves all men. In the preceding paragraph, he had said, "God is light and in him is no darkness at all." We are to understand, then, that as darkness is merely the defect of light, so hatred and evil are mere imperfect stages of *agapē* and *agathon,* love and loveliness. This concords with that utterance reported in John's Gospel: "God sent not the Son into the world to judge the world; but that the world should through him be saved. He that believeth on him is not judged: he that believeth not hath been judged already. [. . .] And this is the judgment, that the light is come into the world, and that men loved darkness rather than the light." That is to say, God visits no punishment on them; they punish themselves, by their natural affinity for the defective. Thus, the love that God is, is not a love of which hatred is the contrary; otherwise Satan would be a coordinate power; but it is a love which embraces hatred as an imperfect stage of it, an Anteros—yea, even needs hatred and hatefulness as its object. For self-love is no love; so if God's self is love, that which he loves must be defect of love; just as a luminary can light up only that which otherwise would be dark. Henry James, the Swedenborgian, says: "It is no doubt very tolerable finite or creaturely love to love one's own in another, to love another for his conformity to one's self: but nothing can be in more flagrant contrast with the creative Love, all whose tenderness *ex vi termini* must be reserved only for what intrinsically is most bitterly hostile and negative to itself." This is from *Substance and Shadow: An Essay on the Physics of Creation.* It is a pity he had not filled his pages with things like this, as he was able easily to do, instead of scolding at his reader and at people generally, until the physics of creation was well-nigh forgot. I must deduct, however, from what I just wrote: obviously no genius could make his every sentence as sublime as one which discloses for the problem of evil its everlasting solution.

The movement of love is circular, at one and the same impulse projecting creations into independency and drawing them into harmony. This seems complicated when stated so; but it is fully summed up in the simple formula we call the Golden Rule. This does not, of course, say, Do everything possible to gratify the egoistic impulses of others, but it says, Sacrifice your own perfection to the perfectionment of your neighbor. Nor must it for a moment be confounded with the Benthamite, or Helvetian, or Beccarian motto, Act for the greatest good of the greatest number. Love is not directed to abstractions but to persons; not to persons we do not know, nor to numbers of people, but to our own dear ones, our family and neighbors. "Our neighbor," we remember, is one whom we live near, not locally perhaps but in life and feeling.

Everybody can see that the statement of St. John is the formula of an evolutionary philosophy, which teaches that growth comes only from love, from I will not say self-*sacrifice,* but from the ardent impulse to fulfill another's highest impulse. Suppose, for example, that I have an idea that interests me. It is my creation. It is my creature; for as shown in last July's *Monist,* it is a little person. I love it; and I will sink myself in perfecting it. It is not by dealing out cold justice to the circle of my ideas that I can make them grow, but by cherishing and tending them as I would the flowers in my garden. The philosophy we draw from John's gospel is that this is the way mind develops; and as for the cosmos, only so far as it yet is mind, and so has life, is it capable of further evolution. Love, recognizing germs of loveliness in the hateful, gradually warms it into life, and makes it lovely. That is the sort of evolution which every careful student of my essay "The Law of Mind" must see that synechism calls for.

The nineteenth century is now fast sinking into the grave, and we all begin to review its doings and to think what character it is destined to bear as compared with other centuries in the minds of future historians. It will be called, I guess, the Economical Century; for political economy has more direct relations with all the branches of its activity than has any other science. Well, political economy has its formula of redemption, too. It is this: Intelligence in the service of greed ensures the justest prices, the fairest contracts, the most enlightened conduct of all the dealings between men, and leads to the *summum bonum,* food in plenty and perfect comfort. Food for whom? Why, for the greedy master of intelligence. I do not mean to say that this is one of the legitimate conclusions of political economy, the scientific character of which I fully acknowledge. But the study of doctrines, themselves true, will often temporarily encourage generalizations extremely false, as the study of physics has encouraged necessitarianism. What I say, then, is that the great attention paid to economical questions during our century has induced an exaggeration of the beneficial effects of greed and of the unfortunate results of sentiment, until there has resulted a philosophy which comes unwittingly to this, that greed is the great agent in the elevation of the human race and in the evolution of the universe.

I open a handbook of political economy—the most typical and middling one I have at hand—and there find some remarks of which I will here make a brief analysis. I omit qualifications, sops thrown to Cerberus, phrases to placate Christian prejudice, trappings which serve to hide from author and reader alike the ugly nakedness of the greed-god. But I have surveyed my position. The author enumerates "three motives to human action: The love of self; The love of a limited class having common interests and feelings with one's self; The love of mankind at large."

Remark, at the outset, what obsequious title is bestowed on greed—"the love of self." Love! The second motive is love. In place of "a limited class" put "certain persons," and you have a fair description. Taking "class" in the old-fashioned sense, a weak kind of love is described. In the sequel, there seems to be some haziness as to the delimitation of this motive. By the love of mankind at large, the author does not mean that deep, subconscious passion that is properly so called; but merely public-spirit, perhaps little more than a fidget about pushing ideas. The author proceeds to a comparative estimate of the worth of these motives. Greed, says he, but using, of course, another word, "is not so great an evil as is commonly supposed. [. . .] Every man can promote his own interests a great deal more effectively than he can promote any one else's, or than any one else can promote his." Besides, as he remarks on another page, the more miserly a man is, the more good he does. The second motive "is the most dangerous one to which society is exposed." Love is all very pretty: "no higher or purer source of human happiness exists." (Ahem!) But it is a "source of enduring injury," and, in short, should be overruled by something wiser. What is this wiser motive? We shall see.

As for public spirit, it is rendered nugatory by the "difficulties in the way of its effective operation." For example, it might suggest putting checks upon the fecundity of the poor and the vicious; and "no measure of repression would be too severe," in the case of criminals. The hint is broad. But unfortunately, you cannot induce legislatures to take such measures, owing to the pestiferous "tender sentiments of man towards man." It thus appears that public-spirit, or Benthamism, is not strong enough to be the effective tutor of love (I am skipping to another page) which must, therefore, be handed over to "the motives which animate men in the pursuit of wealth," in which alone we can confide, and which "are in the highest degree beneficent."[1] Yes, in the "highest degree" without exception are they beneficent to the being upon whom all their blessings are poured out, namely, the Self, whose "sole object," says the writer, in accumulating wealth is his individual "sustenance and enjoyment." Plainly, the author holds the notion that some other motive might be in a higher degree beneficent, even for the man's self, to be a paradox wanting in good sense. He seeks to gloze and modify his doctrine; but he lets the perspicacious reader see what his animating principle is; and when, holding the opinions I have repeated, he at the same time acknowledges that society could not exist upon a basis of intelligent greed alone, he simply pigeon-holes himself as one of the eclectics of inharmonious opinions. He wants his mammon flavored with a soupçon of god.

The economists accuse those, to whom the enunciation of their atrocious villainies communicates a thrill of horror, of being sentimentalists. It may be so: I willingly confess to having some tincture of sentimentalism in me, God be thanked! Ever since the French Revolution brought this leaning of thought into ill repute—and not altogether undeservedly, I must admit, true, beautiful, and good as that great movement was—it has been the tradition to picture sentimentalists as persons incapable of logical thought and unwilling to look facts in the eyes. This tradition may be classed with the French tradition that an Englishman says godam at every second sentence, the English tradition that an American talks about "Britishers," and the American tradition that a Frenchman carries forms of etiquette to an inconvenient extreme; in short, with all those traditions which survive simply because the men who use their eyes and ears are few and far between. Doubtless some excuse there was for all those opinions in days gone by; and sentimentalism, when it was the fashionable amusement to spend one's evenings in a flood of tears over a woeful performance on a candle-litten stage, sometimes made itself a little ridiculous. But what after all is sentimentalism? It is an *ism,* a doctrine, namely, the doctrine that great respect should be paid to the natural judgments of the sensible heart. This is what sentimentalism precisely is; and I entreat the reader to consider whether to contemn it is not of all blasphemies the most degrading. Yet the nineteenth century has steadily contemned it, because it brought about the Reign of Terror. That it did so is true. Still, the whole question is one of *how much.* The Reign of Terror was very bad; but now the Gradgrind banner has been this century long flaunting in the face of heaven, with an insolence to provoke the very skies to scowl and rumble. Soon a flash and quick peal will shake economists quite out of their complacency, too late. The twentieth century, in its latter half, shall surely see the deluge-tempest burst upon the social order—to clear upon a world as deep in ruin as that greed-philosophy has long plunged it into guilt. No post-thermidorian high jinks then!

So a miser is a beneficent power in a community, is he? With the same reason precisely, only in a much higher degree, you might pronounce the Wall Street sharp to be a good angel, who takes money from heedless persons not likely to guard it properly, who wrecks feeble enterprises better stopped, and who administers wholesome lessons to unwary scientific men, by passing worthless checks upon them—as you did, the other day, to me, my millionaire Master in glomery, when you thought you saw your way to using my process without paying for it, and of so bequeathing to your children something to boast about of their father—and who by a thousand wiles puts money at the service of intelligent greed, in his own person. Bernard Mandeville, in his Fable of the Bees, maintains that private vices of all descriptions are public benefits, and proves it, too, quite as cogently as the economist proves his point concerning the miser. He even argues, with no slight force, that but for vice civilization would never have existed. In the same spirit, it has been strongly maintained and is today widely believed that all acts of charity and benevolence, private and public, go seriously to degrade the human race.

The *Origin of Species* of Darwin merely extends politico-economical views of progress to the entire realm of animal and vegetable life. The vast majority of our contemporary naturalists hold the opinion that the true cause of those exquisite and marvelous adaptations of nature for which, when I was a boy, men used to extol the divine wisdom, is that creatures are so crowded together that those of them that happen to have the slightest advantage force those less pushing into situations unfavorable to multiplication or even kill them before they reach the age of reproduction. Among animals, the mere mechanical individualism is vastly reinforced as a power making for good by the animal's ruthless greed. As Darwin puts it on his title-page, it is the struggle for existence; and he should have added for his motto: Every individual for himself, and the Devil take the hindmost! Jesus, in his sermon on the Mount, expressed a different opinion.

Here, then, is the issue. The gospel of Christ says that progress comes from every individual merging his individuality in sympathy with his neighbors. On the other side, the conviction of the nineteenth century is that progress takes place by virtue of every individual's striving for himself with all his might and trampling his neighbor under foot whenever he gets a chance to do so. This may accurately be called the Gospel of Greed.

Much is to be said on both sides. I have not concealed, I could not conceal, my own passionate predilection. Such a confession will probably shock my scientific brethren. Yet the strong feeling is in itself, I think, an argument of some weight in favor of the agapastic theory of evolution—so far as it may be presumed to bespeak the normal judgment of the Sensible Heart. Certainly, if it were possible to believe in agapasm without believing it warmly, that fact would be an argument against the truth of the doctrine. At any rate, since the warmth of feeling exists, it should on every account be candidly confessed; especially since it creates a liability to one-sidedness on my part against which it behooves my readers and me to be severally on our guard. [. . .]

Three modes of evolution have thus been brought before us: evolution by fortuitous variation, evolution by mechanical necessity, and evolution by creative love. We may term them tychastic evolution, or tychasm, anancastic evolution, or anancasm, and agapastic evolution, or agapasm. The doctrines which represent these as severally of principal importance we may term tychasticism, anancasticism, and agapasticism. On the other hand the mere propositions that absolute chance, mechanical necessity, and the law of love are severally operative in the cosmos may receive the names of tychism, anancism, and agapism.

All three modes of evolution are composed of the same general elements. Agapasm exhibits them the most clearly. The good result is here brought to pass, first, by the bestowal of spontaneous energy by the parent upon the offspring, and, second, by the disposition of the latter to catch the general idea of those about it and thus to subserve the general purpose. In order to express the relation that tychasm and anancasm bear to agapasm let me borrow a word from geometry. An ellipse crossed by a straight line is a sort of cubic curve; for a cubic is a curve which is cut thrice by a straight line; now a straight line might cut the ellipse twice and its associated straight line a third time. Still the ellipse with the straight line across it would not have the characteristics of a cubic. It would have, for instance, no contrary flexure, which no true cubic wants; and it would have two nodes, which no true cubic has. The geometers say that it is a degenerate cubic. Just so, tychasm and anancasm are degenerate forms of agapasm.

Men who seek to reconcile the Darwinian idea with Christianity will remark that tychastic evolution, like the agapastic, depends upon a reproductive creation, the forms preserved being those that use the spontaneity conferred upon them in such wise as to be drawn into harmony with their original, quite after the Christian scheme. Very good! This only shows that just as love cannot have a contrary, but must embrace what is most opposed to it, as a degenerate case of it, so tychasm is a kind of agapasm. Only, in the tychastic evolution, progress is solely owing to the distribution of the napkin-hidden talent of the rejected servant among those not rejected, just as ruined gamesters leave their money on the table to make those not yet ruined so much the richer. It makes the felicity of the lambs just the damnation of the goats, transposed to the other side of the equation. In genuine agapasm, on the other hand, advance takes place by virtue of a positive sympathy among the created springing from continuity of mind. This is the idea which tychasticism knows not how to manage.

The anancasticist might here interpose, claiming that the mode of evolution for which he contends agrees with agapasm at the point at which tychasm departs from it. For it makes development go through certain phases, having its inevitable ebbs and flows, yet tending on the whole to a fore-ordained perfection. Bare existence by this its destiny betrays an intrinsic affinity for the good. Herein, it must be admitted, anancasm shows itself to be in a broad acception a species of agapasm. Some forms of it might easily be mistaken for the genuine agapasm. The Hegelian philosophy is such an anancasticism. With its revelatory religion, with its synechism (however imperfectly set forth), with its "reflection," the whole idea of the theory is superb, almost sublime. Yet, after all, living freedom is practically omitted from its method. The whole movement is that of a vast engine, impelled by a vis a tergo, with a blind and mysterious fate of arriving at a lofty goal. I mean that such an engine it *would be,* if it really worked; but in point of fact, it is a Keely motor. Grant that it really acts as it professes to act, and there is nothing to do but accept the philosophy. But never was there seen such an example of a long chain of reasoning—shall I say with a flaw in every link?—no, with every link a handful of sand, squeezed into shape in a dream. Or say, it is a pasteboard model of a philosophy that in reality does not exist. If we use the one precious thing it contains, the idea of it, introducing the tychism which the arbitrariness of its every step suggests, and make that the support of a vital freedom which is the breath of the spirit of love, we may be able to produce that genuine agapasticism at which Hegel was aiming.

* * *

In the very nature of things, the line of demarcation between the three modes of evolution is not perfectly sharp. That does not prevent its being quite real; perhaps it is rather a mark of its reality. There is in the nature of things no sharp line of demarcation between the three fundamental colors, red, green, and violet. But for all that they are really different. The main question is whether three radically different evolutionary elements have been operative; and the second question is what are the most striking characteristics of whatever elements have been operative.

I propose to devote a few pages to a very slight examination of these questions in their relation to the historical development of human thought. I first formulate for the reader's convenience the briefest possible definitions of the three conceivable modes of development of thought, distinguishing also two varieties of anancasm and three of agapasm. The tychastic development of thought, then, will consist in slight departures from habitual ideas in different directions indifferently, quite purposeless and quite unconstrained whether by outward circumstances or by force of logic, these new departures being followed by unforeseen results which tend to fix some of them as habits more than others. The anancastic development of thought will consist of new ideas adopted without foreseeing whither they tend, but having a character determined by causes either external to the mind, such as changed circumstances of life, or internal to the mind as logical developments of ideas already accepted, such as generalizations. The agapastic development of thought is the adoption of certain mental tendencies, not altogether heedlessly, as in tychasm, nor quite blindly by the mere force of circumstances or of logic, as in anancasm, but by an immediate attraction for the idea itself, whose nature is divined before the mind possesses it, by the power of sympathy, that is, by virtue of the continuity of mind; and this mental tendency may be of three varieties, as follows. First, it may affect a whole people or community in its collective personality, and be thence communicated to such individuals as are in powerfully sympathetic connection with the collective people, although they may be intellectually incapable of attaining the idea by their private understandings or even perhaps of consciously apprehending it. Second, it may affect a private person directly, yet so that he is only enabled to apprehend the idea, or to appreciate its attractiveness, by virtue of his sympathy with his neighbors, under the influence of a striking experience or development of thought. The conversion of St. Paul may be taken as an example of what is meant. Third, it may affect an individual, independently of his human affections, by virtue of an attraction it exercises upon his mind, even before he has comprehended it. This is the phenomenon which has been well called the divination of genius; for it is due to the continuity between the man's mind and the Most High.

Let us next consider by means of what tests we can discriminate between these different categories of evolution. No absolute criterion is possible in the nature of things, since in the nature of things there is no sharp line of demarcation between the different classes. Nevertheless, quantitative symptoms may be found by which a sagacious and sympathetic judge of human nature may be able to estimate the approximate proportions in which the different kinds of influence are commingled.

So far as the historical evolution of human thought has been tychastic, it should have proceeded by insensible or minute steps; for such is the nature of chances when so multiplied as to show phenomena of regularity. For example, assume that of the native-born white adult males of the United States in 1880, one-fourth part were below 5 feet 4 inches in stature and one-fourth part above 5 feet 8 inches. Then by the principles of probability, among the whole population, we should expect

216 under 4 feet 6 inches	216 above 6 feet 6 inches
48 under 4 feet 5 inches	48 above 6 feet 7 inches
9 under 4 feet 5 inches	9 above 6 feet 8 inches
less than 2 under 4 feet 3 inches	less than 2 above 6 feet 9 inches

I set down these figures to show how insignificantly few are the cases in which anything very far out of the common run presents itself by chance. Though the stature of only every second man is included within the four inches between 5 feet 4 inches and 5 feet 8 inches, yet if this interval be extended by thrice four inches above and below, it will embrace all our 8 millions odd of native-born adult white males (of 1880), except only 9 taller and 9 shorter.

The test of minute variation, if *not* satisfied, absolutely negatives tychasm. If it is satisfied, we shall find that it negatives anancasm but not agapasm. We want a positive test, satisfied by tychasm, only. Now wherever we find men's thought taking by imperceptible degrees a turn contrary to the purposes which animate them, in spite of their highest impulses, there, we may safely conclude, there has been a tychastic action.

Students of the history of mind there be of an erudition to fill an imperfect scholar like me with envy edulcorated by joyous admiration, who maintain that ideas when just started are and can be little more than freaks, since they cannot yet have been critically examined, and further that everywhere and at all times progress has been so gradual that it is difficult to make out distinctly what original step any given man has taken. It would follow that tychasm has been the sole method of intellectual development. I have to confess I cannot read history so; I cannot help thinking that while tychasm has sometimes been operative, at others great steps covering nearly the same ground and made by different men independently have been mistaken for a succession of small steps, and further that students have been reluctant to admit a real entitative "spirit" of an age or of a people, under the mistaken and unscrutinized impression that they should thus be opening the door to wild and unnatural hypotheses. I find, on the contrary, that, however it may be with the education of individual minds, the historical development of thought has seldom been of a tychastic nature, and exclusively in backward and barbarizing movements. I desire to speak with the extreme modesty which befits a student of logic who is required to survey so very wide a field of human thought that he can cover it only by a reconnaissance, to which only the greatest skill and most adroit methods can impart any value at all; but, after all, I can only express my own opinions and not those of anybody else; and in my humble judgment, the largest example of tychasm is afforded by the history of Christianity, from about its establishment by Constantine to, say, the time of the Irish monasteries, an era or eon of about 500 years. Undoubtedly the external circumstance, which more than all others at first inclined men to accept Christianity in its loveliness and tenderness, was the fearful extent to which society was broken up into units by the unmitigated greed and hard-heartedness into which the Romans had seduced the world. And yet it was that very same fact, more than any other external circumstance, that fostered that bitterness against the wicked world of which the primitive gospel of Mark contains not a single trace. At least, I do not detect it in the remark about the blasphemy against the Holy Ghost, where nothing is said about vengeance, nor even in that speech where the closing lines of Isaiah are quoted, about the worm and the fire that feed upon the "carcasses of the men that have transgressed against me." But little by little the bitterness increases until, in the last book of the New Testament, its poor distracted author represents that all the time Christ was talking about having come to save the world, the secret design was to catch the entire human race, with the exception of a paltry 144,000, and souse them all in a brimstone lake, and as the smoke of their torment went up forever and ever, to turn and remark, "There is no curse any more." Would it be an insensible smirk or a fiendish grin that should accompany such an utterance? I wish I could believe St. John did not write it; but it is his gospel which tells about the "resurrection unto condemnation"—that is of men's being resuscitated just for the sake of torturing them—and at any rate, the Revelation is a very ancient composition. One can understand that the early Christians were like men trying with all their might to climb a steep declivity of smooth wet clay; the deepest and truest element of their life, animating both heart and head, was universal love; but they were continually, and against their wills, slipping into a party spirit, every slip serving as a precedent, in a fashion but too familiar to every man. This party feeling insensibly grew until by about A.D. 330 the luster of the pristine integrity that in St. Mark reflects the white spirit of light was so far tarnished that Eusebius (the Jared Sparks of that day), in the preface to his *History,* could announce his intention of exaggerating everything that tended to the glory of the church and of suppressing whatever might disgrace it. His Latin contemporary Lactantius is worse still; and so the darkling went on increasing until before the end of the century the great library of Alexandria was destroyed by Theophilus,[2] until Gregory the Great, two centuries later, burnt the great library of Rome, proclaiming that "Ignorance is the mother of devotion" (which is true, just as oppression and injustice is the mother of spirituality), until a sober description of the state of the church would be a thing our not too nice newspapers would treat as "unfit for publication." All this movement is shown by the application of the test given above to have been tychastic. Another very much like it on a small scale, only a hundred times swifter, for the study of which there are documents by the library-full, is to be found in the history of the French Revolution.

Anancastic evolution advances by successive strides with pauses between. The reason is that, in this process, a habit of thought, having been overthrown, is supplanted by the next strongest. Now this next strongest is sure to be widely disparate from the first, and as often as not is its direct contrary. It reminds one of our old rule of making the second candidate vice-president. This character, therefore, clearly distinguishes anancasm from tychasm. The character which distinguishes it from agapasm is its purposelessness. But external and internal anancasm have to be examined separately. Development under the pressure of external circumstances, or cataclasmine evolution, is in most cases unmistakable enough. It has numberless degrees of intensity, from the brute force, the plain war, which has more than once turned the current of the world's thought, down to the hard fact of evidence, or what has been taken for it, which has been known to convince men by hordes. The only hesitation that can subsist in the presence of such a history is a quantitative one. Never are external influences the only ones which affect the mind, and therefore it must be a matter of judgment for which it would scarcely be worth while to attempt to set rules, whether a given movement is to be regarded as principally governed from without or not. In the rise of medieval thought, I mean scholasticism and the synchronistic art developments, undoubtedly the crusades and the discovery of the writings of Aristotle were powerful influences. The development of scholasticism from Roscellin to Albertus Magnus closely follows the successive steps in the knowledge of Aristotle. Prantl thinks that that is the whole story, and few men have thumbed more books than Carl Prantl. He has done good solid work, notwithstanding his slap-dash judgments. But we shall never make so much as a good beginning of comprehending scholasticism until the whole has been systematically explored and digested by a company of students regularly organized and held under rule for that purpose. But as for the period we are now specially considering, that which synchronized the Romanesque architecture, the literature is easily mastered. It does not quite justify Prantl's dicta as to the slavish dependence of these authors upon their authorities. Moreover, they kept a definite purpose steadily before their minds, throughout all their studies. I am, therefore, unable to offer this period of scholasticism as an example of pure external anancasm, which seems to be the fluorine of the intellectual elements. Perhaps the recent Japanese reception of western ideas is the purest instance of it in history. Yet in combination with other elements, nothing is commoner. If the development of ideas under the influence of the study of external facts be considered as external anancasm—it is on the border between the external and the internal forms—it is, of course, the principal thing in modern learning. But Whewell, whose masterly comprehension of the history of science critics have been too ignorant properly to appreciate, clearly shows that it is far from being the overwhelmingly preponderant influence, even there.

Internal anancasm, or logical groping, which advances upon a predestined line without being able to foresee whither it is to be carried nor to steer its course, this is the rule of development of philosophy. Hegel first made the world understand this; and he seeks to make logic not merely the subjective guide and monitor of thought, which was all it had been ambitioning before, but to be the very mainspring of thinking, and not merely of individual thinking but of discussion, of the history of the development of thought, of all history, of all development. This involves a positive, clearly demonstrable

error. Let the logic in question be of whatever kind it may, a logic of necessary inference or a logic of probable inference (the theory might perhaps be
shaped to fit either), in any case it supposes that logic is sufficient of itself to
determine what conclusion follows from given premisses; for unless it will
do so much, it will not suffice to explain why an individual train of reasoning should take just the course it does take, to say nothing of other kinds of
development. It thus supposes that from given premisses, only one conclusion can logically be drawn, and that there is no scope at all for free choice.
That from given premisses only one conclusion can logically be drawn is one
of the false notions which have come from logicians' confining their attention to that Nantucket of thought, the logic of non-relative terms. In the logic
of relatives, it does not hold good.

One remark occurs to me. If the evolution of history is in considerable part
of the nature of internal anancasm, it resembles the development of individual men; and just as thirty-three years is a rough but natural unit of time for
individuals, being the average age at which man has issue, so there should
be an approximate period at the end of which one great historical movement
ought to be likely to be supplanted by another. Let us see if we can make out
anything of the kind. Take the governmental development of Rome as being
sufficiently long and set down the principal dates.

B.C. 753, Foundation of Rome.
B.C. 510, Expulsion of the Tarquins.
B.C. 27, Octavius assumes title Augustus.
A.D. 476, End of Western Empire.
A.D. 962, Holy Roman Empire.
A.D. 1453, Fall of Constantinople.

The last event was one of the most significant in history, especially for Italy.
The intervals are 243, 483, 502, 486 491, years. All are rather curiously near
equal, except the first which is half the others. Successive reigns of kings would
not commonly be so near equal. Let us set down a few dates in the history of
thought.

B.C. 585, Eclipse of Thales. Beginning of Greek philosophy.
A.D. 30, The crucifixion.
A.D. 529, Closing of Athenian schools. End of Greek philosophy.
A.D. 1125, (Approximate) Rise of the Universities of Bologna and Paris.
A.D. 1543, Publication of the *De Revolutionibus* of Copernicus. Beginning of
Modern Science.

The intervals are 615, 499, 596, 418 years. In the history of metaphysics, we
may take the following:

B.C. 322, Death of Aristotle.
A.D. 1274, Death of Aquinas.
A.D. 1804, Death of Kant.

The intervals are 1595 and 530 years. The former is about thrice the latter.

From these figures, no conclusion can fairly be drawn. At the same time, they suggest that perhaps there may be a rough natural era of about 500 years. Should there be any independent evidence of this, the intervals noticed may gain some significance.

The agapastic development of thought should, if it exists, be distinguished by its purposive character, this purpose being the development of an idea. We should have a direct agapic or sympathetic comprehension and recognition of it by virtue of the continuity of thought. I here take it for granted that such continuity of thought has been sufficiently proved by the arguments used in my paper on the "Law of Mind" in *The Monist* of last July. Even if those arguments are not quite convincing in themselves, yet if they are reënforced by an apparent agapasm in the history of thought, the two propositions will lend one another mutual aid. The reader will, I trust, be too well grounded in logic to mistake such mutual support for a vicious circle in reasoning. If it could be shown directly that there is such an entity as the "spirit of an age" or of a people, and that mere individual intelligence will not account for all the phenomena, this would be proof enough at once of agapasticism and of synechism. I must acknowledge that I am unable to produce a cogent demonstration of this; but I am, I believe, able to adduce such arguments as will serve to confirm those which have been drawn from other facts. I believe that all the greatest achievements of mind have been beyond the powers of unaided individuals; and I find, apart from the support this opinion receives from synechistic considerations, and from the purposive character of many great movements, direct reason for so thinking in the sublimity of the ideas and in their occurring simultaneously and independently to a number of individuals of no extraordinary general powers. The pointed Gothic architecture in several of its developments appears to me to be of such a character. All attempts to imitate it by modern architects of the greatest learning and genius appear flat and tame, and are felt by their authors to be so. Yet at the time the style was living, there was quite an abundance of men capable of producing works of this kind of gigantic sublimity and power. In more than one case, extant documents show that the cathedral chapters, in the selection of architects, treated high artistic genius as a secondary consideration, as if there were no lack of persons able to supply that; and the results justify their confidence. Were individuals in general, then, in those ages possessed of such lofty natures and high intellect? Such an opinion would break down under the first examination.

How many times have men now in middle life seen great discoveries made independently and almost simultaneously! The first instance I remember was the prediction of a planet exterior to Uranus by Leverrier and Adams. One hardly knows to whom the principle of the conservation of energy ought to be attributed, although it may reasonably be considered as the greatest discovery science has ever made. The mechanical theory of heat was set forth by Rankine and by Clausius during the same month of February, 1850; and there are eminent men who attribute this great step to Thomson.[3] The kinetical theory of gases, after being started by John Bernoulli and long buried in oblivion, was reinvented and applied to the explanation not merely of the laws of Boyle, Charles, and Avogadro, but also of diffusion and viscosity, by at least three modern physicists separately. It is well known that the doctrine of natural selection was presented by Wallace and by Darwin at the same meeting of the British Association; and Darwin in his "Historical Sketch" prefixed to the later editions of his book shows that both were anticipated by obscure forerunners. The method of spectrum analysis was claimed for Swan as well as for Kirchhoff, and there were others who perhaps had still better claims. The authorship of the Periodical Law of the Chemical Elements is disputed between a Russian, a German, and an Englishman; although there is no room for doubt that the principal merit belongs to the first. These are nearly all the greatest discoveries of our times. It is the same with the inventions. It may not be surprising that the telegraph should have been independently made by several inventors, because it was an easy corollary from scientific facts well made out before. But it was not so with the telephone and other inventions. Ether, the first anæsthetic, was introduced independently by three different New England physicians. Now ether had been a common article for a century. It had been in one of the pharmacopoeias three centuries before. It is quite incredible that its anaesthetic property should not have been known; it was known. It had probably passed from mouth to ear as a secret from the days of Basil Valentine; but for long it had been a secret of the Punchinello kind. In New England, for many years, boys had used it for amusement. Why then had it not been put to its serious use? No reason can be given, except that the motive to do so was not strong enough. The motives to doing so could only have been desire for gain and philanthropy. About 1846, the date of the introduction, philanthropy was undoubtedly in an unusually active condition. That sensibility, or sentimentalism, which had been introduced in the previous century, had undergone a ripening process, in consequence of which, though now less intense than it had previously been, it was more likely to influence unreflecting people than it had ever been. All three of the ether-claimants had probably been influenced by the desire for gain; but nevertheless they were certainly not insensible to the agapic influences.

I doubt if any of the great discoveries ought, properly, to be considered as altogether individual achievements; and I think many will share this doubt. Yet, if not, what an argument for the continuity of mind, and for agapasticism is here! I do not wish to be very strenuous. If thinkers will only be persuaded to lay aside their prejudices and apply themselves to studying the evidences of this doctrine, I shall be fully content to await the final decision.

Notes

1. How can a writer have any respect for science, as such, who is capable of confounding with the scientific propositions of political economy, which have nothing to say concerning what is "beneficent," such brummagem generalizations as this?

2. See Draper's *History of Intellectual Development*, ch. 10.

3. Thomson, himself, in his article *Heat* in the *Encyclopedia Britannica* never once mentions the name of Clausius.

6. Philosophy (Lecture XVIII from *The Varieties of Religious Experience*)

WILLIAM JAMES

The subject of Saintliness left us face to face with the question, Is the sense of divine presence a sense of anything objectively true? We turned first to mysticism for an answer, and found that although mysticism is entirely willing to corroborate religion, it is too private (and also too various) in its utterances to be able to claim a universal authority. But philosophy publishes results which claim to be universally valid if they are valid at all, so we now turn with our question to philosophy. Can philosophy stamp a warrant of veracity upon the religious man's sense of the divine?

I imagine that many of you at this point begin to indulge in guesses at the goal to which I am tending. I have undermined the authority of mysticism, you say, and the next thing I shall probably do is to seek to discredit that of philosophy. Religion, you expect to hear me conclude, is nothing but an affair of faith, based either on vague sentiment, or on that vivid sense of the reality of things unseen of which in my second lecture and in the lecture on Mysticism I gave so many examples. It is essentially private and individualistic; it always exceeds our powers of formulation; and although attempts to pour its contents into a philosophic mould will probably always go on, men being what they are, yet these attempts are always secondary processes which in no way add to the authority, or warrant the veracity, of the sentiments from which they derive their own stimulus and borrow whatever glow of conviction they may themselves possess. In short, you suspect that I am planning to defend feeling at the expense of reason, to rehabilitate the primitive and unreflective, and to dissuade you from the hope of any Theology worthy of the name.

To a certain extent I have to admit that you guess rightly. I do believe that feeling is the deeper source of religion, and that philosophic and theological formulas are secondary products, like translations of a text into another tongue. But all such statements are misleading from their brevity, and it will take the whole hour for me to explain to you exactly what I mean.

When I call theological formulas secondary products, I mean that in a world in which no religious feeling had ever existed, I doubt whether any philosophic theology could ever have been framed. I doubt if dispassionate intellectual contemplation of the universe, apart from inner unhappiness and need of deliverance on the one hand and mystical emotion on the other, would ever have resulted in religious philosophies such as we now possess. Men would have begun with animistic explanations of natural fact, and criticised these away into scientific ones, as they actually have done. In the science they would have left a certain amount of "psychical research," even as they now will probably have to re-admit a certain amount. But high-flying speculations like those of either dogmatic or idealistic theology, these they would have had no motive to venture on, feeling no need of commerce with such deities. These speculations must, it seems to me, be classed as over-beliefs, buildings-out performed by the intellect into directions of which feeling originally supplied the hint.

But even if religious philosophy had to have its first hint supplied by feeling, may it not have dealt in a superior way with the matter which feeling suggested? Feeling is private and dumb, and unable to give an account of itself. It allows that its results are mysteries and enigmas, declines to justify them rationally, and on occasion is willing that they should even pass for paradoxical and absurd. Philosophy takes just the opposite attitude. Her aspiration is to reclaim from mystery and paradox whatever territory she touches. To find an escape from obscure and wayward personal persuasion to truth objectively valid for all thinking men has ever been the intellect's most cherished ideal. To redeem religion from unwholesome privacy, and to give public status and universal right of way to its deliverances, has been reason's task.

I believe that philosophy will always have opportunity to labor at this task.[1] We are thinking beings, and we cannot exclude the intellect from participating in any of our functions. Even in soliloquizing with ourselves, we construe our feelings intellectually. Both our personal ideals and our religious and mystical experiences must be interpreted congruously with the kind of scenery which our thinking mind inhabits. The philosophical climate of our time inevitably forces its own clothing on us. Moreover, we must exchange our feelings with one another, and in doing so we have to speak, and to use general and abstract verbal formulas. Conceptions and constructions are thus a necessary part of our religion; and as moderator amid the clash of hypotheses, and mediator among the criticisms of one man's constructions by another, philosophy will always have much to do. It would be strange if I disputed this, when these very lectures which I am giving are (as you will see more clearly from now onwards) a laborious attempt to extract from the privacies of religious experience some general facts which can be defined in formulas upon which everybody may agree.

Religious experience, in other words, spontaneously and inevitably engenders myths, superstitions, dogmas, creeds, and metaphysical theologies, and criticisms of one set of these by the adherents of another. Of late, impartial classifications and comparisons have become possible, alongside of the denunciations and anathemas by which the commerce between creeds used exclusively to be carried on. We have the beginnings of a "Science of Religions," so-called; and if these lectures could ever be accounted a crumb-like contribution to such a science, I should be made very happy.

But all these intellectual operations, whether they be constructive or comparative and critical, presuppose immediate experiences as their subject-matter. They are interpretative and inductive operations, operations after the fact, consequent upon religious feeling, not coordinate with it, not independent of what it ascertains.

The intellectualism in religion which I wish to discredit pretends to be something altogether different from this. It assumes to construct religious objects out of the resources of logical reason alone, or of logical reason drawing rigorous inference from non-subjective facts. It calls its conclusions dogmatic theology, or philosophy of the absolute, as the case may be; it does not call them science of religions. It reaches them in an *a priori* way, and warrants their veracity.

Warranted systems have ever been the idols of aspiring souls. All-inclusive, yet simple; noble, clean, luminous, stable, rigorous, true;—what more ideal refuge could there be than such a system would offer to spirits vexed by the muddiness and accidentality of the world of sensible things? Accordingly, we find inculcated in the theological schools of to-day, almost as much as in those of the fore-time, a disdain for merely possible or probable truth, and of results that only private assurance can grasp. Scholastics and idealists both express this disdain. Principal John Caird, for example, writes as follows in his *Introduction to the Philosophy of Religion*:

> "Religion must indeed be a thing of the heart; but in order to elevate it from the region of subjective caprice and waywardness, and to distinguish between that which is true and false in religion, we must appeal to an objective standard. That which enters the heart must first be discerned by the intelligence to be true. It must be seen as having in its own nature a right to dominate feeling, and as

constituting the principle by which feeling must be judged.[2] In estimating the religious character of individuals, nations, or races, the first question is, not how they feel, but what they think and believe—not whether their religion is one which manifests itself in emotions, more or less vehement and enthusiastic, but what are the *conceptions* of God and divine things by which these emotions are called forth. Feeling is necessary in religion, but it is by the *content* or intelligent basis of a religion, and not by feeling, that its character and worth are to be determined."[3]

Cardinal Newman, in his work, *The Idea of a University,* gives more emphatic expression still to this disdain for sentiment.[4] Theology, he says, is a science in the strictest sense of the word. I will tell you, he says, what it is not—not "physical evidences" for God, not "natural religion," for these are but vague subjective interpretations:—

"If," he continues, "the Supreme Being is powerful or skillful, just so far as the telescope shows power, or the microscope shows skill, if his moral law is to be ascertained simply by the physical processes of the animal frame, or his will gathered from the immediate issues of human affairs, if his Essence is just as high and deep and broad as the universe and no more; if this be the fact, then will I confess that there is no specific science about God, that theology is but a name, and a protest in its behalf an hypocrisy. Then, pious as it is to think of Him while the pageant of experiment or abstract reasoning passes by, still such piety is nothing more than a poetry of thought, or an ornament of language, a certain view taken of Nature which one man has and another has not, which gifted minds strike out, which others see to be admirable and ingenious, and which all would be the better for adopting. It is but the theology of Nature, just as we talk of the philosophy or the *romance* of history, or the *poetry* of childhood, or the picturesque or the sentimental or the humorous, or any other abstract quality which the genius or the caprice of the individual, or the fashion of the day, or the consent of the world, recognizes in any set of objects which are subjected to its contemplation. I do not see much difference between avowing that there is no God, and implying that nothing definite can be known for certain about Him."

What I mean by Theology, continues Newman, is none of these things: "I simply mean the Science *of God*, or the truths we know about God, put into a system, just as we have a science of the stars and call it astronomy, or of the crust of the earth and call it geology."

In both these extracts we have the issue clearly set before us: Feeling valid only for the individual is pitted against reason valid universally. The test is a perfectly plain one of fact. Theology based on pure reason must in point of fact convince men universally. If it did not, wherein would its superiority consist? If it only formed sects and schools, even as sentiment and mysticism form them, how would it fulfill its programme of freeing us from personal caprice and waywardness? This perfectly definite practical test of the pretensions of philosophy to found religion on universal reason simplifies my procedure today. I need not discredit philosophy by laborious criticism of its arguments. It will suffice if I show that as a matter of history it fails to prove its pretension to be "objectively" convincing. In fact, philosophy does so fail. It does not banish differences; it founds schools and sects just as feeling does. I believe, in fact, that the logical reason of man operates in this field of divinity exactly as it has always operated in love, or in patriotism, or in politics, or in any other of the wider affairs of life, in which our passions or our mystical intuitions fix our beliefs beforehand. It finds arguments for our conviction, for indeed it *has* to find them. It amplifies and defines our faith, and dignifies it and lends it words and plausibility. It hardly ever engenders it; it cannot now secure it.[5]

Lend me your attention while I run through some of the points of the older systematic theology. You find them in both Protestant and Catholic manuals, best of all in the innumerable text-books published since Pope Leo's Encyclical recommending the study of Saint Thomas. I glance first at the arguments by which dogmatic theology establishes God's existence, after that at those by which it establishes his nature.[6]

The arguments for God's existence have stood for hundreds of years with the waves of unbelieving criticism breaking against them, never totally discrediting them in the ears of the faithful, but on the whole slowly and surely washing out the mortar from between their joints. If you have a God already whom you believe in, these arguments confirm you. If you are atheistic, they fail to set you right. The proofs are various. The "cosmological" one, so-called, reasons from the contingence of the world to a First Cause which must contain whatever perfections the world itself contains. The "argument from design" reasons, from the fact that Nature's laws are mathematical, and her parts benevolently adapted to each other, that this cause is both intellectual and benevolent. The "moral argument" is that the moral law presupposes a lawgiver. The "argument *ex consensu gentium*" is that the belief in God is so widespread as to be grounded in the rational nature of man, and should therefore carry authority with it.

As I just said, I will not discuss these arguments technically. The bare fact that all idealists since Kant have felt entitled either to scout or to neglect them shows that they are not solid enough to serve as religion's all-sufficient foundation. Absolutely impersonal reasons would be in duty bound to show more general convincingness. Causation is indeed too obscure a principle to bear the weight of the whole structure of theology. As for the argument from design, see how Darwinian ideas have revolutionized it. Conceived as we now conceive them, as so many fortunate escapes from almost limitless process-es of destruction, the benevolent adaptations which we find in Nature sug-gest a deity very different from the one who figured in the earlier versions of the argument.[7] The fact is that these arguments do but follow the combined suggestions of the facts and of our feeling. They prove nothing rigorously. They only corroborate our preexistent partialities.

If philosophy can do so little to establish God's existence, how stands it with her efforts to define his attributes? It is worth while to look at the at-tempts of systematic theology in this direction.

> Since God is First Cause, this science of sciences says, he differs from all his creatures in possessing existence *a se*. From this "a-seity" on God's part, theol-ogy deduces by mere logic most of his other perfections. For instance, he must be both *necessary* and *absolute*, cannot not be, and cannot in any way be deter-mined by anything else. This makes Him absolutely unlimited from without, and unlimited also from within; for limitation is non-being; and God is being itself. This unlimitedness makes God infinitely perfect. Moreover, God is *One*, and *Only*, for the infinitely perfect can admit no peer. He is *Spiritual*, for were He composed of physical parts, some other power would have to combine them into the total, and his aseity would thus be contradicted. He is therefore both simple and non-physical in nature. He is *simple metaphysically* also, that is to say, his nature and his existence cannot be distinct, as they are in finite sub-stances which share their formal natures with one another, and are individual only in their material aspect. Since God is one and only, his *essentia* and his *esse* must be given at one stroke. This excludes from his being all those distinctions, so familiar in the world of finite things, between potentiality and actuality, sub-stance and accidents, being and activity, existence and attributes. We can talk, it is true, of God's powers, acts, and attributes, but these discriminations are only "virtual," and made from the human point of view. In God all these points of view fall into an absolute identity of being.
>
> This absence of all potentiality in God obliges Him to be *immutable*. He is actuality, through and through. Were there anything potential about Him, He would either lose or gain by its actualization, and either loss or gain would contradict his perfection. He cannot, therefore, change. Furthermore, He is *immense, boundless;* for could He be outlined in space, He would be compos-ite, and this would contradict his indivisibility. He is therefore *omnipresent*, indivisibly there, at every point of space. He is similarly wholly present at ev-ery point of time—in other words *eternal*. For if He began in time, He would need a prior cause, and that would contradict his aseity. If He ended, it would contradict his necessity. If He went through any succession, it would contra-dict his immutability.

He has *intelligence* and will and every other creature-perfection, for *we* have them, and *effectus nequit superare causam.* In Him, however, they are absolutely and eternally in act, and their *object,* since God can be bounded by naught that is external, can primarily be nothing else than God himself. He knows himself, then, in one eternal indivisible act, and wills himself with an infinite self-pleasure.[8] Since He must of logical necessity thus love and will himself. He cannot be called "free" *ad intra,* with the freedom of contrarieties that characterizes finite creatures. *Ad extra,* however, or with respect to his creation, God is free. He cannot *need* to create, being perfect in being and in happiness already. He *wills* to create, then, by an absolute freedom.

Being thus a substance endowed with intellect and will and freedom, God is a *person;* and a *living* person also, for He is both object and subject of his own activity, and to be this distinguishes the living from the lifeless. He is thus absolutely *self-sufficient;* his *self-knowledge* and *self-love* are both of them infinite and adequate, and need no extraneous conditions to perfect them.

He is *omniscient,* for in knowing himself as Cause He knows all creature things and events by implication. His knowledge is *previsive,* for He is present to all time. Even our free acts are known beforehand to Him, for otherwise his wisdom would admit of successive moments of enrichment, and this would contradict his immutability. He is *omnipotent* for everything that does not involve logical contradiction. He can make being—in other words his power includes *creation.* If what He creates were made of his own substance it would have to be infinite in essence, as that substance is; but it is finite; so it must be non-divine in substance. If it were made of a substance, an eternally existing matter, for example, which God found there to his hand, and to which He simply gave its form, that would contradict God's definition as First Cause, and make Him a mere mover of something caused already. The things he creates, then, He creates *ex nihilo,* and gives them absolute being as so many finite substances additional to himself. The forms which he imprints upon them have their prototypes in his ideas. But as in God there is no such thing as multiplicity, and as these ideas for us are manifold, we must distinguish the ideas as they are in God and the way in which our minds externally imitate them. We must attribute them to Him only in a *terminative* sense, as differing aspects, from the finite point of view, of his unique essence.

God of course is holy, good, and just. He can do no evil, for He is positive being's fullness, and evil is negation. It is true that He has created physical evil in places, but only as a means of wider good, for *bonum totius præeminet bonum partis.* Moral evil He cannot will, either as end or means, for that would contradict his holiness. By creating free beings He permits it only, neither his justice nor his goodness obliging Him to prevent the recipients of freedom from misusing the gift.

As regards God's purpose in creating, primarily it can only have been to exercise his absolute freedom by the manifestation to others of his glory. From this it follows that the others must be rational beings, capable in the first place of knowledge, love, and honor, and in the second place of happiness, for the knowledge and love of God is the mainspring of felicity. In so far forth one may say that God's secondary purpose in creating is *love*.

I will not weary you by pursuing these metaphysical determinations farther, into the mysteries of God's Trinity, for example. What I have given will serve as a specimen of the orthodox philosophical theology of both Catholics and Protestants. Newman, filled with enthusiasm at God's list of perfections, continues the passage which I began to quote to you by a couple of pages of a rhetoric so magnificent that I can hardly refrain from adding them, in spite of the inroad they would make upon our time.[9] He first enumerates God's attributes sonorously, then celebrates his ownership of everything in earth and Heaven, and the dependence of all that happens upon his permissive will. He gives us scholastic philosophy "touched with emotion," and every philosophy should be touched with emotion to be rightly understood. Emotionally, then, dogmatic theology is worth something to minds of the type of Newman's. It will aid us to estimate what it is worth intellectually, if at this point I make a short digression.

* * *

What God hath joined together, let no man put asunder. The Continental schools of philosophy have too often overlooked the fact that man's thinking is organically connected with his conduct. It seems to me to be the chief glory of English and Scottish thinkers to have kept the organic connection in view. The guiding principle of British philosophy has in fact been that every difference must *make* a difference, every theoretical difference somewhere issue in a practical difference, and that the best method of discussing points of theory is to begin by ascertaining what practical difference would result from one alternative or the other being true. What is the particular truth in question *known as?* In what facts does it result? What is its cash-value in terms of particular experience? This is the characteristic English way of taking up a question. In this way, you remember, Locke takes up the question of personal identity. What you mean by it is just your chain of particular memories, says he. That is the only concretely verifiable part of its significance. All further ideas about it, such as the oneness or manyness of the spiritual substance on which it is based, are therefore void of intelligible meaning; and propositions touching such ideas may be indifferently affirmed or denied. So Berkeley with his "matter." The cash-value of matter is our physical sensations. That is what it is known as, all that we concretely verify of its conception. That, therefore, is the whole meaning of the term "matter"—any other pretended meaning is mere wind of words. Hume does the same thing with causation. It is known as habitual antecedence, and as tendency on our part to look for something definite to come. Apart from this practical meaning it has no significance whatever, and books about it may be committed to the flames, says Hume. Dugald Stewart and Thomas Brown, James Mill, John Mill, and Professor Bain, have followed more or less consistently the same method; and Shadworth Hodgson has used the principle with full explicitness. When all is said and done, it was English and Scotch writers, and not Kant, who introduced "the critical method" into philosophy, the one method fitted to make philosophy a study worthy of serious men. For what seriousness can possibly remain in debating philosophic propositions that will never make an appreciable difference to us in action? And what could it matter, if all propositions were practically indifferent, which of them we should agree to call true or which false?

An American philosopher of eminent originality, Mr. Charles Sanders Peirce, has rendered thought a service by disentangling from the particulars of its application the principle by which these men were instinctively guided, and by singling it out as fundamental and giving to it a Greek name. He calls it the principle of *pragmatism,* and he defends it somewhat as follows:[10]—

Thought in movement has for its only conceivable motive the attainment of belief, or thought at rest. Only when our thought about a subject has found its rest in belief can our action on the subject firmly and safely begin. Beliefs, in short, are rules for action; and the whole function of thinking is but one step in the production of active habits. If there were any part of a thought that made no difference in the thought's practical consequences, then that part would be no proper element of the thought's significance. To develop a thought's meaning we need therefore only determine what conduct it is fitted to produce; that conduct is for us its sole significance; and the tangible fact at the root of all our thought-distinctions is that there is no one of them so fine as to consist in anything but a possible difference of practice. To attain perfect clearness in our thoughts of an object, we need then only consider what sensations, immediate or remote, we are conceivably to expect from it, and what conduct we must prepare in case the object should be true. Our conception of these practical consequences is for us the whole of our conception of the object, so far as that conception has positive significance at all.

This is the principle of Peirce, the principle of pragmatism. Such a principle will help us on this occasion to decide, among the various attributes set down in the scholastic inventory of God's perfections, whether some be not far less significant than others.

If, namely, we apply the principle of pragmatism to God's metaphysical attributes, strictly so called, as distinguished from his moral attributes, I think that, even were we forced by a coercive logic to believe them, we still should have to confess them to be destitute of all intelligible significance. Take God's aseity, for example; or his necessariness; his immateriality; his "simplicity" or superiority to the kind of inner variety and succession which we find in finite beings, his indivisibility, and lack of the inner distinctions of being and activity, substance and accident, potentiality and actuality, and the rest; his repudiation of inclusion in a genus; his actualized infinity; his "personality," apart from the moral qualities which it may comport; his relations to evil being permissive and not positive; his self-sufficiency, self-love, and absolute felicity in himself:—candidly speaking, how do such qualities as these make any definite connection with our life? And if they severally call for no distinctive adaptations of our conduct, what vital difference can it possibly make to a man's religion whether they be true or false?

For my own part, although I dislike to say aught that may grate upon tender associations, I must frankly confess that even though these attributes were faultlessly deduced, I cannot conceive of its being of the smallest consequence to us religiously that any one of them should be true. Pray, what specific act can I perform in order to adapt myself the better to God's simplicity? Or how does it assist me to plan my behavior, to know that his happiness is anyhow absolutely complete? In the middle of the century just past, Mayne Reid was the great writer of books of out-of-door adventure. He was forever extolling the hunters and field-observers of living animals' habits, and keeping up a fire of invective against the "closet-naturalists," as he called them, the collectors and classifiers, and handlers of skeletons and skins. When I was a boy, I used to think that a closet-naturalist must be the vilest type of wretch under the sun. But surely the systematic theologians are the closet-naturalists of the deity, even in Captain Mayne Reid's sense. What is their deduction of metaphysical attributes but a shuffling and matching of pedantic dictionary-adjectives, aloof from morals, aloof from human needs, something that might be worked out from the mere word "God" by one of those logical machines of wood and brass which recent ingenuity has contrived as well as by a man of flesh and blood. They have the trail of the serpent over them. One feels that in the theologians' hands, they are only a set of titles obtained by a mechanical manipulation of synonyms; verbality has stepped into the place of vision, professionalism into that of life. Instead of bread we have a stone; instead of a fish, a serpent. Did such a conglomeration of abstract terms give really the gist of our knowledge of the deity, schools of theology might indeed continue to flourish, but religion, vital religion, would have taken its flight from this world. What keeps religion going is something else than abstract definitions and systems of concatenated adjectives, and something different from faculties of theology and their professors. All these things are after-effects, secondary accretions upon those phenomena of vital conversation with the unseen divine, of which I have shown you so many instances, renewing themselves in *sæcula sæculorum* in the lives of humble private men.

So much for the metaphysical attributes of God! From the point of view of practical religion, the metaphysical monster which they offer to our worship is an absolutely worthless invention of the scholarly mind.

What shall we now say of the attributes called moral? Pragmatically, they stand on an entirely different footing. They positively determine fear and hope and expectation, and are foundations for the saintly life. It needs but a glance at them to show how great is their significance.

God's holiness, for example: being holy, God can will nothing but the good. Being omnipotent, he can secure its triumph. Being omniscient, he can see us in the dark. Being just, he can punish us for what he sees. Being loving, he can pardon too. Being unalterable, we can count on him securely. These qualities enter into connection with our life, it is highly important that we should be informed concerning them. That God's purpose in creation should be the manifestation of his glory is also an attribute which has definite relations to our practical life. Among other things it has given a definite character to worship in all Christian countries. If dogmatic theology really does prove beyond dispute that a God with characters like these exists, she may well claim to give a solid basis to religious sentiment. But verily, how stands it with her arguments?

It stands with them as ill as with the arguments for his existence. Not only do post-Kantian idealists reject them root and branch, but it is a plain historic fact that they never have converted any one who has found in the moral complexion of the world, as he experienced it, reasons for doubting that a good God can have framed it. To prove God's goodness by the scholastic argument that there is no non-being in his essence would sound to such a witness simply silly.

No! the book of Job went over this whole matter once for all and definitively. Ratiocination is a relatively superficial and unreal path to the deity: "I will lay mine hand upon my mouth; I have heard of Thee by the hearing of the ear, but now mine eye seeth Thee." An intellect perplexed and baffled, yet a trustful sense of presence—such is the situation of the man who is sincere with himself and with the facts, but who remains religious still.[11]

We must therefore, I think, bid a definitive good-by to dogmatic theology. In all sincerity our faith must do without that warrant. Modern idealism,

I repeat, has said good-by to this theology forever. Can modern idealism give faith a better warrant, or must she still rely on her poor self for witness?

The basis of modern idealism is Kant's doctrine of the Transcendental Ego of Apperception. By this formidable term Kant merely meant the fact that the consciousness "I think them" must (potentially or actually) accompany all our objects. Former skeptics had said as much, but the "I" in question had remained for them identified with the personal individual. Kant abstracted and depersonalized it, and made it the most universal of all his categories, although for Kant himself the Transcendental Ego had no theological implications.

It was reserved for his successors to convert Kant's notion of *Bewusstsein überhaupt,* or abstract consciousness, into an infinite concrete self-consciousness which is the soul of the world, and in which our sundry personal self-consciousnesses have their being. It would lead me into technicalities to show you even briefly how this transformation was in point of fact effected. Suffice it to say that in the Hegelian school, which today so deeply influences both British and American thinking, two principles have borne the brunt of the operation.

The first of these principles is that the old logic of identity never gives us more than a post-mortem dissection of *disjecta membra,* and that the fullness of life can be construed to thought only by recognizing that every object which our thought may propose to itself involves the notion of some other object which seems at first to negate the first one.

The second principle is that to be conscious of a negation is already virtually to be beyond it. The mere asking of a question or expression of a dissatisfaction proves that the answer or the satisfaction is already imminent; the finite, realized as such, is already the infinite *in posse.*

Applying these principles, we seem to get a propulsive force into our logic which the ordinary logic of a bare, stark self-identity in each thing never attains to. The objects of our thought now *act* within our thought, act as objects act when given in experience. They change and develop. They introduce something other than themselves along with them; and this other, at first only ideal or potential, presently proves itself also to be actual. It supersedes the thing at first supposed, and both verifies and corrects it, in developing the fullness of its meaning.

The program is excellent; the universe *is* a place where things are followed by other things that both correct and fulfill them; and a logic which gave us something like this movement of fact would express truth far better than the traditional school-logic, which never gets of its own accord from anything to anything else, and registers only predictions and subsumptions, or static resemblances and differences. Nothing could be more unlike the methods of dogmatic theology than those of this new logic. Let me quote in illustration some passages from the Scottish transcendentalist whom I have already named.

"How are we to conceive," Principal Caird writes, "of the reality in which all intelligence rests?" He replies: "Two things may without difficulty be proved, viz., that this reality is an absolute Spirit, and conversely that it is only in communion with this absolute Spirit or Intelligence that the finite Spirit can realize itself. It is absolute; for the faintest movement of human intelligence would be arrested, if it did not presuppose the absolute reality of intelligence, of thought itself. Doubt or denial themselves presuppose and indirectly affirm it. When I pronounce anything to be true, I pronounce it, indeed, to be relative to thought, but not to be relative to my thought, or to the thought of any other individual mind. From the existence of all individual minds as such I can abstract; I can think them away. But that which I cannot think away is thought or self-consciousness itself, in its independence and absoluteness, or, in other words, an Absolute Thought or Self-Consciousness."

Here, you see, Principal Caird makes the transition which Kant did not make: he converts the omnipresence of consciousness in general as a condition of "truth" being anywhere possible, into an omnipresent universal consciousness, which he identifies with God in his concreteness. He next proceeds to use the principle that to acknowledge your limits is in essence to be beyond them; and makes the transition to the religious experience of individuals in the following words:—

"If [Man] were only a creature of transient sensations and impulses, of an ever coming and going succession of intuitions, fancies, feelings, then nothing could ever have for him the character of objective truth or reality. But it is the prerogative of man's spiritual nature that he can yield himself up to a thought and will that are infinitely larger than his own. As a thinking, self-conscious being, indeed, he may be said, by his very nature, to live in the atmosphere of the Universal Life. As a thinking being, it is possible for me to suppress and quell in my consciousness every movement of self-assertion, every notion and opinion that is merely mine, every desire that belongs to me as this particular Self, and to become the pure medium of a thought that is universal—in one word, to live no more my own life, but let my consciousness be possessed and suffused by the Infinite and Eternal life of spirit. And yet it is just in this renunciation of self that I truly gain myself, or realize the highest possibilities of my own nature. For whilst in one sense we give up self to live the universal and absolute life of reason, yet that to which we thus surrender ourselves is in reality our truer self. The life of absolute reason is not a life that is foreign to us."

Nevertheless, Principal Caird goes onto say, so far as we are able outwardly to realize this doctrine, the balm it offers remains incomplete. Whatever we may be *in posse*, the very best of us *in actu* falls very short of being absolutely divine. Social morality, love, and self-sacrifice even, merge our Self only in some other finite self or selves. They do not quite identify it with the Infinite. Man's ideal destiny, infinite in abstract logic, might thus seem in practice forever unrealizable.

"Is there, then," our author continues, "no solution of the contradiction between the ideal and the actual? We answer. There is such a solution, but in order to reach it we are carried beyond the sphere of morality into that of religion. It may be said to be the essential characteristic of religion as contrasted with morality, that it changes aspiration into fruition, anticipation into realization; that instead of leaving man in the interminable pursuit of a vanishing ideal, it makes him the actual partaker of a divine or infinite life. Whether we view religion from the human side or the divine—as the surrender of the soul to God, or as the life of God in the soul—in either aspect it is of its very essence that the Infinite has ceased to be a far-off vision, and has become a present reality. The very first pulsation of the spiritual life, when we rightly apprehend its significance, is the indication that the division between the Spirit and its object has vanished, that the ideal has become real, that the finite has reached its goal and become suffused with the presence and life of the Infinite.

"Oneness of mind and will with the divine mind and will is not the future hope and aim of religion, but its very beginning and birth in the soul. To enter on the religious life is to terminate the struggle. In that act which constitutes the beginning of the religious life—call it faith, or trust, or self-surrender, or by whatever name you will—there is involved the identification of the finite with a life which is eternally realized. It is true indeed that the religious life is progressive; but understood in the light of the foregoing idea, religious progress is not progress *towards,* but *within* the sphere of the Infinite. It is not the vain attempt by endless finite additions or increments to become possessed of infinite wealth, but it is the endeavor, by the constant exercise of spiritual activity, to appropriate that infinite inheritance of which we are already in possession. The whole future of the religious life is given in its beginning, but it is given implicitly. The position of the man who has entered on the religious life is that evil, error, imperfection, do not really belong to him: they are excrescences which have no organic relation to his true nature: they are already virtually, as they will be actually, suppressed and annulled, and in the very process of being annulled they become the means of spiritual progress. Though he is not exempt from temptation and conflict, [yet] in that inner sphere in which his true life lies, the struggle is over, the victory already achieved. It is not a finite but an infinite life which the spirit lives. Every pulse-beat of its [existence] is the expression and realization of the life of God."[12]

You will readily admit that no description of the phenomena of the religious consciousness could be better than these words of your lamented preacher and philosopher. They reproduce the very rapture of those crises of conversion of which we have been hearing; they utter what the mystic felt but was unable to communicate; and the saint, in hearing them, recognizes his own experience. It is indeed gratifying to find the content of religion report-ed so unanimously. But when all is said and done, has Principal Caird—and I only use him as an example of that whole mode of thinking—transcended the sphere of feeling and of the direct experience of the individual, and laid the foundations of religion in impartial reason? Has he made religion universal by coercive reasoning, transformed it from a private faith into a public cer-tainty? Has he rescued its affirmations from obscurity and mystery?

I believe that he has done nothing of the kind, but that he has simply re-affirmed the individual's experiences in a more generalized vocabulary. And again, I can be excused from proving technically that the transcendentalist reasonings fail to make religion universal, for I can point to the plain fact that a majority of scholars, even religiously disposed ones, stubbornly refuse to treat them as convincing. The whole of Germany, one may say, has positively rejected the Hegelian argumentation. As for Scotland, I need only mention Professor Fraser's and Professor Pringle-Pattison's memorable criticisms, with which so many of you are familiar.[13] Once more, I ask, if transcenden-tal idealism were as objectively and absolutely rational as it pretends to be, could it possibly fail so egregiously to be persuasive?

What religion reports, you must remember, always purports to be a fact of experience: the divine is actually present, religion says, and between it and ourselves relations of give and take are actual. If definite perceptions of fact like this cannot stand upon their own feet, surely abstract reasoning cannot give them the support they are in need of. Conceptual processes can class facts, define them, interpret them; but they do not produce them, nor can they reproduce their individuality. There is always a *plus*, a *thisness*, which feeling alone can answer for. Philosophy in this sphere is thus a secondary function, unable to warrant faith's veracity, and so I revert to the thesis which I announced at the beginning of this lecture.

In all sad sincerity I think we must conclude that the attempt to demon-strate by purely intellectual processes the truth of the deliverances of direct religious experience is absolutely hopeless.

It would be unfair to philosophy, however, to leave her under this nega-tive sentence. Let me close, then, by briefly enumerating what she can do for religion. If she will abandon metaphysics and deduction for criticism and induction, and frankly transform herself from theology into science of reli-gions, she can make herself enormously useful.

The spontaneous intellect of man always defines the divine which it feels in ways that harmonize with its temporary intellectual prepossessions. Philosophy can by comparison eliminate the local and the accidental from these definitions. Both from dogma and from worship she can remove historic incrustations. By confronting the spontaneous religious constructions with the results of natural science, philosophy can also eliminate doctrines that are now known to be scientifically absurd or incongruous.

Sifting out in this way unworthy formulations, she can leave a residuum of conceptions that at least are possible. With these she can deal as *hypotheses,* testing them in all the manners, whether negative or positive, by which hypotheses are ever tested. She can reduce their number, as some are found more open to objection. She can perhaps become the champion of one which she picks out as being the most closely verified or verifiable. She can refine upon the definition of this hypothesis, distinguishing between what is innocent overbelief and symbolism in the expression of it, and what is to be literally taken. As a result, she can offer mediation between different believers, and help to bring about consensus of opinion. She can do this the more successfully, the better she discriminates the common and essential from the individual and local elements of the religious beliefs which she compares.

I do not see why a critical Science of Religions of this sort might not eventually command as general a public adhesion as is commanded by a physical science. Even the personally non-religious might accept its conclusions on trust, much as blind persons now accept the facts of optics—it might appear as foolish to refuse them. Yet as the science of optics has to be fed in the first instance, and continually verified later, by facts experienced by seeing persons; so the science of religions would depend for its original material on facts of personal experience, and would have to square itself with personal experience through all its critical reconstructions. It could never get away from concrete life, or work in a conceptual vacuum. It would forever have to confess, as every science confesses, that the subtlety of nature flies beyond it, and that its formulas are but approximations. Philosophy lives in words, but truth and fact well up into our lives in ways that exceed verbal formulation. There is in the living act of perception always something that glimmers and twinkles and will not be caught, and for which reflection comes too late. No one knows this as well as the philosopher. He must fire his volley of new vocables out of his conceptual shotgun, for his profession condemns him to this industry, but he secretly knows the hollowness and irrelevancy. His formulas are like stereoscopic or kinetoscopic photographs seen outside the instrument; they lack the depth, the motion, the vitality. In the religious sphere, in particular, belief that formulas are true can never wholly take the place of personal experience.

In my next lecture I will try to complete my rough description of religious experience; and in the lecture after that, which is the last one, I will try my hand at formulating conceptually the truth to which it is a witness.

Notes

1. Compare Professor W. Wallace's "Gifford Lectures," in *Lectures and Essays* (Oxford: Clarendon Press, 1898), 17 ff.

2. Op. cit., 174, abridged.

3. Ibid., 186 abridged and italicized.

4. Discourse II. sect. 7.

5. As regards the secondary character of intellectual constructions, and the primacy of feeling and instinct in founding religious beliefs, see the striking work of H. Fielding, *The Hearts of Men* (London: Hurst and Blackett, 1902), which came into my hands after my text was written. "Creeds," says the author, "are the grammar of religion, they are to religion what grammar is to speech. Words are the expression of our wants; grammar is the theory formed afterwards. Speech never proceeded from grammar, but the reverse. As speech progresses and changes from unknown causes, grammar must follow" (313). The whole book, which keeps unusually close to concrete facts, is little more than an amplification of this text.

6. For convenience' sake, I follow the order of A. Stockl's *Lehrbuch der Philosophie*, 5te Auflage (Mainz, 1881), Band ii. B. Boedder's *Natural Theology* (London, 1891) is a handy English Catholic Manual; but an almost identical doctrine is given by such Protestant theologians as C. Hodge: *Systematic Theology* (New York, 1873) or A. H. Strong: *Systematic Theology*, 5th edition (New York, 1896).

7. It must not be forgotten that any form of disorder in the world might, by the design argument, suggest a God for just that kind of disorder. The truth is that any state of things whatever that can be named is logically susceptible of teleological interpretation. The ruins of the earthquake at Lisbon, for example: the whole of past history had to be planned exactly as it was to bring about in the fullness of time just that particular arrangement of debris of masonry, furniture, and once living bodies. No other train of causes would have been sufficient. And so of any other arrangement, bad or good, which might as a matter of fact be found resulting anywhere from previous conditions. To avoid such pessimistic consequences and save its beneficent designer, the design argument accordingly invokes two other principles, restrictive in their operation. The first is physical: Nature's forces tend of their own accord only to disorder and destruction, to heaps of ruins, not to architecture. This principle, though plausible at first sight, seems, in the light of recent biology, to be more and more improbable. The second principle is one of anthropomorphic interpretation. No arrangement that for us is "disorderly" can possibly have been an object of design at all. This principle is of course a mere assumption in the interests of anthropomorphic Theism.

When one views the world with no definite theological bias one way or the other, one sees that order and disorder, as we now recognize them, are purely human inventions. We are interested in certain types of arrangement, useful, aesthetic, or moral—so interested that whenever we find them realized, the fact emphatically rivets our attention. The result is that we work over the contents of the world selectively. It is overflowing with disorderly arrangements from our point of view, but order is the only thing we care for and look at, and by choosing, one can always find some sort of orderly arrangement in the midst of any chaos. If I should throw down a thousand beans at random upon a table, I could doubtless, by eliminating a sufficient number of them, leave the rest in almost any geometrical pattern you might propose to me, and you might then say that that pattern was the thing prefigured beforehand, and that the other beans were mere irrelevance and packing material. Our dealings with Nature are just like this. She is a vast *plenum* in which our attention draws capricious lines in innumerable directions. We count and name whatever lies upon the special lines we trace, whilst the other things and the untraced lines are neither named nor counted. There are in reality infinitely more things "unadapted" to each other in this world than there are things "adapted"; infinitely more things with irregular relations than with regular relations between them. But we look for the regular kind of thing exclusively, and ingeniously discover and preserve it in our memory. It accumulates with other regular kinds, until the collection of them fills our encyclopaedias. Yet all the while between and around them lies an infinite anonymous chaos of objects that no one ever thought of together, of relations that never yet attracted our attention.

The facts of order from which the psycho-theological argument starts are thus easily susceptible of interpretation as arbitrary human products. So long as this is the case, although of course no argument against God follows, it follows that the argument for him will fail to constitute a knockdown proof of his existence. It will be convincing only to those who on other grounds believe in him already.

8. For the scholastics the *facultas appetendi* embraces feeling, desire, and will.

9. Op. cit., Discourse III. sect. 7.

10. In an article, "How to make our Ideas Clear", in the *Popular Science Monthly* xii (January 1878): 286.

11. Pragmatically, the most important attribute of God is his punitive justice. But who, in the present state of theological opinion on that point, will dare maintain that hell fire or its equivalent in some shape is rendered certain by pure logic? Theology herself has largely based this doctrine upon revelation; and, in discussing it, has tended more and more to substitute conventional ideas of criminal law for *a priori* principles of reason. But the very notion that this glorious universe with planets and winds, and laughing sky and ocean, should have been conceived and had its beams and rafters laid in technicalities of criminality, is incredible to our modern imagination. It weakens a religion to hear it argued upon such a basis.

12. John Caird, *An Introduction to the Philosophy of Religion* (London and New York, 1880), 243–50, and 291–99, much abridged.

13. A. C. Fraser, *Philosophy of Theism*, second edition (Edinburgh and London, 1899), especially part ii, chaps. vii and viii.; A. Seth [Pringle-Pattison], *Hegelianism and Personality* (Ibid., 1890), passim.

The most persuasive arguments in favor of a concrete individual Soul of the world, with which I am acquainted, are those of my colleague, Josiah Royce, in his *Religious Aspect of Philosophy* (Boston, 1885); in his *Conception of God* (New York and London, 1897); and lately in his Aberdeen Gifford Lectures, *The World and the Individual*, 2 vols. (New York and London, 1901–2). I doubtless seem to some of my readers to evade the philosophic duty which my thesis in this lecture imposes on me, by not even attempting to meet Professor Royce's arguments articulately. I admit the momentary evasion. In the present lectures, which are cast throughout in a popular mould, there seemed no room for subtle metaphysical discussion, and for tactical purposes it was sufficient, the contention of philosophy being what it is (namely, that religion can be transformed into a universally convincing science), to point to the fact that no religious philosophy has actually convinced the mass of thinkers. Meanwhile let me say that I hope that the present volume may be followed by another, if I am spared to write it, in which not only Professor Royce's arguments, but others for monistic absolutism shall be considered with all the technical fullness which their great importance calls for. At present I resign myself to lying passive under the reproach of superficiality.

7. From *Darkwater*, Chapter 9

W. E. B. DU BOIS

Once upon a time I took a great journey in this land to three of the ends of our world and over seven thousand mighty miles. I saw the grim desert and the high ramparts of the Rocky Mountains. Three days I flew from the silver beauty of Seattle to the somber whirl of Kansas City. Three days I flew from the brute might of Chicago to the air of the Angels in California, scented with golden flowers, where the homes of men crouch low and loving on the good, broad earth, as though they were kissing her blossoms. Three days I flew through the empire of Texas, but all these shall be tales untold, for in all this journey I saw but one thing that lived and will live eternal in my soul,—the Grand Cañon.

It is a sudden void in the bosom of earth, down to its entrails—a wound where the dull titanic knife has turned and twisted in the hole, leaving its edges livid, scarred, jagged, and pulsing over the white, and red, and purple of its mighty flesh, while down below—down, down below, in black and severed vein, boils the dull and sullen flood of the Colorado.

It is awful. There can be nothing like it. It is the earth and sky gone stark and raving mad. The mountains up-twirled, disbodied and inverted, stand on their peaks and throw their bowels to the sky. Their earth is air; their ether blood-red rock engreened. You stand upon their roots and fall into their pinnacles, a mighty mile.

Behold this mauve and purple mocking of time and space! See yonder peak! No human foot has trod it. Into that blue shadow only the eye of God has looked. Listen to the accents of that gorge which mutters: "Before Abraham was, I am." Is yonder wall a hedge of black or is it the rampart between heaven and hell? I see greens,—is it moss or giant pines? I see specks that may be boulders. Ever the winds sigh and drop into those sun-swept silences. Ever the gorge lies motionless, unmoved, until I fear. It is a grim thing, unholy, terrible! It is human—some mighty drama unseen, unheard, is playing there its tragedies or mocking comedy, and the laugh of endless years is shrieking onward from peak to peak, unheard, unechoed, and unknown.

One throws a rock into the abyss. It gives back no sound. It falls on silence—the voice of its thunders cannot reach so far. It is not—it cannot be a mere, inert, unfeeling, brute fact—its grandeur is too serene—its beauty too divine! It is not red, and blue, and green, but, ah! the shadows and the shades of all the world, glad colorings touched with a hesitant spiritual delicacy. What does it mean—what does it mean? Tell me, black and boiling water! It is not real. It is but shadows. The shading of eternity. Last night yonder tesselated palace was gloom—dark, breeding thought and sin, while hither rose the mountains of the sun, golden, blazing, ensanguined. It was a dream. This blue and brilliant morning shows all those burning peaks alight, while here, shapeless, mistful, brood the shadowed towers.

I have been down into the entrails of earth—down, down by straight and staring cliffs—down by sounding waters and sun-strewn meadows; down by green pastures and still waters, by great, steep chasms—down by the gnarled and twisted fists of God to the deep, sad moan of the yellow river that did this thing of wonder,—a little winding river with death in its depth and a crown of glory in its flying hair.

I have seen what eye of man was never meant to see. I have profaned the sanctuary. I have looked upon the dread disrobing of the Night, and yet I live. Ere I hid my head she was standing in her cavern halls, glowing coldly westward—her feet were blackness: her robes, empurpled, flowed mistily from shoulder down in formless folds of folds; her head, pine-crowned, was set with jeweled stars. I turned away and dreamed—the cañon,—the awful, its depths called; its heights shuddered. Then suddenly I arose and looked. Her robes were falling. At dim-dawn they hung purplish-green and black. Slowly she stripped them from her gaunt and shapely limbs—her cold, gray garments shot with shadows stood revealed. Down dropped the black-blue robes, gray-pearled, and slipped, leaving a filmy, silken, misty thing, and underneath I glimpsed her limbs of utter light.

My God! For what am I thankful this night? For nothing. For nothing but the most commonplace of commonplaces; a table of gentlewomen and gentlemen—soft-spoken, sweet-tempered, full of human sympathy, who made me, a stranger, one of them. Ours was a fellowship of common books, common knowledge, mighty aims. We could laugh and joke and think as friends —and the Thing—the hateful, murderous, dirty Thing which in America we call "Nigger-hatred" was not only not there—it could not even be understood. It was a curious monstrosity at which civilized folk laughed or looked puzzled. There was no elegant and elaborate condescension of—"We once had a colored servant"—"My father was an Abolitionist"—"I've always been interested in *your people*"—there was only the community of kindred souls, the delicate reverence for the Thought that led, the quick deference to the guest. You left in quiet regret, knowing that they were not discussing you behind your back with lies and license. God! It was simple human decency and I had to be thankful for it because I am an American Negro, and white America, with saving exceptions, is cruel to everything that has black blood. [. . .]

There is something in the nature of Beauty that demands an end. Ugliness may be indefinite. It may trail off into gray endlessness. But Beauty must be complete—whether it be a field of poppies or a great life,—it must end, and the End is part and triumph of the Beauty. I know there are those who envisage a beauty eternal. But I cannot. I can dream of great and never-ending processions of beautiful things and visions and acts. But each must be complete or it cannot for me exist.

On the other hand, ugliness to me is eternal, not in the essence but in its incompleteness; but its eternity does not daunt me, for its eternal unfulfilment is a cause of joy. There is in it nothing new or unexpected; it is the old evil stretching out and ever seeking the end it cannot find; it may coil and writhe and recur in endless battle to days without end, but it is the same human ill and bitter hurt. But Beauty is fulfilment. It satisfies. It is always new and strange. It is the reasonable thing. Its end is Death—the sweet silence of perfection, the calm and balance of utter music. Therein is the triumph of Beauty.

So strong is the spell of beauty that there are those who, contradicting their own knowledge and experience, try to say that all is beauty. They are called optimists, and they lie. All is not beauty. Ugliness and hate and ill are here with all their contradiction and illogic; they will always be here—perhaps, God send, with lessened volume and force, but here and eternal, while beauty triumphs in its great completion—Death. We cannot conjure the end of all ugliness in eternal beauty, for beauty by its very being and definition has in each definition its ends and limits; but while beauty lies implicit and revealed in its end, ugliness writhes on in darkness forever. So the ugliness of continual birth fulfils itself and conquers gloriously only in the beautiful end, Death.

At last to us all comes happiness, there in the Court of Peace, where the dead lie so still and calm and good. If we were not dead we would lie and listen to the flowers grow. We would hear the birds sing and see how the rain rises and blushes and burns and pales and dies in beauty. We would see spring, summer, and the red riot of autumn, and then in winter, beneath the soft white snow, sleep and dream of dreams. But we know that being dead, our Happiness is a fine and finished thing and that ten, a hundred, and a thousand years, we shall lie at rest, unhurt in the Court of Peace.

THE PRAYERS OF GOD

Name of God's Name!
Red murder reigns;
All hell is loose;
On gold autumnal air
Walk grinning devils, barbed and hoofed;
While high on hills of hate,
Black-blossomed, crimson-sky'd,
Thou sittest, dumb.

Father Almighty!
This earth is mad!
Palsied, our cunning hands;
Rotten, our gold;
Our argosies reel and stagger
Over empty seas;
All the long aisles
Of Thy Great Temples, God,
Stink with the entrails
Of our souls.
And Thou art dumb.

Above the thunder of Thy Thunders, Lord,
Lightening Thy Lightnings,
Rings and roars
The dark damnation
Of this hell of war.
Red piles the pulp of hearts and heads
And little children's hands.

Allah!
Elohim!
Very God of God!
Death is here!
Dead are the living; deep-dead the dead.
Dying are earth's unborn—
The babes' wide eyes of genius and of joy,
Poems and prayers, sun-glows and earth-songs,
Great-pictured dreams,
Enmarbled phantasies,

High hymning heavens—all
In this dread night
Writhe and shriek and choke and die
This long ghost-night—
While Thou art dumb.

Have mercy!
Have mercy upon us, miserable sinners!
Stand forth, unveil Thy Face,
Pour down the light
That seethes above Thy Throne,
And blaze this devil's dance to darkness!
Hear!
Speak!
In Christ's Great Name—

I hear!
Forgive me, God!
Above the thunder I hearkened;
Beneath the silence, now,—
I hear!

(Wait, God, a little space.
It is so strange to talk with Thee—
Alone!)

This gold?
I took it.
Is it Thine?
Forgive; I did not know.

Blood? Is it wet with blood?
'Tis from my brother's hands.
(I know; his hands are mine.)
It flowed for Thee, O Lord.
War? Not so; not war—
Dominion, Lord, and over black, not white;
Black, brown, and fawn,
And not Thy Chosen Brood, O God,
We murdered.
To build Thy Kingdom,
To drape our wives and little ones,
And set their souls a-glitter—
For this we killed these lesser breeds
And civilized their dead,
Raping red rubber, diamonds, cocoa, gold!

For this, too, once, and in Thy Name,
I lynched a Nigger—
(He raved and writhed,
I heard him cry,
I felt the life-light leap and lie,
I saw him crackle there, on high,
I watched him wither!)

Thou?
Thee?
I lynched Thee?

Awake me, God! I sleep!
What was that awful word Thou saidst?
That black and riven thing—was it Thee?
That gasp—was it Thine?
This pain—is it Thine?
Are, then, these bullets piercing Thee?
Have all the wars of all the world,
Down all dim time, drawn blood from Thee?
Have all the lies and thefts and hates—
Is this Thy Crucifixion, God,
And not that funny, little cross,
With vinegar and thorns?
Is this Thy kingdom here, not there,
This stone and stucco drift of dreams?

Help!
I sense that low and awful cry—
Who cries?
Who weeps?
With silent sob that rends and tears—
Can God sob?

Who prays?
I hear strong prayers throng by,
Like mighty winds on dusky moors—
Can God pray?

Prayest Thou, Lord, and to me?
Thou needest me?
Thou *needest* me?
Thou needest *me?*
Poor, wounded soul!
Of this I never dreamed. I thought—

Courage, God,
I come!

8. Creative Democracy: The Task before Us

JOHN DEWEY

Under present circumstances I cannot hope to conceal the fact that I have managed to exist eighty years. Mention of the fact may suggest to you a more important fact—namely, that events of the utmost significance for the destiny of this country have taken place during the past four-fifths of a century, a period that covers more than half of its national life in its present form. For obvious reasons I shall not attempt a summary of even the more important of these events. I refer here to them because of their bearing upon the issue to which this country committed itself when the nation took shape—the creation of democracy, an issue which is now as urgent as it was a hundred and fifty years ago when the most experienced and wisest men of the country gathered to take stock of conditions and to create the political structure of a self-governing society.

For the net import of the changes that have taken place in these later years is that ways of life and institutions which were once the natural, almost the inevitable, product of fortunate conditions have now to be won by conscious and resolute effort. Not all the country was in a pioneer state eighty years ago. But it was still, save perhaps in a few large cities, so close to the pioneer stage of American life that the traditions of the pioneer, indeed of the frontier, were active agencies in forming the thoughts and shaping the beliefs of those who were born into its life. In imagination at least the country was still having an open frontier, one of unused and unappropriated resources. It was a country of physical opportunity and invitation. Even so, there was more than a

From *The Later Works of John Dewey, 1925–53,* vol. 14 (1939–41). © 1988 by the Board of Trustees, Southern Illinois University Press. Reprinted by permission.

marvelous conjunction of physical circumstances involved in bringing to birth this new nation. There was in existence a group of men who were capable of readapting older institutions and ideas to meet the situations provided by new physical conditions—a group of men extraordinarily gifted in political inventiveness.

At the present time, the frontier is moral, not physical. The period of free lands that seemed boundless in extent has vanished. Unused resources are now human rather than material. They are found in the waste of grown men and women who are without the chance to work, and in the young men and young women who find doors closed where there was once opportunity. The crisis that one hundred and fifty years ago called out social and political inventiveness is with us in a form which puts a heavier demand on human creativeness.

At all events this is what I mean when I say that we now have to re-create by deliberate and determined endeavor the kind of democracy which in its origin one hundred and fifty years ago was largely the product of a fortunate combination of men and circumstances. We have lived for a long time upon the heritage that came to us from the happy conjunction of men and events in an earlier day. The present state of the world is more than a reminder that we have now to put forth every energy of our own to prove worthy of our heritage. It is a challenge to do for the critical and complex conditions of today what the men of an earlier day did for simpler conditions.

If I emphasize that the task can be accomplished only by inventive effort and creative activity, it is in part because the depth of the present crisis is due in considerable part to the fact that for a long period we acted as if our democracy were something that perpetuated itself automatically; as if our ancestors had succeeded in setting up a machine that solved the problem of perpetual motion in politics. We acted as if democracy were something that took place mainly at Washington and Albany—or some other state capital—under the impetus of what happened when men and women went to the polls once a year or so—which is a somewhat extreme way of saying that we have had the habit of thinking of democracy as a kind of political mechanism that will work as long as citizens were reasonably faithful in performing political duties. Of late years we have heard more and more frequently that this is not enough; that democracy is a way of life. This saying gets down to hard pan. But I am not sure that something of the externality of the old idea does not cling to the new and better statement. In any case we can escape from this external way of thinking only as we realize in thought and act that democracy is a personal way of individual life; that it signifies the possession and continual use of certain attitudes, forming personal character and determining desire and purpose in all the relations of life. Instead of thinking of our own dispositions and habits as accommodated to certain institutions we have to learn to think of the latter as expressions, projections and extensions of habitually dominant personal attitudes.

Democracy as a personal, an individual, way of life involves nothing fundamentally new. But when applied it puts a new practical meaning in old ideas. Put into effect it signifies that powerful present enemies of democracy can be successfully met only by the creation of personal attitudes in individual human beings; that we must get over our tendency to think that its defense can be found in any external means whatever, whether military or civil, if they are separated from individual attitudes so deep-seated as to constitute personal character.

Democracy is a way of life controlled by a working faith in the possibilities of human nature. Belief in the Common Man is a familiar article in the democratic creed. That belief is without basis and significance save as it means faith in the potentialities of human nature as that nature is exhibited in every human being irrespective of race, color, sex, birth and family, of material or cultural wealth. This faith may be enacted in statutes, but it is only on paper unless it is put in force in the attitudes which human beings display to one another in all the incidents and relations of daily life. To denounce Naziism for intolerance, cruelty and stimulation of hatred amounts to fostering insincerity if, in our personal relations to other persons, if, in our daily walk and conversation, we are moved by racial, color or other class prejudice; indeed, by anything save a generous belief in their possibilities as human beings, a belief which brings with it the need for providing conditions which will enable these capacities to reach fulfilment. The democratic faith in human equality is belief that every human being, independent of the quantity or range of his personal endowment, has the right to equal opportunity with every other person for development of whatever gifts he has. The democratic belief in the principle of leadership is a generous one. It is universal. It is belief in the capacity of every person to lead his own life free from coercion and imposition by others provided right conditions are supplied.

Democracy is a way of personal life controlled not merely by faith in human nature in general but by faith in the capacity of human beings for intelligent judgment and action if proper conditions are furnished. I have been accused more than once and from opposed quarters of an undue, a utopian, faith in the possibilities of intelligence and in education as a correlate of intelligence. At all events, I did not invent this faith. I acquired it from my surroundings as far as those surroundings were animated by the democratic spirit. For what is the faith of democracy in the role of consultation, of conference, of persuasion, of discussion, in formation of public opinion, which in the long run is self-corrective, except faith in the capacity of the intelligence of the common man to respond with commonsense to the free play of facts and ideas which are secured by effective guarantees of free inquiry, free assembly and free communication? I am willing to leave to upholders of totalitarian states of the right and the left the view that faith in the capacities of intelligence is utopian. For the faith is so deeply embedded in the methods which are intrinsic to democracy that when a professed democrat denies the faith he convicts himself of treachery to his profession.

When I think of the conditions under which men and women are living in many foreign countries today, fear of espionage, with danger hanging over the meeting of friends for friendly conversation in private gatherings, I am inclined to believe that the heart and final guarantee of democracy is in free gatherings of neighbors on the street corner to discuss back and forth what is read in uncensored news of the day, and in gatherings of friends in the living rooms of houses and apartments to converse freely with one another. Intolerance, abuse, calling of names because of differences of opinion about religion or politics or business, as well as because of differences of race, color, wealth or degree of culture are treason to the democratic way of life. For everything which bars freedom and fullness of communication sets up barriers that divide human beings into sets and cliques, into antagonistic sects and factions, and thereby undermines the democratic way of life. Merely legal guarantees of the civil liberties of free belief, free expression, free assembly are of little avail if in daily life freedom of communication, the give and take of ideas, facts, experiences, is choked by mutual suspicion, by abuse, by fear and hatred. These things destroy the essential condition of the democratic way of living even more effectually than open coercion which—as the example of totalitarian states proves—is effective only when it succeeds in breeding hate, suspicion, intolerance in the minds of individual human beings.

Finally, given the two conditions just mentioned, democracy as a way of life is controlled by personal faith in personal day-by-day working together with others. Democracy is the belief that even when needs and ends or consequences are different for each individual, the habit of amicable cooperation—which may include, as in sport, rivalry and competition—is itself a priceless addition to life. To take as far as possible every conflict which arises —and they are bound to arise—out of the atmosphere and medium of force, of violence as a means of settlement into that of discussion and of intelligence is to treat those who disagree—even profoundly—with us as those from whom we may learn, and in so far, as friends. A genuinely democratic faith in peace is faith in the possibility of conducting disputes, controversies and conflicts as cooperative undertakings in which both parties learn by giving the other a chance to express itself, instead of having one party conquer by forceful suppression of the other—a suppression which is none the less one of violence when it takes place by psychological means of ridicule, abuse, intimidation, instead of by overt imprisonment or in concentration camps. To cooperate by giving differences a chance to show themselves because of the belief that the expression of difference is not only a right of the other persons but is a means of enriching one's own life-experience, is inherent in the democratic personal way of life.

If what has been said is charged with being a set of moral commonplaces, my only reply is that that is just the point in saying them. For to get rid of the habit of thinking of democracy as something institutional and external and to acquire the habit of treating it as a way of personal life is to realize that democracy is a moral ideal and so far as it becomes a fact is a moral fact. It is to realize that democracy is a reality only as it is indeed a commonplace of living.

Since my adult years have been given to the pursuit of philosophy, I shall ask your indulgence if in concluding I state briefly the democratic faith in the formal terms of a philosophic position. So stated, democracy is belief in the ability of human experience to generate the aims and methods by which further experience will grow in ordered richness. Every other form of moral and social faith rests upon the idea that experience must be subjected at some point or other to some form of external control; to some "authority" alleged to exist outside the processes of experience. Democracy is the faith that the process of experience is more important than any special result attained, so that special results achieved are of ultimate value only as they are used to enrich and order the ongoing process. Since the process of experience is capable of being educative, faith in democracy is all one with faith in experience and education. All ends and values that are cut off from the ongoing process become arrests, fixations. They strive to fixate what has been gained instead of using it to open the road and point the way to new and better experiences.

If one asks what is meant by experience in this connection my reply is that it is that free interaction of individual human beings with surrounding conditions, especially the human surroundings, which develops and satisfies need and desire by increasing knowledge of things as they are. Knowledge of conditions as they are is the only solid ground for communication and sharing; all other communication means the subjection of some persons to the personal opinion of other persons. Need and desire—out of which grow purpose and direction of energy—go beyond what exists, and hence beyond knowledge, beyond science. They continually open the way into the unexplored and unattained future.

Democracy as compared with other ways of life is the sole way of living which believes wholeheartedly in the process of experience as end and as means; as that which is capable of generating the science which is the sole dependable authority for the direction of further experience and which releases emotions, needs and desires so as to call into being the things that have not existed in the past. For every way of life that fails in its democracy limits the contacts, the exchanges, the communications, the interactions by which experience is steadied while it is also enlarged and enriched. The task of this release and enrichment is one that has to be carried on day by day. Since it is one that can have no end till experience itself comes to an end, the task of democracy is forever that of creation of a freer and more humane experience in which all share and to which all contribute.

9. A Common Faith: Faith and Its Object

JOHN DEWEY

[. . .] The intellectual articles of a creed must be understood to be symbolic
of moral and other ideal values, [. . . and] the facts taken to be historic and
used as concrete evidence of the intellectual articles are themselves symbolic. These articles of a creed present events and persons that have been made
over by the idealizing imagination in the interest, at their best, of moral ideals. Historic personages in their divine attributes are materializations of the
ends that enlist devotion and inspire endeavor. They are symbolic of the reality of ends moving us in many forms of experience. The ideal values that
are thus symbolized also mark human experience in science and art and the
various modes of human association: they mark almost everything in life that
rises from the level of manipulation of conditions as they exist. It is admitted that the objects of religion are ideal in contrast with our present state.
What would be lost if it were also admitted that they have authoritative claim
upon conduct just because they are ideal? The assumption that these objects
of religion exist already in some realm of Being seems to add nothing to their
force, while it weakens their claim over us as ideals, in so far as it bases that
claim upon matters that are intellectually dubious. The question narrows
itself to this: Are the ideals that move us genuinely ideal or are they ideal only
in contrast with our present estate?

The import of the question extends far. It determines the meaning given
to the word "God." On one score, the word can mean only a particular Being. On the other score, it denotes the unity of all ideal ends arousing us to

Originally published in *A Common Faith,* © 1934 by Yale University Press. Reprinted by permission.

desire and actions. Does the unification have a claim upon our attitude and conduct because it is already, apart from us, in realized existence, or because of its own inherent meaning and value? Suppose for the moment that the word "God" means the ideal ends that at a given time and place one acknowledges as having authority over his volition and emotion, the values to which one is supremely devoted, as far as these ends, through imagination, take on unity. If we make this supposition, the issue will stand out clearly in contrast with the doctrine of religions that "God" designates some kind of Being having prior and therefore non-ideal existence.

The word "non-ideal" is to be taken literally in regard to some religions that have historically existed, to all of them as far as they are neglectful of moral qualities in their divine beings. It does not apply in the same literal way to Judaism and Christianity. For they have asserted that the Supreme Being has moral and spiritual attributes. But it applies to them none the less in that these moral and spiritual characters are thought of as properties of a particular existence and are thought to be of religious value for us because of this embodiment in such an existence. Here, as far as I can see, is the ultimate issue as to the difference between a religion and the religious as a function of experience.

The idea that "God" represents a unification of ideal values that is essentially imaginative in origin when the imagination supervenes in conduct is attended with verbal difficulties owing to our frequent use of the word "imagination" to denote fantasy and doubtful reality. But the reality of ideal ends as ideals is vouched for by their undeniable power in action. An ideal is not an illusion because imagination is the organ through which it is apprehended. For all possibilities reach us through the imagination. In a definite sense the only meaning that can be assigned the term "imagination" is that things unrealized in fact come home to us and have power to stir us. The unification effected through imagination is not fanciful, for it is the reflex of the unification of practical and emotional attitudes. The unity signifies not a single Being, but the unity of loyalty and effort evoked by the fact that many ends are one in the power of their ideal, or imaginative, quality to stir and hold us.

We may well ask whether the power and significance in life of the traditional conceptions of God are not due to the ideal qualities referred to by them, the hypostatization of them into an existence being due to a conflux of tendencies in human nature that converts the object of desire into an antecedent reality [...] with beliefs that have prevailed in the cultures of the past. For in the older cultures the idea of the supernatural was "natural," in the sense in which "natural" signifies something customary and familiar. It seems more credible that religious persons have been supported and consoled by the reality with which ideal values appeal to them than that they have been upborne by sheer matter of fact existence. That, when once men are inured to the idea of the union of the ideal and the physical, the two should be so bound together in emotion that it is difficult to institute a separation, agrees with all we know of human psychology.

The benefits that will accrue, however, from making the separation are evident. The dislocation frees the religious values of experience once for all from matters that are continually becoming more dubious. With that release there comes emancipation from the necessity of resort to apologetics. The reality of ideal ends and values in their authority over us is an undoubted fact. The validity of justice, affection, and that intellectual correspondence of our ideas with realities that we call truth, is so assured in its hold upon humanity that it is unnecessary for the religious attitude to encumber itself with the apparatus of dogma and doctrine. Any other conception of the religious attitude, when it is adequately analyzed, means that those who hold it care more for force than for ideal values—since all that an Existence can add is force to establish, to punish, and to reward. There are, indeed, some persons who frankly say that their own faith does not require any guarantee that moral values are backed up by physical force, but who hold that the masses are so backward that ideal values will not affect their conduct unless in the popular belief these values have the sanction of a power that can enforce them and can execute justice upon those who fail to comply.

There are some persons, deserving of more respect, who say: "We agree that the beginning must be made with the primacy of the ideal. But why stop at this point? Why not search with the utmost eagerness and vigor for all the evidence we can find, such as is supplied by history, by presence of design in nature, which may lead on to the belief that the ideal is already extant in a Personality having objective existence?"

One answer to the question is that we are involved by this search in all the problems of the existence of evil that have haunted theology in the past and that the most ingenious apologetics have not faced, much less met. If these apologists had not identified the existence of ideal goods with that of a Person supposed to originate and support them—a Being, moreover, to whom omnipotent power is attributed—the problem of the occurrence of evil would be gratuitous. The significance of ideal ends and meanings is, indeed, closely connected with the fact that there are in life all sorts of things that are evil to us because we would have them otherwise. Were existing conditions wholly good, the notion of possibilities to be realized would never emerge.

But the more basic answer is that while if the search is conducted upon a strictly empirical basis there is no reason why it should not take place, as a matter of fact it is always undertaken in the interest of the supernatural. Thus it diverts attention and energy from ideal values and from the exploration of actual conditions by means of which they may be promoted. History is testimony to this fact. Men have never fully used the powers they possess to advance the good in life, because they have waited upon some power external to themselves and to nature to do the work they are responsible for doing. Dependence upon an external power is the counterpart of surrender of human endeavor. Nor is emphasis on exercising our own powers for good an egoistical or a sentimentally optimistic recourse. It is not the first, for it does not isolate man, either individually or collectively, from nature. It is not the second, because it makes no assumption beyond that of the need and responsibility for human endeavor, and beyond the conviction that, if human desire and endeavor were enlisted in behalf of natural ends, conditions would be bettered. It involves no expectation of a millennium of good.

Belief in the supernatural as a necessary power for apprehension of the ideal and for practical attachment to it has for its counterpart a pessimistic belief in the corruption and impotency of natural means. That is axiomatic in Christian dogma. But this apparent pessimism has a way of suddenly changing into an exaggerated optimism. For according to the terms of the doctrine, if the faith in the supernatural is of the required order, regeneration at once takes place. Goodness, in all essentials, is thereby established; if not, there is proof that the established relation to the supernatural has been vitiated. This romantic optimism is one cause for the excessive attention to individual salvation characteristic of traditional Christianity. Belief in a sudden and complete transmutation through conversion and in the objective efficacy of prayer, is too easy a way out of difficulties. It leaves matters in general just about as they were before; that is, sufficiently bad so that there is additional support for the idea that only supernatural aid can better them. The position of natural intelligence is that there exists a mixture of good and evil, and that reconstruction in the direction of the good which is indicated by ideal ends, must take place, if at all, through continued cooperative effort. There is at least enough impulse toward justice, kindliness, and order so that if it were mobilized for action, not expecting abrupt and complete transformation to occur, the disorder, cruelty, and oppression that exist would be reduced.

The discussion has arrived at a point where a more fundamental objection to the position I am taking needs consideration. The misunderstanding upon which this objection rests should be pointed out. The view I have advanced is sometimes treated as if the identification of the divine with ideal ends left the ideal wholly without roots in existence and without support from existence. The objection implies that my view commits one to such a separation of the ideal and the existent that the ideal has no chance to find lodgment even as a seed that might grow and bear fruit. On the contrary, what I have been criticizing is the identification of the ideal with a particular Being, especially when that identification makes necessary the conclusion that this Being is outside of nature, and what I have tried to show is that the ideal itself has its roots in natural conditions; it emerges when the imagination idealizes existence by laying hold of the possibilities offered to thought and action. There are values, goods, actually realized upon a natural basis—the goods of human association, of art and knowledge. The idealizing imagination seizes upon the most precious things found in the climacteric moments of experience and projects them. We need no external criterion and guarantee for their goodness. They are had, they exist as good, and out of them we frame our ideal ends.

Moreover, the ends that result from our projection of experienced goods into objects of thought, desire and effort exist, only they exist as ends. Ends, purposes, exercise determining power in human conduct. The aims of philanthropists, of Florence Nightingale, of Howard, of Wilberforce, of Peabody, have not been idle dreams. They have modified institutions. Aims, ideals, do not exist simply in "mind"; they exist in character, in personality and action. One might call the roll of artists, intellectual inquirers, parents, friends, citizens who are neighbors, to show that purposes exist in an operative way. What I have been objecting to, I repeat, is not the idea that ideals are linked with existence and that they themselves exist, through human embodiment, as forces, but the idea that their authority and value depend upon some prior complete embodiment—as if the efforts of human beings in behalf of justice, or knowledge or beauty, depended for their effectiveness and validity upon assurance that there already existed in some supernal region a place where criminals are humanely treated, where there is no serfdom or slavery, where all facts and truths are already discovered and possessed, and all beauty is eternally displayed in actualized form.

The aims and ideals that move us are generated through imagination. But they are not made out of imaginary stuff. They are made out of the hard stuff of the world of physical and social experience. The locomotive did not exist before Stevenson, nor the telegraph before the time of Morse. But the conditions for their existence were there in physical material and energies and in human capacity. Imagination seized hold upon the idea of a rearrangement of existing things that would evolve new objects. The same thing is true of a painter, a musician, a poet, a philanthropist, a moral prophet. The new vision does not arise out of nothing, but emerges through seeing, in terms of possibilities, that is, of imagination, old things in new relations serving a new end which the new end aids in creating.

Moreover the process of creation is experimental and continuous. The artist, scientific man, or good citizen, depends upon what others have done before him and are doing around him. The sense of new values that become ends to be realized arises first in dim and uncertain form. As the values are dwelt upon and carried forward in action they grow in definiteness and coherence. Interaction between aim and existent conditions improves and tests the ideal; and conditions are at the same time modified. Ideals change as they are applied in existent conditions. The process endures and advances with the life of humanity. What one person and one group accomplish becomes the standing ground and starting point of those who succeed them. When the vital factors in this natural process are generally acknowledged in emotion, thought and action, the process will be both accelerated and purified through elimination of that irrelevant element that culminates in the idea of the supernatural. When the vital factors attain the religious force that has been drafted into supernatural religions, the resulting reinforcement will be incalculable.

These considerations may be applied to the idea of God, or, to avoid misleading conceptions, to the idea of the divine. This idea is, as I have said, one of ideal possibilities unified through imaginative realization and projection. But this idea of God, or of the divine, is also connected with all the natural forces and conditions—including man and human association—that promote the growth of the ideal and that further its realization. We are in the presence neither of ideals completely embodied in existence nor yet of ideals that are mere rootless ideals, fantasies, utopias. For there are forces in nature and society that generate and support the ideals. They are further unified by the action that gives them coherence and solidity. It is this active relation between ideal and actual to which I would give the name "God." I would not insist that the name must be given. There are those who hold that the associations of the term with the supernatural are so numerous and close that any use of the word "God" is sure to give rise to misconception and be taken as a concession to traditional ideas.

They may be correct in this view. But the facts to which I have referred are there, and they need to be brought out with all possible clearness and force. There exist concretely and experimentally goods—the values of art in all its forms, of knowledge, of effort and of rest after striving, of education and fellowship, of friendship and love, of growth in mind and body. These goods are there and yet they are relatively embryonic. Many persons are shut out from generous participation in them; there are forces at work that threaten and sap existent goods as well as prevent their expansion. A clear and intense conception of a union of ideal ends with actual conditions is capable of arousing steady emotion. It may be fed by every experience, no matter what its material.

In a distracted age, the need for such an idea is urgent. It can unify interests and energies now dispersed; it can direct action and generate the heat of emotion and the light of intelligence. Whether one gives the name "God" to this union, operative in thought and action, is a matter for individual decision. But the function of such a working union of the ideal and actual seems to me to be identical with the force that has in fact been attached to the conception of God in all the religions that have a spiritual content; and a clear idea of that function seems to me urgently needed at the present time.

The sense of this union may, with some persons, be furthered by mystical experiences, using the term "mystical" in its broadest sense. That result depends largely upon temperament. But there is a marked difference between the union associated with mysticism and the union which I had in mind. There is nothing mystical about the latter; it is natural and moral. Nor is there anything mystical about the perception or consciousness of such union. Imagination of ideal ends pertinent to actual conditions represents the fruition of a disciplined mind. There is, indeed, even danger that resort to mystical experiences will be an escape, and that its result will be the passive feeling that the union of actual and ideal is already accomplished. But in fact this union is active and practical; it is a uniting, not something given.

One reason why personally I think it fitting to use the word "God" to denote that uniting of the ideal and actual which has been spoken of, lies in the fact that aggressive atheism seems to me to have something in common with traditional supernaturalism. I do not mean merely that the former is mainly so negative that it fails to give positive direction to thought, though that fact is pertinent. What I have in mind especially is the exclusive preoccupation of both militant atheism and supernaturalism with man in isolation. For in spite of supernaturalism's reference to something beyond nature, it conceives of this earth as the moral centre of the universe and of man as the apex of the whole scheme of things. It regards the drama of sin and redemption enacted within the isolated and lonely soul of man as the one thing of ultimate importance. Apart from man, nature is held either accursed or negligible. Militant atheism is also affected by lack of natural piety. The ties binding man to nature that poets have always celebrated are passed over lightly. The attitude taken is often that of man living in an indifferent and hostile world and issuing blasts of defiance. A religious attitude, however, needs the sense of a connection of man, in the way of both dependence and support, with the enveloping world that the imagination feels is a universe. Use of the words "God" or "divine" to convey the union of actual with ideal may protect man from a sense of isolation and from consequent despair or defiance.

In any case, whatever the name, the meaning is selective. For it involves no miscellaneous worship of everything in general. It selects those factors in existence that generate and support our idea of good as an end to be striven for. It excludes a multitude of forces that at any given time are irrelevant to this function. Nature produces whatever gives reinforcement and direction but also what occasions discord and confusion. The "divine" is thus a term of human choice and aspiration. A humanistic religion, if it excludes our relation to nature, is pale and thin, as it is presumptuous, when it takes humanity as an object of worship. Matthew Arnold's conception of a "power not ourselves" is too narrow in its reference to operative and sustaining conditions. While it is selective, it is too narrow in its basis of selection—righteousness. The conception thus needs to be widened in two ways. The powers that generate and support the good as experienced and as ideal, work within as well as without. There seems to be a reminiscence of an external Jehovah in Arnold's statement. And the powers work to enforce other values and ideals than righteousness. Arnold's sense of an opposition between Hellenism and Hebraism resulted in exclusion of beauty, truth, and friendship from the list of the consequences toward which powers work within and without.

In the relation between nature and human ends and endeavors, recent science has broken down the older dualism. It has been engaged in this task for three centuries. But as long as the conceptions of science were strictly mechanical (mechanical in the sense of assuming separate things acting upon one another purely externally by push and pull), religious apologists had a standing ground in pointing out the differences between man and physical nature. The differences could be used for arguing that something supernatural had intervened in the case of man. The recent acclaim, however, by apologists for religion of the surrender by science of the classic type of mechanicalism[1] seems ill-advised from their own point of view. For the change in the modern scientific view of nature simply brings man and nature nearer together. We are no longer compelled to choose between explaining away what is distinctive in man through reducing him to another form of a mechanical model and the doctrine that something literally supernatural marks him off from nature. The less mechanical—in its older sense—physical nature is found to be, the closer is man to nature.

In his fascinating book, *The Dawn of Conscience,* James Henry Breasted refers to Haeckel as saying that the question he would most wish to have answered is this: Is the universe friendly to man? The question is an ambiguous one. Friendly to man in what respect? With respect to ease and comfort, to material success, to egoistic ambitions? Or to his aspiration to inquire and discover, to invent and create, to build a more secure order for human existence? In whatever form the question be put, the answer cannot in all honesty be an unqualified and absolute one. Mr. Breasted's answer, as a historian, is that nature has been friendly to the emergence and development of conscience and character. Those who will have all or nothing cannot be satisfied with this answer. Emergence and growth are not enough for them. They want something more than growth accompanied by toil and pain. They want final achievement. Others who are less absolutist may be content to think that, morally speaking, growth is a higher value and ideal than is sheer attainment. They will remember also that growth has not been confined to conscience and character; that it extends also to discovery, learning and knowledge, to creation in the arts, to furtherance of ties that hold men together in mutual aid and affection. These persons at least will be satisfied with an intellectual view of the religious function that is based on continuing choice directed toward ideal ends.

For, I would remind readers in conclusion, it is the intellectual side of the religious attitude that I have been considering. I have suggested that the religious element in life has been hampered by conceptions of the supernatural that were imbedded in those cultures wherein man had little control over outer nature and little in the way of sure method of inquiry and test. The crisis today as to the intellectual content of religious belief has been caused by the change in the intellectual climate due to the increase of our knowledge and our means of understanding. I have tried to show that this change is not fatal to the religious values in our common experience, however adverse its impact may be upon historic religions. Rather, provided that the methods and results of intelligence at work are frankly adopted, the change is liberating.

It clarifies our ideals, rendering them less subject to illusion and fantasy. It relieves us of the incubus of thinking of them as fixed, as without power of growth. It discloses that they develop in coherence and pertinency with increase of natural intelligence. The change gives aspiration for natural knowledge a definitely religious character, since growth in understanding of nature is seen to be organically related to the formation of ideal ends. The same change enables man to select those elements in natural conditions that may be organized to support and extend the sway of ideals. All purpose is selective, and all intelligent action includes deliberate choice. In the degree in which we cease to depend upon belief in the supernatural, selection is enlightened and choice can be made in behalf of ideals whose inherent relations to conditions and consequences are understood. Were the naturalistic foundations and bearings of religion grasped, the religious element in life would emerge from the throes of the crisis in religion. Religion would then be found to have its natural place in every aspect of human experience that is concerned with estimate of possibilities, with emotional stir by possibilities as yet unrealized, and with all action in behalf of their realization. All that is significant in human experience falls within this frame.

Note

1. I use this term because science has not abandoned its beliefs in working mechanisms in giving up the idea that they are of the nature of a strictly mechanical contract of discrete things.

10. The Aesthetic Drama of the Ordinary

JOHN J. McDERMOTT

Traditionally, we think of ourselves as "in the world" as a button is in a box, a marble in a hole, a coin in a pocket, a spoon in a drawer; in, always in something or other. And yet, to the contrary, I seem to carry myself, to lead myself, to have myself hang around, furtive of nose, eye, and hand, all the while spending and wasting, eating and fouling, minding and drifting, engaging in activities more descriptive of a permeable membrane than of a box. To feel is to be felt. To be in the world is to "world" and to be "worlded." No doubt, the accepted language of expository prose severely limits us in this effort to describe our situation experientially. Were I to say, for example, my presence in the world or my being in the world, I would still fall prey to the container theory and once again be "in" as over against "out." Is this not why it is necessary to describe an unusual person, situation, or state of being as being "out of this world," or "spaced out" or simply "out of it." Why is it that ordinary language, or our language as used ordinarily, so often militates against the ways in which we actually have, that is, undergo, our experiencing? Why is it that we turn to the more specialized forms of discourse such as jokes, fiction, poetry, music, painting, sculpture, and dance, in order to say what we "really" mean? Does this situation entail the baleful judgment that the comparative bankruptcy of our ordinary language justly points to the comparable bankruptcy of our ordinary experience?

In gross and obvious empirical terms, it is difficult to say no to the necessity of this entailment. Surely it is true that we are surrounded by the banal,

Originally published in *Streams of Experience* (Amherst: University of Massachusetts Press, 1986). © 1986 by John J. McDermott. Reprinted by permission of the author.

monumentalized in a miniature and trivial fashion by the American shopping center. And it is equally, yea, painfully true that the "things" of our everyday experience are increasingly de-aestheticized, not only by misuse and failure to maintain, but forebodingly in their very conception of design and choice of material.

The city of Houston, in paying homage to a long outdated frontier myth of every "building" for itself, proceeds to construct an environment which buries an urban aesthetic in the wake of free enterprise. Houston gives rise to tall and imposing buildings whose eyes of window and light point to the surrounding plains, but whose feet are turned inward. These buildings do not open in a merry Maypole of neighborhood frolic and function. Houston buildings are truly sky-buildings, for they look up and out, leaving only the sneer of a curved lip to waft over the enervated neighborhoods below, most of them increasingly grimy and seedy. As an apparent favor to most of us, Houston provides a way for us to avoid these neighborhoods, allowing us to careen around the city, looking only at the bellies of the titans of glass and steel, astride the circular ribbon of concrete known appropriately as the beltway, marred only by the dead trees, broken car jacks, and the intrusive omnipresence of Texas-sized billboards. Perhaps it is just as well that we, too, rise above the madding crowd, for in that way we miss the awkwardness of wandering into one of those walled-off, sometimes covenanted and patrolled, fancy enclaves which make the city tolerable for the rich. And as we make our "beltway," we miss as well that strikingly sad experience of downtown Houston at 6 P.M. of a weekend evening, when the loneliness and shabbiness of the streets are cast into stark relief by the perimeter of empty skyscrapers and the hollow sounds of the feet of the occasional snow-belt émigré traveler, emerging from the Hyatt Regency in a futile search for action. What is startling and depressing about all of this is that the city of Houston is the nation's newest and allegedly most promising major city.

* * *

Actually, whether it is North, South, East, or West matters little, for in general the archons of aesthetic illiteracy have seen to it that on behalf of whatever other ideology they follow, the presence of aesthetic sensibility has been either ruled out or, where traditionally present, allowed to erode. Further, to the extent that we prehend ourselves as a thing among things or a functioning item in a box, then we get what we deserve. Supposing, however, we were to consider the major metaphorical versions of how we carry on our human experiencing and, in so doing, avoid using the imagery of the box. Instead, let us consider ourselves as being in a uterine situation, which binds us to nutrition in a distinctively organic way. James Marston Fitch, a premier architectural historian, writes about us as follows: "Life is coexistent with the external natural environment in which the body is submerged. The body's dependence upon this external environment is absolute—in the fullest sense of the word uterine."[1]

No box here. Rather we are floating, gestating organisms, transacting with our environment, eating all the while. The crucial ingredient in all uterine situations is the nutritional quality of the environment. If our immediate surroundings are foul, soiled, polluted harbors of disease and grime, ridden with alien organisms, then we falter and perish. The growth of the spirit is exactly analogous to the growth of the organism. It too must be fed and it must have the capacity to convert its experiences into a nutritious transaction. In short, the human organism has need of two livers. The one, traditional and omnipresent, transforms our blood among its 500 major functions and oversees the elimination from our body of ammonia, bacteria, and an assortment of debris, all of which would poison us. The second is more vague, having no physical analogue. But its function is similar and crucial. This second liver eats the sky and the earth, sorts out tones and colors, and provides a filter through which the experienced environment enters our consciousness. It is this spiritual liver which generates our feelings of queasiness, loneliness, surprise, and celebration. And it is this liver which monitors the tenuous relationship between expectations and anticipations on the one hand and realizations, disappointments, and failures on the other. We are not simply in the world so much as we are of and about the world. On behalf of this second type of livering, let us evoke the major metaphors of the fabric, of the uterus, through which we have our natal being. Our context for inquiry shall be the affairs of time and space, as well as the import of things, events, and relations. We shall avoid the heightened and intensified versions of these experiential filters and concentrate on the explosive and implosive drama of their ordinariness.

Time

Time passing is a death knell. With the license of a paraphrase, I ask, For whom does the bell toll? It tolls for thee and me and for ours. We complain about the studied repetition, which striates our lives, and yet, in honesty, we indulge this repetition as a way of hiding from the inexorability of time passing, as a sign equivalent to the imminence of our self-eulogy. Time is a shroud, often opaque, infrequently diaphanous. Yet, from time to time, we are able to bring time into our own self-awareness and to bring time to its knees. On those rare occasions when time is ours rather than we being creatures of time, we feel a burst of singularity, of independence, even perhaps of the eternal import of our being present to ourselves. How has it happened that we have become slaves to time? Surely as children of Kant and Einstein, we should know better. For them and for modern physics, time is a mock-up, an earth phenomenon, no more relevant cosmically than the watches which watch time, supposedly passing. Still, Kant notwithstanding, time is the name given to the process of our inevitable dissolution. On the morrow, our kidney is less quick, our liver less conscientious, our lung less pulsatile, and our brain less alert. Is it possible, without indulging ourselves in a Walter Mittyesque self-deception, to turn this erosive quality of time passing to our own advantage?

I suggest that we can beat time at its own game. Having created time, let us obviate it. Time, after all, rushes headlong into the future, oblivious to its damages, its obsoleting, and its imperviousness to the pain it often leaves in its wake. A contrary view is that in its passing, time heals. But it is not time which heals us, it is we who heal ourselves by our retroactive reconstruction of history. It is here that time is vulnerable, for it has no history, no past. Time is ever lurching into the future. We, however, can scavenge its remains and make them part of ourselves. For us, the past is existentially present if we have the will and the attentiveness to so arrange. I offer here that we recover the detritus of time passing and clot its flow with our freighted self-consciousness. We can become like the giant balloons in the Macy's Thanksgiving Day parade, thick with history and nostalgia, forcing time passing to snake around us, assuring that it be incapable of enervating our deepest feelings of continuity. What, for example, could time do to us if every time we met a person, or thought a thought, or dreamt a dream, we involved every person ever met, every thought ever thought, and every dream ever dreamt? What would happen if every event, every place, every thing experienced, resonated all the events, places, and things of our lives? What would happen if we generated a personal environment in which the nostalgic fed into the leads of the present, a self-created and sustained environment with implications fore and aft? In so doing, we would reduce time passing to scratching on the externals of our Promethean presence. Time would revolve around us rather than passing through us. Time would provide the playground for our activities rather than the graveyard of our hopes. We would time the world rather than having the world time us. And we would reverse the old adage, to wit, if you have the place, I have the time, for time is mine to keep and to give. And, in addition to telling our children now is your time, we would tell ourselves, no matter how old, now is our time.

Space

It is equally as difficult to extricate ourselves from the box of space as it is to escape from the penalties of time. Here too, we have failed to listen to Kant and Einstein, for space, just as time, has no existential reality other than our conception of it. Yet we allow the prepossessing character of space to dwarf us. Nowhere is this more apparent than in Texas, where the big sky of Montana is outdone by the scorching presence of a sun that seems never to set, frying our brains in the oven of its arrogance. In the spring of the year, the bluebonnets and Indian paintbrush state our position: fey, lovely, quiet, reserved, and delicate of manner. The Texas sun indulges this temporary human-scaled assertion while hovering in the background with vengeance on its mind. As the flowers fade, the horizon widens and the sun takes its place at the center of our lives, burning us with the downdraft of its rays. Listen to Larry King on the sun and sky in West Texas.

> The land is stark and flat and treeless, altogether as bleak and spare as mood scenes in Russian literature, a great dry-docked ocean with small swells of hummocky tan sand dunes or humpbacked rocky knolls that change colors with the hour and the shadows: reddish brown, slate gray, bruise colored. But it is the sky—God-high and pale, like a blue chenille bedspread bleached by seasons in the sun—that dominates. There is simply *too much* sky. Men grow small in its presence and—perhaps feeling diminished—they sometimes are compelled to proclaim themselves in wild or berserk ways. Alone in those remote voids, one may suddenly half believe he is the last man on earth and go in frantic search of the tribe. Desert fever, the natives call it. . . . The summer sun is as merciless as a loan shark: a blinding, angry orange explosion baking the land's sparse grasses and quickly aging the skin.[2]

Texans pride themselves as being larger than life. But this is just a form of railing against the sun. The centuries-long exodus from the Northeast and the coastal cities was in part an escape from urban claustrophobia. In that regard, the escape was short-lived and self-deceptive, for it soon became apparent that the West presented a claustrophobia of another kind—paradoxically, that of open space. The box was larger, the horizon deeper, but the human self became even more trivialized than it was among the skyscrapers and the crowded alleyways and alcoves of the teeming urban centers. No, to the extent that we are overshadowed by an external overhang, be it artifact or natural, we cower in the presence of an *other* which is larger, more diffuse, still threatening and depersonalizing. In response, just as we must seize the time, so too must we seize the space, and turn it into a place, our place.

The placing of space is the creating of interior space, of personal space, of your space and my space, of our space. I am convinced, painful though it be, that we as human beings have no natural place. We are recombinant organisms in a cosmic DNA chain. Wrapped in the mystery of our origins, we moved from natural places to artifactual ones, from caves to ziggurats to the Eiffel tower. We moved from dunes to pyramids and then to the World Trade Center. The history of our architecture, big and small, functional and grandiloquent, lovely and grotesque, is the history of the extension of the human body into the abyss. We dig and we perch. We level and we raise. We make our places round and square and angular. We make them hard and soft and brittle. We take centuries to make them and we throw them up overnight. In modern America, the new Bedouins repeat the nomadic taste of old and carry their places with them as they plod the highway vascular system of the nation, hooking up here and there.

Some of our idiomatic questions and phrases tell us of our concern for being in place. Do you have a place? Set a place for me. This is my place. Why do we always go to your place? Would you care to place a bet? I have been to that place. Wow, this is *some* place. Win, place, show. The trouble with him is that he never went any place and the trouble with her is that she never got any place. How are you doing? How is it going? Fine, I am getting someplace. Not so well, I seem to be no place.

Recall that poignant scene in *Death of a Salesman* when Willy Loman asks Howard for a place in the showroom rather than on the road. In two lines, Howard tells Willy three times that he has no "spot" for him. I knew your father, Howard, and I knew you when you were an infant. Sorry, Willy! No spot, no place, for you. Pack it in. You are out of time and have no place.

Listen lady, clear out. But this is my place. No lady, this place is to be replaced. The harrowing drama of eviction haunts all of us as we envision our future out of place and on the street.[3] Dorothy Day founded halfway houses, places somewhere between no place and my place, that is, at least, someplace. And, finally, they tell us that we are on the way to our resting place, a place from where there is no return.

These are only anecdotal bare bones, each of them selected from a myriad of other instances which point to our effort to overcome the ontological *angoisse* which accompanies our experience of *Unheimlichkeit,* a deep and pervasive sense of ultimate homelessness. We scratch out a place and we raise a wall. The windows look out but the doors open in. We hang a picture and stick a flower in a vase. We go from cradle and crib to a coffin, small boxes at the beginning and end of journeys through slightly larger boxes. Some of us find ourselves in boxes underneath and on top of other boxes in a form of apartmentalization. Some of our boxes are official boxes and we call them offices, slightly less prestigious than the advantage of a box seat. Everywhere in the nation, the majority of our houses are huddled together, sitting on stingy little pieces of ground, while we ogle the vast stretch of land held by absentees. One recalls here "Little Boxes," a folksong of the 1960s that excoriates the ticky-tacky boxes on the hillsides, as a preface to the yuppiedom of our own time. For the most part, our relation to external space is timid, even craven. From time to time, we send forth a camel, a schooner, a Conestoga wagon, or a space shuttle as probes into the outer reaches of our environs, on behalf of our collective body. Yet these geographical efforts to break out are more symbolic than real, for after our explorations we seem destined to repeat our limited variety of habitat.

The *locus classicus* for an explication of the mortal danger in a sheerly geographical response to space is found in a story by Franz Kafka, "The Burrow." In an effort to protect his food from an assumed intruder, the burrower walls off a series of mazes sure to confuse an opponent. This attempt is executed with such cunning and brilliance that his nonreflective anality is missed as a potential threat. The food is indeed walled off from the intruder—from the burrower as well. He dies of starvation, for he cannot find his own food.

The way out of the box is quite different, for it has to do not with the geography and physicality of space, but rather with our symbolic utilization of space for purposes of the human quest. We manage our ontological dwarfing and trivialization at the hands of infinite space, and the rush of time passing and obsoleting, by our construction, management, placing, and relating of *our* things. It is to our things, to creating our salvation in a world without guarantee of salvation, that we now turn.

Things

Thing, orthographically and pronouncedly, is one of the ugly words in contemporary American usage. Yet it is also, inferentially and historically, one of the most subtle and beautiful of our words. It is lamentable that we do not speak the way Chaucer spoke. From the year 1400 and a work of Lydgate, *Troy-Book*, the text reads: "That thei with Paris to Greece schulde wende, To Brynge this thynge to an ende." The Trojan War was a thing? Of course it was a thing, for thing means concern, assembly, and, above all, an affair. Thing is a woman's menses and a dispute in the town. Thing is a male sex organ and a form of prayer. (The continuity is not intended, although desirable.) Thing is what is to be done or its doing. I can't give you any thing but love, baby. That is the only thing I have plenty of, baby. When you come, bring your things. I forgot to bring my things. My things are packed away. Everything will be all right. And by the way, I hope that things will be better.

What and who are these things to which we cling? An old pari-mutuel ticket, a stub for game seven of the World Series, a class ring, a mug, a dead Havana cigar, loved but unsmoked. My snuff box, my jewelry drawer, an album, a diary, a yearbook, all tumbled into the box of memories, but transcendent and assertive of me and mine. Do not throw out his things; they will be missed. Put her things in the attic, for someday she will want them as a form of reconnoitering her experienced past. Do you remember those things? I know that we had them. Where are they? They are in my consciousness. Can we find them? We didn't throw them out, did we? How could we?

The making, placing, and fondling of our things is equivalent to the making, placing, and fondling of our world. We are our things. They are personal intrusions into the vast, impersonal reach of space. They are functional clots in the flow of time. They are living memories of experiences had but still viable. They are memorials to experiences undergone and symbolically still present. The renewed handling of a doll, a ticket, a toy soldier, a childhood book, a tea cup, a bubble-gum wrapper, evokes the flood of experiences past but not forgotten.[4] How we strive to say hello, to say here I am, in a cosmos impervious, unfeeling, and dead to our plaintive cry of self-assertion. To make is to be made and to have is to be had. My thing is not anything or something. Your thing is not my thing but it could be our thing. The ancients had it right, bury the things with the person. We should do that again. Bury me with a copy of the *New York Times,* a Willie Mays baseball card, a bottle of Jameson, my William James book, a pipe, some matches, and a package of Seven-Seas tobacco.

The twentieth-century artist Alexander Calder once said that no one is truly human who has not made his or her own fork and knife. Homemade or not, do you have your own fork, your own knife, your own cup, your own bed, desk, chair? You must have your own things! They are you. You are they. As the poet Rilke tells us, "Being here amounts to so much."[5]

Our things are our things. They do not belong to the cosmos or to the gods. They can be had by others only in vicarious terms. Commendable though it may be for those of us who are collectors of other people's things, nonetheless, those who burn their papers or destroy their things just before they die are a testament to both the radical self-presence and transiency of human life. Those of us, myself included, who collect other people's things, are Texas turkey vultures, seizing upon the sacred moments hammered out by transients and eating them in an effort to taste the elixir of memory for our own vapid personal life. Ironically, for the most part their experience of their things were similar efforts, sadly redeemed more by us than by them. Now to the crux of the matter before us.

It is not, I contend, humanly significant to have the primary meaning of one's life as posthumous. We and our things, I and my things, constitute our world. The nectar of living, losing, loving, maintaining, and caring for our things is for us, and for us alone. It is of time but not in time. It is of space but not in space. We and our things make, constitute, arrange, and determine space and time. The elixir garnered by the posthumous is for the survivors. It cannot be of any biological significance to us, although many of us have bartered our present for the ever absent lilt of being remembered. St. Francis of Assisi and John Dewey both taught us the same *thing:* time is sacred, live by the sacrament of the moment and listen to the animals. We may have a future. It is barely conceivable, although I doubt its existence. We do have, however, a present. It is the present, canopied by our hopefully storied past, that spells the only meaning of our lives. Still, the present would be empty without our things.

You, you out there, you have your things. Take note. Say hello, say hello, things. They are your things. Nay, they are you. No things, no you, or in correct grammar, you become *nothing.* So be it. Space and time are simply vehicles for things, our things, your things, my things. These things do not sit, however, in rows upon rows, like ducks in a shooting gallery. These things make love, hate, and tire. Like us, they are involved. We consider now this involvement of persons, things, things and persons, all struggling to time space and space time, namely, the emergence of events as relations.

Things as Events as Aesthetic Relations

We have been in a struggle to achieve nonderivative presence of ourselves and our things over against the dominating worlds of space and time. Fortunately, for us, space and time do not necessarily speak to each other. Our canniness can play them off, one against the other. The triumph is local, never ultimate, although it does give us staying power in our attempt to say I, me, you, we, us, and other asserted pronominal outrages against the abyss.

A happy phenomenon for human life is that things not only are; they also happen. I like to call these happenings events. The literal meaning of event is intended: a coming out, a party, a debutante dance, a *bar mitvah,* a hooray for the time, given the circumstance. In my metaphysics, at least, things are bundles of relations, snipped at the edges to be sure. Usually, we give our things a name and this name takes the place of our experience of the thing. It does not take long to teach a child a list of nouns, each bent on obviating and blocking the rich way in which the child first comes upon and undergoes things. It is difficult to overcome this prejudice of language, especially since row upon row of nouns, standing for things, makes perfectly good sense, if you believe that space is a container and time is the measure of external motion. If, however, you believe as I do, that space and time are human instincts, subject to the drama of our inner lives, then things lose their inert form. Emerson says this best when he claims that every fact and event in our private history shall astonish us by "soaring from our body into the empyrean."[6]

The clue here is the presence of a person. Quite aside from the geographical and physical relationships characteristic of things and creatures, we further endow a whole other set of relations, the aesthetic. I refer to the rhythm of how we experience *what* we experience. The most distinctive human activity is the potentially affective dimension of our experiencing ourself, experiencing the world. I say potentially, for some of us all of the time and most of us most of the time are dead to the possible rhythms of our experiences. We are ghouls. We look alive but we are dead, dead to our things and dead even to ourselves. As John Cage warned us, we experience the names of sounds and not the sounds themselves. It is not the things as names, nouns, which are rich. It is how the things do and how they are done to. It is how they marry and divorce, sidle and reject. The aesthetic drama of the ordinary plays itself out as a result of allowing all things to become events, namely, by allowing all things the full run of their implications. This run may fulfill our anticipations and our expectations. This run may disappoint us. This run may surprise us, or blow us out. Implicitness is everywhere and everywhen. Were we to experience an apparently single thing in its full implicitness, as an event reaching out to all its potential relations, then, in fact, we would experience everything, for the leads and the hints would carry us into the nook and cranny of the implicitness of every experience.[7]

We are caught between a Scylla and Charybdis with regard to the drama of the ordinary. The scions of the bland and the anaesthetic convince us that nothing is happening, whereas the arbiters and self-announcers of high culture tell us that only a few can make it happen, so we are reduced to watching. My version is different. The world is already astir with happenings, had we the wit to let them enter our lives in their own way, so that we may press them backward and forward, gathering relations, novelties, all the while. Our affective presence converts the ordinary to the extraordinary. The world is made sacred by our handling of our things. We are the makers of our world. It is we who praise, lament, and celebrate. Out of the doom of obviousness and repetition shall come the light, a light lit by the fire of our eyes.

> To see a World in a Grain of Sand
> And a Heaven in a Wild Flower,
> Hold Infinity in the palm of your hand
> And Eternity in an hour

Notes

1. Cited in Serge Chermayeff and Christopher Alexander, *Community and Privacy* (New York: Anchor Books, 1965), 29.

2. Larry L. King, "The Last Frontier," *The Old Man and Lesser Mortals* (New York: Viking, 1975), 207.

3. Cf. the moving and poignant scene of "eviction" in Ralph Ellison, *Invisible Man* (New York: Vintage Books, 1972 [1952]), 261–77.

4. The master of "things" and "boxes" is, of course, Joseph Cornell. Indeed, he is the master of things in boxes, known forever as Cornell boxes. Only those who have experienced these "boxes" can appreciate Cornell's extraordinary ability to merge the surrealism of the imagination and the obviousness of things as a "memorial to experience." Cf. Diane Waldman, *Joseph Cornell* (New York: George Braziller, 1977); and Kynaston McShine, *Joseph Cornell* (New York: Museum of Modern Art, 1981). As with Cornell, by "things" we mean, as does William James, bundles of relations. Things are not construed here as Aristotelian essences, much less as conceptually rendered boxes.

5. Rainer Maria Rilke, "The Ninth Elegy," *Duino Elegies* (New York: Norton, 1939), 73.

6. Ralph Waldo Emerson, "The American Scholar," *Works*, vol. 1 (Boston: Houghton Mifflin, 1903–4), 96–97.

7. Cf. William Blake, "Auguries of Innocence," *The Poetry and Prose of William Blake*, ed. David V. Erdman (New York: Anchor Books, 1965), 481.

11. Pragmatism as Romantic Polytheism

RICHARD RORTY

[. . .] I turn now to the other big difference between Nietzsche on the one hand and James and Dewey on the other. Nietzsche thinks religious belief is intellectually disreputable; James and Dewey do not.

In order to defend James and Dewey's tolerance for theism against Nietzsche, I shall sketch a pragmatist philosophy of religion in five brief theses. Then I shall try to relate these theses to what James and Dewey actually said about belief in God. First, it is an advantage of the antirepresentationalist view of belief that James took over from Bain and Peirce—the view that beliefs are habits of action—that it frees us from the responsibility to unify all our beliefs into a single worldview. If our beliefs are all parts of a single attempt to represent a single world, then they must all hang together fairly tightly. But if they are habits of action, then, because the purposes served by action may blamelessly vary, so may the habits we develop to serve those purposes.

Second, Nietzsche's attempt to "see science through the optic of art, and art through that of life," like Arnold's and Mill's substitution of poetry for religion, is an attempt to make more room for individuality than can be provided either by orthodox monotheism, or by the Enlightenment's attempt to put science in the place of religion as a source of Truth. So the attempt, by Tillich and others, to treat religious faith as "symbolic," and thereby to treat religion as poetic and poetry as religious, and neither as competing with science, is on the right track. But to make it convincing we need to drop the idea that some parts of culture fulfill our need to know the truth and others fulfill

Originally published in *The Revival of Pragmatism: New Essays on Social Thought, Law, and Culture,* ed. Morris Dickstein. © 1998, Duke University Press. Reprinted by permission.

lesser aims. The pragmatists' romantic utilitarianism does drop this idea: if there is no will to truth apart from the will to happiness, there is no way to contrast the cognitive with the noncognitive, the serious with the nonserious.

Third, pragmatism does permit us to make another distinction, one that takes over some of the work previously done by the old distinction between the cognitive and the noncognitive. The new distinction is between projects of social cooperation and projects of individual self-development. Intersubjective agreement is required for the former projects, but not for the latter. Natural science is a paradigmatic project of social cooperation: the project of improving man's estate by taking account of every possible observation and experimental result in order to facilitate the making of predictions that will come true. Law is another such paradigm. Romantic art, by contrast, is a paradigmatic project of individual self-development. Religion, if it can be disconnected from both science and morals—from the attempt to predict the consequences of our actions and the attempt to rank human needs—may be another such paradigm.

Fourth, the idea that we should love Truth is largely responsible for the idea that religious belief is "intellectually irresponsible." But there is no such thing as the love of Truth. What has been called by that name is a mixture of the love of reaching intersubjective agreement, the love of gaining mastery over a recalcitrant set of data, the love of winning arguments, and the love of synthesizing little theories into big theories. It is never an objection to a religious belief that there is no evidence for it. The only possible objection to it can be that it intrudes an individual project into a social and cooperative project, and thereby offends against the teachings of *On Liberty*. Such intrusion is a betrayal of one's responsibilities to cooperate with other human beings, not of one's responsibility to Truth or to Reason.

Fifth, the attempt to love Truth, and to think of it as One, and as capable of commensurating and ranking human needs, is a secular version of the traditional religious hope that allegiance to something big, powerful, and nonhuman will persuade that powerful being to take your side in your struggle with other people. Nietzsche despised any such hope as a sign of weakness. Pragmatists who are also democrats have a different objection to such hope for allegiance with power. They see it as a betrayal of the ideal of human fraternity that democracy inherits from the Judeo-Christian religious tradition. That ideal finds its best expression in the doctrine, common to Mill and James, that every human need should be satisfied unless doing so causes too many other human needs to go unsatisfied. The pragmatist objection to religious fundamentalists is not that fundamentalists are *intellectually* irresponsible in disregarding the results of natural science. Rather it is that they are *morally* irresponsible in attempting to circumvent the process of achieving democratic consensus about how to maximize happiness. They sin not by ignoring Mill's inductive methods, but by ignoring his reflections on liberty. I turn now to the question of how the view of religious belief epitomized in my five theses accords with the views of James and Dewey. It would not, I think, have been congenial to James. But I think it might have suited Dewey. So I shall argue that it is Dewey's rather unambitious and halfhearted *A Common Faith,* rather than James's brave and exuberant "Conclusion" to *Varieties of Religious Experience,* that coheres best with the romantic utilitarianism which both accepted.

James says, in that chapter of *Varieties,* that "the pivot round which the religious life revolves . . . is the interest of the individual in his private personal destiny." By "repudiating the personal point of view," however, science gives us a picture of nature that "has no distinguishable ultimate tendency with which it is possible to feel a sympathy." The "driftings of the cosmic atoms" are "a kind of aimless weather, doing and undoing, achieving no proper history, and leaving no result."[1] On the view I have just outlined, he should have followed this up by saying "But we are free to describe the universe in many different ways." Describing it as the drifting of cosmic atoms is useful for the social project of working together to control our environment and improve man's estate. But that description leaves us entirely free to say, for example, that the Heavens proclaim the glory of God.

Sometimes James seems to take this line, as when, with obvious approval, he quotes James Henry Leuba as saying: "*God is not known, he is not understood, he is used*—sometimes as meat-purveyor, sometimes as moral support, sometimes as friend, sometime as an object of love. If he proves himself useful, the religious consciousness can ask no more than that. Does God really exist? How does he exist? What is he? are so many irrelevant questions. Not God, but life, more life, a larger, richer, more satisfying life, is, in the last analysis, the end of religion." Unfortunately, however, almost immediately after quoting Leuba James says "we must next pass beyond the point of view of merely subjective utility and make inquiry into the intellectual content itself." He then goes on to argue that the material he has gathered together in *Varieties* provides empirical evidence for the hypothesis that "the conscious person is continuous with a wider self through which saving experiences come." He calls this "a positive content of religious experience which, it seems to me, is literally and objectively true as far as it goes."[2]

On the view I have been suggesting, this claim to literal and objective truth is unpragmatic, hollow, and superfluous. James should have rested content with the argument of "The Will to Believe." As I read that essay, it says that we have a right to believe what we like when we are, so to speak, on our own time.[3] But we abandon this right when we are engaged in, for example, a scientific or a political project. For when so engaged it is necessary to reconcile our beliefs, our habits of action, with those of others. On our own time, by contrast, our habits of action are nobody's business but our own. A romantic polytheist will rejoice in what Nietzsche called the "free-spiritedness and many-spiritedness" of individuals, and see the only constraint on this freedom and this diversity as the need not to injure others.

James wobbled on the question of whether what he called "the religious hypothesis" was something to be adopted on "passional" or on "intellectual" grounds. This hypothesis says that "the best things are the more eternal things, the overlapping things, the things in the universe that throw the last stone, so to speak, and say the final word."[4] In "The Will to Believe" this is put forward as a hypothesis to which considerations of evidence are irrelevant, and must therefore be turned over to our emotions. But in the "Conclusion" to *Varieties of Religious Experience*, the hypothesis that "God's existence is the guarantee of an ideal order that shall be permanently preserved" is one for which he has accumulated evidence. There he also says that the least common denominator of religious beliefs is that "the solution to the problem presented by a 'sense that there is something wrong about us as we naturally stand' is that we are saved from the wrongness by making proper connection with the higher powers." Again, he says that "the conscious person is continuous with a wider self from which saving experiences come."[5]

James should not have made a distinction between issues to be decided by intellect and issues to be decided by emotion. If he had not, he might have wobbled less. What he should have done instead was to distinguish issues that you must resolve cooperatively with others and issues that you are entitled to resolve on your own. The first set of issues are about conciliating your habits of action with those of other human beings. The second set are about getting your own habits of action to cohere with each other sufficiently so that you acquire a stable, coherent self-image. But such a self-image does not require monotheism, or the belief that Truth is One. It is compatible with the idea that you have many different needs, and that the beliefs that help you fill one set of needs are irrelevant to, and need not be made to cohere with, those that help you to fill another set.

Dewey avoided James's mistakes in this area. One reason he did so is that he was much less prone to a sense of guilt than was James. After he realized that his mother had made him unnecessarily miserable by burdening him with a belief in original sin, Dewey simply stopped thinking that, in James's words, "there is something wrong about us as we naturally stand." He no longer believed that we could be "saved from the wrongness by making proper connection with the higher powers." He thought that all that was wrong with us was that the Christian ideal of fraternity had not yet been achieved—society had not yet become pervasively democratic. That was not a problem to be solved by making proper connection with higher powers, but a problem of men to be solved by men.

Dewey's steadfast refusal to have any truck with the notion of original sin, and his suspicion of anything that smacked of such a notion, is bound up with his lifelong distaste for the idea of authority—the idea that anything could have authority over the members of a democratic community save the free, collective decisions of that community. This antiauthoritarian motif is perhaps clearest in his "Christianity and Democracy"—an early essay to which Alan Ryan has recently called our attention, saying that it is "a dazzling and dazzlingly brave piece of work."[6] Indeed it is. It must have seemed strange to the University of Michigan's Christian Students Association to be told, in 1892, that "God is essentially and only the self-revealing" and that "the revelation is complete only as men come to realize him."

Dewey spelled out what he meant by going on to say, "Had Jesus Christ made an absolute, detailed and explicit statement upon all the facts of life, that statement would not have had meaning—it would not have been revelation—until men began to realize in their own action the truth that he declared—until they themselves began to live it."[7] This amounts to saying that even if a nonhuman authority tells you something, the only way to figure out whether what you have been told is true is to see whether it gets you the sort of life you want. The only way is to apply the utilitarian test for whether the suggestion made proves to be "good in the way of belief." Granted that hearing what such a being has to say may change your wants, you nevertheless test those new wants and that purported truth in the same way: by living them, trying them out in everyday life, seeing whether they make you and yours happier.

Suppose that a source you believe to be nonhuman tells you that all men are brothers, that the attempt to make yourself and those you cherish happier should be expanded into an attempt to make all human beings happy. For Dewey, the source of this suggestion is irrelevant. You might have heard it from a god or a guru, but you might just as well have found it carved out by the waves on a sandy beach. It has no validity unless it is treated as an hypothesis, tried out, and found successful. The good thing about Christianity, Dewey is saying, is that it has been found to work.

More specifically, what has been found to work is the idea of fraternity and equality as a basis for social organization. This worked not just as a Thrasymachian device for avoiding pain—what Rawls calls a "mere modus viven-di"—but as a source of the kind of spiritual transfiguration that Platonism and the Christian churches have told us would have to wait upon a future intersection of time with eternity. It makes possible precisely the sort of nobility of spirit that Nietzsche mistakenly thought could be had only by the exceptional few—those who were capable of being greatly happy.

"Democracy," Dewey says, "is neither a form of government nor a social expediency, but a metaphysic of the relation of man and his experience in nature."[8] The point of calling it a metaphysic is not, of course, that it is an accurate account of the fundamental relation of reality, but that if one shares Whitman's sense of glorious democratic vistas stretching on indefinitely into the future one has everything which Platonists hoped to get out of such an account. For Whitman offers what Tillich called "a symbol of ultimate concern," of something that can be loved with all one's heart and soul and mind.

Plato's mistake, in Dewey's view, was having identified the ultimate object of concern with something unique, atemporal, and nonhuman rather than with an indefinitely expansible pantheon of transitory temporal accomplishments, both natural and cultural. This mistake lent aid and comfort to monotheism. Dewey might well have agreed with Nietzsche that "monotheism, this rigid consequence of the doctrine of one normal human type—the faith in one normal god beside whom there are only pseudo-gods—was perhaps the greatest danger that has yet confronted humanity."[9]

When Christianity is treated as a merely social gospel, it acquires the advantage which Nietzsche attributes to polytheism: it makes the most important human achievement "creating for ourselves our own new eyes," and thereby "honors the rights of individuals." As Dewey put it, "Government, business, art, religion, all social institutions have . . . a purpose[:] . . . to set free the capacities of human individuals. . . . The test of their value is the extent to which they educate every individual into the full stature of his possibility."[10] In a democratic society, everybody gets to worship his or her personal symbol of ultimate concern, unless worship of that symbol interferes with the pursuit of happiness by his or her fellow-citizens. Accepting that utilitarian constraint, the one Mill formulated in *On Liberty,* is the only obligation imposed by democratic citizenship, the only exception to democracy's commitment to honor the rights of individuals.

This means that nobody is under any constraint to seek Truth, nor to care, any more than Sherlock Holmes did, whether the earth revolves around the sun or conversely. Scientific theories become, as do theological and philosophical ones, optional tools for the facilitation of individual or social projects. Scientists thereby lose the position they inherited from the monotheistic priesthood, as the people who pay proper tribute to the authority of something "not ourselves."

"Not ourselves" is a term that tolls like a bell throughout the text of Arnold's *Literature and Dogma,* and this may be one of the reasons Dewey had a particular dislike for Arnold.[11] Once he got out from under his mother's Calvinism, Dewey distrusted nothing more than the suggestion that there was a non-human authority to which human beings owed respect. He praised democracy as the *only* form of "moral and social faith" that does *not* "rest upon the idea that experience must be subjected at some point or other to some form of external control; to some 'authority' alleged to exist outside the processes of experience."[12] This passage in an essay of 1939 echoes one written forty-seven years earlier. In "Christianity and Democracy" Dewey had said that "the one claim that Christianity makes is that God is truth; that as truth He is love and reveals Himself fully to man, keeping back nothing of Himself; that man is so one with the truth thus revealed that it is not so much revealed *to* him as *in* him; he is its incarnation."[13] For Dewey God is in no way Kierkegaard's Wholly Other. Nor is he One. Rather, he is all the varied sublimities human beings come to see through the eyes that they themselves create.

If atheism were identical with antimonotheism, then Dewey would have been as aggressive an atheist as has ever lived. The idea that God might have kept something back, that there might be something not ourselves that it was our duty to discover, was as distasteful to him as was the idea that God could tell us which of our needs took priority over others. He reserved his awe for the universe as a whole, "the community of causes and consequences in which we, together with those not born, are enmeshed." "The continuing life of this comprehensive community of beings," he said, "includes all the significant achievement of men in science and art and all the kindly offices of intercourse and communication."

Notice, in the passages I have just quoted, the phrase "together with those not born" and also the adjective "continuing." Dewey's distaste for the eternity and stability on which monotheism prides itself is so great that he can never refer to the universe as a whole without reminding us that the universe is still evolving—still experimenting, still fashioning new eyes with which to see itself.

Wordsworth's version of pantheism meant a great deal to Dewey, but Whitman's insistence on futurity meant more. Wordsworth's pantheism saves us from what Arnold called "Hebraism" by making it impossible to treat, as Dewey put it, "the drama of sin and redemption enacted within the isolated and lonely soul of man as the one thing of ultimate importance." But Whitman does something more. He tells us that nonhuman nature culminates in a community of free men, in their collaboration in building a society in which, as Dewey said, "poetry and religious feeling will be the unforced flowers of life."[14]

Dewey's principal symbol of what he called "the union of the ideal and the actual" was the United States of America treated as Whitman treated it: as a symbol of openness to the possibility of as yet undreamt of, ever more diverse, forms of human happiness. Much of what Dewey wrote consists of endless reiteration of Whitman's caution that "America . . . counts, as I reckon, for her justification and success, (for who, as yet, dare claim success?) almost entirely on the future. . . . For our New World I consider far less important for what it has done, or what it is, than for results to come."[15]

Notes

1. William James, *Varieties of Religious Experience* (Cambridge, Mass.: Harvard University Press, 1985), 387–88.

2. Ibid., 399 and 405, respectively.

3. See my "Religious Faith, Intellectual Responsibility, and Romance," in *The Cambridge Companion to William James*, ed. Ruth Anna Putnam (Cambridge, Mass.: Harvard University Press, 1997).

4. William James, *The Will to Believe* (Cambridge, Mass.: Harvard University Press, 1979), 29.

5. James, *Varieties of Religious Experience*, 407, 400, 405 respectively.

6. Alan Ryan, *John Dewey and the High Tide of American Liberalism* (New York: Norton, 1995), 102.

7. John Dewey, *The Early Works of John Dewey, 1882–1898*, vol. 9, ed. Jo Ann Boydston (Carbondale: Southern Illinois University Press, 1969), 6–7.

8. Dewey, "Maeterlinck's Philosophy of Life," *The Middle Works of John Dewey, 1899–1924*, vol. 6. Dewey says that Emerson, Whitman, and Maeterlinck are the only three to have grasped this fact about democracy.

9. Nietzsche, *The Gay Science*, section 143: "Der Monotheismus . . . diese starre Konsequenz der Lehre von einem Normalmenschen—also der Glaube an einen Normalgott, neben dem es nur noch falsche Luegengoetter gibt—war vielleicht die groesste Gefahr der bisherigen Menscheit."

10. Dewey, *Reconstruction in Philosophy*, in *The Middle Works of John Dewey, 1899–1924*, vol. 12, ed. Jo Ann Boydston (Carbondale: Southern Illinois University Press, 1986), 186.

11. See Dewey, "A Common Faith," in *The Later Works of John Dewey, 1925–1953*, vol. 9, ed. Jo Ann Boydston (Carbondale: University of Illinois Press, 1989), 36, and also Dewey's early essay "Poetry and Philosophy." In the latter Dewey says that "the source of regret which inspires Arnold's lines is his consciousness of a twofold isolation of man—his isolation from nature, his isolation from his fellow-man" (*The Early Works of John Dewey*, vol. 3, ed. Jo Ann Boydston [Carbondale: University of Illinois Press, 1969], 115).

12. "Creative Democracy—The Task before Us" (1939). The passage cited is in *The Later*

Works of John Dewey, vol. 14, ed. Jo Ann Boydston (Carbondale: University of Illinois Press, 1983), 229. Dewey says that he is here "stating briefly the democratic faith in the formal terms of a philosophic position."

13. Dewey, *The Early Works of John Dewey,* vol. 4, ed. Jo Ann Boydston (Carbondale: University of Illinois Press, 1972), 5.

14. Dewey, *Reconstruction,* 201.

15. Walt Whitman, "Democratic Vistas," in *Complete Poetry and Selected Prose* (New York: Library of America, 1982), 929.

PART 2

Contemporary Essays on the
American Tradition of Religious Thought

Notes on Authors

RICHARD J. BERNSTEIN is a professor and the chair of the Department of Philosophy at New School University. Professor Bernstein has authored numerous books and articles; his books include *Freud and the Legacy of Moses* (Cambridge: Cambridge University Press, 1998), *Hannah Arendt and the Jewish Question* (Cambridge, Mass.: MIT Press, 1996), *The New Constellation: The Ethical-Political Horizons of Modernity-Postmodernity* (Cambridge, Mass.: MIT Press, 1992), *Philosophical Profiles: Essays in a Pragmatic Mode* (Philadelphia: University of Pennsylvania Press, 1986), *Habermas and Modernity* (Cambridge, Mass.: MIT Press, 1985), *John Dewey* (Atascadero, Calif.: Ridgeview, 1966), and others.

DOUGLAS R. ANDERSON is an associate professor of philosophy at Pennsylvania State University. Professor Anderson has authored two books, *Strands of System: The Philosophy of Charles Peirce* (Ashland, Ohio: Purdue University Press, 1995) and *Creativity and the Philosophy of C. S. Peirce* (The Hague: Martinus Nijhoff, 1987), as well as numerous journal articles.

WILLIAM D. DEAN is a professor of constructive theology at Illif School of Theology. His publications include *American Religious Empiricism* (Albany, N.Y.: SUNY Press, 1986), *History Making History: The New Historicism in American Religious Thought* (Albany, N.Y.: SUNY Press, 1988), and *The Religious Critic in American Culture* (Albany, N.Y.: SUNY Press, 1994).

STUART ROSENBAUM is a professor of philosophy at Baylor University. His publications include journal essays and the coedited volumes *Hatred, Bigotry, and Prejudice* (Amherst, N.Y.: Prometheus, 1999), *Gay Marriage* (Amherst, N.Y.: Prometheus, 1998), *Animal Experiment* (Amherst, N.Y.: Prometheus, 1996), and *Abortion* (Amherst, N.Y.: Prometheus, 1989).

ROBERT WESTBROOK is a professor in the Department of History at the University of Rochester. His publications include *John Dewey and American Democracy* (Ithaca, N.Y.: Cornell University Press, 1991) and the coedited volume *In Face of the Facts: Moral Inquiry in American Scholarship* (Cambridge: Cambridge University Press, 1998).

12. Pragmatism's Common Faith

RICHARD J. BERNSTEIN

The noun *pragmatism* and especially the adjective *pragmatic* have become well integrated into our everyday discourse. Pick up a newspaper and you are likely to read about so and so who is very pragmatic or has just made a pragmatic decision. Sometimes the adjective is used as a term of praise to indicate that the decision was a practical one given the circumstances. A pragmatic person is someone who knows how to get things done. Sometimes it has a slightly negative connotation, where it indicates that a person may slight matters of principle, theory, or ideology. In a religious or moral context the term is frequently used with great suspicion: pragmatism is often taken to mean some sort of relativism that threatens religion. Or to be a bit more blunt, pragmatism is demonized as the doctrine of "secular humanism" that is abhorred as the enemy of Christianity and indeed, the enemy of all religion. Is pragmatism, along with postmodernism, just one more intellectual threat to the moral and religious values of our communities and our country? Is it perhaps, as critics have charged, an invitation to the kind of relativism that undermines social and political order? These questions presume that when pragmatism is unmasked—when it is shown for what it "really" is—it turns out to be little more than the doctrine of "aggressive atheism." (I return later to this idea of "aggressive atheism.")

* * *

The first question I want to raise is this: what does this popular conception of pragmatism—namely, as an invidious doctrine that undermines morality and religion—have to do with the American intellectual tradition represented by such figures as Ralph Waldo Emerson, Charles Sanders Peirce,

William James, John Dewey, and George Herbert Mead? The answer, and I state this loudly, clearly, and distinctly, is nothing at all.

I want to show that if we read what the classic figures of the American pragmatic tradition actually said (rather than what has been said about them), we will see how they all repudiated "aggressive atheism." In differing ways, each of them took the religious life seriously and made vital contributions to understanding what it means. I will focus primarily on William James, Charles Sanders Peirce, and John Dewey. Still, although I want to set the record straight, this is not my primary aim. I hope to show that the insights of the pragmatic thinkers ought to be integrated into any reflective conception of the religious life. And today, when dangerous forms of fundamentalism and fanaticism present threats throughout the world, it is even more vital to infuse our religious convictions with a spirit of pragmatic tolerance, openness, and critical fallibilism.

Let me begin by turning to the historical task that will serve as the basis for my argument. It was William James who, more than anyone else, popularized pragmatism as a distinctive philosophic orientation. In a classic paper, "Philosophical Conceptions and Practical Results," which he delivered at the University of California on August 26, 1898, James introduced pragmatism to a wider public. He began by generously acknowledging Peirce to be the founder of the pragmatic movement and went on to outline what he meant: "There can be no difference which doesn't make a difference, no difference in abstract truth which does not express itself in a difference of concrete fact, and of conduct consequent upon the fact, imposed on somebody, somehow, somewhere, and somewhen."[1]

An example James used to clarify a pragmatic approach was the debate concerning the following question: "Is matter the producer of all things, or is a God there too?" And listen to what he says:

> Many of us, most of us, I think, now feel as if a terrible coldness and deadness would come over the world were we forced to believe that no informing spirit or purpose had to do with it, but it merely accidentally had come. The actually experienced details of fact might be the same on either hypothesis, some sad, some joyous; some rational, some odd and grotesque; but without a God behind them, we think they would have something ghastly, they would tell no genuine story, there would be no speculation in those eyes that they do glare with. With the God, on the other hand, they would grow solid, warm, and altogether full of real significance.[2]

James seeks to apply his version of "the pragmatic principle" to elaborate a concrete understanding of the meaning of God—what God means for us in our practical, everyday lives. His reflections are intended to show the superiority of "the religious hypothesis" over the cold indifferent forms of materialism. For the moment, I am not primarily concerned about evaluating James's reasoning and his assertions. But I do want to emphasize that James never thought of pragmatism as hostile to religion. On the contrary, it was a way of making religious convictions concrete, practical, and intimately related to experience.

Religious issues were always in the foreground of James's thinking. James, who suffered from bouts of severe depression, which was then called "melancholia," tells us: "I have always thought that this experience of melancholia of mine had a religious bearing. I mean that the fear was so invasive and powerful that if I had not clung to scripture texts like 'The eternal God is my refuge,' etc., 'Come unto me, all ye that labor and are heavyladen,' etc., 'I am the resurrection and the life,' etc., I think I should have grown really insane."[3] It was James who staunchly defended the legitimacy and the necessity of "faith and the right to believe." He declared: "Faith thus remains as one of the inalienable birthrights of our mind. Of course it must remain a practical, and not a dogmatic attitude. It must go with the toleration of other faiths, with the search for the most probable, and with the full consciousness of responsibilities and risks."[4]

James also introduced the famous distinction between the "tough-minded" and "tender-minded," and he claimed that the great advantage of pragmatism is that it combines the virtues of both these attitudes. Nevertheless, many philosophers have thought that James himself was a bit too tender-minded, too "optimistic," too "religious," too "free-willist."

The pragmatist who best exemplifies the really tough-minded thinker is Peirce, a logician and practicing scientist who, as he himself tells us, was shaped by the "laboratory habit of mind." When James popularized his version of pragmatism, Peirce was so indignant and outraged that he renamed his own doctrine *pragmaticism,* declaring that it was a name ugly enough to be safe from kidnappers. So one might think that Peirce would be far more skeptical about the "religious hypothesis," far more materialist and reductionist. But once again, an examination shows this to be false. Peirce proposed what he called a "neglected argument for the reality of god," and in a striking phrase he declares: "As to God, open your eyes and your heart, which is a perceptive organ and you see him."[5] Furthermore, Peirce integrated his religious outlook into his cosmological speculations. He elaborated a conception of what he called "evolutionary love," which he based in part on his reading of the Gospels. This is the way in which Peirce formulates his "religious hypothesis":

Here, then, is the issue. The gospel of Christ says that progress comes from every individual merging his individuality in sympathy with his neighbors. On the other side, the conviction of the nineteenth century is that progress takes place by virtue of every individual's striving for himself with all his might and trampling his neighbour under foot whenever he gets a chance to do so. This may accurately be called the Gospel of Greed. Much is to be said on both sides. I have not concealed, I could not conceal, my own passionate predilection. Such a confession will probably shock my scientific brethren.[6]

John Dewey, the educator, radical reformer, and committed naturalist, is frequently taken to be the pragmatist who was most indifferent to religious questions. It is certainly true that his voluminous writings include very few texts that deal explicitly with religious questions. But once again we must be cautious about jumping to the wrong conclusion. Bruce Kuklick, the eminent historian of American philosophy, was one of the first to argue that many of Dewey's fundamental ideas emerged from and were shaped by his religious upbringing.[7] And Steven Rockefeller's magnificent comprehensive study of John Dewey shows the necessity of approaching "Dewey's thought from the perspective of its religious meaning and value."[8] Earlier I used the phrase "aggressive atheism." That phrase is taken from John Dewey's book *A Common Faith,* where Dewey severely criticizes both "aggressive atheism" and "supernaturalism" as betraying the genuinely religious dimension of experience. Listen carefully to what Dewey says:

One reason why personally I think it fitting to use the word "God" to denote that uniting of the ideal and actual which has been spoken of, lies in the fact that aggressive atheism seems to me to have something in common with traditional supernaturalism. I do not mean merely that the former is mainly so negative that it fails to give positive direction to thought, though that fact is pertinent. What I have in mind especially is the exclusive preoccupation of both militant atheism and supernaturalism with man in isolation. For in spite of supernaturalism's reference to something beyond nature, it conceives of this earth as the moral centre of the universe and man as the apex of the whole scheme of things. It regards the drama of sin and redemption enacted within the isolated and lonely soul of man as the one thing of ultimate importance. Apart from man, nature is held either accursed or negligible. Militant atheism is also affected by lack of natural piety. The ties binding man to nature that poets have always celebrated are passed over lightly. The attitude taken is often that of man living in an indifferent and hostile world and issuing blasts of defiance. A religious attitude, however, needs the sense of a connection of man, in the way of both dependence and support, with the enveloping world that the imagination feels is a universe. Use of the words "God" or "divine" to convey the union of actual with ideal may protect man from a sense of isolation and from consequent despair or defiance.[9]

I hope that I have said enough to show that the classical pragmatic thinkers were not hostile to religion. This is simply false. But my main purpose is to show the philosophic relevance and importance of what we can derive from their thinking. So I want to stand back and reflect on what they all share despite the many significant differences among them.

The American pragmatic movement developed during the late nineteenth century, when the most important scientific discovery to shape intellectual life was Darwin's theory of evolution. *The Origin of Species* was published in 1859, the year of John Dewey's birth. Darwin's discoveries and his evolutionary hypotheses profoundly influenced the thought of Peirce, James, and Dewey. They were not, however, "Social Darwinians." Each of them was ruthlessly critical of this ideology, with its popular slogans about the "survival of the fittest." This ideology was what Peirce called "The Doctrine of Greed." The nineteenth century was also a time of raging debates about the "conflict" between science and religion. Science, which was frequently characterized as "materialistic" and "atheistic," was taken to pose a dramatic threat to the integrity of religion. The point I want to emphasize is that *none* of the classical pragmatists thought that science, including Darwin's evolutionary science, posed any threat to genuine religious life. On the contrary, they categorically rejected any conception of religion and religious life that was incompatible with the critical experimental spirit of the sciences. They were, however, enemies of dogmatism in all its forms, religious and secular. But this still does not get to the core of pragmatism's contribution to the understanding of religious life. And here we must turn briefly to some of the central themes of the pragmatic movement.

The pragmatists rejected all forms of epistemological foundationalism, what Dewey called the "quest for certainty." They knew full well how much of the history of philosophy and the history of religion had been dominated by and obsessed with the quest for certainty. This quest was marked by the search for necessary, indubitable, and incorrigible truths that could serve as a firm foundation for knowledge and faith. The pragmatists sought to show that such "absolute truths," ones immune to criticism, questioning, and revision, are illusory.

The primary claim of the pragmatists is even more radical. It is not simply that as finite human beings we cannot know whether something is absolutely true. Rather, they argued that the very idea of "absolute truth" is incoherent, for it is based on a misconception of the knowing process, which

the pragmatists called inquiry. There are no absolute or definitive epistemological beginnings or endings in human inquiry. In a famous series of papers that he published as early as 1868, Peirce argued that all signs (including propositional signs) are always open to further interpretation.[10] Inquiry
itself is an ongoing, critical, and self-corrective enterprise. Pragmatists are
committed fallibilists. They would all agree with Wilfrid Sellars's famous
claim that "empirical knowledge, like its sophisticated extension, science, is
rational, not because it has a *foundation*, but because it is a self-correcting
enterprise which can put any claim in jeopardy, though not all at once."[11] And
this is true not just for empirical knowledge and science but for all types of
inquiry, whether scientific or religious.

It is precisely because they are fallibilists that the pragmatists emphasized
cultivating critical communities of inquirers. Every validity claim, every hypothesis, ought to be open to public critical discussion. More forcefully, the
pragmatists advocated the need to subject our most cherished beliefs and
convictions to public critical scrutiny. This imperative rests on both epistemological and ethical grounds. Furthermore, we need to develop communities in which individuals have the imagination to create new hypotheses
and theories and the courage to give up their most cherished beliefs when
they have been refuted. This is the only way in which we can properly test
our beliefs, including religious ones. The pragmatists were deeply suspicious
of all forms of monism; they advocated and practiced *engaged* pluralism,
where individuals could risk and test their hypotheses and beliefs in critical
encounters with other points of view. No one can claim to have a God's-eye
view of the universe. There is an irreducible plurality of perspectives. But we
can engage in critical dialogue where we seek to learn from others the differing ways in which our fellow human beings understand their experience.

Although pragmatists are strongly committed to engaged pluralism, they
are not relativists (in the pejorative sense of this term) or nihilists. They certainly do not believe that "anything goes." Hilary Putnam correctly lists the
following as one of the cardinal principles of pragmatism: "Our norms and
standards of anything *including* warranted assertability are capable of reform.
There are better and worse norms and standards."[12] This is the very antithesis of what the relativist claims. On the basis of what I have said, we can understand why the pragmatists, especially Dewey, placed so much emphasis on
the educational process that takes place throughout our lives. The cultivation
of the virtues, requiring ongoing critical engagement, is a process that begins
with one's earliest education and continues throughout one's life.

Let me sum up what I have been arguing. Pragmatists underscore the need
for a pluralistic, fallibilistic, critical orientation to questions concerning re-

ligious life. Pragmatists condemn all forms of dogmatism and fundamentalism. Any religious conviction that cannot embrace this critical spirit, that fears open critical examination, betrays its own principles. To put the issue in theological terms, a faith that excludes critical examination is a form of idolatry.

Still, another question may haunt us. Someone who agrees with what I have said thus far may nevertheless object that the pragmatic reflections on religious life miss something. The pragmatists emphasize the religious aspect of experience rather than religious "beliefs" and "truths." But the great world religions are not merely about experience or attitudes; they make crucial cognitive claims about the nature of ultimate reality. To play down this aspect of religion is to ignore what is most important about the great religions. I can well imagine a critic making the following objection. "Bernstein, you yourself have noted that Dewey is hostile to what he calls 'supernaturalism.' But what does he really mean by 'supernaturalism'? Isn't this just a pejorative way of referring to what is essential to a serious religious conviction— namely, the belief in a being that really does transcend human experience?" Such a critic might add: "Let me apply the pragmatic criterion to your claims. You say that Dewey, and the other pragmatists, oppose 'aggressive atheism.' But what is the difference that makes a difference between aggressive atheism and the diaphanous pragmatic conception of religion?"

Such a challenge strikes me as eminently fair and appropriate. It brings us to the heart of the matter. Drawing on the insights of the pragmatists and especially Dewey, I want to defend the idea of a common faith central to the spirit of pragmatism. I am certainly not claiming that this is the only viable or acceptable conception of religious faith. To do so would violate the engaged pluralism central to a pragmatic orientation. But I hope to show that this common faith does not reduce itself to the caricature of "secular humanism" often but falsely projected onto it.

One of the most frequently reiterated objections to secular humanism is that it is anthropomorphic. Humanity becomes the new god. This arrogant humanism takes humanity to be the measure of all things. Such a form of human idolatry has disastrous moral and political consequences. And these consequences are not merely abstract or theoretical; they are all too practical, encouraging greed and wanton materialism. The twentieth century has taught us that when humankind becomes a god, when we think of ourselves as omnipotent and act accordingly, disaster follows. I believe that this is a gross caricature of secular humanism, but more important, I deny that this caricature has anything to do with the pragmatists.

Let me return to the previously cited passage from *A Common Faith*. Ironically Dewey rejects supernaturalism as well as militant atheism by arguing that both these extremes conceive of "man as the one thing of ultimate importance," "the apex of the whole scheme of things." They lack "natural piety." Dewey's robust naturalism is not a form of reductive materialism or physicalism. Rather, it is an orientation that appreciates the grandeur and variety of the natural world. Dewey's naturalism was shaped not only by Darwin and the experimental spirit of inquiry but also by the imaginative portrayal of nature found in the romantic poets, whom Dewey especially cherished. His naturalism opposes the "sin of pride" where human beings are taken to be the masters of the universe. He draws out the profound sense of the contingency and fragility of human life and of our dependency on natural forces beyond our control. The natural piety of which Dewey speaks is an attitude of respect, awe, and humility. This natural piety is the very antithesis of human arrogance, which exaggerates the significance of human beings. As a result, Dewey is critical of all doctrines that take human beings and their concerns to be at the center of the universe. Dewey does reject the idea of *God* as the name of a particular supreme being, but this is not quite as heretical as it may sound, for many theologians of various religions would agree with him. Positively, Dewey advocates that we should think of the word *God* as referring to the "ideal ends that at a given time and place one acknowledges as having authority over his volition and emotion, the values to which one is supremely devoted, as far as these ends, through imagination, take on unity."[13] Dewey recognizes that we imaginatively conceive and acknowledge ideals that have authority over our volitions and emotions, ideals to which we may be supremely devoted. Such ideals, then, can transcend our current limited experience. Stated in another way, these ideal ends are at once regulative, insofar as they guide our conduct, and constitutive of our very being in the world. Any form of reductive materialism that limits our understanding of human beings to what now exists in space and time is rejected because it fails to recognize the power of ideal ends in shaping who we are. Furthermore, Dewey affirms the reality of ideal ends. He tells us that "the reality of ideal ends as ideals is vouched for by their undeniable power in action."[14]

Dewey's understanding of the religious dimension of experience offers us something important. Dewey is rightly skeptical of the idea that historical religions share a common essence. If we examine the enormous variety of beliefs and practices of religions past and present, we discover that the "differences among them are so great and so shocking that any common element that can be extracted is meaningless."[15] When we try to state what is common to the range of heterogeneous religions, we end up with vacuous generalizations and clichés. "There is no such thing," Dewey tells us "as religion in general"; "a religion . . . always signifies a special body of beliefs and practices having some kind of institutional organization, loose or tight.[16] But the adjective *religious* can be used to signify a special, pervasive integrating quality of experience. According to Dewey (and I agree with him), it is possible to profess a specific religion without being religious. It is also possible to be religious without professing the doctrines of a specific religion. This is not nearly as paradoxical as it may initially appear. I suspect that we all know persons who profess the beliefs of a specific religion and participate in its rituals in such a mechanical and unreflective manner that we hesitate to call them religious. There are also persons who do not profess the beliefs of a specific religion but who nevertheless exhibit a genuinely religious attitude in their actions, in the way in which they conduct their lives and treat their fellow human beings and the rest of nature. Of course, the pragmatists do place a special emphasis on conduct, on the ways in which we act, but this is consistent even with the biblical injunction "by their fruits ye shall know them."

We must be careful not to misinterpret Dewey by ascribing to him an understanding of religious experience that he categorically rejects. He is not affirming that there is a special type or *kind* of experience that can be labeled "religious." And he certainly rejects the idea that special kinds of experiences are by themselves *sufficient* to justify religious beliefs. Experience does not come in neatly separated kinds, such as moral experience, aesthetic experience, or intellectual experience. The term *religious* signifies a quality that can interpenetrate the entire range of experience. Too frequently we think of religious experience as something that is set aside for special occasions, times, and places separate from the rest of our lives. As Dewey tells us, however, the religious aspect of experience "completely interpenetrates all elements of our being." (Perhaps he should have said that a religious attitude is one that *ought* to interpenetrate all elements of our being.) To appreciate fully what Dewey is claiming, we would have to explore in detail what he means by experience, the most central notion of his philosophy. Let me indicate just a few of its highlights. Experience is never merely just subjective or private. Nor is it just a matter of knowledge. One of Dewey's major complaints with the epistemological tradition is that it distorts the variety of experiences by concentrating exclusively on the epistemic significance of experience. But experience is much richer and far more extensive than knowing. There are what Merleau-Ponty calls prereflective experiences. The conflicts and tensions that arise within our prereflective experiences yield the problems that systematic inquiry seeks to resolve. Experience consists of complex transactions with temporal and spatial depth. Experience does not consist of a monotonous, continuous flow. Experience comprises moments of conflict and tension as well as culminations and consummations. Sometimes Dewey uses the expression "an experience" to single out these heightened consummatory phases of experience. Seeing an extraordinary sunset, witnessing a great performance of *King Lear,* and solving a difficult intellectual problem are all examples of such heightened experiences. These experiences are filled with emotion and funded with meaning. Our experiences may be slack, humdrum, and tedious, of course, but they need not be so. Dewey's concern with education and social reform is primarily motivated by the desire to make experience more meaningful and vital. There are pervasive qualities that interpenetrate experiences and provide them with an integrated sense of wholeness. And here we come close to grasping what Dewey means by the religious dimension of experience. Dewey is calling attention to the imaginative wholeness that harmonizes the self.

> The *whole* self is an ideal, an imaginative projection. Hence the idea of a thoroughgoing and deepseated harmonizing of the self with the Universe . . . operates only through imagination which is one reason why this composing of the self is not voluntary in the sense of an act of special volition or resolution. An "adjustment" possesses the will rather than is its express product. . . . And it is pertinent to note that the unification of the self throughout the ceaseless flux of what it does, suffers, and achieves, cannot be attained in terms of itself. The self is always directed toward something beyond itself and so its own unification depends upon the idea of the integration of the shifting scenes of the world into that imaginative totality we call the Universe.[17]

For Dewey then, "any activity pursued in behalf of an ideal end against obstacles and in spite of threats to personal loss because of conviction of its general and enduring value is religious in quality."

Although I have been defending Dewey's understanding of the religious as an attitude or dimension of experience that can interpenetrate our entire being and range of experience, I also want to express some of my disagreements with Dewey. I think that Dewey tends to caricature what he calls "supernaturalism." Furthermore, like Robert Westbrook, I think that Dewey does not do justice to the importance of religious communities in providing the shared experience—the emotional and motivational sustenance—in nurturing a democratic faith.[18] We need to recognize the positive role that religious communities have played in lives of democratic citizens. And we also need to recognize that such communities have frequently been based on the belief in a transcendent God, what Dewey labels "supernaturalism." The early civil rights movement in the United States would not have been possible without the religious support provided by local black churches. Not only have progressive religious social-reform movements been vital in our history; they have been powerful sites for democratic reform throughout the world.[19] Consider the role of grassroots liberation theology movements in Latin America. Even today many of the islands of democratic communal activism in the United States are spiritually vitalized by committed religious believers. Think of Dorothy Day's Catholic Worker movement or the interfaith community organizers inspired by Ernie Cortez and his colleagues.

There is a further issue. Dewey objected to supernaturalism because he thought it was committed to an objectionable form of dualism and harbored the quest for certainty. He was also worried about antidemocratic institutional authoritarian practices. He was not attacking a straw man. There were and are powerful institutional forms of religion opposed to pragmatism and Deweyan democracy. We ought to resist the temptation to caricature all religious believers, however, just as we ought to resist the temptation to demonize secular humanists. It is more consonant with the engaged pluralism that I am advocating to avoid condemning all forms of supernaturalism—that is, all professions of faith based on belief in a transcendent Supreme Being. Engaged pragmatists must always be open to the discourse of others with radically different beliefs. Pragmatism is not a "party line." Rather, it consists of a firm set of commitments about the character of critical inquiry that is compatible with differing religious beliefs and attitudes. This was true for the classical pragmatists, who disagreed with each other about religious life and religious beliefs, and it is just as true for such leading contemporary pragmatists as Cornel West, Hilary Putnam, and Richard Rorty. The crucial issue for a pragmatist ought to be whether a religious believer (or a nonbeliever) is committed to the type of open critical dialogue that has been central to the pragmatic tradition.

There is one more theme to consider before concluding. One of the most frequent accusations brought against the pragmatists is that they are far too optimistic. They have an excessive faith in human intelligence. They lack—or so it is claimed—an adequate sense of evil and sin. No program of social reform will ever completely eliminate or eradicate the stain of original sin. Roughly speaking, this is the sort of objection Reinhold Niebuhr brought against Dewey, and it has been reiterated by many others. Frankly, this charge of naive optimism is a slander, for it misses what is most central in a robust pragmatic outlook. Dewey and the other classical pragmatists are neither optimistic nor pessimistic. Such epithets are completely inappropriate. Pragmatism does not diminish our sense of evil in the world. On the contrary, it heightens this sense by making us acutely aware of the obligation to eliminate or ameliorate existing evils. The primary issue, however, is how we are to *respond* to the real social evils that we encounter in our daily lives. It is the issue of *response* and responsibility that stands at the heart of pragmatism. If we fail to make a serious attempt to eradicate the sources of the evils that we encounter, then we are failing in our responsibilities. There is not, nor can there be, any *guarantee* of success. If we become passive, indifferent, or sink into despair, however, we are failing in our capacity as agents who can make a difference, who can seek to ameliorate suffering. We are neither complete masters of our own fates nor passive playthings of forces beyond our control. In a world in which there are many signs that we are becoming indifferent and numb to existing evils, the cultivation of an active pragmatic attitude can further a sense of solidarity with the suffering of our fellow human beings.

Let me conclude by emphasizing a few key points. Pragmatism is not indifferent or hostile to the religious life. It is not a form of "aggressive atheism." On the contrary, all the classical pragmatists argued that a pragmatic orientation can help us to clarify the concrete meaning of religious life. A major contribution of pragmatism has been its insistence on ongoing, open, fallibilistic public criticism. Pragmatism opposes all forms of dogmatism, fanaticism, and fundamentalism. In this respect, pragmatism ought to be incorporated into any adequate religious orientation. I also believe that there is much that can be appropriated from the pragmatists in understanding and cultivating the religious dimension of experience. Rather than promote the caricature of "secular humanism," where humanity is taken to stand at the center of the universe, Dewey teaches us the importance of a natural piety that is sensitive to the contingency of human life and our responsibility to ameliorate human suffering. Dewey, like the other pragmatists, knew that his own most central convictions require faith, but it is a reflective faith in the creative intelligence of the common man. "Intelligence," Dewey tells us, "as distinct from the older conception of reason, is inherently involved in action. Moreover, there is no opposition between [intelligence] and emotion. There is such a thing as passionate intelligence"[20] It is a common faith in the democratic sense that no one is excluded from it and everyone can share it. But it is not "common" in the sense that it is easily acquired. On the contrary, it is a very demanding faith, because it means giving up the quest for certainty. We must learn to live with the contingency and ambiguity from which there is no escape. It requires courage, persistence, imagination, and active responsibility in confronting social evils. In this respect Dewey's common faith is a demanding faith that unfortunately is all too uncommon. Let me conclude with Dewey's own final remarks in *A Common Faith*.

> We who now live are parts of a humanity that extends into the remote past, a humanity that has interacted with nature. The things in civilization we most prize are not of ourselves. They exist by grace of the doings and sufferings of

the continuous human community in which we are a link. Ours is the responsibility of conserving, transmitting, rectifying and expanding the heritage of values we have received that those who come after us may receive it more solid and secure, more widely accessible and more generously shared than we have received it. Here are all the elements for a religious faith that shall not be confined to sect, class, or race. Such a faith has always been implicitly the common faith of mankind. It remains to make it explicit and militant.[21]

Notes

This essay originated in a talk at the Pruit Memorial Symposium, November 13, 1997, at Baylor University.

1. William James, *The Writings of William James,* ed. John J. McDermott (Chicago: University of Chicago Press, 1977), 349.

2. Ibid., 350.

3. Ibid., 7.

4. Ibid., 737.

5. Charles Sanders Peirce, *Collected Papers of Charles Sanders Peirce,* vol. 6, ed. Charles Hartshorne and Paul Weiss (Cambridge, Mass.: Harvard University Press, 1935), 493.

6. Ibid., 294–95.

7. Bruce Kuklick, *Churchmen and Philosophers: From Jonathan Edwards to John Dewey* (New Haven, Conn.: Yale University Press, 1985).

8. Steven Rockefeller, *John Dewey: Religious Faith and Democratic Humanism* (New York: Columbia University Press, 1991), x.

9. John Dewey, *A Common Faith,* in *The Later Works of John Dewey, 1925–1953,* vol. 9, ed. Jo Ann Boydston (Carbondale: Southern Illinois University Press, 1986), 36.

10. Charles Sanders Peirce, "Questions Concerning Certain Faculties Claimed for Man," "Some Consequences of Four Incapacities," and "Grounds of Validity on the Laws of Logic," in *Collected Papers of Charles Sanders Peirce,* vol. 5, ed. Charles Hartshorne and Paul Weiss (Cambridge, Mass.: Harvard University Press, 1958).

11. Wilfrid Sellars, "Empiricism and the Philosophy of Mind," *Science, Perception, and Reality* (New York: Humanities Press, 1963), 170.

12. Hilary Putnam, *Realism with a Human Face,* ed. James Conant (Cambridge, Mass.: Harvard University Press, 1990), 21.

13. Dewey, *A Common Faith,* 29.

14. Ibid., 30.

15. Ibid., 7.

16. Ibid., 8.

17. Ibid., 14.

18. See Robert Westbrook's "An Uncommon Faith: Pragmatism and Religious Experience," chapter 16 of this volume.

19. See Richard J. Bernstein, "The Meaning of Public Life," in *Religion and American Public Life,* ed. Robin W. Lovin (New York: Paulist, 1986).

20. Dewey, *A Common Faith,* 52.

21. Ibid., 57–58.

13. Awakening in the Everyday: Experiencing the Religious in the American Philosophical Tradition

DOUGLAS R. ANDERSON

The tradition of American thought tells an interesting yet sometimes over-looked story concerning the nature of religious experience and religious life. Although it is probably not a new story, in its American incarnation it gives voice to a conception of religious life that may yet speak to our late twenti-eth-century experience. This way of looking at religious experience does not focus on the content of belief, and it does not pretend to settle intra- or interdenominational quarrels. Rather, it focuses on what used to be called the conduct of life, on how one lives in what we might call a religious attitude. The story suggests that what is at the heart of religious experience is not any particular belief or set of beliefs but a willingness to leave oneself open to an ongoing process of conversions or awakenings. Interestingly, this account appears in a variety of places that otherwise seem quite incompatible: in Puritanism and its subsequent cultural Calvinism, among the transcenden-talists, and most recently, in the work of pragmatic thinkers. To illustrate this outlook in abbreviated form, I focus here on three figures: Jonathan Edwards, Henry Thoreau, and John Dewey.

Edwards is an unlikely but necessary place to begin—unlikely because the story seems to undermine the Puritan search for eternal stability and neces-sary because Edwards seems to have been the first to fully articulate a ver-sion of the story. Edwards was born into a culture in which religious living was, implicitly at least, already as important as religious doctrine. As W. H.

Werkmeister notes: "While Puritanism was alive in New England it was vastly more than a mere matter of doctrine or rigoristic rules and hairsplitting logic. It was a living faith and a basic piety, deeply grounded in a realistic feeling of man's depravity and of his need for salvation. Its theology was but the external expression of an inward attitude or mood—of a mood which gave strength and fortitude in adversity but which was also the cause of intolerance and persecution."[1]

What first drew my attention in the direction of Edwards was my ongoing perplexity in reading his diary and "Personal Narrative." Edwards's version of the religious attitude is often obscured by a focus on his philosophical argumentation or the "fire-and-brimstone" side of his work. Edwards was indeed committed to a particular, doctrinal understanding of Christianity. Yet his religious life was lived in the semiwilderness of the Connecticut valley, in an unusual family circumstance in which he felt called to constrain the liberality of his grandfather. This life served as the basis of his thinking, and in the irony of his most personal writings, his own way of looking at religious experience and the religious attitude emerges. Edwards believed himself an authority (if not the authority) on the conditions of true salvation—he claimed to grasp the nature of the religious affections. Yet his own conversion remained incomplete, precarious. That is, his "Personal Narrative" reveals a conversion process that remains ongoing; one awakening after another supplants—or, better, enlarges on—the previous one. Edwards achieved no closure. Instead of establishing the kind of hard and fast "one-off" life change one might expect among cultural Calvinists, he disclosed a career of awakenings. Out of this Edwards came to create an original understanding of conversion as a process. After all his inquiry into his own and others' conversions, however, he established no human certainty concerning their genuineness.

From one angle, this is not a surprising consequence of the religious doctrines into which Edwards was educated. For Edwards, God is present but never fully revealed to us directly and overtly. That is, we may reveal through our beliefs and actions the traits of salvation, but we cannot *know* that we are saved; at best we become hermeneuts of the religious affections. Thus religious experience for Edwards becomes a very human, finite, and precarious experience. It is a living toward a consequence and from a condition, but always without certainty. It is not a static way of being but a movement, a lived altering that yet hangs together enough to describe a career or a history.

The "Personal Narrative" discloses an ever-present undercurrent of frustration, and I suspect it stems from Edwards's own confrontation with this irony in which he finds his religious life. What Edwards reveals is not the stasis

and steadiness that might seem to constitute a religious life but an adjustment to the presence of awakening. His own experience, even as it describes
the model process of a saving conversion, runs counter to much of New
England Calvinist theology. As he reflects on his experience, we see him
maintaining a capacity for self-overcoming and self-recovery. Edwards is able
to gather up earlier conversions and see them as a narrative, as having continuity. His sense of his life is expansive even when it is shot through with
self-doubt; were he to lose this sense through success or failure, his narrative would end either in consummation or cessation. Instead he finds his life
creating its own sort of infinity, a place into which we can move with him as
the narrative unfolds. At the same time, within the continuity of the narrative, there are very clear fractures—failures and losses. He sees in his childhood conversion the virtue of innocence and purity, but it is accompanied
by an innocence concerning the real demandingness of a religious life. He
delighted, he says, in praying "five times a day" and spending "much time in
religious talk with other boys"; but as he gathers up that youthful religiosity,
he declares its inadequacy: "And I am ready to think, many are deceived with
such affections, and such a delight as I then had in religion, and mistake it
for grace."[2] He sees in his college years an awakening to an intellectual dimension of religious experience but fears the intellectualism toward which
this awakening moves him. Throughout this almost dialectical movement,
we see Edwards learning to come to grips with his own failures—including
his perceived inability to deal with failure—and the losses of certain features
of his lived experience, his beliefs and habits of conduct, to which he thought
he had been committed. In short, he attends to his own fatality.

In attending to this fatality, Edwards reveals another feature of the religious
attitude—an acknowledgment of dependence. On the one hand, Edwards
recognizes the need to keep oneself open to awakening; despite his Spinoza-
like account of freedom, he is no fatalist. On the other hand, he understands
that no effort on his part alone is sufficient to constitute a life in grace. "I now
sought," he tells us, "an increase in grace and holiness, and a holy life, with
much more earnestness than ever I sought grace before I had it." "And yet,"
he adds, he undertook this pursuit "with too great a dependence on my own
strength; which afterwards proved a great damage to me."[3] In living through
the transitions, Edwards comes to see that experiencing the religious requires
his strength to be in league with that which defines his finitude.

In part unwittingly, perhaps, Edwards thus discloses that religious experience is not a static way of being, nor is it merely an unyielding commitment
to certain doctrines. Experientially the religious life is for Edwards revealed
as the maintenance of an attitude of openness to the possibility of self-overcoming, to ongoing awakening or conversion. It demands both a tremendous

discipline to maintain continuity in one's finitude and a tremendous flexibility in dealing with one's failures and losses. Edwards's hope is that he may "grow in grace," and he recognizes that he must attend to this growth always in his present status, even when this status itself reveals some inadequacy. "Though it seems to me," he says, "that, in some respects, I was a far better Christian, for two or three years after my first conversion, than I am now. . . . yet, of late years, I have had a more full and constant sense of the absolute sovereignty of God."[4] Furthermore, as William Clebsch contends, Edwards ultimately saw that his conversion process was guided by a fundamentally aesthetic attitude—that it was a matter not merely of fulfilling duty but of feeling "at home with God" in the world. For Edwards, Clebsch argues, "the genuinely virtuous person lived true to the beauty of the universe. The difference lay neither in the deed done nor even in the psychological motive behind it, but rather in the frame of mind—whether one was in or out of tune with the universe."[5] Here, then, in seminal form is an American version of religious experience: the maintenance of a religious attitude in the conduct of a finite life. It is not the life of a dogmatist that we usually associate with Puritanism. My guess is that, given his internal wars with himself, Edwards understood this. Moreover, he understood that this version of religious experience, which left him open to the possibility of indefinite awakenings, presented a much more difficult challenge than the living of a formulaic life according to unchanging beliefs. This is the central irony of Jonathan Edwards; he kept questing and seeking when his doctrines told him explicitly that there was no need to do so. As Clebsch puts it: "Only God could search the hearts of men and women. But Edwards could not help wondering!"[6]

The notion of an American religious attitude put in another appearance in the works of the transcendentalists. It appears in Bronson Alcott's unending quest for a concrete utopia and, with more effect, in Emerson's persistent reference to movement to "higher platforms" and outer circles, from whose vantage points one can begin to gauge one's self-development. But it is Henry Thoreau, I think, who takes the presentation of this religious attitude as his central task. Throughout *Walden* and in a number of his essays, Thoreau makes constant, if indirect, reference to the religious cast of his thinking. Indeed, in "Life without Principle" he relates how in various lectures he had done his "best to make a clean breast of what religion I have experienced, and the audience never suspected what I was about."[7] With Edwards the attitude of openness to conversion seems out of place because of Edwards's apparent commitment to a single doctrine of the world. In Thoreau's case what is unusual is his reticence regarding the standard, formal religions. With more subtlety and indirectness than Edwards employs, he tries to distinguish what American culture explicitly supposes religious life to be from what is revealed in the way it is actually lived. Thoreau is not unlike an artist reminding us to draw what we see, not what we *think* we see. I take Thoreau to be saying initially that religion is not about particular doctrines or belief content but is a question of the way one conducts one's life. His essay "Walking" takes up this difference.

Walking serves as an analogue for a religious life, for "every walk is a sort of crusade, preached by some Peter the Hermit in us, to go forth and reconquer this holy land from the hands of the Infidels."[8] Walkers are, for Thoreau, "Holy-Landers" who seek in themselves a redemption of their own lives. The focus of the walker's seeking is a dimension of wildness with which one can face experience and nature. It is here that we find Thoreau's account of salvation in finitude: "What I have been preparing to say is, that in Wildness is the preservation of the World."[9]

What the walker seeks and, if successful, seeks to maintain is the inner wildness that can effect a life of awakening, a religious life. In such a seeking the walker, like Edwards and the Calvinists, undergoes a submissive moment: "I believe that there is a subtle magnetism in Nature, which, if we unconsciously yield to it, will direct us aright. It is not indifferent to us which way we walk."[10] Thoreau substitutes nature for Edwards's sovereign God as that to which we must remain open and with which we must work. In both cases we cannot merely direct ourselves or our environment; for Thoreau, we must achieve an orientation or attitude that will permit and enable our development, our movement toward the wild. This attitude resembles the functioning openness to self-overcoming and self-recovery manifested in Edwards's "Personal Narrative." It is not mere passivity but a disciplined attitude of abandonment: "If you are ready to leave father and mother, and brother and sister, and wife and child and friends, and never see them again—if you have paid your debts, and made your will, and settled all your affairs, and are a free man—then you are ready for a walk."[11]

If we recall that Thoreau faced death while revising this text, some of the apparent callousness of the passage is softened, but the severity of the discipline remains. Thoreau asks not that we leave people behind but that we be ready to go where called. It is, I take it, Thoreau's attempt to bring a sense of the eternal directly into our concrete, finite, everyday experience. That which religions have often made transcendent is to be made immanent in the ordinary and the everyday: "We should go forth on the shortest walk, perchance, in the spirit of undying adventure, never to return, prepared to send back our embalmed hearts only as relics to our desolate kingdoms."[12] Again, our finitude, when religiously oriented, begins to constitute its own infinity. The creative act of the walking life is one of risk and possible loss;

we must advance with an attitude that is awake and attentive to this. For Thoreau, this is a religious attitude.

This attitude is the condition for further awakening—for conversion— whose achievement was the central aim of Thoreau's move to Walden Pond: "Only that day dawns to which we are awake. There is more day to dawn."[13] It is not, however, a game of "capture the flag." What is to be won, on a dialectical basis, is an awakening to the possibility of ongoing awakening, to being always awake. In "Walking" Thoreau refers to this awakened state as being alive: "Life consists with wildness. The most alive is the wildest."[14]

Occasionally Thoreau is interpreted as defending a simple escapism, sheer negative freedom. The move toward wildness is taken as a movement back to nature, a romance with primitivism. This seems to me a strong misreading of his aim. Both in *Walden* and in "Walking" Thoreau disavows such an intention. The wildness is itself a condition not for abandoning civilization but for recivilizing one's self and one's culture: "When I would recreate myself, I seek the darkest wood, the thickest and most interminable and, to the citizen, most dismal, swamp. . . . A town is saved, not more by the righteous men in it than by the woods and swamps that surround it."[15] Our wildness is not a mere savagery but the very condition of our acting freely, of maintaining our aliveness. The upshot of Thoreau's religious life is not a monastic retreat from the civilized world but a life disciplined in remaining alive to its own possibilities in the world that confronts it.[16] We are creative only when our wildness is in league with our own heritage and history, and it is in this living conjunction that we can make our lives religious: "So we saunter toward the Holy land, till one day the sun shall shine more brightly than ever he has done, shall perchance shine into our minds and hearts, and light up our whole lives with a great awakening light."[17]

Thoreau's emphasis on free but disciplined action as defining religious experience is highlighted by the role he assigns to the devil: "Who but the Evil One has cried 'Whoa!' to mankind?" This emphasis brings into view a feature of religious experience implicit both in Edwards's life and in Thoreau's disclosure of the meaning of walking: its ontic or constitutive feature. The religious life not only engages the real—whether construed as sovereign God or nature—but, in part, constitutes the real. The religious life is the making of one's self and its consequences through a religious attitude. On leaving Walden Thoreau surmised that he might have "several more lives to live" and, in a much quoted passage, spoke of this making of life as follows:

> I learned this, at least, by my experiment; that if one advances confidently in the direction of his dreams, and endeavors to live the life which he has imagined, he will meet with a success unexpected in common hours. He will put

some things behind, will pass an invisible boundary; new, universal, and more liberal laws will begin to establish themselves around and within him; or the old laws be expanded, and interpreted in his favor in a more liberal sense, and he will live with the license of a higher order of beings.[18]

Given its repetition, it may be difficult to hear this passage afresh, but we should note the terms Thoreau employs: *learned, advances, endeavors, imagined, meet with, put behind, establish,* and *expand.* Together they take us toward the possibility of a sort of divinity in our ordinary, everyday existence. Edwards bore witness to the need for an openness to self-recovery; Thoreau gave fuller articulation to the discipline this openness to awakening requires and alludes to the constitutive, "recivilizing" effect of "walking"; the significance of this constitutive dimension, however, receives more direct attention in the experiential pragmatism of John Dewey.

Dewey's work *A Common Faith* serves, then, as the final source for the version of American religious life I am trying to sketch. I begin by taking Dewey's Terry Lectures to be sermons aimed at those who had lost faith in their traditional religions but who yet found significance in being religious, among whom Dewey counted himself. As Dewey wrote to Private Charles E. Witzell in 1943: "It may be of help if I say whom I had in mind in writing the book. I have taught many years and I don't think that any of my students would say that I set out to undermine anyone's faith. . . . The lectures making up the book were meant for those whose religious beliefs had been abandoned, and who were given the impression that their abandonment left them without any religious beliefs whatsoever. I wanted to show them that religious values are not the monopoly of any one class or sect and are still open to *them.*"[19] Thus *A Common Faith* not only *talks* about Dewey's conception of the religious but also, at least in part, *performs* this conception. This performance exemplifies the actualizing of ideals that is central to Dewey's religious dimension of experience.

The general pragmatic upshot of Dewey's conception of the religious is that the religious attitude, when lived through one's character and career, makes an important difference in the world of experience and nature that we both inhabit and confront. The attitude, when pervasive in a life, enables free and constitutive action on our part. It is precisely this constitutiveness that, in the framework of Dewey's pragmatism, reveals to us a religious life; after all, for the pragmatists, it is the fruits of our experience that declare our meaning. Dewey, more openly than Thoreau and more knowingly than Edwards, focuses on the active and constitutive nature of the religious attitude. Generally, for Dewey, the quality of an attitude "is displayed in art, science, and good citizenship."[20] In particular, a religious attitude effects ameliorization: "The aims of philanthropists, of Florence Nightingale, of Howard, of Wilberforce, of Peabody, have not been idle dreams. They have modified institutions. Aims, ideals, do not exist simply in 'mind'; they exist in character, in personality and action."[21] Here, in this constitutive activity, is where Dewey located the divine in human experience: "It is this *active* relation between ideal and actual to which I would give the name 'God.'"[22] And it is this active relation that, from its finitude, declares an infinity in which possibilities come to light.

So far as Dewey locates the divine in our finite experience, he carries on the story begun by Edwards and Thoreau. Where the pragmatic upshot makes a notable revision is in its emphasis on imagination as a feature of the religious life. It is through imagination that we are able to produce the ideals on which we can act. However, imagination under the sway of a religious attitude is not wanton. Imaginative ideals are constrained by the heritages and natural surroundings in which they emerge: "The new vision does not arise out of nothing, but emerges through seeing, in terms of possibilities, that is, of imagination, old things in new relations serving a new end which the new end aids in creating."[23] Thus the religious in experience is both experimental and traditional; for Dewey, though it is often overlooked, a general apprenticeship to the past is requisite for our own self-revision: "the process of creation"—the divine constitutive activity of the religious life—"is experimental and continuous."[24] It is this continuity with a heritage and a history—akin to that which underwrites Edwards's narrative—that marks Dewey's own use of the term *God*. He was reprimanded by theists and atheists alike for his use of the term, but he stood by its use as a way of revealing the continuity of his own new conception of the religious with his own earlier experiences of religion in a more narrowly Christian upbringing. To reject the term altogether would mark for Dewey not self-overcoming and self-revision in the face of an experienced loss but a denial of the loss itself. "The essentially unreligious attitude," Dewey says, "is that which attributes human achievement and purpose to man in isolation from the world of physical nature and his fellows."[25]

Although Dewey adamantly resists attributing any specific beliefs to the religious attitude, he does focus on articulating several features that condition the constitutive, creative, and meliorative activity he presents. The first is the positive nature of the attitude: that which is meliorative about it. It is an attitude "more outgoing, more ready and glad," than "stoic resolution," and "it is more active than the former."[26] I take Dewey to be offering a more detailed and perhaps more mundane account of Thoreau's "aliveness"; again, the religious orientation is not one of reclusiveness. The second feature is its pervasiveness. It is not merely one attitude among others; rather, it supervenes on our other attitudes. Dewey thus retains an element of traditional views of conversion in saying that it is the whole person that undergoes change by way of a religious attitude. As Edwards's experience impresses on us, religious self-revision involves the whole self. "It is," Dewey says, "a change *of* will conceived as the organic plenitude of our being, rather than any special change *in* will."[27]

Finally, the result of the attitude's presence is the quality of openness and attentiveness to one's own possibilities and a willingness to undergo change—what Edwards experienced but was unable to articulate fully, except in the revealing pages of his "Narrative." This is the quality requisite for constitutive, meliorative activity. The religious attitude "includes a note of submission" which "is voluntary, not externally imposed."[28] Herein again lies the possibility of openness to self-revision. Ironically, Dewey takes aim at religions precisely because, when their theological doctrines and formulas for living are dogmatically operative, they foreclose the possibility of living with this openness. They play the role of Thoreau's Evil One, who yells "Whoa!": "Religions now prevent, because of their weight of historic encumbrances, the religious quality of experience from coming to consciousness and finding the expression that is appropriate to present conditions, intellectual and moral."[29] It is just this sort of closure that forced the thoughtful and live-minded Edwards into crisis after crisis. Insofar as the doctrines under which he lived demanded adherence rather than thought, his own self-aversion and openness to thoughtful revision and correction ran up against his belief in and hope for a certainty regarding the features of true salvation. From the vantage of Thoreau and Dewey, Edwards lived religiously—awakened, alive, and constitutive—in spite of, not because of, his religion.

Concluding Remarks

So, in brief, goes the story of American religious life from another angle of vision. My aim is not to show that Edwards, Thoreau, and Dewey are of a piece but rather to exhibit for consideration the ongoing career of an account of experience that is religious. Needless to say, many others help constitute this career, Emerson, Peirce, James, and Whitehead among them. The story has been given voice in the twentieth century by other, more neglected thinkers; Ernest Hocking in *The Meaning of God in Human Experience* and Henry Bugbee in *The Inward Morning* describe versions of this account that are well worth our attention. How is one, except apologetically in the pejorative sense, to write one's own personal narrative in a culture that has in most quarters almost forgotten the constraining element of experience? The account of religious experience at hand describes a life that, under the guidance of a religious attitude, actively remakes itself and its world in league with the constraints and resistances it encounters. It is willing to risk failure and to countenance loss; it is, consequently, a moral life, but not a merely moral life. We at once willingly submit to our limitations and possibilities and take on the responsibility for creating our own way. The story of our seasons of awakening seems to me central enough to our cultural heritage that we might, in a variety of ways, take up its retelling. And the fact that it has survived such radical alterations in our cultural outlook says something of its durability and malleability. On this score, Dewey's closing remarks in *A Common Faith* speak *to* us and both *for* and *about* Edwards and Thoreau: "Ours is the responsibility of conserving, transmitting, rectifying and expanding the heritage of values we have received that those who come after us may receive it more solid and secure, more widely accessible and more generously shared than we have received it."[30]

Notes

1. W. H. Werkmeister, *A History of Philosophical Ideas in America* (New York: Ronald, 1949), 10–11.

2. Jonathan Edwards, *Selected Writings of Jonathan Edwards,* ed. Harold P. Simonson (New York: Ungar, 1987), 27.

3. Ibid., 33.

4. Ibid.

5. William A. Clebsch, *American Religious Thought* (Chicago: University of Chicago Press, 1973), 53.

6. Ibid., 34.

7. Henry David Thoreau, *The Portable Thoreau,* ed. Carl Bode (New York: Penguin Books, 1982), 644.

8. Ibid., 593.

9. Ibid., 609.

10. Ibid., 602.

11. Ibid., 593.

12. Ibid.

13. Ibid., 572.

14. Ibid., 611.

15. Ibid., 613.

16. It is interesting to note that neither Edwards's forced retreat to Stockbridge nor Thoreau's stay at Walden Pond resulted in social isolation—their religious lives were bound up with their communities.

17. Thoreau, *Portable Thoreau,* 630.

18. Ibid., 562.

19. This letter resides in W. E. Hocking's personal library at the home of Richard Hocking, Madison, N.H.

20. John Dewey, *The Later Works of John Dewey, 1925–1953,* vol. 9, ed. Jo Ann Boydston (Carbondale: Southern Illinois University Press, 1989), 17.

21. Ibid., 33.

22. Ibid., 34.

23. Ibid.

24. Ibid.

25. Ibid., 18

26. Ibid., 13.

27. Ibid.

28. Ibid., 12.

29. Ibid., 8.

30. Ibid., 57–58.

14. Pragmatism, History, and Theology

WILLIAM DEAN

The French, treasuring their national identity, have developed a natural suspicion of the growing power of Anglo-Saxon pragmatism. With Gallic humor, a French diplomat recently turned the tables and said of pragmatism, "It will work in practice. But will it work in theory?"[1] Theologians, treasuring their own identity, have developed an ardent suspicion of those neopragmatist philosophers bent on punishing theologians who break their laws. These theologians say of the new pragmatism, "It may work in philosophy. But will it work in religion?"

As theologians know, pragmatists believe not only that ideas should work in practice but that they will arise in practice. However, these pragmatists live in an American landscape both awash in a sea of faith and populated by people who believe ideas arise from faith as well as practice. In *Achieving Our Country* the pragmatist Richard Rorty eloquently argued that we all should attend to our country's interests. But American theologians might question whether he and other neopragmatic philosophers attend seriously to the country's theological interests.

Once, casually addressing theological interests, Rorty characterized the theologian as one who "believes in an order beyond time and change which both determines the point of human existence and establishes a hierarchy of responsibilities," and he characterized religious faith as based on just such a universal and eternal order.[2] In short, for Rorty, theology and religion are foundationalist by definition, grounding their ideas outside history and therefore outside the circle of the practices alone worthy of serious attention by pragmatists. Later—this time speaking before a number of theologians expressly interested in pragmatism—Rorty conceded that some religious thinkers, including John Dewey, had set God within rather than beyond history. Nevertheless, Rorty quickly nullified that concession, this time claiming that religious thinkers are nostalgic and antiquated, that they refer to God only "to link their days each to each," and that they fail to recognize that God is "a perhaps obsolete name for a possible human future" or "an external guarantor of some such future."[3]

In the following pages I seek to accomplish three purposes: (1) to suggest, however briefly, that from its very beginning and through its history much Western theology has placed God in, rather than beyond, history; (2) to illustrate, through a discussion of the concept of God, that theology neither has always been nor is always now a nostalgic act venerating a static thing but is also an anticipatory effort open to revision; and (3) to propose that even today a basically pragmatic theology must acknowledge that some religious ideas arise mysteriously. My efforts should not be overinterpreted. First, I invoke biblical and orthodox theologies not to claim that, as they stand, they can be laid over wholesale into the twenty-first century but only to refute the assumption that Judaism and Christianity have always invested themselves in an "order beyond time and change." Second, I argue that just because a theology accepts some pragmatic styles some of the time does not mean it must adhere to all pragmatic styles all of the time. Theology may often adhere to the letter of the new pragmatic law, but it certainly does not live or intend to live within the spirit of that law. Religious thought, after all, is the mother of philosophical pragmatism, not its client—and should not act as if it were.[4]

The Pragmatist God of the Israelites and of the Early Church

The American Puritans have been called "proto-pragmatists,"[5] but in a broader and older world the title should be awarded to the ancient Israelites. The most ambitious exercise of the Israelites' pragmatism lay in their belief that God is real not because God is rational, sublime, or otherwise fit for divinity but because God made a difference in Israel's life.

The pragmatism of the Old Testament, or Hebrew Bible (arbitrarily I will use the term *Old Testament*) worked out of a religion of history, where God was known and identified through God's role in history. The Israelites viewed God not as a reality living beyond historical time and change, waiting to be represented, but as a changing reality within historical time and change. God was not represented symbolically through history, as though history were a window displaying God on the other side or a mirror reflecting God's eternal and universal truth. There was nothing but the stage of history, and there were no wings to the stage. God is not a visible player, but God nevertheless plays on that stage, and this can be demonstrated by the plot unfolding on the stage. For some of the ancient Israelites, God was named the original creator of history because history made that name seem true. No one, it was reasoned, but one powerful enough to create history could act in history with such sovereignty and caprice.[6] Whether or not one reads the stories of God's acts in history literally (most modern pragmatists would not), that they were understood to transpire in the historical process cannot be denied.

Particularly for the earliest Israelites, the meaning of history was spelled out primarily by the covenant, or contract, between Israel and God. The covenant stated Israel's obligations to God and set the terms for God's response when Israel fulfilled or failed to fulfill its covenant obligations. Israel's obedience to the covenant was rewarded with historical successes, and its disobedience to the covenant was punished with historical failures in what could be a very rough justice. The covenant's logic was spelled out in Israel's retributive philosophy of history, according to which God always gets retribution and Israel always suffers retribution. The covenant's truth was tested by seeing whether its implicit predictions were fulfilled. For example, according to the Book of Joshua, when Israel violated the covenant by stealing its enemies' "devoted things," God caused the Israelites to fall in battle and those who had participated in the theft to be stoned or burned to death. Further, Joshua implies, if Israel would repent and uphold the covenant, God would cause the Israelites to slaughter their opponents (Josh. 7–8). The Book of Judges sets up the following four-part causal sequence: (1) Israel's apostasy—its worship of other gods—is followed by (2) God's judgment, which causes Israel to be defeated in battle; this defeat, in turn, is followed by (3) Israel's repentance for its apostasy; and this is followed by (4) God's deliverance of Israel, manifest in Israel's conquest of its enemies (Judg. 2). Thus God's interactions with Israel occurred in history largely through acts of retribution. Further, the covenant is the instrument through which Israel's retributive philosophy of history is exercised, and the covenant's truth is to be tested through examining whether its predictions are fulfilled.

Given this pragmatic historicism, it is not surprising that the Jewish scholar Mordecai Kaplan would say, "The people of Israel was the first people to discover the God of history."[7] According to G. Ernest Wright, the Israelites' God is simply the "God who acts," not the God who speaks, if speaking is a means of conveying ideas that can be dissociated from acts and thereby "dissociated from history and dealt with as an abstraction" for theological contemplation.[8] God not only acts in history; God *is* God's action. God's famous answer to Moses's request for God's name is translated in the Revised Standard Version as "I am who I am" (Exod. 3:14). The Old Testament scholar Jack Miles argues that this should be translated "I am what I do," for God "is indeed defined by what he does." "Even to himself," Miles claims, "he is a mystery that is revealed progressively only through his actions and their aftermath."[9] That is, God is "known" as a mystery within history and believed not because God is directly experienced or symbolically represented but because God's will is executed.

It was the experience of God's acts felt in and interpreted by Israel's spiritual culture that counted, not the belief that God existed or had supernatural power. For example, the important thing about a political or military victory or defeat for Israel was not the theory that God was directing physical events but the fact that in victory or defeat Israel knew itself to be vindicated or punished by God. When Nathan found David guilty of killing Uriah, David was not miraculously struck down or removed from his kingly office, but he knew he had been judged. When the prophets judged Israel, they may have adroitly analyzed impending military and political events, but their intention was to show that Israel had been or would be judged.

The prophets, in short, tended to be pragmatic, judging an idea true not because it corresponded to an eternal truth but because believing it brought results. This pragmatism was important because it gave the Israelites a way to guide their national life. If Israel wanted its history to improve, it should act as though God acted in history through the retributive structure of the covenant. For the prophets, faith in God is not about belief in God but about the way to live better. In the life of Israel, one possibility is most threatening to theological truth: that the retribution pragmatics would not work or, to say the same thing, that obedience or disobedience to God would have no consequences. The Book of Job toyed with this eventuality. Job's counselors, following the pragmatic logic of retribution, inferred that Job must be guilty because, normally, suffering would be the consequence of guilt, but Job challenged that retributive interpretation.[10] Throughout most of their scriptures, however, the pragmatic logic worked for the Israelites, as they adopted the theory that obedience to God would cause Israel to flourish and disobedience to God would cause Israel to deteriorate.

Thus the Israelites were interested not in referring to God but in using God. They would never ask whether God is known by some equivalent to historical sonar—historical clues sounding out a God beyond history. Nor would they ask whether God is an echo—merely their own voices misheard as God's voice. These questions were a matter of indifference for the Israelites, even if not for those who would later be their Greek contemporaries and their twentieth-century cultural children.

The New Testament, at least where it is most Jewish, is informed by a similar pragmatic spirit. Jesus argued pragmatically that, if people want to inherit the Kingdom of God, they should treat his message as true. But Jesus was also interested in a pragmatic approach to more immediate questions. He seemed to argue, for example, that some prophets were false because they were unable to make sense of history. "You will know them," Jesus said, "by their fruits. Are grapes gathered from thorns, or figs from thistles? . . . Every tree that does not bear good fruit is cut down and thrown into the fire" (Matt. 7:16–19). In Matthew he generalized on this pragmatic criterion, saying, "The good man out of his good treasure brings forth good, and the evil man out of his evil treasure brings forth evil" (Matt. 12:35).

When the Apostle Paul rejected "works righteousness," he was not rejecting pragmatism. Paul assumed that salvation does flow pragmatically from good works (after all, it is "the doers of the law who will be justified" [Rom. 2:13]). The problem with works righteousness lies not in its pragmatic logic but in its premise that good works are possible. It is because the Jews failed to do good works that they were in trouble. Paul's solution, righteousness through faith, is itself pragmatic, connecting that righteousness with salvation (God "justifies him who has faith in Jesus" [Rom. 3:26]).

The Pragmatist God of the Americans

Echoing this biblical pragmatism, the American pragmatist William James joked: "By their fruits ye shall know them, not by their roots."[11] James was conscious that this fruits-roots axis guided an American theological procedure as well. He traced his pragmatism to Jonathan Edwards, whose *Treatise on Religious Affections* was for James "an elaborate working out of this [pragmatist] thesis," for it was Edwards who argued, "*The degree* in which our experience is productive of practice shows *the degree in which our experience is spiritual and divine.*"[12] Later in the eighteenth century, Benjamin Franklin captured the extremes to which Americans would take this when he explained, "The people have a saying, that God Almighty is himself a mechanic, the greatest in the universe; and he is respected more for the variety, ingenuity and utility of his handiworks than for the antiquity of his family."[13]

This pragmatic logic had been adopted by many American Puritans, who tended to have a pragmatic streak—partly due, no doubt, to their deep consciousness of the parallels between their own story and that of the Israelites. Like the Israelites, they entered into a covenant that lay at the heart of their spiritual culture and required their loyalty. Thus they knew their material success in the wilderness was to be seen as a reward for their faithfulness to God and that their material failures—especially natural disasters, such as rainstorms, disease, and earthquakes—should be seen as a punishment for violating their covenant with God. In short, it is because of divine mediation that action and consequence are causally linked. Thus the historian Perry Miller said that for the Puritans, "there is implicit recognition of a causal sequence: the sins exist, the disease breaks out; the sins are reformed, the disease is cured." Eventually the punishments became less external and more internal; then punishment was found in spiritual rather than material deprivation, so that the unfaithful Puritan was given over to hard-heartedness, sloth, sensuality, indifference, and hypocrisy. Later still the punishment was manifested in the failure of their "public spirit."[14] All this was just as John Winthrop's early sermon aboard the *Arbella* said it would be: "The Lord will surely break out in wrath against us, be revenged of such a perjured people and make us know the price of the breach of such a Covenant."[15]

This pragmatic stance made particular sense to many later Americans not only because of their biblical past but because they found mere custom unconvincing. Immigrants arrived in America with their religious traditions, but they faced circumstances radically different from those of the Old World, where those traditions had developed. Of course, current environs always partially invalidate received traditions, but the radically new American environs did this more profoundly. Consequently, the early immigrants could not easily carry on European theologies and then test the truth of their own theologies by correspondence to those older theologies. They needed to augment their received religious traditions, and in fact they did, amplifying their theologies in ways that had little correspondence to traditions of the countries they had left. For example, the Americans had their evangelical Great Awakenings in the eighteenth and nineteenth centuries, and they adopted various species of religious naturalism; experiential and naturalistic theologies abound to this day.

Thus, both because they were influenced by Israel's retributive philosophy of history and because they needed to test ideas by their uses in a new environment rather than by their congruence with Old World customs, it is not surprising that Americans looked to history for evidence of their salvation. Although they made much of salvation beyond history—that is, after death—their religious thinking was typically oriented not to truths beyond history, as Platonic and Augustinian theologies are, but toward truths found and tested in history, as Hebraic and Calvinist theologies are.

Calvinists had always found evidence for their salvation in their good works. For them, to quote R. H. Tawney, "good works are not a way of attaining salvation, but they are indispensable as a proof that salvation has been attained."[16] Like the Israelites, the Calvinist Puritans and their various American successors built their theologies around what they believed was a covenant and the recognition that fulfilling or not fulfilling covenant obligations has consequences. Therein lay the ideas and the logic for pragmatic reasoning: one can test whether one's salvation is real by looking at whether one flourishes in this world.

It was from this religious history and not from any philosophers' inventiveness that America derived its philosophical pragmatism. The American historian Bruce Kuklick, in *Churchmen and Philosophers*, demonstrates the dependence of American thought on the Calvinist orientation, which came to be "the most sustained intellectual tradition the United States has produced," providing "the one systematic body of thinking in America, as well as the only sustained intellectual debate."[17] John Dewey, whom Kuklick calls "the preeminent philosopher in the United States and the twentieth century's foremost American intellectual," works as a prime instance of this Calvinist-pragmatist linkage. Although academicians wanted to see Dewey as "the quintessential secular liberal," he was a Calvinist in attitude, quietly importing "what were recognized at the time as religious values into a scientific conception of man and nature."[18]

With only slight exaggeration it could be said that Calvinism provided the world for which pragmatism was the method. Classical pragmatism's linkage between God and the world is no less real and no more complicated than the Calvinist Puritans' linkage. Pragmatism's God, however, is leveraged by natural faculties such as the imagination rather than by the sinful heart, and its God was set in the cosmology of modern science rather than in that of the Bible.

Under Darwin's new influence, Dewey saw society as a kind of species threatened with extinction. Just as a species faces extinction when it and/or its natural environment has changed, a society faces extinction when it and/or its social and natural environment has changed. The society's only hope is then to change itself or its environment. A new adjustment to the universe cannot be accomplished piecemeal, however, by tinkering with societies alone or environments alone, until they better fit each other. What must be found is some larger view of the universe, which will become that canopy under which society and its environment can be reconceived and altered, so that they can be related in new ways.[19]

If a society reaches this new vision imaginatively, it has not by itself simply invented that vision but has been somehow contextualized and lured, prompted both to remember the past and to revise it creatively. This prompting is usually provided by the same spiritual tradition or heritage that was largely formative of the society in the past. This tradition, which Dewey calls "the unity of all ideal ends arousing us to desire and actions,"[20] guides and sparks the social imagination, which will go on to outrun it, causing it to be slightly reenvisioned. Thus the imagination, instead of working in isolation, responds creatively to a living and active heritage. Something like this no doubt occurred in the eighteenth century, as America developed an implicit vision under which it moved from being a parochial Puritan society to becoming a biblical Enlightenment society with enough coherence and unity to revolt from England and create a new democracy.

This tradition, as it leads the social imagination, does virtually all that a transcendent God is believed to do for a society. The tradition prompts a society to do what otherwise it could not do. It affects the social imagination, informs it of the local past to which it must relate, and spurs it to introduce needed novelty. Out of this comes a new vision contributing to the society's spiritual culture. When traditions do this for societies, the societies receive just the sort of influence commonly attributed to a God, and they often say they have been affected by God. As known pragmatically, God is the living tradition that is meaningful when it changes the society and that is true when these changes are satisfactory.

Ultimately God is the sense of the whole that gives to a society a vision for organizing and promoting its new possibilities. Dewey knew that religions tend to rivet themselves to some past and now useless sense of the whole, or God, but he argued that such adherence need not be the case. Dewey named the faith participating in the continuous growth of a society's spiritual culture and of its God "religiousness" and opposed to it "religion," which is loyal to an earlier God and spiritual culture. Dewey was convinced that religiousness was pragmatic, allowing people to contribute to the growth of their spiritual culture and of their God-like spiritual tradition.[21] Most important, for Dewey, God is real because God makes religiousness possible.

For both Calvin and Dewey, God saves the world, and humans need to look primarily to God to be saved. For Dewey, God is a living religious tradition, and at the same time, God prods the society to move beyond that tradition to generate new social ideals.[22]

Dewey was not original in using a pragmatic argument to establish the reality of God. He was preceded not only by the Calvinists but by the pragmatists William James and Charles Sanders Peirce, working out of the same biblical, Puritan, Calvinist tradition. Dewey was original, nonetheless, in showing through pragmatic argument how a historical God works in a social and historical context. Dewey's God is set thoroughly in history and is about public life and the ways in which societies should meet their challenges. Although James proposed a God who acts from within history, this God is manifest in the private life of individuals, not the public world of society.[23]

Peirce's God can deal with public problems but is embodied outside the flow of historical change, in a world of eternal ideas.[24]

The Pragmatist God and Theology

The single most important theological characteristic of the pragmatists' God is historicity. Pragmatist theology tests the truth of ideas about God by asking whether holding an idea brings the society holding that idea good historical consequences.

Like any other theologians, pragmatist theologians must first locate the ideas they will test in history. But how are they to discover which ideas to test? Typically they mine the history of religious thought about God, finding standard ideas about the divine and then examining the consequences that follow when those ideas are believed. When quite new situations arise, however, situations unanticipated in the history of theology, these theologians must find ideas about God not previously considered to be true.

The discovery of new candidates for truth can be undertaken by what C. S. Peirce called "retroduction"—reasoning that moves "from consequent to antecedent." When religious thinkers need new ideas about God, they treat certain historical events as possible religious consequences and then attempt to guess what in God might have caused those consequences.[25] Such reasoning guided William James's *Varieties of Religious Experience,* arguably the most important study of religion in the twentieth century. There James examined people's testimonies about their religious experience and then allowed the believers to retroduce the beliefs that might have issued in those experiences.

In seeking new candidates for religious truth, Dewey looked more to the society than to the person and said that a society needs to develop ideas that contribute to the health of what I am calling its spiritual culture. In doing this, pragmatist theology uses social history both to acquire and to confirm ideas about God. This only reiterates what most Israelites believed: God is discovered in history, and ideas about God are tested by seeing their results in history. The Israelites were historicists, taking the view that what is real is both composed and destroyed by historical events and that knowledge of what is real is tested through historical inquiry.

What concept of God is suggested by such a historical approach? It is at least that God, as a historical reality or tradition, is shaped as any other historical reality is shaped, by a combination of what it receives from history and its own innovation. God works in history through guiding and spurring the spiritual culture, and God's identity continually changes to meet the changing needs of societies and environments.

Admittedly, it is puzzling first to claim that God is a tradition (Dewey's "unity of all ideal ends arousing us to desire and actions") and then to say that God can change, especially by innovating. But why should a living tradition, even if it is called God, not change and innovate? After all, humans are walking, talking traditions, collections of genetic and environmental inheritances from the past—they are formed and constituted by these inheritances, much as a tradition is—and yet they change and innovate. Traditions, if they live, need not be static or forever the same. To say here that God changes is only to say that God is a growing tradition rather than a static tradition. To put it in contemporary language, God is not a social construction, which is created in a moment of time and then remains fixed forever, but a social convention, a social reality that evolves through time.

Of course, like many theological conclusions, the idea that God is a social convention is a speculation, using principles of pragmatism, historicism, and retroduction. When it is developed, this idea must eventually be challenged by historical accounts showing how peoples developed their thought about God and the sacred.[26]

This conventionalist concept of God may be better understood through a metaphor. God, it might be said, is a "sacred convention," "the spirit of history," the vital soul of a community's past. This spirit offers the society a sense of the whole, a perfectly general vision that colors everything a society thinks or does.

How can the activity of "the spirit of history" be understood? Perhaps by comparing it to "the spirit of the law." Like the spirit of the law, which inspires the legal culture, the spirit of history inspires the spiritual culture. In each case a spirit is alive, so that when new situations are encountered, they prompt changes in a culture, sometimes through innovation and sometimes through a new insistence on past practices. New historical situations create legal predicaments for the legal culture, which in turn either codifies new laws or insists that legal precedents be honored. The formation of laws, therefore, does not occur out of the blue; it is accomplished by the legal culture in, as they say, the spirit of the law. Similarly, new historical situations create spiritual predicaments for the spiritual culture, which in turn either develops a slightly different sense of the whole or retains a time-honored sense of the whole. But this development of the sense of the whole does not come as a raw invention; it is accomplished by the spiritual culture interacting with the spirit of history. Thus the spirit of the law and the spirit of history prompt a culture either to innovate beyond the past or to mandate that the past be honored. The spirit of history differs from the spirit of the law primarily in scope: it provokes a sense of the whole pertaining to all aspects of life, whereas the spirit of the law provokes only a legal culture as it establishes laws for the public order.

Such a pragmatic and historicist concept of God gives new meaning to standard theological terms.

Accordingly, what theologians call *faith* is knowledge, but it is more than knowledge. Faith is a sensitivity, even a kind of sensibility, that discerns the spirit of history as it is manifest in history. Just as an appreciative teacher is able to a read the attitudes that shape a class, or a deft politician is able to intuit the heartbeat of a political audience, faith senses what spurs and guides the spiritual culture. This faith is a form of perception, but it is perception as understood by what William James called "radical empiricism," discerning the elemental impact of the past before it is sorted out by sense organs to become clear, distinct, and cognitive.[27] Faith seeks clarity but distrusts it and usually settles for vagueness, adumbration, wildness. Faith is primarily an emotional, bodily, intuitive response to the spiritual convention that drives an entire historical process.

If a society is always freighted with a synthetic vision that admonishes it to orient its life this way and not that, then faith is the receptor of the reality that drives that vision. If a society's historical activity is more than a dumb and static aggregation of isolated events, the temporary unity it has, making it "this spiritual culture" rather than "that spiritual culture,"[28] is provided by faith as faith perceives the living and transcendent cause of that unity.

In summary, faith is a sense of history that interacts with the spirit of history.[29] If a society's historical activity is affected by a spirit of history, then faith is the reception of that spirit, and over time it can alter that spirit.

Revelation can be understood as a manifestation or disclosure of the spirit of history received by faith. If a revelation is acted on and has desirable historical consequences, then that revelation becomes true.

Equally, *prayer* is the process whereby people attune themselves to the spirit of history, particularly as it has been revealed. Prayer enlivens the sense of history, puts people in a frame of mind where they are more likely to interact with the spirit of history.

When the pragmatic approach places God thoroughly within history, it suggests characteristics or *attributes* of God. These have been recognized by a variety of religion scholars, and they must be stated here without the development they deserve and with only a passing recognition of the serious objections they have elicited.[30]

First, God's interaction with history entails the *moral ambiguity* of the

divine. This ambiguity follows from God's interaction with a morally ambiguous human history, whether God is seen as a cause or a consequence of
that history. If God helps shape history, so that history is partly a consequent
of a divine cause, then it is legitimate to reason backward, from the historical consequent that people can see to the divine cause that they cannot see.
Because history's moral record is thoroughly ambiguous, this suggests that
history's most important moral influence is ambiguous. Equally and more
obviously, if God is seen as affected by history and if causes shape consequences, then the moral ambiguity of history seems to entail the moral ambiguity of God. Commentary on the moral ambiguity of God is long-standing and emanates from people ranging from skeptics, such as Voltaire, to
Holocaust survivors, such as Elie Wiesel, to a few theologians.

The moral ambiguity of God is not an idea strange to the Bible or to Christianity. The Old Testament repeatedly implicates God in evil and finds divine acts of repentance quite appropriate. The New Testament focuses on the
execution of an innocent man and suggests God's involvement in that execution. The Calvinism endemic to American religious thought, as well as
Lutheranism, has acknowledged God's involvement in history's evil. Luther's
and Calvin's insistence on God's sometimes predestining control of history
makes God in some sense responsible not only for history's goodness but also
for its evil. For them, a truly sovereign God must be responsible for all that
occurs in history, including its evils.[31]

Second, a pragmatic historical theology suggests that *God's power is limited,* so that God is not omnipotent. If God lives in history, God is affected
by history. And if God is affected by history, then real power exists outside
God, so that God's power is limited or finite.[32] This leaves open the possibility that, at particular moments in history, God will be unable to affect history in appropriate ways, as well as the possibility that people can make communities more receptive to God's influence.[33] In short, if God cannot do
everything, then humans may be able to do something to aid God. (To quote
William James, why else *be* religious?)[34]

But to deny divine omnipotence is hardly to abandon theology as it has
been practiced in much of the Western world. The Old Testament assumes
that God's power is limited when it pictures Israel defying God's will and sees
God as having to respond to that defiance. All biblical stories are historical
in spirit, not playing out the predetermined script of an omnipotent God but
working in free space where human decisions are unpredictable and make a
difference. To state it otherwise, if God were to have all power, then the people involved in biblical history would have no power, making biblical history merely a puppet show, not the drama of free people interacting with a liv-

ing God. To defend God's majesty by claiming God's power is unlimited is to sacrifice the Bible on the altar of theological compliments.

Third, God can be called *transcendent.* God is not metaphysically transcendent, transcending the realm of history, but historically transcendent, temporally superceding any past history or historical account of God. Just as the spirit of the law cannot be tied to legal opinions or precedents of the past or to any grand generalizations about the law, so the divine spirit of history cannot be tied to past religious thought or thinkers. Just as lawyers (with the possible exception of strict constructionists) believe the spirit of the law transcends any particular rendition of the law, religious people act as though their God transcends any particular society's view of the divine spirit of history.

Fourth, despite the fact that God changes, God has an *identity.* For example, the Old Testament prophets believed God spoke in new ways in new historical circumstances but never suspected that the God who spoke in new ways was a new God. Equally, Jesus, like most of the Christians who eventually followed him (but unlike the Gnostics), believed that his God, even if seen in new ways, remained also the God of the Jews. For God's identity to endure amid change means that God does not die with each move beyond a past identity. To say that "God is dead" each time it becomes clear that an earlier definition of God is no longer tenable is ultraconservative, presuming that old definitions are the only definitions.

Fifth, God is *living,* if to live means both to change and transcend the past and to change in ways that are unpredictable, so that God is not only unpredicted but in principle unpredictable. God is free in the sense that when God changes, those changes cannot be entirely anticipated even through exhaustive examination of past influences on God. For this reason the spirit of history can be said to take on a life of its own. Like any living thing, including the spirit of the law, the spirit of history is partially independent of, as well as partially dependent on, past and present historical situations. Thus, when societies seek the spirit of history, they sometimes wait to see how it will disclose itself in their spiritual culture, just as those who attend a trial sometimes wait to see how the spirit of the law will disclose itself in their courtroom. Metaphorically, societies wait for God to speak, and when God speaks, it is often in ways that were not required by history.

Sixth, God is *not an idol.* To make God into an idol deprives God of the capacity to live and to transcend histories. Idolatry arises when a society identifies its interpretation of God with God itself. Idolatry denies the possibility that God has an independent life and transcends the particular historical situation of the idolater. Idolatry, whether conservative or liberal, encourages people simply to identify the living God with their own interpretation of God.

The Pragmatist God and Mystery

Of course, this conventionalist concept of God is theoretical, setting forth an idea of God that would make sense within pragmatism. Similar theoretical gestures are made by any theology as it proposes a God that would fit its assumed worldview—and any theology must assume some worldview. My proposal to view God as a sacred convention reconceives what Dewey called a "unity of all ideal ends arousing us to desire and action." This and other highly theoretical definitions never make God available, however, for they never can arouse us to desire and action. Ironically, pragmatic theology's theoretical representation of God is pragmatically and religiously of little use.

A religiously useful theology proposes a God that is psychologically and socially effective. To represent God in this way carries pragmatic theology into nonintellectual and mysterious territory, an area sometimes distasteful for academic pragmatists.[35] In the spirit of William James in *The Varieties of Religious Experience,* however, if religious thought is to be pragmatically significant, it must be discussed with regard to its psychological and social effectiveness, even if this makes it academically suspect.

In what follows, I propose that American theology becomes religiously useful after it allows God to be utterly secularized by a historical analysis that reduces God to its historical causes and deprives God of any transcendent status or truth.

Most modern historians, when speaking as historians, tend to be reductionists at heart, going as far as they can to explain religious myth, symbol, or ritual as nothing but the functions of historical causes. They tend to cleanse religion of its mystery by washing it in the currents of history. Religion, the historical and other reductionists say, worships what is merely a psychological or social construction. What religion calls God is the mundane consequence of a long and complicated sequence of mundane historical decisions and accidents. The so-called divine judgments may lacerate the present, but these lacerations are simply the imaginings of an earlier community chastising a present community. God is like a tidal wave that began as a human creation beyond the horizon of remembered history but now thunders onto today's shore, posing as a mighty presence. The reductionists view the idea of God as inseminated by earlier generations, carried through a long ecclesiastical conduit, and then delivered into the present as something only ostensibly alive. When the gospel song "Steal Away" speaks of men and women called by the thunder, that thunder is only the present crack of a whip shaken by a human hand far in the past. When it speaks of their being called by the lightning, that lightning is not God's grandeur but only a reflection of another generation's wisdom that, like illumination from a distant star, finally reaches this generation.

During the nineteenth and twentieth centuries, when liberal theologans began to treat theology historically, they may have intended to expose the merely human origins of a false, supernatural, and absolute God only better to defend their own true, natural, and historically grounded God. But the reductionists are now reducing the liberals' God much as the liberals once reduced the God of the conservatives.

The success of such reduction is especially obvious when applied to the pragmatic liberals, even to my effort to defend Dewey's God by calling it a living social convention. After all, the pragmatic liberals have deemed God to be real for one simple reason: God passed their thoroughly secular test. But they have reduced God to what secular pragmatism judges to be plausible, while normally God judges the secular world, especially its philosophies. In addition, the pragmatic liberals often gave God what God needed to become God (for example, by calling God a sacred convention). But while the God of religions normally brings to the secular world what it needs but cannot otherwise acquire, here God receives from secular society the reality it needs but cannot otherwise acquire.

Of course, pragmatic, historicist theologians intended to escape the shallow waters of mere history—waters only deep enough to float secular historical causes. But their historical analysis does not pull them out of these waters; it pushes them in. Of course, liberal theologians wanted a theology that spoke to secular history, not a secular history that spoke to theology. Theology was to take the last word away from secular history, not yield it to secular society. Once the decision was made to study religion in terms of its social causes, however, historical reduction was bound to undo even historicist theologians.

Admittedly, the enterprise of historical reduction is a problematic business, for the particular truth that everything can be explained by history can itself be explained by history and become no longer true. Nevertheless, reductionists will go on making God simply the product of a meaningless sequence of historical causes and effects, stripping not just orthodox theologies but even pragmatic, historicist theologies of their claims to religious truth.

I contend that it is just at this moment—just when a theology is explained away by history, just when it is most humiliated—that theological claims can mean something once again, but this time as religious rather than theoretical expressions. Just as, according to the writer Flannery O'Connor, the novelist "will realize eventually that fiction can transcend its limitations only by staying within them," the religious community will realize that a theology can transcend its secular limits by staying within them.[36] A theology can become more than a theology when it is accepted as a merely historical writing that can be explained by history. A fiction writer is obligated to seek historical realism above all, to present society's manners and the environment's nature. But it is just then, according to O'Connor, that it becomes apparent that "there always has to be left over that sense of Mystery which cannot be accounted for by any human formula," that there is discovered "mystery through manners, grace through nature." Equally, it is just when a theology is understood to lie thoroughly within a causal sequence of ordinary historical events that it can rise above such ordinary, secular history and expose an extraordinary, sacred history. A story can become a good story when it appears to be not art but only a portrayal of peoples' real-life motives, predicaments, and contexts. Equally, a theology can acquire religious meaning when it fails as an independent demonstration of religious truth and becomes merely a fragment from secular history susceptible to historical explanation. In other words, it is just when theology is consumed by its historical causes and loses its formal argument that there can appear "a depth where these things have been exhausted."[37]

Theology will interpret a religious story that suggests a sense of the whole, argue for the story's theological truth, but then see its argument reduced to the history from which it arose. After theology has been utterly sacrificed to secular history, however, it may become religiously viable as it was not before, or it may unexpectedly make obvious something beyond the secular history to which it has been reduced.

When people read a story, they read no more than a story. They read, "Once upon a time, this happened to these people and, unexpectedly, they did this." The story explains how the people's actions were caused by their pasts and how later unanticipated causes and other consequences followed. Although these elements stay within the story's literary, secular, and historical limits, some people find that the story transcends those limits. The story itself does not pretend to offer anything that transcends its limits, nor does it insert a deus ex machina to close its explanatory gaps. In fact, it usually insists that what it tells can be explained by what lies within the story; it precludes anything that transcends its history—especially, any true God. But such a story can transcend its limits anyway, and religious faith is one possible response to a story when it transcends its limits. For example, Ernest Hemingway's short story "A Clean, Well-Lighted Place" is an atheistic tale that can have vivid transcendent meaning.

Jesus offered a model for the ironic twist I am proposing. It was not as miracle worker, the Messiah-in-waiting, the man born of a virgin, or the heroic heir to King David's throne entering Jerusalem before Passover that Jesus most clearly showed himself to live within the limits of history—for these stories tempted people to see Jesus as triumphant over history. The Jesus who lived within history was the one who had to drink from, rather than let pass, history's bitter cup, who was helpless before his captors, who was willingly doomed by the consequences of his own promise to sacrifice himself in and for secular history. Jesus may have recognized his confinement within secular history when he cried out in virtual atheistic distress, "My God, why have you forsaken me?" But the Jesus who was crucified in history and who died in and for history was the Jesus, some argue, who transcended secular history and whose story was believed by the church.

Israel also lived within the limits of history. It was not as a light to the nations, a nation that successfully heeded the prophetic judgment, a nation ready to inherit the ancient promises given to Abraham—it was not as these that Israel most clearly lived within the limits of history. In fact, these possibilities tempted people to see Israel as triumphant over history. The Israel that lived within history was the one that abandoned its imperial pretensions, that suffered under judgment, that was first divided and then conquered in 722 B.C.E. by Assyria and in 587 by Babylon, and that was finally shattered, leaving the Israelites, like Cain, to become "wanderers on the Earth," a dispersed people whose country was lost to history and was carried only in the people's imagination. This was the Israel whose story transcended its secular limits and was told in synagogues and churches.

If these narrative details suggest a biblical theory about history, it is that those who eventually transcended their secular history were the ones who renounced hope of living beyond that history and accepted their confinement to it. Sometimes, it appears, the most atheistic, secular stories are the ones best fitted to assume sacred meaning. This is the irony of atheism. When God, the story goes, was reduced to nothing but a player in secular history, a mere social convention of history, then God, in the language of the Old Testament, became active in history or, in the language of the New Testament, became incarnate in history.

Of course, most theologians insist that God somehow exists in part beyond all history, even sacred history, rather than entirely within history. They consistently resist history's effort to explain God, seeking a divinity who will explain what history cannot. Many natural theologians insert God into the gaps of science, seeking thereby to explain what science cannot. God never succumbs to natural history, allowing it to explain everything, but violates or works outside the order of that history from the outset. Not only does history fail to explain God, but from the outset God must explain history. The unhappy consequence of this reasoning is that it locates God outside all history. It strips history of any inherent religious meaning, robs the ordinary human dwelling of the capacity to contain a spiritual culture and of a God who might inspire that culture.

A theology that accepts history proceeds in a different way. The biblical picture that places God thoroughly within history leads to a properly atheistic stance. But there is an ironic sequel: out of this atheism may arise a new theism. The postmodern despair encouraged by a pragmatic, historicist stance can lead, ironically, to religious affirmation. Just as the God reduced to secular history is the God who transcends that history, the history that reduces God to itself becomes a larger, more-than-secular history, one with sacred meaning.

Faith cannot make history intelligible (the historians do that), but it can make history meaningful by giving to it a sense of the whole. The biblical point is that faith can arise and secular history can be transcended when one gives oneself to other people as they stand in history. Only when Jesus sacrifices himself to history does he become the Christ; this is a historicist way of understanding the antique saying of John 1:14, "The Word became flesh and dwelt among us." The story of Jesus transcends history's limitations by accepting those limitations. When others go and do likewise, the same is said to happen. When you feed the hungry, give drink to the thirsty, welcome the stranger, clothe the naked, and visit the sick and those in prison, then, whether you know it or not, you find in them a sacred presence ("when you did it to one of the least of these . . . , you did it to me" [Matt. 25:40]). Or take another story: on the road to Jericho, a Samaritan traveler stopped for a stranger (presumably a conventional Jew and therefore his enemy) who was beaten and lying beside the road. He gave his money and risked his life to help the stranger, sacrificed himself to a particular historical happenstance on a particular dark road. Thus limited to history, the Samaritan discovered that he not only found God in "one of the least of these" but became a true neighbor, embodied the love that found history sufficient (Luke 10:29–37).[38] The biblical point is that, with the devotion of a historical reductionist, one must accept the Jesus who truly dies on the cross and the Israel that is truly dispersed in the Diaspora, recognizing that each was irrevocably and utterly lost to the forces of history. This reduction to history destroys all hope that theological argument is sufficient or that a God can be meaningful beyond history. Nevertheless, and ironically, this death at the hand of history gives to history a sacred value.[39]

In this process no extrahistorical reality is introduced, for the new meaning of history is offered by a reality that is itself historical, even if it is more than secular. The reduction of God or religious figures to history allows history to become meaningful but with a meaning absent from secular history. No theoretical explanation can, by itself, yield religious meaning; when it attempts to do so, it becomes idolatrous. Nevertheless, there can be a mystery that transcends secular history after all religious things have been reduced to historical explanations. To put it in Flannery O'Connor's words, "faith is a 'walking in darkness' and not a theological solution to mystery."[40]

Finally, however, the real test of a mystery, even when it transcends secular history, is whether it works within secular history. To avoid that test would be to retreat to an idealism foreign to both the biblical and the American contexts and to ignore the history from which mystery arose. The only true test of faith will be seen in the benefits it yields for ordinary, secular historical practice, so that pragmatic and historicist standards must be introduced once again.

The God of convention and the God that transcends secular history—presumably the same—cannot be called true unless they return to secular history and make a practical and beneficial difference, acquiring what William James called "cash value." Whether or not this actually happens is a question this essay cannot answer.

Notes

1. See Alan Riding, "Where Are the Beret Factories of Yesteryear," a review of Jonathan Fenby, *France on the Brink, New York Times Book Review*, August 1, 1999, p. 6.

2. Richard Rorty, *Contingency, Irony, and Solidarity* (New York: Cambridge University Press, 1989), xv.

3. Richard Rorty, "Religious Faith, Intellectual Responsibility, and Romance," *American Journal of Theology and Philosophy* 17, no. 2 (May 1996): 139, 135. The article was originally a paper delivered at a conference of the Highlands Institute for American Religious and Philosophical Thought.

4. Much biblical thought, for example, was pragmatist before pragmatism was formulated. For a recent instance of pragmatic theology, see Victor Anderson, *Pragmatic Theology* (Albany, N.Y.: SUNY Press, 1998); for a summary analysis of pragmatic theology, see Sheila Davaney, *Pragmatic Historicism* (Albany, N.Y.: SUNY Press, 2000).

5. Andrew Delbanco, *The Real American Dream: A Meditation on Hope* (Cambridge, Mass.: Harvard University Press, 1999), 35.

6. Referring to several Old Testament accounts of creation, Gerhard von Rad speaks of "the theological derivation of Jahweh's power over history from his authority as Creator." Later he says, "Only by referring history to the creation of the world could the saving action within Israel be brought into its appropriate theological frame of reference, because creation is part of Israel's etiology" (Gerhard von Rad, *Old Testament Theology*, 2 vols. [New York: Harper, 1962], 1:138, 2:342).

7. Mordecai M. Kaplan and Arthur A. Cohen, *If Not Now, When?* (New York: Schocken Books, 1973), 22.

8. G. Ernest Wright, *God Who Acts: Biblical Theology as Recital* (London: SCM, 1960), 12.

9. Jack Miles, *God: A Biography* (New York: Knopf, 1995), 99.

10. Some accept even today the pragmatics of retribution and use it to debate the meaning of the Nazi death camps. See Richard L. Rubenstein, *After Auschwitz: Radical Theology and Contemporary Judaism* (Indianapolis: Bobbs-Merrill, 1966), esp. chap. 2.

11. William James, *The Varieties of Religious Experience* (Cambridge, Mass.: Harvard University Press, 1985), 25.

12. Ibid. The emphasis appears in James's text.

13. In H. W. Brands, *The First American: The Life and Times of Benjamin Franklin* (New York: Doubleday, 2000), 634.

14. Perry Miller, *The New England Mind: From Colony to Province* (Cambridge, Mass.: Harvard University Press, 1981), 27–28, 37.

15. Ibid., 23.

16. R. H. Tawney, *Religion and the Rise of Capitalism: A Historical Study* (New York: Harcourt, Brace, 1952), 109.

17. Bruce Kuklick, *Churchmen and Philosophers: From Jonathan Edwards to John Dewey* (New Haven, Conn.: Yale University Press, 1985), 222, 9.

18. Ibid., xx, 256, xv–xvi. Like Jonathan Edwards, Dewey found God in nature, although unlike Edwards's, his God was not supernatural.

19. In Dewey's words, "some complex of conditions that have operated to effect an adjustment in life, an orientation, that brings with it a sense of peace" (John Dewey, *A Common Faith* [New Haven, Conn.: Yale University Press, 1952], 13). More conscious than his Calvinist predecessors that everything changes, Dewey was angered by orthodox Christians who perpetuated an earlier and now obsolete view of the universe, particularly when it falsely and dangerously promised supernatural assistance in today's naturalistic world. But while the new view never simply copied earlier visions, it did preserve much of their substance—something Dewey continually underrated.

20. Dewey, *Common Faith*, 42.

21. Ibid., 85.

22. Ibid.

23. James had several arguments for the existence of God, all of which have God affecting history. First, God "is not merely ideal, for it produces effects in this world. . . . But that which produces effects within another reality must be termed a reality itself." In short, "God is real since he produces real effects" (James, *Varieties*, 406–7). Second, if you are forced to chose between two vitally important options, but lack normal evidence, then it is legitimate for you to act from faith in God, if that brings desirable consequences that do not conflict with other beliefs (William James, "The Will to Believe," in *The Will to Believe and Other Popular Essays* [Cambridge, Mass.: Harvard University Press, 1979]). Third, you are entitled to believe in God if you sense "that we inhabit an invisible spiritual environment from which help comes, our soul being mysteriously one with a larger soul whose instruments we are" (William James, *A Pluralistic Universe* [Cambridge, Mass.: Harvard University Press, 1977], 139). The last possibility—that of working "mysterious-

ly" within history itself—is of the sort described in James's "radical empiricism." In all these arguments James refers to pragmatic tests of choices made by individuals rather than by societies.

24. Peirce seeks, even in his quest for God, "real generals" and objects to James's belief in the mutability of truth and the capacity of the will to alter truth (Charles Peirce, *Collected Papers of Charles Sanders Peirce*, vol. 6, ed. Charles Hartshorne and Paul Weiss [Cambridge, Mass.: Harvard University Press, 1963], 332). Peirce's pragmatic approach to the reality of God comes down to a simple, two-step argument. First, we have the mental capacity to examine ordinary facts and to intuit, fallibly but uncannily, the general ideas those facts suggest, even though they are not in the facts; this capacity drives us to the simple, unsophisticated conclusion that the facts of mind and world must be ordered by a God. Second, Peirce's pragmatism enters when he argues that the belief that the world has been so ordered can be tested by examining how it alters our conduct (*Collected Papers*, 6:311–47.)

25. Peirce, *Collected Papers*, 6:321.

26. For example, regarding non-Western religion, see Émile Durkheim, *The Elementary Forms of Religious Life*, trans. Karen E. Fields (New York: Free Press, 1995); regarding Christianity, see Shailer Mathews, *The Growth of the Idea of God* (New York: Macmillan, 1931).

27. Radical empiricism was defined by William James and developed, as "immediate empiricism," by John Dewey. It describes what Jonathan Edwards called a sense of the heart, what Alfred North Whitehead called causal efficacy, and what the theologian Bernard Meland called appreciative awareness. See my *American Religious Empiricism* (Albany, N.Y.: SUNY Press, 1986), chap. 1.

28. For John Dewey's similar use of *that*, see John Dewey, *The Later Works of John Dewey*, vol. 10 (New York: Capricorn Books, 1958), 35–37.

29. As an empirical faculty, faith can be prompted by a reality beyond itself; but the truth of its reference to reality is tested not by a correspondence test of truth but pragmatically, by its consequences. This was recognized by James and Dewey, each of whom tested beliefs acquired through immediate experience not by tests of correspondence but through examining the consequences of holding such beliefs. I argue that religious empiricists must exercise a sense of history in *American Religious Empiricism* (42, 62, 118) and attempt to do just that in William Dean, *The American Spiritual Culture: And the Invention of Jazz, Football, and the Movies* (New York: Continuum, 2002).

30. See, e.g., Bernard M. Loomer, "The Size of God," in *The Size of God: The Theology of Bernard Loomer in Context*, ed. William Dean and Larry Axel (Indianapolis, Ind.: Mercer University Press, 1987); and the writings of Charles Hartshorne, especially *Omnipotence and Other Theological Mistakes* (Albany, N.Y.: SUNY Press, 1984).

31. See James L. Crenshaw, *A Whirlpool of Torment: Israelite Traditions of God as an Oppressive Presence* (Philadelphia: Fortress Press, 1984); Judith Plaskow, "Facing the Ambiguity of God," *Tikkun* 6, no. 5 (Sept.–Oct. 1991): 70, 96; Terence E. Fretheim, "The Repentance of God: A Key to Evaluating Old Testament God-Talk," *Horizons in Biblical Theology* 10 (1988): 47–70; and my book *The Religious Critic in American Culture* (Albany, N.Y.: SUNY Press, 1994), 140–48. Jack Miles reports, "If we were forced to say in one word who God is and in another what the Bible is about, the answer would have to be

that God is a *warrior*, and the Bible is about *victory* (*God*, 106 [emphasis is Miles's]; see also 81, 104),

32. For such reasoning, see James, *Pluralistic Universe*, 144.

33. "Take, for example, any one of us in this room with the ideals which he cherishes, and is willing to live and work for. Every such ideal realized will be one moment in the world's salvation. But these particular ideals are not bare abstract possibilities. They are grounded, they are *live* possibilities, for we are their live champions and pledges, and if the complementary conditions come and add themselves, our ideals will become actual things. What now are the complementary conditions? They are first such a mixture of things as will in the fullness of time give us a chance, a gap that we can spring into, and, finally, *our act*" (William James, *Pragmatism* [Cambridge: Harvard University Press, 1975], 137–38; emphasis is James's). See also James, *Will to Believe*, 55.

34. James, *Will to Believe*, 55. See also James, *Pragmatism*, 137–38

35. However, to emphasize mystery is not necessarily to take a nonacademic or even a conservative approach to theology. Bernard Meland, a University of Chicago theologian called both a liberal and "a theologian's theologian," damned the constraints theology placed on an essentially mysterious God. Interestingly, he often fails to note the constraints his own religious naturalism placed on God. See Bernard Meland, *Fallible Forms and Symbols: Discourses on Method in a Theology of Culture* (Philadelphia: Fortress, 1976), particularly chap. 4.

36. Flannery O'Connor, *Flannery O'Connor: Collected Works* (New York: Literary Classics of America, 1988), 808.

37. Flannery O'Connor, *Mystery and Manners: Occasional Prose*, ed. Sally Fitzgerald and Robert Fitzgerald (New York: Farrar, Straus and Giroux, 1975), 153.

38. For Andrew J. Mattill Jr. the true neighbor is the Samaritan, not the beaten man, and the beaten man is the representative of the divine. See "The Anonymous Victim (Luke 10:25–37): A New Look at the Story of the Good Samaritan," *Unitarian Universalist Christian* 34 (1979): 38–54.

39. This dynamic resembles that described by Thomas Altizer when he sees the incarnation as the death of God and the birth of history. Unlike Altizer's God, however, the God who is the spirit of history does not, as I see it, arise from Hegel's extrahistorical absolute. See Thomas J. J. Altizer, *The Gospel of Christian Atheism* (Philadelphia: Westminster, 1966).

40. O'Connor, *Mystery and Manners*, 184.

15. Morality and Religion: Why Not Pragmatism?

STUART ROSENBAUM

Pragmatism is a distinctively American contribution to the intellectual life of the West. Unfortunately it endures general caricature as the intellectual expression of American capitalist efficiency. When pragmatism is attributed distinctive content beyond this "businesslike" caricature, it is usually associated with scientism, atheism, and humanism. The idea that the American pragmatic tradition might offer serious resources for expressing and understanding humanity's deepest moral and religious convictions is seldom taken seriously.

Reasons for these caricatures and the customary neglect are not hard to find. In the contemporary world, for example, Richard Rorty is a well-known representative of pragmatism. Rorty's thought, rhetoric, and honesty put him at odds with a wide range of earnest, more traditional thinkers. He is well known, for example, for claiming that truth is "what our peers will . . . let us get away with saying,"[1] a claim guaranteed to irritate those who take their intellectual responsibilities seriously. Rorty also confesses his atheism, and he does so with an apparent insouciance that suggests the issue of God's existence does not matter, providing yet another way this prominent pragmatist alienates those working more squarely in Western theological traditions.[2] Rorty's rhetoric and honesty, however, provide only one reason for the caricature and neglect of pragmatism's resources.

Pragmatism is the American expression of a more general movement away from intellectual traditions that have been dominant in many ways since Plato and Aristotle. Those dominant traditions are in many respects diverse, but they also share important commitments. For example, they are committed to the ideas that reality has a distinct character, that a divine being is responsible for it, that humans are capable of knowing both this reality and the divine being, and that there are fixed and knowable limits of correct behavior. Since the last half of the nineteenth century, intellectual culture has gradually been turning away from these intellectual traditions. On the Continent Nietzsche was the lonely critic who gave impetus to that turning. In the New World Emerson may have been the first clearly identifiable spokesperson for the turn away from those traditions. Each of these seminal thinkers was instrumental in the origin of slightly different traditions of thought—postmodernism and pragmatism—that have in common their rejection of the earlier traditions. The earlier traditions have nevertheless resisted the suggestion that they are defective. We see around us evidence of their resistance in, for example, the activities of creationists, fundamentalists, and other broadly "reactionary" sorts. I begin by broadly sketching the intellectual traditions pragmatists think are dying, and I also explain why those traditions do not die gracefully, despite fatal illnesses repeatedly diagnosed by pragmatists and others. This task includes defending pragmatism against the claim that it is committed to moral and religious relativism. The second, and larger, part of my task is to offer an account—of necessity a sketchy one—of the moral and religious energy simmering untapped beneath the caricature and neglect of the pragmatic tradition.

The Intellectual Tradition and Pragmatism's Critique

One way of seeing the intellectual traditions that pragmatists reject is as a kind of "rearguard" action designed to save humanity from the need to face its own responsibility. Pragmatists, like existentialists, will countenance no dissembling about the starkness of the human condition or about the need to take responsibility for ourselves and for the conditions under which we live. A large part of human culture, according to pragmatists, has been dedicated to finding ways to stave off the need to face our responsibility for ourselves and our communities. Since Galileo and Newton signaled that the human world is not so amenable to human hopes as people had thought, intellectuals have ingeniously sought ways to avoid human responsibility for the human condition; they have sought reassurance that somebody or something else—God, the categorical imperative, the principle of utility, or the Golden Rule—was responsible and should be followed or obeyed. To be sure, their search has gone on under the guise of efforts to know the truth or to certify actions and practices as universally right and good. Nevertheless, the pragmatic tradition of thought points to the failure of these efforts and seeks to face constructively human responsibility for the human community.

The effort to shift responsibility that pragmatists find objectionable begins with epistemology. Epistemology studies how persons are able, if they use their intellects responsibly, to get in touch with a reality beyond themselves. This reality may be a law-driven physical reality that reduces persons to insignificance, a moral reality to which they must be responsible, or a religious reality they must serve.[3] Epistemology has been the heart of philosophy at least since Galileo, and its goal has been to establish cognitive contact with a reality that persons must accommodate and to which they must be responsible. John Dewey makes this point throughout his work. Here is a sample from *The Quest for Certainty:* "Thus philosophy in its classic form became a species of apologetic justification for belief in an ultimate reality in which the values which should regulate life and control conduct are securely enstated."[4]

The pragmatists' reaction to these efforts at epistemology is similar to Willard Quine's reaction in "Two Dogmas of Empiricism" to efforts at explicating the idea of a semantic rule: "We might just stop tugging at our bootstraps altogether."[5] The pragmatic tradition of thought enables us, as Quine put it, to "stop tugging at our bootstraps" and to turn our attention to, as Dewey put it, "the problems of men." The pragmatic tradition asks us to stop trying to get in touch with a reality beyond ourselves and to turn our efforts toward building a world in which we, along with our fellow humans and our progeny, can be at home. This goal we are yet far from realizing.

The issue, however, is more intricate than my brief account acknowledges. The pragmatic critique of what Dewey calls "philosophy in its classic form" is a genealogical critique; it seeks a psychological explanation for the origin of this "classic" philosophy. The title of Dewey's Gifford Lectures, *The Quest for Certainty*, conveys the substance of that critique. Since Dewey views epistemology as the intellectual pathology of grasping for security in a transcendent realm, he finds the cure for that pathology in reconstituting our understanding of knowledge and inquiry so that in knowing we no longer seek to get in touch with such realities. The term I have chosen to describe Dewey's critique of traditional epistemology—*pathology*—is one Dewey himself, so far as I know, did not use. The point of using it and of giving such a raw account of Dewey's critique is to show why the targets of his critique might properly feel he has gone too far.

The targets of Dewey's critique see him as not taking seriously our intellectual responsibility to know the truth. They feel that even if insecurity motivates our desire to know the truth, the search for truth has integrity apart from issues of its psychological origin.

Furthermore, when the targets of Dewey's critique turn aggressive, they charge him with relativism. They see relativism in Dewey's view because they see him advising us not to hope for knowledge of any reality beyond the natural world and human culture. It follows, they reason, that when we regard something as true, right, good, or beautiful, we do so because of local cultural values, values we have no reason to expect other people in different cultures to respect. We might, they fear, end up saying that Muslim, Buddhist, or Jewish religions are as "good" as Christianity—or even, as Gilbert Harman has said, that Hitler's guiding principles of action were correct for him.[6] By way of illustrating this problem that traditional thinkers find in pragmatism's critique, I can do no better than to quote the president of the Southern Baptist Theological Seminary, Albert Mohler:

> As postmodern philosopher Richard Rorty asserts, truth is made rather than found. . . . What has been understood and affirmed as truth, argue the postmodernists, is nothing more than a convenient structure of thought intended to oppress the powerless. Truth is not universal, for every culture establishes its own truth. Truth is not objectively real, for all truth is merely constructed. As Rorty stated, truth is made, not found. Little imagination is needed to see that this radical relativism is a direct challenge to the Christian gospel.[7]

Mohler's suspicion of Rorty, pragmatism, and postmodernism leads him straight to the relativism charge.

This charge is a standard critique of pragmatism, and also of postmodernism, and it is usually accompanied by the claim that such relativism is "self-defeating," or "self-referentially incoherent." This claim has been made by such eminent philosophers as Alvin Plantinga and Nicholas Wolterstorff,[8] as well as many others. Here is how the charge goes. If pragmatism is true, then either what you pragmatists say about truth is true absolutely, or it is true just for you or your culture. If it is true just for you or your culture, then the rest of us who take truth seriously need not be concerned about your opinion. If it is true absolutely, then you have defeated your own view that truth is relative. You must say one or the other. In either case, your view is inconsequential for serious thinkers, and we may ignore your relativism. The point here is that strategies designed to show that truth is relative can prove nothing to anyone unless they assume that truth is not relative; in short, any such strategy is self-defeating, or self-referentially incoherent.

The Self-Defeating Relativism Charge

The standard way pragmatists respond to this charge is to point out that it simply begs the question in favor of the kind of absolutism pragmatists reject. It does so by assuming that there are only two ways of thinking about truth: truth is either absolute or relative; either it is reality we find, or it is opinion we make. For pragmatists, both alternatives depend on conceptions of truth, knowing, and the objects of knowledge that they reject, making the charge a classic case of question begging. Pragmatists think truth is not an object of any kind to be either found or made; rather, it is an outcome of successful inquiry. Nor do they think knowing is having true, justified belief; rather, it is having a result of successful inquiry. And they think that what is known is not an object with which one manages to make cognitive contact; rather, it is something one is entitled to take for granted in future inquiry because it is a fruit of successful inquiry. William James makes this point a bit awkwardly but distinctly in "Pragmatism's Conception of Truth."[9] Dewey makes the point repeatedly; one astute expression appears in his *Logic: The Theory of Inquiry.* As Dewey puts it there, the good, the true, and the beautiful in classical theory are "hypostatizations" of "the three most generalized forms of appreciation."

> The actual basis of these absolutes is appreciation of concrete consummatory ends. In the case of intellectual, esthetic and moral experiences, the objective completion of certain unsettled existential conditions is brought about with such integrity that the final situation is possessed of peculiar excellence. There is the judgment "This is true, beautiful, good" in an emphatic sense. Generalizations are finally framed on the ground of a number of such concrete realizations. Being true, beautiful, or good, is recognized as a common character of subject-matters in spite of great differences in their actual constituents. They have, however, no meaning save as they indicate that certain subject-matters are outstanding consummatory completions of certain types of previously indeterminate situations by means of the execution of appropriate operations. Good, true, beautiful, are, in other words, abstract nouns designating characters which belong to three kinds of actually attained ends in their consummatory capacity.[10]

Though I love reading Dewey aloud—as my students can attest—I am occasionally struck by the impenetrability of his prose for those unaccustomed to hearing or reading it and by the aptness of Justice Oliver Wendell Holmes's remark on reading Dewey's *Experience and Nature:* "So methought God would have spoken had he been inarticulate but keenly desirous to tell you how it was."[11] I thus feel compelled to supply some illustrations of his point in this passage. What exactly is a "consummatory experience" anyway?

In the play *Amadeus,* when Salieri examined Mozart's music, he judged it without hesitation to be completely perfect—to be, as he put it, "the mind of God." Salieri's experience on looking at Mozart's manuscript was an instance of the experience Dewey spoke of as consummatory: a musical experience than which Salieri could conceive no better. Similarly, when Steven Weinberg, the Nobel Prize–winning physicist at the University of Texas, embraced the quark theory of particulate matter, he judged it true even if confirming evidence for all six quarks was not available; the theory was, as he put it, too beautiful not to be true. Weinberg's theory was, in Dewey's terms, an outstanding consummatory completion of a previously indeterminate situation. Thomas Kuhn quotes Wolfgang Pauli from the time just before Heisenberg resolved central issues in quantum mechanics; Pauli wrote to a friend: "At the moment physics is again terribly confused. In any case, it is too difficult for me, and I wish I had been a movie comedian or something of the sort and had never heard of physics." Less than five months later, Pauli wrote, "Heisenberg's type of mechanics has again given me hope and joy in life."[12] In Dewey's language, Pauli saw Heisenberg's quantum mechanics as consummatory; it brought harmony and order to a previously indeterminate situation. Heisenberg's theory is true, Weinberg's theory is true, and Mozart's compositions are beautiful; and they are all so because they are outstanding consummatory completions, not because they match a preexisting reality. These examples may seem to have taken us far from issues of philosophy, but they have not. For pragmatists, and especially for Dewey, these consummatory experiences, in all the guises in which they come into human experience, are focal centers of all human activities. Pragmatism is largely an effort to put words to this idea.

Pragmatists respond to the traditional thinkers' charge of relativism by saying that it is not a critique at all; it is simple, and sometimes simple-minded, question begging.

Pragmatism's Moral and Religious Resources

I promised at least a tentative account of pragmatism's moral and religious resources. The starting point for those resources must be consistent with pragmatism's rejection of the traditional idea of truth as a collection of propositions, such as those contained in the Apostle's Creed, Newton's *Principia,* or Weinberg's quark theory. Those resources must be consistent with two pragmatic tenets: the idea that belief is not an intellectual embrace of propositions and the idea that justification—by evidence or by faith—is not a special kind of relation that brings fortunate beliefs into contact with the reality they intend, the kind of relation many suppose physicists and theologians ought to provide for their claims about the world or about God. Richard Rorty puts these points succinctly by saying, "We can no longer believe that some larger power is on the side of those who pursue knowledge."[13] What is pragmatism's alternative?

One way to begin characterizing pragmatism's alternative is to say it is experiential rather than intellectual, concrete rather than abstract. A pragmatic reorientation of our moral and religious lives will thus enable and support specific ways of thinking about morality and religion that have previously received little encouragement. Still, although these ways of thinking about morality and religion differ from conventional ways, they need not undermine or compromise morality or religion. Dewey expresses this point as follows: "I have enough faith in the depth of the religious tendencies of men to believe that they will adapt themselves to any required intellectual change."[14] The pragmatic tradition shows us that an intellectual change is required, and it shows us how to make the required change.

Since a pragmatic alternative must be experiential and concrete, let me begin experientially and concretely. Each of us knows what it means to be emotionally attached to another—a child, a parent, a mentor, or a friend. In addition, our emotional attachments appear in relationships other than personal ones. During the first week of September 1997, much of the world mourned the passing of two women, Princess Diana and Mother Teresa. These women had become focal points for something almost universal in human psyches; millions all over the world genuinely grieved at their deaths. What might explain this emotional attachment to people we did not know as we know our children, our parents, and our friends? The beginnings of an account might suggest that Princess Diana and Mother Teresa were in obvious and different ways noble or virtuous or pure and that each of them expressed something fundamental in our grieving psyches. This account might extend to many other icons of contemporary culture, such as Jimmy Stewart, Martin Luther King, John and Robert Kennedy, or Mohandas Ghandi. Each of these, like Princess Diana and Mother Teresa, also became focal points for something almost universal in human psyches.

For pragmatists, however, this emotional focus on such people need not be explained. In fact, efforts to *explain* the emotionally focusing character of special individuals are, for pragmatists, a sign of the grip that the traditional Western understanding of moral and religious value has on our intellects. Philip Lawler, in a *Wall Street Journal* editorial, sought to explain the almost universal reverence for Mother Teresa by reference to her purity.[15] He claimed that many revered her deeply *because* she was pure or *because* she embodied the characteristic of purity. A pragmatist might say, by way of offering a contrasting perspective, that Mother Teresa *was* purity. Even this way of characterizing a contrasting perspective, however, is misleading without additional commentary. How might we think of Mother Teresa as herself purity? The statement seems almost oxymoronic to our conventionally Western psyches. But remember that pragmatists insist on being experiential and concrete in matters intellectual as well as practical. What makes for our grief at Mother Teresa's death is that she is herself a focal center for our values. She is not a host of something abstract—purity or virtue or love; rather, she herself *is* one focus of our moral and religious lives. She *is* a moral and religious value for us. The same may be said of the others I mentioned as possible cultural icons. Ghandi, Martin Luther King, Jimmy Stewart, John Kennedy—all are foci of our moral and religious lives. This pragmatic alternative to more conventional moral and religious thought may appear too dramatically experiential and concrete. None of the well-known pragmatists, so far as I know, says anything quite so explicit as I have said here in explicating their common commitment to the experiential and the concrete. Some do, however, point clearly in this direction.

Consider, for example, what Dewey says about moral deliberation in *Ethics:* "Deliberation is actually an imaginative rehearsal of various courses of conduct. We give way, *in our mind,* to some impulse; we try, *in our mind,* some plan. Following its career through various steps, we find ourselves in imagination in the presence of the consequences that would follow: and as we then like and approve, or dislike and disapprove, these consequences, we find the original impulse or plan good or bad. Deliberation is dramatic and active, not mathematical and impersonal."[16]

Few moral thinkers have spoken as explicitly as Dewey about what moral deliberation is, I think, because traditional Western moral thought has assumed that moral deliberation is dialectical and intellectual, that it is, to use an ugly word, ratiocinative. Again, in the pragmatic tradition, as the quotation from Dewey suggests, the experiential and the concrete come to the fore in the conception of deliberation as dramatic and active. To extend Dewey's remark about deliberation in a way he does not, as far as I know, explicitly do, we may consider how our values enter into the process of deliberation conceived as dramatic and active. They must enter that deliberative process in a form that enables them to guide our imaginative dramas—dramas that are, according to Dewey, the center of our moral deliberation. Entry into such imaginative dramas is possible only for what is concrete and experiential. To put the situation quite bluntly, we must be able to converse with our values, to see them (imaginatively) in situations about which we are deliberating, to pretend they are in our shoes or we are in their shoes. How should we treat the poor? With charity? No. We should treat the poor as Mother Teresa treated the poor. How should we behave in the presence of religious conflict? With tolerance? No. We should behave toward those who differ religiously from us as did Ghandi. Mother Teresa and Ghandi can—and do—enter into our imaginative deliberations; we can converse with them, we can imagine what they would do in our situation, and we can pretend we are in their shoes or they are in ours. Insofar as ideas such as purity, justice, courage, duty, and love (among others) are embodied, and only insofar as they are embodied, may they enter into our deliberations about action. Charity is Mother Teresa; tolerance is Ghandi. Those values are those characters, although they are not only those particular characters.

An obvious implication of this suggestion is that our values "differ." Many of us have among our values Mother Teresa and Ghandi, but for each of us there are others who also beckon toward the same goals as do Mother Teresa and Ghandi; to some extent we might say that our values differ as the characters that constitute them differ. Many of us share Ghandi and Mother Teresa. Probably only I have my father, my grandfather, and some specific others who have contributed to the shaping of my character. Fortunately, our values not only differ but also cohere and overlap, because many of us do share Mother Teresa, Ghandi, and numerous others.

The idea I am characterizing as pragmatic—as concrete and experiential—is the idea that our values are our "imagination guides," the "inner" representations who live with us and help us through our daily rounds. I should probably add that this suggestion is not the result of an effort to analyze or see into the "essence" of ideas such as purity, courage, justice, and love; rather, it is simply an effort to follow Dewey's account of moral deliberation. It is, in short, a phenomenology of moral value. In being phenomenological and descriptive, however, it challenges traditional moral philosophers to find contact between their theorizing and the phenomenologically normal sort of moral deliberation Dewey describes.

In contemporary philosophy the pragmatic perspective about morality, as I have characterized it, is represented by a diverse group of thinkers, many of whom do not see themselves as heirs of the American pragmatic tradition. Annette Baier and Martha Nussbaum, in their respective accounts of Hume and Aristotle, sympathize with the pragmatic understanding of moral value as concrete and experiential.[17] Mark Johnson argues that our understanding of moral value is irreducibly metaphorical and seeks to construct a theory of morality that takes this metaphorical content into account.[18]

This suggestion about morality is equally plausible when applied to religion. On this issue, unfortunately, prominent sources within the pragmatic tradition are vague and not as helpful as one would like. William James probably comes closest to making the suggestion in his *Varieties of Religious Experience,* where his respect for the concrete and the experiential approaches a mania. In spite of his near obsession with the religious possibilities of experience, James falls short of giving us a way of *thinking about* our religious lives. He does tell much that is useful about the religious life, but he does not tell how to move away from the idea that religious life is a matter of beliefs affirmed as true and justified—in the usual senses of truth and justification that give rise to conundrums of epistemology. He does unquestionably turn us in the right direction, for he tells us, "Philosophy lives in words, but truth and fact well up into our lives in ways that exceed verbal formulation."[19] In this respect, James's *Varieties of Religious Experience* echoes David Hume's insight that reason is at best a tool for helping us guide our passions or for making intentional headway through our already value-laden experience.

James is quite clear that our religious lives are experiential and concrete. He does not, however, connect dramatic expressions of the concrete and experiential possibilities of religious life—over which he labors at great length—to the more ordinary religious lives lived by ordinary people. What concrete and experiential possibilities of religious life do we express in our ordinary everyday trafficking with churches, synagogues, mosques, and shrines? On this issue, James is silent.

Dewey is clearer but still indirect. His book *A Common Faith* intentionally transcends religion and suggests that the religious life is self-conscious about realizing ideal goals in our communities, goals we naturally think of as part of the religious life. He even provides a conception of God alternative to that of the Western epistemological tradition; instead of viewing God as did St. Anselm, "the being than which no greater can be conceived," he offers "the unity of all ideal ends arousing us to desire and action." Many (in my experience, anyway) are completely befuddled by Dewey's offering, and sometimes they are aggressively inimical to it. Two questions arise here. (1) How does Dewey enable our thought about ordinary religious life in a way James does not? (2) How credible is Dewey's account of God?

We may begin with the latter question by asking why Dewey's formulation is somehow more obscure than Anselm's. Does one of these formulations simply better express the object of our religious commitments or sentiments? Admittedly Dewey's formulation is less familiar to us, but is it any less familiar than is, say, Dvorak to those accustomed to hearing Boccherini, Vivaldi, or Bach? Given its inevitable epistemological entanglements, Anselm's formulation is, and from the contemporary perspective appears to be, seriously burdened with theoretical difficulties we should be glad to set aside. Dewey's formulation offers an opportunity to set aside those cumbersome difficulties; it frees us from the epistemological shackles Anselm's formulation clamps on us.

Indeed, the central point of Dewey's intellectual work is precisely to free us from those shackles and related intellectual entanglements. His "unity of ideal ends" is one particular way Dewey self-consciously seeks to do so. His formulation is especially suggestive when construed in the concrete and experiential way earlier found useful in connection with moral value. In fact, reading *A Common Faith* with this thought in mind lights up many of that work's passages that might remain otherwise obscure. Consider, for example, this passage:

> Historic personages in their divine attributes are materializations of the ends that enlist devotion and inspire endeavor. They are symbolic of the reality of ends moving us in many forms of experience. . . . It is admitted that the objects of religion are ideal in contrast with our present state. What would be lost if it were also admitted that they have authoritative claim upon conduct just because they are ideal? The assumption that these objects of religion exist already in some realm of Being seems to add nothing to their force, while it weakens their claim over us as ideals, in so far as it bases that claim upon matters that are intellectually dubious.[20]

Let us ask this: for Christians, who is Jesus? Dewey's response in this passage is straightforward: Jesus is a materialization of ends that enlist devotion and inspire endeavor. Another way of putting Dewey's point is to say that Jesus is the focal center of Christians' religious lives. Jesus is the concrete and experiential religious value who serves, along with Mother Teresa, Ghandi, and others, as a central moral and religious value for Christians. This way of thinking about Jesus is not foreign to Christians, but it is controversial, and I believe it to be so because of the epistemological burdens Christianity carries in Western religious culture.

Let me put the point in summary fashion: Jesus is the center of Christians' moral and religious lives in just the way I earlier suggested Mother Teresa and Ghandi are centers of moral lives. These three are, in Dewey's words, ideal ends, and their *unity as ideal ends* is God. Mother Teresa and Ghandi sought to "follow Jesus"; accordingly, Jesus himself is the ideal end, the central religious value for Christians. Others, however, are central also—not only Mother Teresa but also St. Francis, St. Benedict, and so on. What we found to be true of moral values—that they both cohere and differ—is true also of religious values. The examples of Mother Teresa, Ghandi, St. Francis, and St. Benedict suggest that some religious values mediate others. In Dostoyevsky's novel *The Brother's Karamazov,* for example, Father Zossima mediates Jesus for Alexi; Zossima's elder brother, Markov, mediates Jesus for the priest; and Markov finds himself, in a way James would deeply appreciate, in direct contact with Jesus himself. The center of all these characters' religious lives is Jesus, but Jesus is mediated for them in different ways by different others.

Another way to think about the unity of ideal ends is not as something already achieved—as Jesus, Mother Teresa, and Ghandi are for us already achieved—but as something yet to be achieved. This conception comes to the fore when we think about religious diversity in the world. Not only is Jesus a focal center of Christians' religious lives, but Abraham and Moses are focal centers of Jews' lives, Mohammed is a focal center of Muslims' lives, and so on. The diversity of these ideal ends in different religious traditions needs mediation in the direction of unity, the unity of all ideal ends. The responsibility to effect this unity is a human responsibility. For pragmatists as I am representing them, this human responsibility involves casting off the epistemological and metaphysical conundrums of the Western philosophical tradition. Only when Christians, Muslims, Jews, and others can cast off their epistemological burdens, the burdens that require them to affirm propositional truths that others benightedly lack, will they be able to take up this essential task of seeking the unity of all ideal ends.

The last few lines of the previously quoted passage from *A Common Faith* give force to an implication of Dewey's way of thinking about God that is too little appreciated in the contemporary world. He says this: "The assumption that these objects of religion exist already in some realm of Being seems to add nothing to their force, while it weakens their claim over us as ideals, in so far as it bases that claim upon matters that are intellectually dubious."

Contemporary America is rife with people who have abandoned their religious heritage because they can no longer accept its intellectual content. They cannot believe the things they think they must believe in order to be authentic members of Jewish, Christian, Muslim, or Hindu communities. In this passage Dewey predicts and explains this phenomenon. His point is that when these religions are conceived epistemologically—as a matter of correct propositional content—they must languish; without that epistemological burden, he would add, those religions may yet flourish. He would add, I believe, that they may yet find unity.

A point similar to this one focuses on the stereotypic conflict between religion and science. The point is captured in admitting that science has already won this epistemological conflict, as it has been destined to do. Abandon the epistemological burden, the idea of correct propositional content, and the idea of a winner in that conflict loses meaning; science and religion may both flourish without worries concerning how or whether they might interfere with one another. Dewey and James also intend to save religious institutions from the ignominious fate they have suffered, and continue to suffer, at the hands of the contemporary culture of science.

I began this section by asking how credible was Dewey's account of God.

My answer is perhaps obvious. Not only is Dewey's account of God credible, but it is constructive and fruitful in efforts to *build* a kingdom of God, by comparison with which one can see that Anselm's account is an endless distraction from that task. Now, and in conclusion, I can finally move to the other question I wanted to address, how Dewey's understanding of the religious life enables our *thinking about* our religious lives.

The short answer to this question is that Dewey's understanding opens the religious life to our own understanding and empowers our religious communities by recognizing them for what they are, namely, constituents of our psyches. Dewey's religious communities are the loci of religious value; they are the loci of the stories that enable our understandings of ourselves as the historical people we are, people who possess worth and dignity because of our roles in those stories and our creative abilities to extend those stories beyond their traditional content. The communities themselves are primary, however, not because they are means to understanding the truth but because they are the locus of moral and religious value; they are our best tools in our efforts deliberately to constitute our psyches, our children, and our futures. What pragmatism tells us is that we depend completely on our communities for our values, for the stories that mold our psyches around those values, and for the continuity that makes us as well as our values possible. Our everyday religious lives are possible only in the religious communities that nurture us, our everyday moral lives become possible only in the moral communities that nurture us, our political lives become possible only in the political communities that nurture us, and so on.

This "communitarian" commitment of the American pragmatic tradition long antedates the work of those we think of in the contemporary world as communitarians; that tradition's communitarian commitment is—unlike the more reactionary-appearing thought of other contemporary communitarians—a direct result of its thought about value as freed from epistemological burdens.

Notes

1. Richard Rorty, *Philosophy and the Mirror of Nature* (Princeton, N.J.: Princeton University Press, 1979), 176; see also 174: "Explaining rationality and epistemic authority by reference to what society lets us say, rather than the latter by the former, is the essence of what I shall call 'epistemological behaviorism,' an attitude common to Dewey and Wittgenstein."

2. See the interview by Stephen Louthan, "On Religion—a Discussion with Richard Rorty, Alvin Plantinga and Nicholas Wolterstorff," reprinted in *The Christian Scholars Review* 26, no. 2 (Winter 1996): 177–83.

3. In fairness to many contemporary epistemologists, I should probably add that they think of the reality with which they seek cognitive contact as having neither moral nor religious dimensions but only physical ones. I have in mind here the Churchlands, Alvin Goldman, Fred Dretske, Lawrence Bonjour, and many others. These diminished expectations have probably been responsible for the decline of interest in developments in epistemology among not only intellectuals and academicians but also well-informed people generally.

4. John Dewey, *The Later Works of John Dewey, 1925–1953*, vol. 4, ed. Jo Ann Boydston (Carbondale: Southern Illinois University Press, 1984), 23.

5. Quine's essay is "Two Dogmas of Empiricism" and appears in his collection of essays *From a Logical Point of View* (New York: Harper and Row, 1953).

6. Gilbert Harman, "Moral Relativism Defended," *Philosophical Review* 84, no. 1 (Jan. 1975): 3–22. This essay is the first of a series in which Harman defends this view.

7. Albert Mohler, "Ministry Is Stranger Than It Used to Be: The Challenge of Postmodernism," *Southern Seminary Magazine,* Spring 1997, 4. Mohler says more in this essay about the unacceptability of postmodernism. This issue of the *Southern Seminary Magazine* contains two other essays that also criticize postmodern tendencies of thought, one by another faculty member of Southern Seminary, Thom S. Rainer, and one by Win Corduan, a professor of philosophy and religion and an associate dean of general studies at Taylor University.

8. See Alvin Plantinga's "How to Be an Anti-Realist," presidential address to Central Division, American Philosophical Association, April 29, 1982, *Proceedings and Addresses of the American Philosophical Association* 56, no. 1 (Sept. 1982): 47–70; Wolterstorff made the claim in "What Business Does Christian Learning Have in a Pluralist Society?" his presentation at the Pruit Symposium at Baylor University, November 1997.

9. In H. S. Thayer, ed., *Pragmatism: The Classic Writings* (Indianapolis, Ind.: Hackett, 1982), 227–44, esp. 236.

10. John Dewey, *The Later Works of John Dewey, 1925–1953*, vol. 12, ed. Jo Ann Boydston (Carbondale: Southern Illinois University Press, 1986), 178–79.

11. I owe this quotation to Robert Westbrook, *John Dewey and American Democracy* (Ithaca, N.Y.: Cornell University Press, 1991), 341.

12. Thomas Kuhn, *The Structure of Scientific Revolutions* (Chicago: University of Chicago Press, 1962), 84.

13. Richard Rorty, "Nietzsche and the Pragmatists," *The New Leader,* May 19, 1997, p. 9.

14. In Steven Rockefeller, *John Dewey: Religious Faith and Democratic Humanism* (New York: Columbia University Press, 1991), 75.

15. Philip Lawler, "A Life of Purity," *Wall Street Journal,* September 8, 1997. Philip Lawler is the editor of *Catholic World Report.*

16. John Dewey, *The Later Works of John Dewey, 1925–1953*, vol. 7, ed. Jo Ann Boydston (Carbondale: Southern Illinois University Press, 1985), 275.

17. Annette Baier presents her perspective on Hume in *Postures of the Mind: Essays on Mind and Morals* (Minneapolis: University of Minnesota Press, 1985) and *A Progress of Sentiments* (Cambridge, Mass.: Harvard University Press, 1991); Nussbaum's Aristotle seem to me very close to Dewey, but there are scholarly issues here that I have not adequately

addressed. Her works include *The Fragility of Goodness* (Cambridge: Cambridge University Press, 1986) and *Love's Knowledge: Essays on Philosophy and Literature* (New York: Oxford University Press, 1990).

18. Mark Johnson, *Moral Imagination* (Chicago: University of Chicago Press, 1994). I believe that Johnson's theoretical account of metaphor puts an unfortunate spin on Dewey's thought, one antithetical to the deepest spirit of Dewey's pragmatism. Dewey, I believe, intended not to reshape moral theory but to put it fully into historical and cultural perspective as a limited and no longer useful approach to thinking about morality.

19. William James, *The Varieties of Religious Experience* (New York: Penguin Books, 1983), 456.

20. John Dewey, *A Common Faith* (New Haven, Conn.: Yale University Press, 1934), 41.

16. An Uncommon Faith: Pragmatism and Religious Experience

ROBERT WESTBROOK

Before secular audiences, the pragmatists William James and John Dewey have often been called to account for sentimental squishiness on the subject of religion. Even Dewey thought James too "tender-minded" when "theological notions are under consideration," a judgment echoed widely by many since. Dewey in turn drew fire from secular comrades in the radical politics of the 1930s when, after long silence, he himself again ventured to speak well of God in *A Common Faith* (1934). "*Every* defence or justification of the idea of God, even the most refined and well-intentioned, is a justification of reaction," thundered Corliss Lamont. Nothing Dewey had ever done more clearly indicated "the necessity for honest and uncompromising minds to repudiate his leadership."[1]

On the other hand, those whose lives and thought are cast within particular religious traditions have been inclined to number Dewey, and less often James, among the cultured despisers of religion. To cite an extreme example of such criticism, Mortimer Adler declared in a notorious speech, "God and the Professors" (1940), that Dewey was an antireligious philosopher who posed a greater threat to democracy than did Hitler and called for his "liquidation."[2]

How do we explain this cross fire? How is it that these pragmatists have been numbered in our century among both the leading friends and foes of religion? As one might expect, much of the answer to this question depends on what we—or to be more precise, James and Dewey—take religion to be. The explanation for the cross fire, that is, lies in their *uncommon* faith. Three features of their engagement with religion seem to me—especially in combination—to go to the heart of the peculiarity of their faith and to the mixed reception it has received over the last hundred years. First, James and Dewey were loath to deny the unique character of religious experience, attributing to it distinctive and irreducible qualities. This view put them at odds with secular critics, especially those whom Dewey termed "aggressive atheists," eager to dismiss "everything of a religious nature."[3] Second, although they provided ample space within their philosophy for religious faith, their pragmatism made them unable (and in Dewey's case, unwilling) to warrant any theological truth claims. This theological agnosticism distanced them from more conventional religious thinkers, even those liberal Christian theologians eager to embrace them. And third, James and Dewey were disposed to treat religious experience and belief as individual experience and belief, slighting or even disparaging their communal manifestations. This disposition set them against the interests of institutionalized religion. Let me consider each of these peculiarities in turn. I will direct the preponderance of my own criticism at the last of these features of the pragmatists' thinking about religion since I think it does the most disservice to the democratic faith in which I find myself a fellow communicant with Dewey.

Religious Experience

Neither James nor Dewey can be said to have been conventionally religious. James, the son of the iconoclastic and sometimes weird Henry James Sr., followed his father in never committing himself to a creed not of his own devising. Dewey, lacerated by the piety of his evangelical mother, escaped first to a liberal Protestantism underpinned by rarified Hegelian abstractions and then to a "natural piety" that knew no church.[4] In at least one important respect, however, the religious thought of James and Dewey was resolutely and quite typically American. That is, both philosophers centered their attention on religious *experience.* In this they were at one with a deep-seated tradition in American thought, at one with Edwards, Emerson, Bushnell, and other major figures who preceded them. As William Clebsch remarked, American religious thought

> has typically asked what went on when people acted religiously. It has subordinated strictly theological questions about God to more experiential ones about men and women. . . . American religious thinkers typically adjusted their ideas of deity to religious experience, not vice versa. Typically they resisted collapsing the significance of the human spirit's earnest exercises into something other than religiousness itself, not psychology or morality, not metaphysics or theology, not doctrine or liturgy, not social or ecclesiastical institutions. . . . And typically they interpreted religious experience as coming to terms with, not as escaping from, the whole of mankind's environing universe.[5]

James and Dewey emphasized the variety of religious experience, in both its objects and emotions, yet both attributed some general, distinguishing qualities to it. "The essence of religious experiences, the thing by which we finally must judge them," James said, "must be that element or quality in them which we can meet nowhere else."[6]

Although it does considerable violence to the richness of James's religious investigations to reduce them to the sort of bare generalizations that satisfied Dewey, I think these two pragmatists shared a view of the distinctive, empirical features of religious experience. In the conclusion to *The Varieties of Religious Experience,* James argued that the "essence" of religious experience is to be found in what Dewey might have characterized as a particular sort of "problematic situation," a situation of general uneasiness about selfhood—"a sense that there is *something wrong about us* as we naturally stand"—and its resolution. As James described the dynamic of this situation, it entailed a perceived reunification of a divided self, torn between a lower "wrongness" and a higher "rightness," by means of conjoining the higher self with "a MORE of the same quality, which is operative in the universe outside of him, and which he can keep in working touch with, and in a fashion get on board of and save himself when all his lower being has gone to pieces in the wreck." This union with the "MORE" was marked by solemn joy and a surrender of will. "There is a state of mind, known to religious men, but to no others," James observed, "in which the will to assert ourselves and hold our own has been displaced by a willingness to close our mouths and be as nothing in the floods and waterspouts of God. In this state of mind, what we most dreaded has become the habitation of our safety, and the hour of our moral death has turned into our spiritual birthday."[7]

James was a "twice-born soul" disposed to dwell on the divisions and conflicts besetting the self, as Dewey, a "once-born soul," was not. The notion that "there is something wrong about us as we naturally stand" has about it the whiff of a conception of original sin, which Dewey could not abide. Dewey was also disposed to speak not of "lower" and "higher" selves but of "narrower" and "wider" selves, though the valorizations were the same. Nonetheless, Dewey's brief account of religious experience has much the same character as that ventured by James.[8] Experience, he argued, has a religious quality when it takes shape as a profound "adjustment" of self and world in the face of the problematic conditions of existence, "changes in ourselves that are much more inclusive and deep seated" than the ordinary adjustments we might make in our lives. Such changes "relate not to this or that want in relation to this and that condition of our surroundings, but pertain to our being in its entirety. Because of their scope, this modification of ourselves is enduring. It lasts through any amount of vicissitude of circumstances, internal and external. There is a composing and harmonizing of the various elements of our being such that, in spite of changes in the special conditions that surround us, these conditions are also arranged, settled, in relation to us." There is a note of "ready and glad" submission in such experience, as well as "a sense of security and peace." Such an adjustment is not the product of will but the possession of will, "a change *of* will . . . rather than any special change *in* will"; it is, moreover, "an influx from sources beyond conscious deliberation and purpose." It marks "a thoroughgoing and deep-seated harmonizing of the self with the Universe (as a name for the totality of conditions with which the self is connected)."[9]

This talk of union with the "MORE" and a harmonizing of the self with the "Universe" drew theologians, particularly such demythologizing liberal theologians as Henry Wieman, to the pragmatists.[10] (The capital letters no doubt had something to do with it). Conversely, such talk has also unnerved sympathetic secular critics, who see it as a troubling flirtation with the foundationalism that pragmatists should be determined to undermine.

The neopragmatist Richard Rorty is a good example of such a critic. Although he has of late written provocatively of the relationship between pragmatism and religion, Rorty has nothing to say about religious experience, and he wishes James and Dewey had not rooted their religious thought in its investigation. For him, religion is strictly a matter of beliefs. Experience—religious or otherwise—is a notion that he has explicitly repudiated, lamenting that James and Dewey clung to it. He numbers himself among those philosophers who "tend to talk about *sentences* a lot but to say very little about ideas or experiences, as opposed to such sentential attitudes as beliefs and desires." Having made this "linguistic turn," he regrets that his pragmatist forebears remained empiricists and, especially, that they insisted on the philosophical significance of immediate, noncognitive, nondiscursive experience, particularly insofar as it seems to him that in so doing they were attempting to ground knowledge in such experience. This strikes Rorty as the sort of epistemological foundationalism that James and Dewey in their better moments repudiated, and he will have none of it. For him, the appreciative account that James and Dewey offered of religious experience concedes too much respect to a world "not of ourselves"—by Rorty's lights, a world well lost.[11]

Religious Belief

James and Dewey both understood religious experience as nondiscursive, noncognitive experience—immediate experience that is "had" rather than "known," as Dewey put it.[12] And reflection on the meaning and implication of such experience is irresistible, even for mystics who insist on its ineffability. Religious experience, James observed, "spontaneously and inevitably engenders myths, superstitions, dogmas, creeds, and metaphysical theologies, and criticisms of one set of these by the adherents of another."[13] But if James and Dewey were guilty of the sort of foundationalist move that concerns Rorty, one might expect them to have grounded some significant truth claims in religious experience. Yet neither did so—James because, try as he might, he could not convincingly do so, and Dewey because he had no interest in even trying.

As pragmatists James and Dewey had little choice but to be theological agnostics. Their pragmatism took truth to be a human artifact and truth making to be human artifice. Reality is neither true nor false; it is simply there. Truth is a predicate not of the world but of propositions about the world. Truth making is a function, a habit of action, an evolutionary adaptation that serves to enable human beings as communities of inquiry to map their world and negotiate it in the interests of human flourishing. Propositions are true insofar as they serve as good maps, insofar as they make for untroubled journeys through the experienced world by rendering that world explicable. The only evidence for the truth of a proposition lies in present human experience, and propositions about any reality that lie outside that experience, such as the human past, can be tested only insofar as they intrude on present experience in such a way as to enable a community of inquiry to verify those propositions.

Theological propositions are for the pragmatist unverifiable because the existents they posit—God, immortal souls, and so forth—do not, even if they exist, intrude on human experience in such a way as to provide compelling evidence for their verification. James found it difficult to rest content with this conclusion. On the one hand, the only quasi-theological hypothesis that he was willing to offer for verification at the close of *The Varieties of Religious Experience* is the proposition that the subconscious self is the door through which the "more" of religious experience (whatever it is) arrives with its saving effects. On the other hand, he looked to psychic research for more compelling evidence of verifiable intrusions of incorporeal spirits, and on occasion he fudged his pragmatism so as to suggest that the rewarding consequences that follow on religious beliefs are sufficient evidence of their truth. Brought up short on this point even by fellow pragmatists such as Dewey, however, he expressed regret for any misunderstandings engendered by the looseness of his language and acknowledged that the satisfactions a belief provides are, if not incidental to its truth, insufficient to establish it.[14]

Dewey never fudged his pragmatism. Although he admitted that he could not deny "the logical possibility of the existence of a personal will which is causative and directive of the universe and which is devoted to the promotion of moral ends," he doubted that pragmatists would ever confront evidence sufficient to justify belief in such a God. Moreover, he said, "if the future of religion is bound up with really finding such justificatory evidence, I fear for the future of religion."[15]

Nevertheless, although pragmatism might fail to warrant religious beliefs as truth claims, James and Dewey were not disposed to dispense with them as faith claims, claims that both philosophers thought essential to the moral life. Although neither left much room for religious truth, both gave religious faith a wide berth. As these pragmatists saw it, this denial of truth to religion was no cause for alarm, for as Dewey said, "the realm of meanings is wider than that of true-and-false meanings; it is more urgent and more fertile. . . . A large part of our life is carried on in a realm of meanings in which truth and falsity as such are irrelevant."[16]

Both James and Dewey were willing to venture beyond the modest true-and-false meanings yielded by an empirical account of religious experience and into the realm of what James termed "overbeliefs," that is, speculative "buildings-out performed by the intellect into directions of which feeling originally supplied the hint."[17] And it was in this realm of overbeliefs that James and Dewey most clearly parted company with one another.

James's overbeliefs, if by no means orthodox or sectarian, were more conventional than Dewey's, which no doubt accounts for his greater appeal to those we would most commonly call religious. Ever eager to distinguish his views from the barren gnosticism of absolute idealism, James counted himself a "crass supernaturalist," committing himself to a theology that "admits miracles and providential leanings, and finds no intellectual difficulty in mixing the ideal and the real worlds together by interpolating influences from the ideal region among the forces that causally determine the real world's details." More peculiarly, James saw no need for an infinite God, maintaining a need only for one "both other and larger than our conscious selves." Nor was he unwilling to entertain the possibility of polytheism or of a less than omnipotent god who could not guarantee salvation. For James, "the *chance* of salvation" was enough.[18]

Dewey categorically repudiated supernaturalism. His was a religious naturalism, centered above all in moral faith. Moral faith grows out of an imaginative insight into the ideal possibilities inherent in nature and the convictions such insight engenders. "Conviction in the moral sense," Dewey said, "signifies being conquered, vanquished, in our active nature by an ideal end; it signifies acknowledgment of its rightful claim over our desires and purposes. Such acknowledgment is practical, not primarily intellectual. It goes beyond evidence that can be presented to *any* possible observer." Moral conviction takes on religious qualities when it arouses intense emotions that are "actuated and supported by ends so inclusive that they unify the self." The "unseen power" that vanquishes the will is "the power of an ideal."[19]

For Dewey religiously charged moral faith carries no guarantees; it is a faith in the possible, not the actual, the necessary, or the inevitable. An imagined possibility is not, however, an imaginary possibility; rather, it is made of "the hard stuff of the world of physical and social experience." The sense of dependence characteristic of religious experience reflects the necessary support afforded the undertakings and aspirations of individuals by the universe of relations—natural and social—in which they are embedded. "The religious experience is a reality in so far as in the midst of effort to foresee and regulate future objects we are sustained and expanded in feebleness and failure by the sense of an enveloping whole." Such experience calls for a "natural piety" that rests on "a just sense of nature as the whole of which we are parts, while it also recognizes that we are parts that are marked by intelligence and purpose, having the capacity to strive by their aid to bring conditions into greater consonance with what is humanly desirable."[20]

The controversy that swirled around *A Common Faith* centered primarily on the notion of God that Dewey offered his readers—almost as an afterthought—within this larger conception of religion as imaginative moral faith. The inclusive ends that constitute the objects of religious sentiment, he argued, are generated and supported by forces at work in nature and society and are unified by action that uses these forces. This "*active* relation between ideal and actual" is what Dewey thought merits the name *God* or *the divine,* if anything does—although he did not insist on the terms. Such a God is not a being or an antecedent existence; rather, it is a process, and usually an incomplete one at that, "a *uniting,* not something given." On the basis of this olive branch thrown to conventional religious language, Dewey found himself embroiled in debate with Wieman and other liberal theologians who declared him a closet theist. In this context he insisted that he did not mean to suggest that there is a single integrative force at work in the universe; rather, the action uniting ideal and actual is "the work of human imagination and will."[21]

As far as Dewey himself is concerned, democracy was his inclusive ideal end, the ideal that fired his moral conviction and unified his self (and his philosophy). He understood democracy to be an ethical ideal that calls on men and women to build communities in which the necessary opportunities and resources are available for every individual to realize fully his or her particular capacities and powers through participation in political, social, and cultural life; as he saw it, democracy thus construed is not an imaginary ideal but an imaginative one, a vision of possibilities in experience. Democracy, he said, "simply projects to their logical and practical limit forces inherent in human nature and already embodied to some extent in human nature. It serves accordingly as basis for criticism of institutions as they exist and of plans of betterment."[22]

Both James and Dewey exercised what James called "the will to believe" in their overbeliefs. James argued that when a belief affords a live, forced, and momentous option that cannot be decided on intellectual grounds—as religious beliefs often do—individuals are entitled to adopt the belief without awaiting a warrant to do so from human truth-making practices. "The most interesting and valuable things about a man are usually his over-beliefs," James said, and hence "we should treat them with tenderness and tolerance so long as they are not intolerant themselves." Dewey was a good deal less inclined than James to be tender toward the religious overbeliefs of others, since he found them all too often an invitation to intolerance and a premature underestimation of the range and power of the truth-making practices of scientific inquiry. Nonetheless, he did not object on principle to the will to believe and certainly exercised it himself on behalf of his own democratic faith. Both James and Dewey took especial note, in both their thought and their own faiths, of those instances in which believing that a belief will be confirmed is essential to confirming it, those cases "where a fact cannot come at all unless a preliminary faith exists in its coming, . . . where faith in a fact can help create the fact." Certainly Dewey's faith in the possibility of realizing his democratic ideal is a case in point of such belief.[23]

Affirmation of a "will to believe" (or as James sometimes wished he had put it, a "right to believe") complicates the pragmatists' distinction between warranted truth claims and unwarranted faith claims, for it suggests that in some circumstances the faithful are justified in believing the latter to be true though they are as yet unwarranted and perhaps will forever be unwarrantable by human practices. One might call this a faith claim to a truth claim. In this respect, truth and falsity are more relevant to religious belief than Dewey suggested, albeit in a distinctively pragmatic sense. According to the pragmatists, faith that an unwarranted and unfalsified belief is true can sometimes be justified by the valuable consequences that follow on believing that belief to be true, including perhaps consequences that will eventually warrant its truth. Not all consequences of a faith claim are pertinent to warranting its truth, of course, and they might establish only the benefits of believing a proposition to be true (even if it turns out to be false). But some consequences of believing a proposition to be true might be pertinent to judging its veracity, particularly in those cases where faith galvanizes truth-testing action.[24]

In any case, James and Dewey argued, unwarranted and unfalsified assumptions or postulates are essential to the moral life—and even natural science needs a few of them. Indeed, ethical and religious postulates are akin to the assumption of a uniform and law-bound natural world that governs the work of scientists and makes science possible. Like the scientist's assumption that the world is lawlike and that these laws are accessible to human intelligence, such moral and religious postulates are propositions that one must believe to be true to engage in the action necessary to test them, and the proof is in the pudding of this experimental evidence.[25] James and Dewey thus readily conceded the importance of the faithful's conviction that their beliefs are true, while at the same time rendering the warrants for such beliefs far more provisional than many believers would be willing to accept.[26]

The differences in the overbeliefs of James and Dewey are attributable, above all, to their disagreement about the usefulness to the moral life of an unwarranted belief in a supernatural God (or gods). In his conclusions to *The Varieties of Religious Experience,* James endorsed the view of his colleague James Henry Leuba that "so long as men can *use* their God, they care very little who he is, or even whether he is at all." As Leuba put it:

> *God is not known, he is not understood; he is used*—sometimes as meat-purveyor, sometimes as moral support, sometimes as friend, sometimes as an object of love. If he proves himself useful, the religious consciousness asks for no more than that. Does God really exist? How does he exist? What is he? are so many irrelevant questions. Not God, but life, more life, a larger, richer, more satisfying life, is, in the last analysis, the end of religion. The love of life, at any and every level of development, is the religious impulse.[27]

James believed that, all things considered, a belief in supernatural powers is useful to a larger, richer, more satisfying life. Dewey came to the opposite conclusion. James believed that a limited supernatural divinity—a power bigger and higher than ourselves that can promise if not guarantee salvation—provides essential support for a strenuous moral life. Dewey believed that such a life needs only the support of a natural "enveloping whole," rich in possibilities. James, in sum, believed a measure of supernaturalism serves us well. Dewey believed that supernaturalism "stands in the way of an effective realization of the sweep and depth of the implications of natural human relations."[28]

James was a liberal in the tradition of John Stuart Mill (to whom he dedicated *Pragmatism*). He was willing to let a thousand overbeliefs bloom on the condition only that no one attempt to impose his or her overbeliefs on others. He was satisfied with a neutral public sphere, naked of religious faith. Dewey was not such a liberal. He was, in the first instance, a democrat and religiously so. At the very least, he believed that democracy requires a public sphere of cooperative inquiry, deliberation, and judgment clothed in a faith in democracy itself, a naturalist civic religion. Appeals to supernatural authority have no place in such a sphere. Such appeals are, as Richard Rorty has said, a "conversation stopper" or, as Charles Peirce might have put it, a roadblock in the road of inquiry—and no charge was more damning for Dewey.[29] Because Dewey believed that supernatural overbeliefs often threaten the democratic ideals in which he vested his own faith, he tied the fate of democracy to the defeat of supernaturalism and the growth of a catholic natural piety. Unlike James's faith, Dewey's faith was a fighting faith.[30]

Religious Community

One of the most striking blind spots in the religious thought of James and Dewey is their neglect of—and sometimes contempt for—shared religious experience. This too might be said to be a characteristically American note in their thought. "It is already beginning to indicate character and religion to withdraw from the religious meetings," Emerson wrote in 1838. "Let me admonish you, first of all, to go alone; to refuse the good models, even those which are sacred in the imagination of men, and dare to love God without mediator or veil."[31] Ours after all is a religious landscape long dominated by an evangelical Protestantism favoring a largely unmediated relationship between the believer and his or her God. Even so, religious experience and belief as it appears in the analysis of James and Dewey is uncommonly un-common.

James's *Varieties of Religious Experience* is, among other things, a massive and impressive gathering of documentary evidence of religious experience. But no individual in the book is saved in church or by the ministrations of others. For the purposes of his analysis, James adopted what he admitted was an arbitrarily Emersonian definition of religion: "the feelings, acts, and experiences of individual men *in their solitude,* so far as they apprehend themselves to stand in relation to whatever they may consider the divine."[32] His is a story in which "the individual transacts the business by himself alone, and the ecclesiastical organization, with its priests and sacraments and other go-betweens, sinks to an altogether secondary place. The relation goes direct from heart to heart, from soul to soul, between man and his maker." James's account of religious experience is, moreover, an account largely of religious "geniuses." He had, he said, no interest in "your ordinary religious believer," for "his religion has been made for him by others, communicated to him by tradition, determined to fixed forms by imitation, and retained by habit." As far as James was concerned, "it would profit us little to study this second-hand religious life."[33]

Dewey's perspective on institutionalized religion was even more jaundiced than that of James. Quite early in his career Dewey became disenchanted with the Christian church, whose particularism and political conservatism he perceived as impeding the realization of his democratic ideals. In 1893 he declared that "the function of the church is to universalize itself, and thus pass out of existence."[34] By this he meant that Christians should abandon the sectarian elements of their religion and commit themselves to the universal truth embodied in scientific inquiry and democracy, an erasure of the lines dividing the secular and the spiritual that he claimed was the Christian message in the first place. Jesus taught "no special religious truths" but undivided truth, Dewey said, and "it is in democracy, the community of ideas and interest through community of action that the incarnation of God in man (man, that is to say, as organ of universal truth) becomes a living, present thing, having its ordinary and natural sense. This truth is brought down to life; its segregation removed; it is made a common truth enacted in all departments of action, not in one isolated sphere called religious."[35] Although Dewey dropped this sort of language when he stopped going to church a couple years after making these remarks, he continued to contest the divide between the sacred and the profane and the authority of the Christian church to police this boundary. In *A Common Faith* he distinguished sharply between the "religious" qualities of natural experience and institutional "religions" committed to supernaturalism, and he argued for the "emancipation" of the former from the latter and the integration of religious meanings and values into every sphere of human experience.

Given the threat that Dewey thought supernatural religion posed to his own faith, his adversarial stance toward institutionalized supernaturalism is understandable. What is less explicable in his case than in that of James is his inattentiveness to the role that institutional forms and practices—traditions, rituals, creeds, and so forth—seem of necessity to play in any faith such as his own commitment to democracy, which took its cues from "the miracle of shared life and shared experience."[36] Despite its title, *A Common Faith* treats religious experience chiefly as individual religious experience, an affair of the self, and has little to say —and even less good to say—about the common life of religious communities. One might have expected more from a critic who believed that "shared experience is the greatest of human goods" and who suggested that "the future of religion is connected with the possibility of developing a faith in the possibilities of human experience and human relationships that will create a vital sense of the solidarity of human interests and inspire action to make that sense a reality." If, as Dewey said, intersubjective human communication is "a wonder by the side of which transubstantiation pales," then it requires a sacrament.[37] So hostile was Dewey to the churches of his day that he failed to consider that they might have something to teach about the ways and means of making any faith—including his own secular democratic faith—a common one.

Had Dewey been more attentive than he was to what one might term the "expressive" dimension of democratic life, he might have been more willing to profit from the lessons that institutional religion could have provided him. This is not to say that he was altogether blind to the expressive requirements of a democratic faith. He noted with favor the saying that "if one could control the songs of a nation, one need not care who made its laws," and because he believed that "imagination is the chief instrument of the good," he burdened artists with a central role in envisioning and expressing a democratic faith.[38] But he said too little of the means by which such imaginative visions might be spread, sustained, and integrated into everyday life.

Democracy, like all faiths, requires its "geniuses." Our American democracy has been blessed with several. To my mind, these would include the following, at least: Thomas Jefferson, Ralph Waldo Emerson, Frederick Douglass, Elizabeth Cady Stanton, Abraham Lincoln, Walt Whitman, Eugene Debs, Jane Addams, Martin Luther King Jr., and John Dewey himself.[39] But a faith must be attentive to the needs of its ordinary believers as well and provide them with rituals, festivals, hymns, prayers, passion plays, and scriptural documents, including sacred books and tales of saints and martyrs. For if a democratic faith is to survive, it must shape the building of an unsteepled church.

Notes

1. John Dewey, "What Pragmatism Means by Practical" (1908), in *The Middle Works of John Dewey, 1899–1924*, vol. 4, ed. Jo Ann Boydston (Carbondale: Southern Illinois University Press, 1977), 109; Corliss Lamont, "John Dewey Capitulates to God," *New Masses,* July 31, 1934, p. 23; Lamont, "The Right Reverend Re-Definer," *New Masses,* October 2, 1934, p. 38. I will say nothing about the religious thought of the third of pragmatism's founders, Charles S. Peirce, partly out of ignorance and partly because what I do know of Peirce's religious philosophy strikes me as less "uncommon" than that of the three pragmatists I do consider. For example, Peirce's "Neglected Argument for the Reality of God," while peculiar in some important respects, is still an "argument from design," a long-standing pillar of religious belief within American culture. See Peirce, "A Neglected Argument for

the Reality of God," in *Peirce on Signs*, ed. James Hoopes (Chapel Hill: University of North Carolina Press, 1991), 260–78. For evidence of the persistence of the argument from design at all levels of American culture, see James Gilbert, *Redeeming Culture: American Religion in an Age of Science* (Chicago: University of Chicago Press, 1997). See also a recent, controversial version of this argument by the biologist Michael J. Behe in his book *Darwin's Black Box: The Biochemical Challenge to Evolution* (New York: Free Press, 1996).

2. Mortimer Adler, "God and the Professors," *Vital Speeches*, December 1, 1940, pp. 100, 102. One imagines that while Adler might have been willing to offer James a stay of execution and Dewey a relatively painless death, he would be inclined to have the neopragmatist Richard Rorty drawn and quartered.

3. John Dewey, *A Common Faith*, in *The Later Works of John Dewey, 1925–1953*, vol. 9, ed. Jo Ann Boydston (Carbondale: Southern Illinois University Press, 1986), 3, 36.

4. The fullest accounts of the religious thought of James and Dewey are Henry S. Levinson, *The Religious Investigations of William James* (Chapel Hill: University of North Carolina Press, 1981); and Steven C. Rockefeller, *John Dewey: Religious Faith and Democratic Humanism* (New York: Columbia University Press, 1991).

5. William A. Clebsch, *American Religious Thought* (Chicago: University of Chicago Press, 1973), 3–4.

6. William James, *The Varieties of Religious Experience* (1902), in James, *Writings, 1902–1910* (New York: Library of America, 1987), 8.

7. Ibid., 454, 49–50.

8. Although Dewey did not say so explicitly, there is some evidence that he built on *The Varieties of Religious Experience*. See Dewey, *A Common Faith*, 10, 14. As Steven Rockefeller says, what Dewey found in James's investigations was "the demonstration that by adopting an empirical and functional approach and by defining what is distinctly religious about an experience with reference to its consequences and quality, it is possible to develop a naturalistic theory of religious experience which does not necessarily require the idea of the supernatural or presuppose one special object, emotion, or kind of action that is uniquely religious" (Rockefeller, *John Dewey*, 471). Richard Rorty denies that Dewey would endorse the account of religious experience James offered ("Pragmatism as Romantic Polytheism," in *The Revival of Pragmatism*, ed. Morris Dickstein [Durham, N.C.: Duke University Press, 1998], 31). But if one lends that account a once-born, "healthy-minded" reading, I think Dewey could accept it—provided, of course, he was afforded the opportunity to repudiate any "overbeliefs" attached to terms such as the "MORE." In his description of Dewey's religious thought, Rorty seems to me to neglect those aspects of Dewey's metaphysics—his "natural piety," his respect for that in nature which is "not ourselves"—that put him in sympathy with such accounts. This neglect is not surprising since Rorty has little sympathy with Dewey's metaphysics.

9. Dewey, *A Common Faith*, 12–14.

10. On Dewey's debate with liberal theologians, see Rockefeller, *John Dewey*, 512–40.

11. Richard Rorty, "Dewey between Hegel and Darwin," in *Modernist Impulses in the Human Sciences, 1870–1930*, ed. Dorothy Ross (Baltimore, Md.: Johns Hopkins University Press, 1994), 55; Rorty, "Romantic Polytheism," 30–34. As I noted, Rorty thinks Dewey avoided James's "mistakes," whereas I do not. His response to my suggestion that James and Dewey shared an account of religious experience more similar than different would

no doubt be something like this: "Well, I am not so sure, but if you are right, then Dewey too made a bad move." Richard Shusterman offers an effective rebuttal to Rorty's claim generally to find epistemologically foundational intentions or consequences in Dewey's account of immediate, nondiscursive experience, as well as a set of compelling reasons pragmatists might want to hang onto a notion of such experience. See "Somatic Experience: Foundation or Reconstruction?" in Shusterman, *Practicing Philosophy: Pragmatism and the Philosophical Life* (New York: Routledge, 1997), 157–77. Shusterman does, however, take note of one important instance in which he finds Dewey guilty as charged; see John Dewey, "Qualitative Thought" (1930), in *The Later Works of John Dewey, 1925–1953,* vol. 5, ed. Jo Ann Boydston (Carbondale: Southern Illinois University Press, 1984), 243–62.

12. See John Dewey, *Experience and Nature* (1929), in *The Later Works of John Dewey, 1925–1953,* vol. 1, ed. Jo Ann Boydston (Carbondale: Southern Illinois University Press, 1981), 27–28.

13. James, *Varieties,* 389.

14. Dewey, "What Pragmatism Means," 104–12; William James, *The Meaning of Truth* (1909), in James, *Writings, 1902–1910,* 925.

15. John Dewey, "Dr. Dewey Replies" (1933), in *The Later Works of John Dewey,* 9:227–28.

16. Dewey, *Experience and Nature,* 307.

17. James, *Varieties,* 388.

18. Ibid., 464–69.

19. Dewey, *A Common Faith,* 15, 17.

20. Ibid., 15, 17.

21. Ibid., 34–35; Dewey, "Dewey Replies," 226.

22. John Dewey, *Ethics* (1932), in *The Later Works of John Dewey, 1925–1953,* vol. 7, ed. Jo Ann Boydston (Carbondale: Southern Illinois University Press, 1985), 349. See also J. H. Randall Jr., "The Religion of Shared Experience," in *The Philosopher of the Common Man,* ed. Sidney Ratner (New York: Putnam's, 1940), 106–45.

23. James, *Varieties,* 460; William James, "The Will to Believe" (1897) in James, *Writings, 1878–1899* (New York: Library of America, 1992), 458, 464, 474.

24. In defending religious belief, James sometimes muddled his pragmatist defense of the right to believe so as to lend truth-testing authority to consequences of belief that could not bear it. See William James, *Pragmatism* (1907), in James, *Writings, 1902–1910,* 606–19. James was much more willing than Dewey to lend the support of pragmatism to the right to beliefs that were not only (at present) unwarranted and unfalsified but might well be forever unwarrantable and unfalsifiable—on the grounds that holding such beliefs to be true had desirable consequences other than testing their truth.

25. Dewey made this comparison between scientific and ethical or religious postulates early in his career in his *Outlines of a Critical Theory of Ethics* (1891), in *The Early Works of John Dewey, 1882–1898,* vol. 3, ed. Jo Ann Boydston (Carbondale: University of Illinois Press, 1969), 320–23.

26. The critic James Wood has said dubiously of the "as-if" religious thinking characteristic of the pragmatists that "in religion, a belief that is only 'as if' is either the prelude to a loss of faith, or an instance of bad faith (in both senses of the phrase). If religion is

true, one must believe" (*The Broken Estate: Essays on Literature and Belief* [New York: Modern Library, 2000], xii). For pragmatists, faith is as-yet-unwarranted belief (which is not to say that it is belief without any evidence). Faith is plagued by doubt. James might say to Wood that "as-if" belief is a prelude to a loss of faith only insofar as acting as if a belief is true fails to produce the anticipated consequences. He would argue that often one must believe if religion is to be "made" true.

27. James, *Varieties*, 453.

28. Dewey, *A Common Faith*, 53. As Dewey saw it, "the extreme position on one side is that apart from relation to the supernatural, man is morally on a level with the brutes. The other position is that all significant ends and all securities for stability and peace have grown up in the matrix of human relations, and that the values given a supernatural locus are in fact products of an idealizing imagination that has laid hold of natural goods. There ensues a second contrast. On the one hand, it is held that relation to the supernatural is the only finally dependable source of motive power; that directly and indirectly it has animated every serious effort for the guidance and rectification of man's life on earth. The other position is that goods actually experienced in the concrete relations of family, neighborhood, citizenship, pursuit of art and science, are what men actually depend upon for guidance and support, and that their reference to a supernatural and other-worldly locus has obscured their real nature and has weakened their force" (*A Common Faith*, 47).

29. Richard Rorty, "Religion as Conversation-Stopper," *Common Knowledge* 3 (1994): 1–6. Rorty seems to me want to have it both ways in his recent work on religion and pragmatism. On the one hand, he wants a kind of Millian division between a self-regarding private sphere in which religious belief may flourish and an other-regarding public sphere in which it is banned. "In a democratic society," he says, "everybody gets to worship his or her personal symbol of ultimate concern, unless worship of that symbol interferes with the pursuit of happiness by his or her fellow-citizens" ("Romantic Polytheism," 33). On the other hand, he endorses Dewey's democratic faith and explicitly labels it a "civic religion" ("Something to Steer By," *London Review of Books*, June 20, 1996, p. 8). Rorty tries in good liberal fashion to avoid the contradiction this implies by reducing democratic public life and its civic religion to little more than a commitment to tolerance. Dewey imagined a considerably thicker democratic public life, but be that as it may, even a thin civic religion that takes tolerance as its ultimate concern remains a civic religion. Liberalism, as a number of critics have said of the notion of a "neutral state" advanced by some liberal theorists, can never be fully neutral regarding what constitutes a good life. Moreover, Rorty at times conceives of public life as a realm of social cooperation and practices designed to reach intersubjective agreement. This thicker notion of the public sphere seems to me—as it did to Dewey—to rest on the faith that such practices ("conversation") are a better means for guiding our common life than appeals to authority, divine or otherwise. In sum, it seems to me that Rorty's project is much the same as Dewey's: he wants to drain democracy of supernaturalism. Unlike Dewey, however, Rorty tries to avoid the conclusion that this itself is an act of faith. Hence, if Rorty owns up to the fact that even the thin liberal democracy he advocates cannot do without some sort of civic religion, then his thinking points to a "polytheism" in which different gods would be worshiped in different spheres. Dewey thought such a polytheism is unstable since the gods in question will be warring gods, ever eager to invade the spheres of the others. The recent char-

acter of American politics suggests that he was correct. See also Richard Rorty, "Religous Faith, Intellectual Responsibility, and Romance," in *The Cambridge Companion to William James,* ed. Ruth Anna Putnam (New York: Cambridge University Press, 1997), 84–102.

30. He used the language of war to describe his struggle. For example, "I cannot understand how any realization of the democratic ideal as a vital moral and spiritual ideal in human affairs is possible without *surrender* of the conception of the basic division [between the saved and the lost] to which supernatural Christianity is committed" (Dewey, *A Common Faith,* 55–56, my emphasis).

31. Ralph Waldo Emerson, "Divinity School Address" (1838), *Essays and Lectures* (New York: Library of America, 1983), 87, 88–89.

32. James, *Varieties,* 36 (my emphasis).

33. Ibid., 34, 15.

34. John Dewey, "The Relation of Philosophy to Theology" (1893), in *The Early Works of John Dewey, 1882–1898,* vol. 4, ed. Jo Ann Boydston (Carbondale: Southern Illinois University Press, 1971), 367.

35. John Dewey, "Christianity and Democracy" (1892), in *Early Works,* 4:9.

36. John Dewey, *Reconstruction in Philosophy* (1920), in *The Middle Works of John Dewey, 1899–1924,* vol. 12, ed. Jo Ann Boydston (Carbondale: Southern Illinois University Press, 1982), 201.

37. Dewey, *Experience and Nature,* 145, 132; John Dewey, "What I Believe" (1930), in *The Early Works of John Dewey 1882–1898,* vol. 5, ed. Jo Ann Boydston (Carbondale: Southern Illinois University Press, 1984), 273–74.

38. John Dewey, *Freedom and Culture* (1939), in *The Later Works of John Dewey, 1925–1953,* vol. 13, ed. Jo Ann Boydston (Carbondale: Southern Illinois University Press, 1988), 70; John Dewey, *Art as Experience* (1934), in *The Later Works of John Dewey, 1925–1953,* vol. 10, ed. Jo Ann Boydston (Carbondale: Southern Illinois University Press, 1987), 350.

39. As some of these exemplars suggest, a supernaturalist religious faith is not incompatible with democratic commitments. Dewey argued that figures such as these had "supernaturalized" their democratic faith, that their beliefs were "an idealization of things characteristic of natural associations, which have then been projected into a supernatural realm for safe-keeping and sanction" (*A Common Faith,* 48). He argued that such a supernaturalization does more harm than good in the long run. Like Rorty, he called for a "de-theologized" social gospel that will disengage Christian ideals of fraternity from Platonism (Rorty, "Romantic Polytheism," 26–27).

PART 3

Theism, Secularism, and Religion: Seeking a Common Faith

Notes on Authors

RAYMOND D. BOISVERT is a professor of philosophy at Siena College. His published works include *John Dewey: Rethinking our Time* (Albany, N.Y.: SUNY Press, 1998) and *Dewey's Metaphysics* (New York: Fordham University Press, 1988).

SANDRA B. ROSENTHAL is the provost and a Distinguished Professor of Philosophy at Loyola University. Her publications include *Time, Continuity, and Indeterminacy: A Pragmatic Engagement with Contemporary Perspectives* (Albany, N.Y.: SUNY Press, 2000), *Charles Peirce's Pragmatic Pluralism* (Albany, N.Y.: SUNY Press, 1994), *Mead and Merleau-Ponty: Toward a Common Vision* (Albany, N.Y.: SUNY Press, 1991), and *Speculative Pragmatism* (Amherst: University of Massachusetts Press, 1986).

NANCY K. FRANKENBERRY is a professor of religion at Dartmouth College. Her published works include *Religion and Radical Empiricism* (Albany, N.Y.: SUNY Press, 1987) and the coedited anthologies *Interpreting Neville* (Albany, N.Y.: SUNY, 1999) and *Language, Truth, and Religious Belief: Studies in Twentieth-Century Theory and Method in Religion* (Atlanta: Scholars, 1999).

CARL G. VAUGHT is a Distinguished Professor of Philosophy at Baylor University. His publications include *The Quest for Wholeness* (Albany, N.Y.: SUNY Press, 1982), *The Sermon on the Mount: A Theological Interpretation* (Albany, N.Y.: SUNY Press, 1986), and *The Journey toward God in Augustine's Confessions* (Albany, N.Y.: SUNY Press, 2003).

ROBERT C. NEVILLE is a professor of philosophy and the dean of the School of Theology at Boston University. His publications include *The Cosmology of Freedom: New Edition* (Albany, N.Y.: SUNY Press, 1996), *Creativity and God: A Challenge to Process Theology* (Albany, N.Y.: SUNY Press, 1995), *Eternity and Time's Flow* (Albany, N.Y.: SUNY Press, 1993), and *The High Road around Modernism* (Albany, N.Y.: SUNY Press, 1992).

STEVEN C. ROCKEFELLER is an emeritus professor of religion at Middlebury College. His publications include *John Dewey: Religious Faith and Democratic Humanism* (New York: Columbia University Press, 1991); the coauthored volume *The Christ and the Bodhisattva* (Albany, N.Y.: SUNY Press, 1998); and the coedited volume *Spirit and Nature: Why the Environment Is a Religious Issue* (Boston: Beacon, 1992).

17. What Is Religion?
A Pragmatist Response

RAYMOND D. BOISVERT

Venice is home to a church with the unusual name "Madonna of the Orchard." Initially it was to be consecrated to St. Christopher, the patron of travelers, but he was displaced by a miraculous event. Wanderers in a nearby orchard found a statue of the Madonna. Such a find would lead today's parishioners to ask a simple question: who put it there? To long-ago parishioners, however, the event evinced supernatural intervention. The statue, they believed, could only have fallen out of heaven. This "miracle" was an event best commemorated by renaming the church.

John Searle, who heard this story while teaching in Venice, relates it to show how removed we are from our medieval ancestors. Today not only ordinary people but even church officials would express skepticism. The statue-falling-out-of-the-sky story "is not a possible thought for us because, in a sense, we know too much."[1] Knowing so much leads us to take for granted a natural, nonmiraculous view of things. We no longer need fall back on faith or religious mysteries to explain what seems inexplicable. The puzzling has been transformed into the someday-to-be-explained. "Odd occurrences," according to Searle, "are just occurrences that we do not understand."[2] We have traveled so far that even our immediate predecessors seem antiquated. John Stuart Mill and Bertrand Russell had "mounted polemical and eloquent attacks on traditional religion." "Nowadays nobody bothers, and it is considered in slightly bad taste to even raise the question of God's existence."[3] God and religion, Searle is saying, were once formidable foils for the liberated intellect. They have now dwindled to the status of mere irrelevancies, nothing but cultural remnants from a less enlightened time.

Within the world of neopragmatism, Richard Rorty echoes the Searle-style attitude about frowned-upon topics. The main hero for his neopragmatist revival has been the most secular of the seminal figures, John Dewey. Rorty, though, goes one step further than the nuanced Dewey, who sought to preserve the "religious" without "religion."[4] When Rorty's own predilections are factored in, the multidimensional Dewey who left us subtle formulations is transformed into a one-dimensional thinker whose work was an attempt to redescribe America in terms of "thoroughgoing secularism."[5] The case is now closed. Although "privatized religious belief" is tolerated, secularism is the only real public position for pragmatists.[6] Religion was once a robust and intellectually respectable force in culture. The Enlightenment changed all that. Of course, something that had been "central to Western intellectual life" was lost, but "the Enlightenment thought, rightly, that what would succeed religion would be *better*."[7] Having inherited this "better" legacy, we would act in bad taste indeed by reintroducing a topic that, presumably, can only make things worse.

Hoping neither to make things worse nor violate canons of good taste, I nonetheless wish to revisit the position that Searle and Rorty so neatly relegate to an outdated past. Contemporary descendants of pragmatism, drawing both on their own heritage as well as on wider philosophical developments, can reconceptualize the issues of religion and secularism in a way that makes them once again respectable topics of discussion. Such, at least, will be the aim of this essay. If it is provocative enough to restore these issues to the realm of good taste, then it will have been generally successful. Success in a more specific manner will result if religious perspectives remain open options, as they have been from the beginning of pragmatism. The manner of reaching this destination may offer some surprises. Theism and atheism will be largely ignored and considered marginal in determining the dividing line between secularism and religion. Clues for reconceptualizing religion and secularism will come from an area usually slighted by philosophers, reflection on food. Creating a neologism by switching one vowel, I will provide a terminological key for the transformation. I will then link this neologism, *symbal*, to the construction of the "ligature line," a pragmatically suitable way of sorting out the secular from the religious. Without settling whether one should adhere to any particular point on the ligature line, this essay will provide the groundwork for avoiding disjunctive formulations and for embracing the testimony of various religious traditions.

Pragmatism is well suited for pluralizing an issue and keeping it an open question. It is built around a web of principles that discourage totalizing pronouncements. That web, briefly summarized, includes the following dimensions. (1) Pragmatism is rooted in the *life world,* a realm that is thick, rich, and so multidimensional that intellectual attempts to categorize it are bound to oversimplify. Our formulations, according to William James, "are like stereoscopic or kinetoscopic photographs seen outside the instrument; they lack the depth, the motion, the vitality."[8] Eliminative or exclusionary attitudes, especially those substituting the result of some specialized study as *the* only story about reality, are immediately suspect in pragmatism. (2) Consistent with its emphasis on the life world, pragmatism highlights the centrality of *practice.* Humans are considered as engaged individuals, concerned with, as Dewey puts it, "use and enjoyment." Our practices are both a source of philosophical inspiration and a component to consider in adopting any philosophical position. (3) Because practice is taken seriously, *experience* becomes the most adequate term for describing human interaction with the world. Dewey selected experience to block the more typical philosophical attitude that he called the "spectator" view. Pragmatism here counters the tendency, prominent since the seventeenth century, of reducing humans to *epistemological subjects,* that is, essentially minds receiving and processing data from the external world. A botanist may take a detached, specialized attitude in examining the cellular structures of flowers, but this must not be confused with human experience in "in all its heterogeneity and fullness."[9] (4) If we pay attention to experience, refusing to fit data into preconceived categories, *pluralism* becomes the most defensible statement of pragmatist ontology. Pragmatism resists what I have elsewhere called the "Plotinian temptation,"[10] the fascination with always seeking unities that underlie multiplicity. It is comfortable with the testimony of experience, which admits an irreducible multiplicity. Thinking in terms of a *range* of possibilities is a position congenial to pragmatists.

This cluster of traits, *rootedness in the life world, the centrality of practice, experience as revelatory,* and *the irreducibility of pluralism,* identifies the background assumed for any pragmatist discussion. Of these traits, the centrality of practice is the most significant in a discussion of pragmatism's grappling with religion. What does it mean for pragmatists to claim that the life world is conditioned continually by praxis? It means that, unlike academic philosophers, who tend to overgeneralize from their self-appointed roles as specialized thinkers, most humans most of the time (and even professional philosophers much of the time) are engaged participants in varied life processes concerned with meaning and direction. The farmer milking a cow or tapping a maple tree, the father building a swing set in the backyard, the friend helping repair a car, the mother balancing a checkbook, city planners worried about congestion, rural residents digging a well, neighbors gathered for a Fourth of July cookout—these exemplify the practices that pragmatism wishes to recognize. The academic philosopher, by contrast, wondering whether the objects of the world are real, or what the world would be like if it were blue, or whether a brain in a vat, suitably wired to receive impulses, would be fooled into thinking it has a body, assumes if not the irrelevance of daily practices then at least their marginalization for the purposes of philosophizing. Many problems occupying professional philosophers, especially those related to skepticism, would simply disappear if the representative actions of humans were those of doing or working with things, not those of standing apart and wondering about them.

The two ambients, that of the ordinary individual and that of the professional philosopher, offer themselves as alternative starting points for philosophical work. The anecdote about the Madonna of the orchard helps crystallize the difference. For Searle, religion depends on ignorance. It is not primarily a set of practices reflecting and reinforcing a grasp of our place in the whole scheme of things. Instead, religion is primarily a cognitive alternative to science. As such, its prominence in history would crest in periods that could take seriously the divine act of dropping a statue into an orchard. Our world, however, "has become demystified."[11] We now "know too much" to consider puzzling events and occurrences as "expressions of supernatural meaning."[12] They are simply events not yet understood.

This is a sensible position. If religion, at its center, is a cognitive enterprise dependent primarily on miraculous intrusions into everyday life, then there is not much room for it in our demystified world. In this context religion depends on the existence of a divinity who not only intervenes but does so in ways that, by definition, are beyond human powers of comprehension. Such a divinity will always be retreating in the face of more refined techniques of explanation. In a sense this divinity must retreat, since it has been predefined as the alternative to science. Credulous religious followers tend make this characterization easy, as does the predilection of the epistemological subject to dismiss as irresolvable issues that cannot be made amenable to scientific treatment.[13] Pragmatists, by contrast, do not assume the status of epistemological subjects as the primordial one for humans. Thinking of humans as participants in practices, the pragmatist can, without sacrificing thought and truths, rethink the formulations of central philosophical questions.

For the present discussion, a key move will be to think of religion not primarily in terms of belief in a divinity as source of the miraculous and as explanation of the inexplicable. Rather, religions (now pluralized) are to be considered initially as characterized by practices. In this way what was once figure becomes ground, and vice versa. The pattern for thinking of religions in this way is not unusual. It has been made prominent by anthropologists such as Clifford Geertz. "Whatever role divine intervention may or may not play in the creation of faith—and it is not the business of the scientist to pronounce upon such matters one way or the other—it is, primarily at least, out of the context of concrete acts of religious observance that religious conviction emerges on the human plane."[14] The concrete acts Geertz mentions do not develop in a vacuum. They grow within contexts that accept a particular awareness of the way things are. By listening to commentators on religious traditions, we can gain some sense of the attitudes toward things in general that are coordinated with the practices.

Describing the world of African peoples, John Mbiti claims that "because traditional religions permeate all the departments of life, there is no formal distinction between the sacred and the secular, between the religious and non-religious, between the spiritual and the material areas of life. . . . To be human is to belong to the whole community, and to do so involves participating in the beliefs, ceremonies, rituals and festivals of that community."[15] The last part of this quotation is the most significant. Beliefs are recognized. They are important, but they form only one component in a way of life carried out via practices: ceremonies, rituals, and festivals. The practices, in other words, are not incidental accompaniments, accidental appendages to the centerpiece, a separate entity called religion, and defined primarily in terms of one aspect of life, that devoted to an individualized relationship with a divinity. Indeed, so pervasive is the religious dimension in traditional cultures that many African languages have no separate word for religion.[16]

"More than a form of belief, religion is a matter of practice," Catherine Albanese asserts in her study of religions in America. "Body and emotions play as large a role in a living religion as philosophical concepts."[17] This is a puzzling assertion unless it is understood in the wider context supplied by Mbiti. Emphasis on beliefs is not denied. Creeds are not ignored. On the widest perspective, however, taking into account religions of all sorts, from the religion of the Hopi to Tibetan Buddhism, Vodou, and that of the Yoruba or the Wolof, what emerges as integral are sets of practices associated with a way of grasping the overall situatedness of the community within what it accepts as the pervasive pattern of reality. Childbirth, puberty, marriage, death, disease, and the seasons are accompanied by practices that solidify the community and reinforce a self-understanding of its place within the nature of things.

Matthieu Ricard is a Buddhist monk. He also holds a Ph.D. in molecular biology and is the son of Jean-François Revel, the French philosopher noted for his book *Neither Marx nor Jesus*. Revel's work has contributed eloquently to the liberal post-Enlightenment tradition that has cast suspicion on both religion and totalitarian politics. His son, unhappy with what he perceived to be the emptiness of a secular attitude, decided as a mature man to leave the laboratory for life as a Buddhist monk. An engaging dialogue between father and son has been translated as *The Monk and the Philosopher: A Father and Son Discuss the Meaning of Life.*

What Ricard says early in the book reinforces the importance of practice. "There are a lot of very interesting things in Buddhism, but it's important not to lose yourself in purely theoretical book study. It might distract you from practice, which is the very heart of Buddhism and all inner transformation."[18] This reverses the usual way of thinking. Instead of knowledge followed by practice, there is practice leading to enlightenment. Without the practice, the enlightenment cannot come. Such stress on the importance of practice, although often overlooked by intellectuals who see themselves (and by extension all others) as epistemological subjects, is nonetheless present even in the religious traditions familiar to Western philosophers. Consider the testimony of Kathleen Norris, the poet who has left us some remarkable lessons from her rediscovery of religion's power, in her case that of Christianity. "Conversion doesn't offer a form of knowledge that can be bought and sold, quantified or neatly packaged. It is best learned slowly and in community, the way a Native American child learns his or her traditional religion, the way an adult learns to be a Benedictine, not by book learning or weekend workshops but by being present at the ceremonies."[19]

The phrase "being present at the ceremonies" should not be taken to eliminate the cognitive dimension of religious practices. Rather, it should be taken as a way of underscoring what the epistemological subject tends to marginalize, the embodied and encultured mode of responding to a general conception of the way things are. Religions, practitioners tell us, are not just matters of responding in awe to a divinity who can dispense miracles and explain the inexplicable. Indeed, the Tibetan Buddhism practiced by Ricard dispenses not only with divinity of this sort but with any divinity at all.[20]

To accommodate Buddhism as a religion, and to provide some concrete manner for sorting out secularism from religion, I will begin in a way most philosophers would consider unusual: discussing an ordinary practice celebrated yearly. As with all practices, it is embodied and encultured. What is special in this case is that the practice occurs in a situation where individuals are denied the opportunity for ceremonies of situatedness. We are in what Jaspers called *Grenzsituationen,* those ultimate or boundary conditions that tend to occasion serious reflection about the human condition and our place in it. The scene is as follows: a child holds in her hand a lump of mashed potatoes to which some sugar has been added. Circumstances, though, occasion the participants to violate, symbolically at least, the principle of noncontradiction. It is the early 1940s. The place is Terezin, a transit camp for Jews in Czechoslovakia. The date is an anniversary of the child's birth. The food in her hand is no longer a serving of potatoes. It has become a birthday cake.[21] The inmates are celebrating what might be called a "ceremony of situatedness." Not only is a birthday being commemorated, but the child's place within social geography is being reinforced. Processes of dehumanization and ceremonies of situatedness are inversely related to one another. Although lacking physical weapons for fighting their captors, the prisoners fought dehumanization by attempting to preserve practices associated with ordinary life.

One commentator, attempting to explain inmate life at Terezin, uses the language of spirit. A simple event, in this case the practice of commemorating a birthday, becomes a "revolt of the spirit."[22] *Spirit* and *spiritual* are words with a lengthy history. Originally *spirit* translated the Greek *pneuma*, which means "breath." Eventually it came to be associated with the soul and with an aspect of life opposed to matter. But the original meaning of breath is still relevant when speaking of the "spiritual revolt" at Terezin.[23] The prisoners realized that the ultimate purpose of incarceration was to extinguish their communal breath. That wider spirit resided not in any single individual but in a people with overlapping inspirations and aspirations, clusters of criss-crossing traditions and beliefs, rituals, and holidays. How did the inmates combat asphyxiation? Under impossible conditions, some camp women developed an imaginative way to keep the community breathing: they remembered recipes. In fact, they not only remembered them but had heated discussions about the "right" way to prepare favorite foods such as Viennese dumplings and chocolate strudel. They also wrote down the recipes, hoping that the spirit embodied in the written word would survive this ordeal.[24]

The book that relates the story of these women is called *In Memory's Kitchen*. Neither philosophically rigorous nor sophisticated, it consists of recipes copied down in the camp. Prominent academic philosophers would almost certainly dismiss it as marginal to their professional interests. This would be a mistake. Precisely because these women situate us in a life world different from that of professional philosophy, they can help open new paths for philosophical reflection. Caught in an extreme and deadly environment, their response can guide us toward the reconfiguration of the conceptual network commonly associated with discussions of religion. The reconfigured web of concepts will allow a different, more nuanced, and more open approach than that provided by Searle and Rorty. Two images from the realm of practice will guide my reflections: the little girl's handful of potatoes and the women's copying down recipes on hard-to-find paper. Conceptually the terms *symbol* and *religion* will play key roles. Etymologies will help retrieve meanings useful in guiding my analysis. One neologism, the transformation of *symbol* into *symbal,* will minimize ambiguity (if Derrida can switch vowels, so can pragmatists). *Symbal* will provide the terminological catalyst for removing us from the orbit that has been dominant in post-Enlightenment philosophy. If successful, the new approach will be consistent with a pluralism that does not identify a single alternative as *the* genuinely pragmatist one. At the same time, it will provide novel yet definitive criteria for distinguishing secularity from religion.

For articulating such an alternative, we must return to Terezin and the book *In Memory's Kitchen.* "Food" says the introduction, "is who we are in the deepest sense, and not because it is transformed into blood and bone. Our personal gastronomic traditions—what we eat, the foods and foodways we associate with the rituals of childhood, marriage, and parenthood, moments around the table, celebrations—are critical components of our identities."[25] Indeed, the ingredients in our identities extend even beyond the social plane articulated in this quotation. Food and food practices take us further than social relationships. If we take them seriously as philosophical starting points, they attest not only to a sociology of alliances and connections but to an ontology that admits ligatures, threads of conjunction between ourselves and the life world at large.

Much of modern philosophy, in its anthropocentric pursuit of epistemological questions, has marginalized important metaphysical issues that occupied classical philosophers such as Aristotle. Asking "What is being?" does not set off a flurry of excitement today. Still, we work with a set of assumptions that take for granted some answers about the character of the ambient of which we form a part. The question, "What are the generic traits of existence that must be taken into account if we are to situate ourselves properly?" may be a nonexciting mouthful, but it is important. In his essay on religion, Geertz pointed out that "religion tunes human actions to an envisaged cosmic order."[26] He might have added that all of us, religious or not, tune human actions to whatever cosmic construal we accept as most reasonable. Assuming, for example, that the components of our ambient are related to one another as are the constituents of a "pile of shot," to use a happy phrase from Russell, gives a particular handle on things that leads to some version of social atomism as a consistent extension. Another response, one closer to pragmatist philosophy and postecological science, is that the life world is marked to a great degree by interconnections and interrelationships. It is more like a cell than a pile of shot.

Testimony supporting the latter characterization can be found in the sciences. Peter Coveney and Roger Highfield put it this way in their explanation of contemporary developments in physics: "Even the behavior of some of the simplest of mechanical systems cannot be described in the complete and deterministic Newtonian manner previously thought possible. There is no simple algorithm to turn to. Instead, we must try to understand the world in more global terms, through the *interactions* between its components."[27] Introducing a discussion on the Foucault pendulum and the Einstein-Podolsky-Rosen paradox, the astronomer Trinh Xuan Thuan states the matter straightforwardly: "Science is constantly in pursuit of new interconnections. Indeed, the universe that it purports to describe appears to be totally interconnected. The whole universe appears to be mysteriously present everywhere and at any time. Each part reflects the whole. . . . Reality is no longer local, but global. There is no longer a distinct 'here' or 'there.' Everything is interconnected and 'here' is identical to 'there.'"[28]

Of course, such formulations need not have any deep impact on the lived experience of human beings. Whether they have ramifications for metaphysics or ordinary lives will depend greatly on the philosophical orientation with which one begins. For someone who follows in the Deweyan tradition of pragmatism, however, they can be used to provide corroboration for defending, as Dewey did, a metaphysics highlighting interconnections, interrelationships, and interactions as characteristic of entities at all levels of existence. The correctness of such a metaphysics is crucial to the mode of thinking about religion that I am seeking to introduce, a mode of thinking growing out of practices.

Are the practices woven together with a grasp of the way things are? Some examples suggest that this is indeed the case. A version of what might be called co-ontogeny, admitting the interlocking growth and understanding of self and other, is particularly prominent in these examples. Let's take, to begin with, two examples from different continents, a Native American tobacco ritual and a postpartum head shaving among Africa's Kikuyu. In the former the tobacco is smoked and then exhaled in specific ways. First, it is exhaled in each of the four cardinal directions. This is followed by exhalations above, below, and finally on the smoker himself. Why this practice? Dennis Tedlock explains that the individual thus joins "the self to the cosmos."[29] A Kikuyu mother goes through a ceremonial head shaving after giving birth. The child's unique relationship to the mother, symbolized by the hair, is now being severed, and the infant enters a thick web of kinship interconnections "so that it has a hundred mothers, a hundred fathers, a hundred brothers and hundreds of other relatives."[30]

Of religious articulations that recognize interdependence as central, none is more direct than the Buddhist notion of *pratitya samutpada,* the "conditional or causal interdependence of all things."[31] Matthieu Ricard describes phenomena as arising "through a process of interdependent causes and conditions, but nothing exists in itself or by itself."[32] Dostoyevsky's Father Zossima, the model religious man in *The Brothers Karamazov,* expresses a similar sentiment: "My brother asked the birds to forgive him; that sounds senseless, but it is right; for all is like an ocean, all is flowing and blending; a touch in one place sets up movements at the other end of the earth."[33] The Native American, the Kikuyu mother, the Buddhist monk, and the Russian Orthodox priest are central to the case I am making. It is a case whose core was expressed poetically by Francis Thompson:

> All things by immortal power,
> > Near or far,
> > Hiddenly
> To each other linkèd are,
> That thou canst not stir a flower
> Without troubling of a star.[34]

When we leave the academic halls for a more embodied, praxis-centered environment, and we situate ourselves in a life world that takes seriously the predominance of interconnections, important ramifications for thinking about religion ensue. Most important, this perspective allows us to identify fruitful criteria, occluded by prevailing philosophical assumptions, for reformulating discussions about religion and secularity.

Let's go back to Terezin. The handful of mashed potatoes is a nexus for intertwining linkages. In the strictly etymological sense of the word, it is a symbol (*sumballein,* the Greek original, indicates the movement of throwing things together). Because the word *symbol* has multiple uses, I will use the neologism *symbal* to indicate the single, etymologically inspired sense of "that which links together." *Symbal* and *symbalic* will identify occasions in which multiple strands are not only present but celebrated and brought to consciousness. The Native American smoking tobacco and exhaling in a ritualistic manner is engaged in a symbalic action. Eating a handful of potatoes to celebrate a birthday becomes for the young girl and her community a symbal, a conjunction of dimensions, physiological, moral, cultural, personal, social, and agricultural. These are all connections her captors hoped to sever. Their work, quite literally, was "diabolical," the effort to divide or throw things apart. What they sought was a progressive deligaturing aimed ultimately at severing the link with life itself.

The prisoners' response of celebrating birthdays and copying down recipes, even if it meant doing so on Nazi propaganda flyers, involved the contrary move of religaturing. The child is not an isolated individual. Women remembering recipes think of themselves as allied to a wider whole. Both belong to a community, and the community is linked to others in the outside world, to ancestors, and to those not yet born. But the links embodied in recipes, if recognized, go further still. They blur the nature-culture boundary. Recipes and birthday cakes link not only memory, tradition, and community but also the soil, sun, and rainfall, as well as the work of people planting, cultivating, and harvesting. Celebrating a birthday, under conditions of impossible hardship, not only signals the importance of one particular individual but makes manifest connections that are usually only tacit. It symbalizes, that is, embodies the connections in practices.

When a powerful enemy is attempting to sever linkages, the response of restoring them by reverting to ordinary life practices is a natural and worthy antidote. Those of us not faced with such terror may take the linkages for granted. Our time, says Michel Serres, is one characterized by negligence.[35] *Negligence* here carries the specific etymological sense of ignoring linkages. For Serres, negligence exemplifies the opposite of religion. The post-Enlightenment practices associated with industrialization and urbanization do nothing but reinforce and accelerate this negligence. "Agriculture is a religious practice," says Serres. The farmer cannot overlook the interconnections and multiple dependencies on which success at raising crops and livestock depends. "Every religious crisis is a crisis of agriculture, all religious residue is a way of resisting, at the same time, to the metastases of the city and those of industry."[36] Life, even in a port city like New York, can be lived in total neglect of the tides and can surely be lived in neglect of optimal planting seasons. Linkages with the farmers who grow food, laborers who harvest it, and truckers who deliver it need not be paid more than scant attention. If each connection on which we depend is thought of as a ply, our lives are literally "multiple," composed of many folds. Neglect of the folds, their gradual elimination until there is a single flat line, signals in ordinary life just what it signals on an electroencephalogram: death. The women of Terezin attempted to restore, via practices, as many folds as possible from their ordinary, preinternment lives. In these practices they could celebrate who they were. Food was not only a biological necessity. It was also an occasion for acknowledging the linkages that affiliated the residents of a household with a particular community, then with other humans, and finally with the world itself. Neglecting the practices meant losing one's identity, an identity that was an interlacing of the various strands folded over, under, and within one another.

This concrete struggle to maintain ceremonies of situatedness provides the clues to sketch a more adequate map for discussing questions too often constructed, as in Searle's analysis, within a binary context. The separation there is clear cut. On one side we find belief in miraculous occurrences requiring *super*natural explanations. On the other we find good sense coupled with scientific research. Phrased in this way the issue of locating oneself is already settled. The latter camp is the only defensible one. Set out schematically, the options would look like this:

secularism ———————————————————— religion

Content for determining membership at one pole or the other can be registered on a parallel line:

atheism ———————————————————— theism

There are really only two camps, and inclusion or exclusion depends on the issue of God's existence. In the world of Bertrand Russell and John Stuart Mill, the choices were stark: "either an atheistic attack on or a theistic defense of traditional religion."[37] For Searle, the contemporary situation goes beyond any such line. Secularism is taken so much for granted that the option associated with the older thinkers is no longer important. "The fact that the world has become demystified to the point that religion no longer matters in the public way that it once did shows not so much that we are all becoming atheists but that we have moved beyond atheism to a point where the issues have a different meaning for us."[38]

What is important about even the updated position is the continued identification of religion and theism. Of course, this identification does fit versions of many religions, especially the Abrahamic triad of Judaism, Christianity, and Islam. But it also ignores major religions such as Buddhism, isolates belief in divinity from important practices of self-understanding, and finally, constructs the issue as a sharp dilemma. Neat bifurcations make for imposing rhetorical flourishes, but they are rarely consistent with the range of human experience as it manifests itself across the globe. A more suitable schematic outline, one recognizing the importance of practices and incorporating the ontology of interconnections, can be drawn. I call it simply the ligature line. It offers a spectrum for purposes of classification. Occupying a particular place on this continuum does not automatically identify one as more or less good, more or less immersed in the sensual, more or less ascetic. It has nothing to do with embracing or escaping the here and now. There is no necessary connection between one's place on the continuum and belief in or denial of occurrences or phenomena in daily life that can be explained only by recurring to a transcendent force. Having had a religious experience or not, despite its personal significance, is not essential to a place on the religion end of the spectrum.

In place of the usual antitheses, the line encourages sorting out the various positions according to *kinds of ligatures.* The trajectory toward the religion end is marked by acceptance of linkages requiring dependence on and alignment with what are thought to be lineaments built into the structure of things. Passage from the secular end to the religious one comes at the point where anthropocentric affiliations (social solidarities) are complemented by cosmocentric ones. Acceptance of cosmocentric affiliations identifies the transitional period. People occupying this position straddle the secular-religious divide. Moving fully into the religion end of the ligature line requires acceptance of two further linkages. Religion (likely from *ligare,* "to bind") in the fullest sense is embraced when the bundle of ligatures includes (a) dependence on some path or way that gives our lives direction but is not of our making and (b) some version of what Buddhists identify as the "three jewels," the Buddha, the Dharma, and the Sangha. Generalized, these three jewels identify (1) an inspirational center, whether an individual or a guiding mythology; (2) a cluster of convictions about the place humans occupy in the scheme of things; and (3) conscious identification with the pattern of life embodied in a particular community. In place of a theism-atheism split mirroring the secular-religion opposition, the two versions of the ligature line, one for categories and the other for content, would look like this:

secularism——secular——minimally secular/minimally religious——religious——religion

world as alien——social solidarity——solidarity with natural forces——path not of our making——"three jewels"

The ends of the ligature line are anchored, as in the Searle-inspired case, by secularism and religion, but a range of options separates them. Increasing levels and kinds of ligatures mark the distinctions as one moves from secularism to religion. There are some important implications related to the suggested spectrum. It is possible to occupy the religion end of the spectrum whether one is a monotheist, polytheist, or even a nontheist. Islam, Vodou, and Buddhism, despite their differences, all fall within the religion end of the spectrum. On the other hand, belief in God as a wholly private attitude is consistent with membership in the secular end of the line, not the religious.

Robert Bellah and his colleagues interviewed someone they named Sheila Larson, who described her faith as "Sheilaism."[39] Hers was a wholly private attitude, a perspective reduced mostly to Sheila's relationship to her divinity. Such a compartmentalized and isolated relation with the divine need not be labeled religious except in the most equivocal sense. If the belief is not complemented by a recognition of linkages that extend beyond that between the self and the divinity, it has very little in common with religions as they have manifested themselves in human experience. The same may be said of Rorty's "privatized form of religious belief" in which "pragmatist theists" embrace a faith "which is hard to distinguish from love for, and hope for, the human community."[40] Such a faith, whether theist or not, lacks the dimensions that would situate it on the religious side of the spectrum (a place where Rorty, at any rate, does not want to be). The symbolic dimension is here explicitly limited to consciously chosen connections, ones that are made, not found. Symbala, practices signaling connection, would halt at this level. Linkages beyond social solidarity are simply not thought to be part of the way things are. An important contrasting case, atheists at the religious end of the spectrum, is supplied by old-fashioned communism in its full Marxist-Leninist amplification. Its understanding of history, its acceptance of forces situated deep within the nature of things, its worship of inspirational figures, its set of ideological doctrines, and its emphasis on a community of like-minded practitioners would easily place it within the category of religion.

Whereas Sheilaism and communism represent surprising classifications that emerge from the ligature line, most of the categorizations would fit familiar patterns. A Navajo singer of the blessing way, a Vodou priestess, and the Dalai Lama are examples of individuals who occupy the religion end of the spectrum. Each is aligned with a path not thought to be a human creation, recognizes a thick network of linkages that blur the human-nature boundary, and belongs to a self-conscious community of like-minded individuals. Shading away from this end there is an extent that, following Dewey's example, I have identified as religious. Situating people at this position involves distinguishing, as ordinary language does not, between the religious and religion. Membership in this stretch of the line depends on embracing a cluster of links to other persons and to the natural world while resisting the furthest reaches of the continuum. We are now at the border where secular and religious overlap. Situatedness on this extent of the continuum, while a precondition for access to the religion end, is itself neatly identifiable neither as secular nor as religious. This is the position Dewey articulates in *A Common Faith*, where he says that the religious attitude "needs the sense of a connection of man, in the way of both dependence and support, with the enveloping world that the imagination feels is a universe."[41] Translated into the language of this essay, Dewey's words suggest minimal criteria for belonging to the range identified as religious but not religion. The two furthest reaches on the right side of the line are troublesome for Dewey. Thinking in terms of alignment with some set of standards that are simply woven into the fabric of things and acceding to some version of the three jewels—that is, belonging to an officially organized community of belief—are now considered indefensible. Nonetheless, there is allegiance to a set of ligatures between humans and the wider world. Effort toward enhancing the good can then be understood as cooperating with what is best in the universe.

This is admittedly a borderline attitude. The perspective Dewey articulates, one that goes beyond mere social solidarity but stops short of explicitly recognizing our human need to align ourselves to some dimension not of our making, allows Dewey scholars to judge him as both secular and religious. Michael Eldridge has recently provided a strong case for the former, as Steven Rockefeller earlier provided a strong case for the latter.[42] What is important in clarifying the boundaries on the ligature line is that, for Dewey, humans are not considered, as some existentialists had suggested, to be strangers or outsiders, radically antithetical to the natural ambient that is their home.[43]

The existentialist position, at least that expressed in Sartre's *Nausea,* serves as an example of another threshold, that which moves an individual from the borderline stretch of the spectrum into that of the secular. In this grasp of things, humans and the world are alien to each other in the deepest possible way. Sitting in a park, Sartre's character Roquentin suddenly realizes the gap between his subjectivity's longing for Cartesian purity and the recalcitrance of all that is around him. The park bench, the gates and grass, "the diversity of things, their individuality, were only an appearance, a veneer. This veneer had melted, leaving soft, monstrous masses, all in disorder—naked in a frightful, obscene nakedness."[44] Not surprisingly, the subject construes the objective world he encounters as little more than a series of obstructions: "*In the way,* it was the only relationship I could establish between these trees, these gates, these stones."[45] When the world around us can be thought of only as "in the way," we have arrived at the paradigmatic deligatured state that characterizes the secular end of the continuum. Human beings as subjects stand in opposition to a world composed of objects. We can be described, in other words, as strangers in a strange land. Once again, the scope of symbolic activities is limited. If connections are to be signaled, they will be only those we have explicitly created, ones restricted to the human-human realm. The nonhuman world is now understood as radically other, radically antithetical to the nature and needs of the subject. It makes little sense to ally oneself to nature's presumed forces, to rely on what might be best in them. Allegiance beyond the human realm is out of the question. Good can be created, but, Camus-style, it involves rebellion and is wholly a human product.

More recent examples at the secular end of the spectrum can be found in *Spirituality and the Secular Quest*, a volume in an important publication series entitled World Spirituality. The generous nature of the series is attested by its willingness to explore spirituality outside the context of organized religion. Even generous criteria, however, do not mean that everyone is included. The volume's editor asserts that while the rubric "secular spirituality" comprises individuals such as Einstein, Dewey, Bessie Smith, and Nietzsche, it leaves out others, such as Steven Weinberg and Richard Rorty.[46] What these last two share is acceptance of a Sartrean rupture between humans and the natural world, the latter being understood as either meaningless mechanism or radically contingent other. That is, Weinberg and Rorty are fully consistent secularists because they deny the ontological significance of ligatures and continuities with nonhuman reality. "The essentially unreligious attitude," as Dewey says, "is that which attributes human achievement and purpose to man in isolation from the world of physical nature and his fellows."[47] I would amend this and separate the two dimensions mentioned by Dewey. The essentially unreligious attitude is one that attributes human achievement and purpose to humans in isolation from the world of physical nature. Social solidarity, cooperation with one's "fellows" in the struggle for good, is an important ingredient that serious, well-meaning individuals will hardly ever overlook. It does not push them to the religious side of the spectrum. The anthropocentricity of their efforts is what allows them to embrace the secular position as the most intellectually defensible one.

For understanding the essential components of the secular position, we need to recall the Deweyan quotation cited earlier. The religious attitude is marked by a "sense of connection of man, in the way of both dependence and support, with the enveloping world that the imagination feels is a universe."[48] The key terms Dewey uses are *dependence* and *support*. The Sartrean existentialist is an inveterate foe of dependence. Whatever humans achieve in the direction of good, they achieve it in the face of surroundings that are indifferent or recalcitrant. Attitudes that are religious, on the other hand, accept both dependence on and need for support from forces that are made neither by nor for us. The point articulated in *A Common Faith* was echoed by one of Dewey's students, John Herman Randall. Central to the religious vision, says Randall, is what allows us to live in a way that we recognize ourselves as "cooperating with what is most real in the universe. It is this ideal perspective born of religious vision, and this sense of partnership with the best the world contains, that gives to life that central and unifying meaning which men find in their religion."[49] There can be real debates regarding whether the secular or religious position is the most defensible one. Ultimately it is a question determined by the sort of metaphysical position (as a general grasp how things are) that one can accept as reasonable. The advantage of the ligature line is that it allows for a novel way of asking where to situate oneself.

By emphasizing the Deweyan claim concerning what characterizes the essentially religious and unreligious attitudes, we open a path for getting beyond the secular juggernaut that has dominated much of post-Enlightenment philosophy. The old position uttered by the epistemological subject was always an echo of Laplace's claim regarding God, "I do not need that hypothesis." The most pressing question seemed to be this: must we resort to a supernatural agency for explaining what we cannot now understand? An alternative question can now be formulated, a question building on, but not identical to, the position of Randall: "Is the sacred an integral component of existence?" *Sacred* here indicates the conjunction of dependence and support that, if real, brings several ramifications in its wake. (1) It relativizes the "everyday" aspect of our lives, that is, the prosaic, literal-minded, utilitarian workaday world. This is accomplished by justifying a wider significance. (2) It serves as a lure toward wholeness, or full, inviolate health, the etymological source for *holiness*. (3) It minimizes the Promethean situating of humans in a realm so separate from and superior to the rest of things that thinking primarily in terms of power and control becomes an immediate temptation. Whatever imagery is adopted for articulating an understanding of a community's place in the grand scheme of things, the sacred is accepted when there is open admission of dependence coupled with a sense that humans must adjust themselves to some harmony that is not of their making.

Secularists, who find no support for the sacred, would also continue the work of enhancing good in the world. This effort would go on as a cooperative endeavor of human solidarity, carried out heroically in the face of a surrounding reality that is neutral, if not outright hostile, to their efforts. Whether religion in general or secularism in general is good or bad cannot be determined by the ligature line. The ligature line nevertheless accomplishes several things. It allows for religions to be understood in terms of dimensions other than mere belief in a miracle-producing deity. It provides a scheme for tracking the multitude of positions embraced by humans. Finally, it so restructures the issue of secularism and religion that an open question replaces the closed rejection of the supernatural that is one legacy of the Enlightenment.

If all this makes sense, we can understand why cherishing practices by preserving recipes was a proper way of resisting diabolic forces fomenting genocide. Ordinary kitchen practices have much to teach us involving links and liaisons, if only we will pay attention. Beyond the table, ligatures of all sorts present themselves as candidates for acknowledgment. How far will this symbalic dimension go? For the secularist, it extends to humans and their striving for companionship and constructing goods. For those on the border, it includes, in addition, awe, appreciation, and some cooperation with the nonhuman natural world. Those who have moved into the religious stretch of the line admit as well some link to a dimension that defines propriety, a dimension to which they must adjust themselves. For those who can consistently be classified as embracing religion in the fullest sense, the ligatures extend to some central figure or figures, some teaching, and a community of like-minded believers. Conceived in this way, the issues surrounding religion and secularism can be formulated as an open question, even within the context of pragmatism. Borrowing the image from an Italian pragmatist, James compared pragmatism to a corridor that opens up to a variety of rooms. "In one you may find a man writing an atheistic volume; in the next some one on his knees praying for faith and strength."[50] There is no reason the variety embraced by James at the turn of the last century should be rejected as we move into a new one.

Notes

1. John Searle, *Mind, Language, and Society* (New York: Basic Books, 1998), 34.

2. Ibid.

3. Ibid.

4. See John Dewey, *A Common Faith*, in *The Later Works of John Dewey, 1925–1953*, vol. 9, ed. Jo Ann Boydston (Carbondale: Southern Illinois University Press, 1986).

5. See Richard Rorty, *Achieving Our Country* (Cambridge, Mass.: Harvard University Press, 1998), 15. This resolutely secular reading of Dewey has recently received corroboration from a source usually critical of Rorty, Michael Eldridge. In *Transforming Experience* (Nashville, Tenn.: Vanderbilt University Press, 1998), Eldridge defends a reading of Dewey that is "more pragmatic and more secular" than that of most Dewey interpreters. For a detailed account, see especially his chapter 6, "The Secularity of Deweyan Criticism."

6. Richard Rorty, *Consequences of Pragmatism* (Minneapolis: University of Minnesota Press, 1982), 142.

7. Ibid., xxxviii.

8. William James, *The Varieties of Religious Experience* (New York: Modern Library, 1902), 497. When Hamlet chides his friend by telling him, "There are more things in heaven and earth, Horatio, than are dreamt of in your philosophy," he is uttering a pragmatist-friendly position (William Shakespeare, *Hamlet*, ed. G. R. Hibbard [Oxford: Oxford University Press, 1987], act 1, sc. 5, ll. 74–75).

9. "If experience actually presents esthetic and moral traits, then these traits may also be supposed to reach down into nature, and to testify to something that belongs to nature as truly as does the mechanical structure attributed to it in physical science" (John Dewey, *The Later Works of John Dewey, 1925–1953*, vol. 1, ed. Jo Ann Boydston [Carbondale: Southern Illinois University Press, 1986], 13).

10. See the introduction in Raymond Boisvert, *John Dewey: Rethinking Our Time* (Albany, N.Y.: SUNY Press, 1988).

11. Searle, *Mind, Language, and Society*, 34.

12. Ibid., 35.

13. "Much of philosophy is concerned with questions that we do not know how to answer in the systematic way that is characteristic of science, and many of the results of philosophy are efforts to revise questions to the point that they can become scientific questions" (ibid., 157–58).

14. Clifford Geertz, *The Interpretation of Cultures* (New York: Basic Books, 1973), 112–13.

15. John Mbiti, *African Religions and Philosophy*, 2d ed. (London: Heinemann, 1990), 2.

16. Ibid.

17. Catherine Albanese, *America: Religions and Religion* (Belmont, Calif.: Wadsworth, 1981), 8.

18. Jean-François Revel and Matthieu Ricard, *The Monk and the Philosopher: A Father and Son Discuss the Meaning of Life* (New York: Shocken Books, 1999), 9.

19. Kathleen Norris, *Dakota: A Spiritual Geography* (New York: Ticknor and Fields, 1993), 131–32.

20. Revel and Ricard, *Monk and Philosopher*, 89.

21. Cara Da Silva, ed., *In Memory's Kitchen: A Legacy from the Women of Terezin* (Northvale, N.J.: Aronson, 1996), xxxvii.

22. Ibid., xxiv.

23. Ibid., xv.

24. Ibid., xxxi.

25. Ibid., xxvi.

26. Geertz, *Interpretation of Cultures*, 90.

27. Peter Coveney and Roger Highfield, *Frontiers of Complexity: The Search for Order in a Chaotic World* (New York: Fawcett Columbine, 1995), 330.

28. Trinh Xuan Thuan, *The Secret Melody: And Man Created the Universe*, trans. Storm Dunlo (New York: Oxford University Press, 1995), 270, 273.

29. Dennis Tedlock and Barbara Tedlock, eds. *Teachings from the American Earth: Indian Religion and Philosophy* (New York: Liveright, 1975), xii.

30. Mbiti, *African Religions*, 112.

31. T. Kasulis, *Zen Action, Zen Person* (Honolulu: University of Hawaii Press, 1981), 43.

32. Revel and Ricard, *Monk and Philosopher*, 122.

33. Fyodor Dostoyevsky, *The Brothers Karamazov*, trans. Constance Garnett (New York: Modern Library, 1950 [1880]), 383–84.

34. Francis Thompson, "The Mistress of Vision," *The Complete Poems of Francis Thompson* (New York: Modern Library, n.d.).

35. Michel Serres, *Le Contrat naturel* (Paris: François Bourin, 1990), 81.

36. Michel Serres, *Hermes III: La Traduction* (Paris: Éditions du Minuit, 1974), 246.

37. Searle, *Mind, Language, and Society*, 34.

38. Ibid., 36.

39. Robert Bellah, Richard Madsen, William Sullivan, Ann Swidler, and Steven Tipton,

Habits of the Heart: Individualism and Commitment in American Life (New York: Harper Perennial, 1985), 221.

40. Richard Rorty, "Religious Faith, Intellectual Responsibility, and Romance," in *The Cambridge Companion to William James*, ed. Ruth Anna Putnam (Cambridge: Cambridge University Press, 1997), 92, 96.

41. Dewey, *Later Works*, 9:36.

42. See Michael Eldridge, *Transforming Experience: John Dewey's Cultural Instrumentalism* (Nashville, Tenn.: Vanderbilt University Press, 1998); and Steven Rockefeller, *John Dewey: Religious Faith and Democratic Humanism* (New York: Columbia University Press, 1991).

43. If the early Dewey were considered definitive, then classifying him as religious in the light of the ligature line would be a case more easily made. The clearest statement of the way Dewey moves beyond mere social solidarity is found in his response to T. H. Huxley's claim of a radical opposition between the "cosmic process" and the "ethical process." Ethics, Huxley argued, must struggle against cosmic processes. Dewey responded that this thesis is too grandiose and ignores important distinctions. "We have rather the modification by man of one part of the environment with reference to another part. . . . It still holds true that 'nature is made better by no mean, but nature makes that mean.'" The essay's final sentence is ample justification for placing Dewey on the religious stretch of the ligature line: "But I question whether the spiritual life does not get its surest and most ample guarantees when it is learned that the laws and conditions of righteousness are implicated in the working processes of the universe; when it is found that man in his conscious struggles, in his doubts, temptations, and defeats, in his aspirations and successes, is moved on and buoyed up by the forces which have developed nature; and that in this moral struggle he acts not as a mere individual but as an organ in maintaining and carrying forward the universal process" (John Dewey, *The Early Works of John Dewey, 1895–1898*, vol. 5, ed. Jo Ann Boydston [Carbondale: Southern Illinois University Press, 1972], 36, 37–38, 53).

44. Jean-Paul Sartre, *Nausea*, trans. Lloyd Alexander (New York: New Directions, 1964), 127. This position is particularly well described by Alan Ryan: "The morality of the modern world is an ethic of authenticity, and this demands that we face the grim truth about the world—particularly the grim truth that it cares nothing for us and our purposes. Sartre, the best-known exponent of this view, claimed that what we discover when we look hard at the world is that it is meaningless" (Alan Ryan, *John Dewey and the High Tide of American Liberalism* [New York: Norton, 1995], 360).

45. Sartre, *Nausea*, 128.

46. Peter Van Ness, ed., *Spirituality and the Secular Quest*, World Spirituality: An Encyclopedic History of the Religious Quest, vol. 22 (New York: Crossroad, 1996), 12–13.

47. Dewey, *Later Works*, 9:18.

48. Ibid., 36.

49. John Herman Randall, *The Meaning of Religion for Man* (New York: Harper Torchbooks, 1968), 74.

50. William James, *Pragmatism* (Indianapolis: Hackett, 1981 [1907]), 29.

18. Spirituality and the Spirit of American Pragmatism: Beyond the Theism-Atheism Split

SANDRA B. ROSENTHAL

Classical American pragmatism[1] is noted for its focus on experimental or scientific inquiry, and largely as a result of this it is too often considered as housing a scientific spirit that precludes a religious dimension of experience. Thus this focus on scientific method may seem a treacherous path by which to search for a basic religious spirit that pervades and unifies the spirit of American pragmatism. Nevertheless, this pragmatic focus offers an important way to understand the pervasive religious quality of human existence.[2]

While pragmatism is concerned with the findings of science and its import for concrete human existence, its *systematic* focus on this domain is not on the contents of science but rather on science as *method* or as lived through human activity, on what the scientist *does* to gain knowledge.[3] Pragmatic naturalism views knowledge as continuous with science in terms not of contents but of method, a method that in itself implies no particular type of content.

Pragmatism arose in part as a reaction against the modern worldview, namely, the Cartesian understanding of science and the scientific object that emerged from conflating the experimental method that formed the backbone of modern science with the content of the first "lasting" modern scientific view—the Newtonian mechanistic universe. Such a confusion, based largely on the presuppositions of a spectator theory of knowledge, led to a realistic philosophic interpretation of scientific content, resulting in a quantitatively characterized universe and either dualistic causal accounts of knowledge in terms of correlations between mental contents and material objects or reductionist causal accounts in terms of stimulus and response. In rejecting the spectator theory of knowledge and the illicit reifications to which it gives rise, pragmatism rejects all forms of dualisms and reductionisms that are parasitic on the scientific characterization of nature. For the pragmatist, the human being is within nature, not outside nature and causally linked to it, but neither nature nor humans within it can be reduced to the categories of scientific explanation.

In turning to scientific or experimental inquiry, what pragmatism finds is that the very first stage of scientific inquiry requires human creativity. We are not mere passive spectators gathering ready-made data; rather, we bring creative theories that enter into the very character and organization of the data grasped. Second, the theory dictates directed or goal-oriented activity. Finally, the test for truth is in terms of consequences: does the theory work in integrating the relevant experience? Valid conceptualizations are not something passively attained, either by the contemplation of absolutes or by the passive accumulation of data. Instead, we attain them by activity shot through with the theory that guides it. This role of purposive activity in thought and the resultant appeal to relevance and selective emphasis that must ultimately be justified by workability are key pragmatic tenets.

Such creativity involved in scientific method thus implies a radical rejection of the "passive-spectator" view of knowledge and an introduction of the active, creative agent who, through meanings, helps structure the objects of knowledge and who cannot be separated from the world in which such objects emerge.[4] The world of objects with which the scientist deals is not a substitute for, or more real than, our lived qualitative experience. Rather, it is a conceptual articulation of ways in which the operations of nature can be understood, a product of creative intelligence in its attempt to understand its world, and it contents are verified in the richness of qualitative, everyday experience. Scientific creativity arises out of the matrix of ordinary experience and in turn refers back to this everyday lived experience.[5] In this way, a proper understanding of the lessons of scientific method reveals that the nature into which the human organism is placed contains the qualitative fullness revealed in lived experience, and the grasp of nature within the world is permeated by the meaning structures by which humans and their world are bound and hence is perspectival, at the levels of both science and commonsense experience.[6]

To use scientific method as a model is in no way to assert that perceptual experience is really a highly intellectual affair. To the contrary, although scientific objects are highly sophisticated, intellectualized, abstractive tools for dealing with experience at a "second level," they are not the product of any isolated intellect. Rather, the total biological organism in its behavioral response to the world is involved in the ordering of any level of conceptual awareness. In describing the lived experience within which the objects of science emerge, pragmatism uncovers the essential aspects of the emergence of any objects of conceptual awareness, even in the most rudimentary dealings with things in primordial experience.

For all the pragmatists, the irreducibly meaningful behavior of the human organism in interaction with its natural environment is the foundation of the noetic unity by which humans are bound to their world. Human behavior is meaningful behavior, and it is in behavior that meaning is rooted. The human biological organism bound to a natural environment cannot be separated from the perceiver who constitutes a world. Interactional unity at a primordial behavioral level provides the context from which unity at the conscious level emerges. From the context of organic activity and behavioral environment emerge irreducible meanings that allow the universe to come to conscious awareness in significant ways,[7] a universe rich with ontologically real value-laden qualities that span the gamut of the rich fullness of human existence, qualities that themselves emerge in the interactive contexts of humans with the universe in which they are enmeshed. Value qualities are contextually emergent facts, and so-called brute facts are value laden through the contexts in which they emerge. There is no fact-value distinction.

Seen from the backdrop of the nonspectator understanding of human experience, humans and their environment—organic and inorganic—take on an inherently relational aspect. To speak of organism and environment in isolation from each other is always to miscast the situation, for no organism can exist in isolation from an environment, and an environment is what it is in relation to an organism. The properties attributed to the environment belong to it in the context of that interaction. Interaction remains an indivisible whole, and experience and its qualities function within such interactional contexts.

Only within such contexts can the pragmatic focus on the human biological organism and organism-environment adaptation be understood. The human being is within nature. Neither human activity in general nor human knowledge can be separated from the fact that this being is a natural organism dependent on a natural environment. But the human organism and the nature within which it is located are both rich with the qualities and values of our everyday experience. Distinctively human traits such as mind, thinking, and selfhood are emergent characteristics of nature and part and parcel of its richness. None of the pragmatists views the self as a self-enclosed entity. Rather, they see it as a body-self that is "located," if one speaks of location, throughout the biological organism with its reflexive ability as this emerges from and opens onto the relational contexts in which it functions. While humans are understood as biological organisms within nature, then, this behavior is not reducible to the contents of science any more than is the universe at large.

With the rejection of the spectator theory of knowledge comes the rejection of the correspondence theory of truth and, instead, a view of reality as richer than, or overflowing, our conceptual demarcations. Diverse perspectives grasp the richness of reality in different ways, but they all must be judged in terms of their abilities to expand and harmonize interactive contexts. Growth of self also is understood as a harmonizing expansion, for it involves the sympathetic internalization of the standpoints of "the other" into the very dynamics of selfhood.[8] Growth cannot be reduced to mere accumulation; rather, it is best understood as an increase in the moral-aesthetic and—as I will discuss shortly—ultimately spiritual dimension of the richness of human existence.

In its most concrete exemplification in human existence, growth involves the ongoing integration and expansion of the self through a deepening attunement to, and incorporation of, "the other." This other ultimately includes the whole of the universe, for human activity, with its functions of consciousness, intelligence, and selfhood, opens onto the thick reality in which it is embedded; the interactive ontological unity at the heart of experience provides the open corridor from one to the other. Such an interactional unity contains a two-directional openness: the primordial openness of the character of experience itself opens in one direction toward the features of the human modes of existing within the independently real universe and in the other direction toward the features of the independently real, for the character of experience emerges from an interaction of these two poles and thus reflects characteristics of each, though it mirrors neither exactly. In the interactional unity that constitutes our worldly experience, both poles are thus manifest: the independently there otherness onto which worldly experience opens and the structure of the human way of being within whose purposive activity worldly experience emerges.

Because of an intellectual tradition that has truncated the richness of existence into isolated abstractions, the pragmatic stress both on the pervasive aesthetic-moral nature of existence and on its pervasive experimental nature may remain to some a bit paradoxical despite what I have said thus far. However, growth requires the cultivation of a deepening attunement to the "felt" dimensions of experience, to the general pulse of human existence. This requires a sensitivity to the aesthetic dimension pervading human existence, to experiencing what Dewey calls the qualitative character of *an* experience as a unified whole. The enhancement of this can not be separated from the method of experimental inquiry, for the qualitative character of *an* experience as a unified, integrated whole involves a sense of its own little past and a sense of the creatively organizing and ordering movement that brings to a harmonizing fruition its internal integration and fulfillment.[9] In learning to integrate experience through goal-oriented, experimental activity, one at once enhances its aesthetic dimension. Moreover, the enhancement of the aesthetic dimension enhances other dimensions, for the aesthetic involves the emotional, and the emotional enters into the unity of attitudes and outlooks.

Humans can thus use experimental method to produce consequences that lead to contextual integration through reconstruction of the situation, infusing experience with enriched meaningfulness and harmonization and thereby increasing the aesthetic-moral dimension of existence. In addition, attunement to the aesthetic-moral richness of existence is itself a tool for guiding ongoing experimental activities and hence productive of the types of consequences to which these give rise. Perhaps a way of briefly summarizing all the above is to say that the artful functioning of experience cannot be truncated into isolable skills, for it is holistic through and through.

Working within this pragmatic context, I now turn to pragmatism's common spirituality, which underlies and eludes the theism-atheism split, focusing primarily on the theistic position of James and the atheistic position of Dewey. While they offer contrasting—indeed, contradictory—interpretations of the object of religious experience, James's abstraction of religious experience from institutionalized or "secondhand" religion finds its analogue in Dewey's separation between religions as bodies of doctrine and the religious quality of experience.

James's concern with firsthand religion is to be found in his characterization of religion as meaning "the feelings, acts, and experiences of individual men in their solitude, so far as they apprehend themselves to stand in relation to whatever they may consider the divine. Since the relation may be either moral, physical, or ritual, it is evident that out of religion in [this] sense . . . , theologies, philosophies and ecclesiastical organization may secondarily grow."[10] Established churches "live at secondhand upon tradition."[11]

James's beginning characterization of the object of religious experience does not place him in opposition to Dewey. He states that "the divine shall mean for us only such a primal reality as the individual feels impelled to respond to solemnly and gravely," as well as "tenderly."[12] Although James's position becomes clear in the third lecture—the primal reality is for him clearly supernatural—this is not implied by his general characterizations. He speaks of the "belief that there is an unseen order, and that our supreme good lies in harmoniously adjusting ourselves thereto,"[13] adding that the religious attitude is precisely "this belief and this adjustment."[14] He elaborates on this point, however, by stating, "All our attitudes, moral, practical or emotional, as well as religious, are due to the 'objects' of our consciousness, the things which we believe to exist, whether really *or ideally,* along with ourselves."[15] This "unseen order" as ideal is not alien to the Deweyan context of ideal factors in experience.

Dewey emphatically separates the religious dimension of human existence from any particular religion and from religion in the generic sense. He proposes "the emancipation of elements and outlooks that may be called religious."[16] In this way he rejects the common assumption, held by theists and atheists alike, that God and religious experience stand or fall together. For Dewey as for James, religious experience involves a basic attitude of adjustment, but that attitude need not be correlated with any particular type of object. Rather, the religious attitude "may be taken toward every object and every proposed end or ideal."[17] As he again stresses, "The positive lesson is that religious qualities and values if they are real at all are not bound up with any single item of intellectual assent, not even that of the existence of the God of theism."[18] Indeed, as soon as one has a religion, be it that of "the Sioux Indian or of Judaism or of Christianity," the religious dimension of human existence takes on an irrelevant load of beliefs or practices not inherent to it.[19] In a sense there is no metaphysical reality correlated with Dewey's understanding of religious experience; nevertheless, religious experience does involve an ideal that enters into the adjustment process, and this needs to be explored. This exploration returns us to the pragmatic view of the self as incorporating an openness onto the other, as inherently social or communal.[20]

This relational self emerges in the context of an ongoing social process between the individual and the other. Selfhood derives from communicative interaction. This socially emergent self is an ontologically thick center of purpose, power, creativity, agency, and change. The reconstruction of situations involving the incompatibility of self and other cannot be imposed by eliciting abstract principles but must be developed by calling on a deepened attunement to a more fundamental level of human rapport. The deepening process frees intelligence from the bonds of rigidities and rule applications, as well as from artificial self-enclosures, allowing us to grasp different contexts, to take the perspective of the other, to participate in dialogue with the other, to utilize liberated possibilities. Such a deepening does not negate the use of intelligent inquiry but rather opens it up and focuses it on the vital pulse of concrete human existence. Our primal interactive openness onto the ontologically dense universe, then, is simultaneously a primal interactive openness onto the other. In addition, the deepening process of reason can regain touch with the concrete richness of experience in its full qualitative dimensions.

The expansion of the self, which involves the ongoing incorporation of the perspective of others, though not independent of intelligent inquiry, is not merely a change in an intellectual perspective; rather, it is a change that affects and is affected by the organism in its total concreteness. This receives its most intense form in Dewey's understanding of experiencing the world religiously as a way of relating one's self with the universe as the totality of conditions with which the self is connected. This unity can be neither apprehended in knowledge nor realized in reflection, for it involves such a totality not as a literal content of the intellect but as an imaginative extension of the self, not as an intellectual grasp but as a deepened attunement.[21]

Such an experience brings about a change in consciousness, a deeply embedded change is one's orientation toward the world. It allows one to "rise above" the divisiveness we impose through arbitrary and illusory in-group and out-group distinctions to a "delving beneath," to the sense of the possibilities of a deep-seated harmonizing of the self with the totality of the conditions to which it relates. For all the pragmatists, this involves the entire universe, for their emphasis on continuity reveals that at no time can we separate our developing selves from any part of the universe and claim that it is irrelevant.

The adjustment that can be termed religious is unique, involving "our being in its entirety" rather than particular wants in relation to particular conditions of our surroundings. Dewey explains that it is not merely a change *in* will but a change "*of* will, conceived as the organic plentitude of our being."[22] The ideal involved in religious experience is not, then, one more ethical ideal among others. Not all moral faith in ideals is religious in quality.[23] Rather, "the religious is 'morality touched by emotion' only when the ends of moral conviction arouse emotions that are not only intense but are actuated and supported by ends so inclusive that they unify the self. . . . The inclusiveness of the end in relation to both self and the 'universe' to which an inclusive self is related is indispensable."[24]

As he elaborates, "Infinite relationships of man with his fellows and with nature already exist. The ideal means, as we have seen, a sense of these encompassing continuities with their infinite reach. This meaning even now attaches to present activities because they are set in a whole to which they belong and which belongs to them."[25] As a result, "even in the midst of conflict, struggle and defeat a consciousness is possible of the enduring and comprehending whole."[26] James makes a similar point in his claim that

"God's existence is the guarantee of an ideal order that shall be permanently preserved. . . . tragedy is only provisional and partial, and shipwreck and dissolution are not the absolutely final things."[27] Thus James holds that the broadest forms of moral commitment are held by those who appreciate the religious dimension of existence.

For both Dewey and James, the self is always directed toward something beyond itself.[28] For Dewey, the unseen power that extends beyond and controls our destiny is the power of an "ideal," while for James it is the power of "the real," but the religious experience that gives rise to their conflicting objects of belief is fundamentally the same for both. For Dewey and James alike, the primordial awareness of ultimacy of some sort, with the adjustive response of the whole person this elicits, is a dimension of concrete human existence, irrelevant to the issue as to whether that ultimacy exists "really or ideally." For both, moreover, this involves a "wider self."

This wider self is the focal point for Mead's understanding of the religious dimension of human experience, which he, like Dewey, views as incorporating ideal factors within existence. Regarding "an exalted religious attitude" in which we feel we experience "the meaning of life," he states, "We get into an attitude in which everyone is at one with each other in so far as all belong to the same community."[29] This attitude is "universal in its working character, not universal because of any philosophical abstraction involved."[30] In discussing "how very wide the actual universality of this attitude is," he states: "It takes in practically everything, every possible being with whom one can have a personal relation."[31] The "universal attitude of neighborliness," which for Mead is inherent in the social nature of the self, "passes over into the principle of religious relationship, the attitude which made religion as such possible."[32] The religious attitude "takes you into the immediate inner attitude" of the other." It is "always universal" in character and tends to "build up in some sense a common community which is as universal as the attitudes themselves."[33]

What comes into play in the diverse interpretations of the objects of the religious attitude is what James calls overbelief,[34] belief about the nature of the "more" or "beyond" that is not part of the experience itself. An overbelief is thus a hypothesis as to the nature of that with which in religious experience we feel ourselves connected. The various theologies, as well as James's own theistic hypothesis, "all agree that the 'more' really exists," though they differ in the various specifics attached to this real existence,[35] while Dewey and Mead characterize the more as an ideal. The pragmatic understanding of the concrete fullness of human existence and the qualitative richness of the cosmos in which it is embedded thus provides an existential or experiential basis for theism and atheism alike.

James's characterization of the God of his own overbelief manifests the way in which for him the features of the pragmatic understanding of the universe take precedence over the usual understanding of God. The pragmatic understanding of the restless, pluralistic, open-ended universe in which we live leads him to accept, "along with the superhuman consciousness," the notion that it is not all embracing, all powerful, and all knowing but rather finite and that it has an external environment.[36] For the universe is "*many* everywhere and always" and "*nothing* real escapes from having an environment."[37]

Despite his fundamental commitment to the spirit of pragmatism, however, James peculiarly fails to comprehend the possibility of an enriched atheism based on the pragmatic understanding of human existence and the universe in which it is embedded. Despite pragmatism's distinction between scientific method and scientific content and its consequent rejection of the reification of scientific contents, James views the alternative to theism as a scientism that absolutizes the contents of science and reduces humans to a scientific universe, as was done with the spectator understanding of knowledge in the modern worldview. Theism, according to James, in contrast to the sectarian attitude, rejects scientific bounds and believes that "the real world is of a different temperament—more intricately built than physical science allows." The world interpreted theistically as opposed to atheistically "is not the materialistic world," one in which "scientific laws and objects may be all."[38] But pragmatic atheism does not fit within the sectarian attitude characterized by James, for its understanding of scientific method itself rules out such a scientism in understanding human existence and the universe at large.

James at times seems to realize that the alternative to theism need not be scientism, for he holds that "whether a God exist, or whether no God exist, in yon blue heaven about us bent, we form at any rate an ethical republic here below. And the first reflection which this leads to is that ethics have as genuine and real a foothold in a universe where the highest consciousness is human, as in a universe where there is a God as well. 'The religion of humanity' affords a basis for ethics as well as theism does."[39] For James, though, from the perspective of his own theistic option, "in a merely human world without a God, the appeal to our moral energy falls short of its maximal stimulating power."[40] The atheistic option ultimately means, for James, the option of scientific materialism.

At the same time, the pervasive functioning of scientific method as understood by pragmatism ultimately accounts for James's understanding of the dynamics of one's acceptance of a theistic or atheistic option. The overbelief either way is an experimental hypothesis, with features similar to those "a good hypothesis in science must have."[41] In terms of scientific method, the overbelief or hypothesis is the creative, interpretive stance from which one views so-called objective evidence or facts. This hypothesis directs purposive activity, leading the theist, according to James, to respond to the world differently than would an atheist. Hence the choice between theism and atheism is a "momentous" option.[42] Finally, the test of its truth is via consequences: does the hypothesis work? Absent such verification, the belief will not be sustained, because it will not function in a workable way. To the extent that belief in God's existence works in one's life, that belief is true in the only sense a pragmatist can admit.

In this instance, the content or "facts" that verify the truth of the hypothesis accepted are precisely the kinds of data that scientism rules out as unreal—one's sense of unity, harmony, meaningfulness, inwardness, and so forth. The ontologically thick reality that we seek to integrate and whose integration serves as verification concerns the nature, direction, interrelation, and focus of the dynamic tendencies of a concrete human organism as incorporating types of integrative unities, meaningful perspectives, and so forth. What operates here is an absolute distinction between scientific method and scientific content. What differs in the case of the technically scientific hypothesis and the theistic or atheistic overbelief is not the dynamics of creative constitution, directed activity, and verification in the ongoing course of experience. Rather, there is a great difference in the nature of the consequences that verify. In brief, the data whose integration serves as verification of the types of belief at issue here are precisely those types of data that technical science, in focusing on its own particular type of evidential data, rules out of court.

James holds that the belief in God may produce God as a living force in one's life, verified through its functioning as an organizing and unifying perspective in the ongoing course of experience. Relevant here is James's stress on the point that scientific method strongly distinguishes verification, which causes the preservation of scientific conceptions, from creativity, which causes their production.[43] He summarizes the dynamics of theistic belief thus: "A conception of the world arises in you somehow, no matter how. Is it true or not? you ask." From there, "It might be true somewhere"; "It may be true even here and now"; "It is fit to be true"; It must be true"; "It shall be held for true." "And your acting thus may in certain special cases be a means of making it securely true in the end."[44]

Peirce's essay "A Neglected Argument for the Reality of God" can be seen as analogous to James's understanding of the will to believe and equals the latter in its pragmatically based richness. The argument is really a "nest of three arguments."[45] The first Peirce calls the humble argument; the second, the neglected argument in the narrow sense; the third, the scientific argument. The first argument, which is an immediate and direct experience for the muser, is "entirely honest, sincere and unaffected . . . meditation upon the Idea of God, into which the Play of Musement will inevitably sooner or later lead, and which will produce a truly religious" belief in the reality of God.[46] The second concerns the universality and naturalness of the experience involved in the first. It is "a vindicatory description—of the mental operations which the Humble Argument actually and actively lives out."[47] The third argument identifies the humble argument as exemplifying induction, which is the first step of scientific method.[48] In this way the living belief in God is a first step for scientific inquiry.

That the humble argument is seen as an argument at all shows the inseparable intermingling of reason and feeling at the primal level. The "argument" is not rationally developed but felt in the immediacy of experience; what is emphasized is the emotive, spiritual nature of religious belief, the source of its vitality. The neglected argument offers a vindication of the instinctive nature of the humble argument but provides no "scientific hypothesis" of the existence of God. Religious belief begins with the emotional vitality of felt experience, which provides its living force, and culminates in a belief founded in the full nature of scientific inquiry. This focus on scientific method has led critics to object that Peirce seems to scientize religion. However, here again the focus is not on scientific contents but on scientific method, analogous to James's use of the model of scientific method in understanding overbelief and the will to believe. Religious belief must have verifiable consequences not in offering its own kind of abstract, formalized "explanation" of the world but in the kind of effects it has on the vitality of concrete human existence.

For pragmatic atheism and pragmatic theism alike, then, religious experience is a dimension of the vitality of human existence, and the real or ideal object to which one relates this dimension takes one beyond the features and structures within experience to a personal overbelief; differing perspectives "make sense" of the religious dimension within experience through the functioning of differing types of overbeliefs. Human existence and the universe in which it is embedded share features that underlie both theistic and atheistic overbeliefs within pragmatic philosophy; these common features perhaps lead to a rethinking of James's view that the option between theism and atheism is momentous, affecting our entire mode of existing in the world. Just how would or should a Jamesian theist and a Deweyan atheist respond differently to the world they understand human existence to inhabit? The

momentous option seems to that between a philosophy celebrating the relational, qualitative, value-laden richness of human existence and the universe in which it is embedded and one that attempts to explain away this richness through barren intellectual abstractions.

Notes

1. Throughout this essay, I will use the term *pragmatic philosophy* to mean classical
American pragmatism, that position incorporating the works of its five major contributors: Charles Peirce, William James, John Dewey, C. I. Lewis, and G. H. Mead.

2. I support the unity underlying the various pragmatists in some detail in my book
Speculative Pragmatism (Amherst: University of Massachusetts Press, 1986; repr., Peru, Ill.:
Open Court, 1990).

3. This stress on pure method is not intended to deny that pragmatism is influenced
by the findings of various sciences. Indeed, it pays careful attention to these findings.
Pragmatic philosophy's inextricable linkage to the model of scientific method as pure
method is one thing, however; its attention to various findings of various sciences achieved
by the general method is something quite different. These two issues should not be conflat-
ed, and it is the *method* of science that provides the key to pragmatism.

4. John Dewey, *The Later Works of John Dewey, 1925–1953*, vol. 4, ed. Jo Ann Boydston
(Carbondale: Southern Illinois University Press, 1984), 163–65.

5. G. H. Mead, "The Definition of the Psychical," in *Mead, Selected Writings*, ed. A. J.
Reck (New York: Bobbs-Merrill, 1964), 34; Mead, *The Philosophy of the Act* (Chicago:
University of Chicago Press, 1938), 32; John Dewey, *The Later Works of John Dewey 1925–
1953*, vol. 1, Jo Ann Boydston (Carbondale: Southern Illinois University Press, 1981), 37.

6. Mead, *Philosophy of the Act*, 25; C. S. Peirce, *Collected Papers of Charles Sanders Peirce*,
vol. 5, ed. Charles Hartshorne and Paul Weiss (Cambridge, Mass.: Harvard University
Press, 1958), 181.

7. Thus, both Dewey and Mead stress that meanings can be expressed both in terms
of the ongoing conduct of the biological organism immersed in a natural universe and
in terms of the phenomenological description of the appearance of what is meant. See
Dewey, *Later Works*, 4:142; John Dewey, "The Experimental Theory of Knowledge," in *The
Middle Works of John Dewey, 1899–1924*, vol. 3, ed. Jo Ann Boydston (Carbondale: Southern Illinois University Press, 1976), 114–15; Mead, *Philosophy of the Act*, 115–16.

8. See G. H. Mead, *Mind, Self, and Society*, ed. Charles Morris (Chicago: University of
Chicago Press, 1934), for the development of these points.

9. Thus Dewey notes that "scientific and artistic systems embody the same fundamental
principles of the relationship of life to its surroundings," and indeed the differences between the work of the scientist and the work of the artist are "technical and specialized,
rather than deep-seated" (John Dewey, "Affective Thought," in *The Later Works of John
Dewey 1925–1953*, vol. 2, ed. Jo Ann Boydston (Carbondale: Southern Illinois University
Press, 1985), 106–7.

10. William James, *The Varieties of Religious Experience*, The Works of William James,
ed. Frederick Burkhardt (Cambridge, Mass.: Harvard University Press, 1985), 34.

11. Ibid., 33.

12. Ibid., 39.

13. Ibid., 51.

14. Ibid.

15. Ibid.

16. John Dewey, *A Common Faith*, in *The Later Works of John Dewey, 1925–1953*, vol. 9, ed. Jo Ann Boydston (Carbondale: Southern Illinois University Press, 1986), 8.

17. Ibid.

18. Ibid., 23.

19. Ibid., 8.

20. It is frequently held that James, in distinction from the other pragmatists, stresses the individual in a way that excludes the social. His essay "Great Men and Their Environment" (in James, *The Will to Believe and Other Essays in Popular Philosophy*, ed. Frederick H. Burkhardt, Fredson Bowers, and Ignas K. Skrupskelis [Cambridge, Mass.: Harvard University Press, 1979], 163–89) is taken as an instance of this individualism. However, the whole thrust of this essay revolves around James's support of Darwin over Spencer and his rejection of Spencer's understanding of "the fatal way in which the mind, supposed passive, is molded by its experiences of 'outer relations.'" This essay is a defense not of rugged individualism but of human creativity. As James stresses, the self is always stretched outward toward others. Its integrity can be understood only in terms of the social; it is never felt in isolation but always as extending outward toward others. Indeed, for James, as for all the classical pragmatists, individuals exist in their social relations (James, *The Principles of Psychology*, vol. 1 [Cambridge, Mass.: Harvard University Press, 1981], 279–82).

21. Dewey, *A Common Faith*, 14.

22. Ibid., 13.

23. Ibid., 16

24. Ibid.

25. Dewey, "Human Nature and Conduct," in *The Middle Works of John Dewey, 1899–1924*, vol. 14, ed. Jo Ann Boydston (Carbondale: Southern Illinois University Press, 1986), 226.

26. Ibid.

27. James, *Varieties*, 407.

28. Dewey, *A Common Faith*, 14; James, *Varieties*, 403.

29. Mead, *Mind, Self, and Society*, 274.

30. Ibid., 289.

31. Ibid., 289–90.

32. Ibid., 292–93.

33. Ibid., 296–97.

34. James, *Varieties*, 404–5.

35. Ibid., 401.

36. William James, *A Pluralistic Universe* (Cambridge, Mass.: Harvard University Press, 1977), 40–41.

37. Ibid., 144; emphasis is James's.

38. Ibid., 408.

39. William James, "The Moral Philosopher and the Moral Life," in *The Will to Believe*, 150.

40. Ibid., 160.

41. James, *Varieties*, 407.

42. James, *The Will to Believe*, esp. p. 28.

43. William James, *Principles of Psychology*, vol. 2 (Cambridge, Mass.: Harvard University Press, 1981), 1232–34.

44. James, *A Pluralistic Universe*, 148.

45. Charles Peirce, *Collected Papers of Charles Sanders Peirce*, vol. 6, ed. Charles Hartshorne and Paul Weiss (Cambridge, Mass.: Harvard University Press, 1958), 486.

46. Ibid.

47. Ibid., 487.

48. Peirce's term *abduction* is much more appropriate here, for what is involved is creative hypothesis formation.

19. Pragmatism, Truth, and the Disenchantment of Subjectivity

NANCY K. FRANKENBERRY

In 1908 Arthur Lovejoy could list thirteen pragmatisms, all standing for different doctrines. Today that list can be expanded by including the versions of pragmatism associated with the work of Willard V. O. Quine, Nelson Goodman, Hilary Putnam, Donald Davidson, and Richard Rorty in philosophy and of Cornel West, Henry Levinson, Jeffrey Stout, Sheila Davaney, and others in religious studies. This proliferation is a development that William James and John Dewey would applaud but that Charles Sanders Peirce might deplore, complaining as he did in 1905 that the word *pragmatism* had already begun "to be met with occasionally in the literary journals, where it gets abused in the merciless way that words have to expect when they fall into literary clutches."[1]

In addition, pragmatism has fallen into the hands of positivists, functionalists, and relativists who throughout much of the twentieth century confused its theory of truth with their own. Despite a history of tangled relations with these three flawed "isms," pragmatism has evolved toward holism. I contend that the new pragmatism, apparent only by the last century's end, is for the first time clearly a thoroughgoing holism, distinguishable from the empiricist assumptions of positivism, the utilitarian aspects of functionalism, and the relativism of scheme-content dualism. This places it in a unique position to offer methodological and theoretical directions for overcoming some of philosophy of religion's worst myths, dualisms, and dogmatisms.

In recent decades the old epistemological toils over language, truth, and meaning have come to look very different because of important shifts in epistemology, philosophy of science, philosophy of language, and semantics. Perhaps most profound has been epistemology's shift from foundationalism

to holism. In the American pragmatic tradition, the shift away from foundationalism and the evolution toward holism was begun by Peirce, James, and
Dewey in the first decades of the twentieth century. It was completed in the
second half of the century by the combined work of Quine, Davidson, and
Rorty. Quine's pragmatism is what remains when modern empiricism is
purified of its two dogmas of reductionism and the analytic-synthetic distinction. Davidson's pragmatism is what remains when empiricism is further purified of the third dogma of scheme-content dualism. In Rorty's convincing narrative, the same dialectic that led Dewey away from a spectator
theory of knowledge also led the later Wittgenstein and Davidson away from
the picture theory of language.[2] A radically antirepresentationalist philosophy of language is the common theme in neopragmatic writings.

Contemporary pragmatists do not think that language is primarily an
expression of thought or that subjects and subjectivity can exist apart from
the signs of subjectivity in the intersubjective exchange of speech and reply.
Pragmatists do not see anything as having an intrinsic, ineluctable nature.
Quine taught us to give up the myth of the museum: the image of some object
(the meaning) and next to it some label (the word). Davidson taught us to
give up the scheme-content dualism: the dogma that our beliefs are formed
when we use a contentless scheme to organize a schemeless content. Rorty
taught us that by following Davidson's truth-conditional semantics, we could
even give up a pragmatic theory of truth, and, with it, a set of semantic problems that the older pragmatisms never overcame.

Positively characterized, the new pragmatism is a holism in which all entities are nodes in a network of relations. Knowledge or belief is more like a
"raft" (Neurath) than a "pyramid." We can pull up and repair or scrap any
or all of the planks on the raft, although not all at once, for we must at least
provisionally stand on one or another. Or knowledge and belief is more like
a "web" (Quine) than a building. Every belief is supported by its ties to its
environing beliefs and ultimately to the whole web, but nothing serves as a
ground or architectonic foundation. Holist theories of meaning in the philosophy of language parallel the epistemological antifoundationalism first
seen when Peirce, James, and Dewey rejected both sense experience and rational ideas as privileged, authoritative bases of knowing or as foundations
for the truth of a philosophical system. These American pragmatists also
criticized the definition of truth as an isolated correspondence between self
and world and affirmed instead an understanding of truth as a social context of meaning shaped by the practical implications of ideas.

Having deconstructed all forms of foundationalism, pragmatists argue for
the contingency of language, self, and community. Truth is no more a prop-

erty of statements than sentences are a representation of reality. For those who have been convinced by Quine, Davidson, and Rorty, all that pragmatism needs is Tarski's semantic conception of truth according to which to say "X is true" is equivalent to *assenting* to the statement. Truth, then, is a notion that allows us to talk about sentences instead of "facts," but it has no normative or epistemological import. This introduces an important revision to efforts—by James, Dewey, Peirce, and others down to Putnam—to defend a pragmatic theory of truth. The new pragmatism generates no theory of truth, views the idea of assessing "correspondence with reality" as hopeless, and accents the holistic character of belief and meaning. The new pragmatism is neither realism nor antirealism; still less is it a form of linguistic idealism.

Pragmatism and Truth

Pontius Pilate's vexing question, "What is truth?" concerns the nature of truth, not our ways of discovering it. Pragmatic theories of truth were once mistakenly thought to form a third type of answer to this question, along with correspondence and coherence theories. In this section I argue that as *theories of* truth all three are flawed and that pragmatism means *never having to offer a full-fledged theory of truth.*. I agree with John P. Murphy and Richard Rorty in characterizing Davidson as the first pragmatist to give a satisfactory account of truth.[3]

Correspondence theories depend on an agreement between a proposition and a state of affairs. They have faltered over what "facts" are and what it means to "correspond." The existence of a correspondence relation cannot be established by confronting an assertion with an object and then noticing that a relation called corresponding holds or fails to hold. What would such a confrontation look like? How can we compare a belief with a nonbelief to see whether they match? We have no way to pair off sentences or beliefs with things in the world in order to answer such questions as, Which objects made that sentence true? or, Which objects does that sentence accurately represent? There is no way to divide language from world in such a way as to resolve the question at issue between correspondence theories and coherence theories: which is the truth maker—the word or other beliefs? Nor is there any way to answer the question, Is it the object in itself or the object under a description that is represented?

Coherence theories define truth in terms of a relation among beliefs that fit together in an ideally coherent system of representations. This cannot mean, however, that all the sentences in a consistent set of sentences are true. Rather, proponents of coherence theories of truth are concerned with sets of beliefs, or of sentences held to be true, whose consistency is supposed to be enough to make them true. Unfortunately, many different consistent sets of belief are possible that are inconsistent with one another.[4] Worse still, the argument for coherence as constitutive of the *nature* of truth depends on raising the specter of radical relativism. Having raised this specter once, what is to prevent us from raising it again to ask what makes even an ideally coherent system of propositions true? The best answers to this question, according to Davidson, have the defect of inviting back an idealist metaphysics that makes ideas or mental data the source and criterion of knowledge. But if we have to embrace idealism to evade skepticism, coherentism is not a happy account.

Pragmatic theories of truth have often been presented as an alternative to correspondence and coherence theories, but from the beginning, critics have found fault with pragmatism's conception of truth. In Bertrand Russell's caricature of pragmatism, there is no need "to trouble our heads about what really is true; what is *thought* to be true is all that need concern us." Russell understood William James to believe that "although there is no evidence in favor of religion, we ought nevertheless to believe it if we find satisfaction in so doing."[5] James, for his part, called this kind of interpretation of his pragmatism "the usual slander" and adamantly complained of critics who, he wrote, "accuse me of summoning people to say 'God exists,' even when he doesn't exist, because forsooth in my philosophy the 'truth' of the saying doesn't really mean that he exists in any shape whatever, but only that to say so feels good."[6] Indeed, careful readers of James understand that the notion that a proposition could be factually false but emotionally useful and consequently true never entered into James's formulation, not even in the controversial "Will to Believe" writings, which *do* call for satisfaction of an emotional, moral, or aesthetic sort, but only when a hypothesis is factually or logically *in*determinate *and* when "reality is led to." With regard to the religious hypothesis, James insisted that "the truth of 'God' has to run the gauntlet of all our other beliefs."[7]

Contributing to the logical positivist caricature of pragmatism, A. J. Ayer understood James to be saying that asserting God's existence amounts to no more than claiming people have spiritual requirements that religious belief may be found to satisfy; the pragmatic content of the belief in God's existence, in other words, consists merely in the feeling of optimism it induces. Not surprisingly, Ayer himself regarded religious beliefs as "purely subjective" cases in which "no discernible" facts are available.[8]

While it is not possible to make everything James said on the subject of truth totally consistent, the best understanding of his version of pragmatic truth aligns it with statements about open possibilities rather than settled facts. That is, James's remarks about truth address one of two classes of propositions: those about settled facts or those about open possibilities. The first class is factually and logically determinate, but the second class concerns indeterminate matters where "faith in a fact can help create the fact." Religious fundamentalists, realists, and literalists all locate the question of the truth or falsity of religious beliefs in the first class, of settled facts, as though a definite fact of the matter obtains whether we know it or not. By contrast, religious pragmatists throughout the twentieth century have made a different, more interesting move, tying religious beliefs to the second class, open possibilities or ideals, *not* facts antecedently given. This opens up the reinterpretation of the doctrinal and creedal side of religious life as dealing not with matters of fact but with matters of aspiration, not with matters of *faith* but with matters of *hope*. The most common pragmatist critique of all forms of traditional religious thought, therefore, is that they transpose matters of aspiration too solidly into matters of fact, converting ideal aims into actual powers.

Consistent with this interpretation, we would have to dismiss James's confusing use of the words *truer* and *truest* to mean, roughly, "better" and "best" and concede that overall James simply failed to produce a satisfactory definition or theory of truth. Charles Sanders Peirce and John Dewey also failed. Peirce proposed that "the opinion which is fated to be ultimately agreed to by all who investigate is what we mean by the truth, and the object represented in this opinion is the real."[9] Peirce assumed there *is* some true opinion to be found, but this assumption is challenged by many contemporary neopragmatists. Why should we posit convergence to a single result? The idea that truth is a *goal* of inquiry seems odd, insofar as it refers to something we could not recognize when we had found it and from which we shall never be able to measure our distance. Furthermore, as Hilary Putnam has pointed out in his "naturalistic fallacy" argument, it is always possible to say, "Yada, yada, yada _____ but maybe not true" no matter what is put in the blank. The argument applies also to Putnam's own definition of truth as idealized rational acceptability.

Turning to Dewey, we find a pragmatic definition of truth as warranted assertibility (of our sentences). This confuses truth with a property that accrues to an idea when it is confirmed by inquiry. Wanting to reject the notion of truth as an immutable property, Dewey made it a mutable property, but from the standpoint of later pragmatists such as Davidson, the mistake was in making truth any kind of property at all. To label a statement true is not to describe it but to endorse it. The early pragmatists all erred in treating truth as a property rather than as a redundant, cautionary, or disquotational expression. To say "It is true that this paper is forty pages" means no more than that this paper is forty pages, and to say, "It is false that this paper is forty pages" means that this paper is not forty pages. On this alternative account, truth has no normative or epistemological import. Nothing is said about what it is to *be* true, which may seem a weakness but is really a merit, for it allows us to talk about sentences instead of objects and to avoid the futility involved in trying to compare language and reality as two distinct realms.

Neopragmatism and Holism

One of the principal advances of the new pragmatism has been to free itself from correspondence, coherence, or even pragmatic theories of truth. Thus freed, pragmatism can be usefully described in terms of the three-part characterization offered by Richard Rorty.[10] First, it is *antiessentialism applied to notions such as truth, knowledge, language, morality, and similar objects of philosophical theorizing.* Antiessentialism by any name is holism, the attempt to replace a distinction between schemes and content with a seamless, indefinitely extensible web of relations. The second characterization shows that holism's espousal of relationalism is not an assertion of relativism: pragmatism, according to Rorty, *denies any epistemological difference between truth about what ought to be and truth about what is or any metaphysical difference between morality and science.* In other words, in the new pragmatism ethics and physics are equally objective. No antirelativist could want more. Third, according to Rorty, *there are no constraints on inquiry save conversational ones.* This, too, should be interpreted in a nonrelativistic manner to mean that even following the deaths of all the former underwriters (God, the Forms, the Absolute, Being), we still have constraints that keep us on this side of "anything goes," and they are all socially evolved and consensually decided for pragmatic purposes. As Davidson shows perhaps better than Rorty, the condition for our knowing any language for conversation or inquiry of any kind is the ascription to it of truth conditions, without which we could not even get started on translation, let alone succeed.

Davidson's answer to Pontius Pilate's question utilizes the device called Convention T, taken from the logician Alfred Tarski, which consists of rendering any declarative sentence in the form of a tautology, for example, "'snow is white' is true if and only if snow is white." The proposition thus satisfies its own truth conditions simply by virtue of its logical structures. According to Davidson, Convention T requires that a satisfactory theory of truth for a language L "must entail, for every sentence s of L, a theorem of the form 's is true if and only if p' where 's' is replaced by a description of s and 'p' by s itself if L is English, and by a translation of s into English if L is not English."[11] Obviously, this is neither a definition of truth, pragmatic or otherwise, nor a way of testing for truth in any given instance. It is something altogether more pragmatically useful: it shows us, contrary to relativist confusions, that the attitude of *holding-true* is a primitive concept that logically precedes questions of semantic interpretation. To relativize truth to a language, conceptual scheme, paradigm, or framework is to forget this priority and incoherently try to reverse it. What is new and improved in Davidson's version of truth conditional semantics, therefore, is the starting point: instead of assuming that meaning determines truth, one starts with truth, so that the attitude of holding-true is the basis of all understanding and translation. This explains how we can and do translate from one conceptual scheme to another.

Like James and Dewey, Davidsonian pragmatists reject the subject-object dualism that creates the need to explain truth as consisting in some relation such as "fitting" or "organizing" the world to "mind" or "language." Instead of referring to a state of affairs that explains the practical successes of those who hold true beliefs, the term *true* is more like praise or endorsement. Rorty thinks that pragmatists may also add two other categories to this endorsing use: a cautionary use, and a disquotational use.[12] The cautionary use of *true* occurs in such remarks as "I agree that your belief that Mary is the mother of God is perfectly justified on the basis of Scripture; still, it may not be true." The disquotational use of *true* occurs in such remarks as "If the testimony of the last witness is true, then at least one of the parties is lying."[13]

Pragmatists thus have an account of truth that has a place for each of these uses while avoiding the early Jamesian idea that the expediency of a belief can be explained by its truth. Saying this much tallies with the characterization of pragmatism as antiessentialism with respect to truth. In other words, *true* has no explanatory uses; it is not the name of a distinct norm.

Furthermore, pragmatists think we understand all there is to know about the relation of beliefs to the world when we understand their causal relations with the world. Our knowledge concerning how to apply terms such as *about* and *true of* to sentences is fallout from a naturalistic account of linguistic behavior. On this account no relations of being made true are needed between beliefs and the world. Therefore, pragmatists can safely abjure all epistemological and metaphysical differences between facts and values.

Finally, if the idea of being made true is empty and misleading, then there is no point to the debates between realism and antirealism, that is, debates between those who claim that an objective world (one that exists independent of our thought and language) makes our true statements true (the realists) and those who take issue with that claim (the antirealists). Accordingly, pragmatists are committed to renouncing all constraints on inquiry save conversational ones, just as Rorty has recommended.

Both Davidson and Rorty, on my reading, regard the question, "What *makes* sentence S true?" as nothing more than a confused version of the question, "What is it for sentence S to be true?" It is confused because it suggests "that truth must be explained in terms of a relation between a sentence as a whole and some entity, perhaps a fact, or state of affairs."[14] In the history of philosophy this is the move that has spawned what have been termed "representations," and that has always returned us to a correspondence theory. "It is good to be rid of representations," according to Davidson, "and with them the correspondence theory of truth, for it is thinking that there are representations which engenders thoughts of relativism."[15] Even more explicitly, in a passage that deserves repeated attention, Davidson writes: "Nothing, . . . no *thing*, makes sentences and theories true: not experience, not surface irritations, not the world, can make a sentence true. *That* experience takes a certain course, that our skin is warmed or punctured, that the universe is finite, these facts, if we like to talk that way, make sentences and theories true. But this point is put better without mention of facts. The sentence 'My skin is warm' is true if and only if my skin is warm. Here there is no reference to a fact, a world, an experience, or a piece of evidence."[16] In other words, by attending to the holistic character of language, belief, and meaning, something all pragmatists have urged, we can drop the idea of states of the world serving as truth makers.

Pragmatic Justifications of Religious Belief

Even though pragmatism is often no longer taken as a theory of meaning or of truth, for reasons that Davidson has supplied, it is still frequently taken as a mode of justification. The application of pragmatic norms to the evaluation and justification of religious beliefs is advocated by many recent Anglo-American theologians and philosophers of religion who have given up on capital-T Truth but who still care about reasons and warrants. Justified belief is said to be what passes as true. In this section I argue that the appeal to pragmatic norms in the justification of religious belief either warps pragmatism into functionalism or winds up with conclusions so trivial as to be useless.

Pragmatic justifications of religious beliefs have usually been specified as a matter of the practical effects, fruitfulness, interest, or value of the beliefs held by individuals. According to this approach, a religious belief is true because we find that we must act as if it were true; because it is most consistent with certain practical purposes; because it is most beneficial in helping us cope; or because when coherent with other beliefs, it makes our vision of reality a satisfying whole. From there is but a short step into a functionalist theory of religion according to which "religion is what it does" or "religion exists to do these things." Such arguments turn pragmatism into a version of functionalism, a theory whose flaws have been thoroughly exposed in recent decades.[17] Pragmatists can avoid falling into functionalist analysis if their appeals to consequences take the form of saying only something like "religion does these things," not "religion persists because it does these very things." In that case, however, they have succeeded in explaining not the phenomenon of religion but only something about a society in which religion is present.

Even when the functionalist fallacy is not explicitly committed in the course of formal reasoning, informal appeals of a vulgar pragmatic type fail to explain religious beliefs. At best, the appeal to presumed benefits, consequences, or fruits of beliefs as implicitly justificatory of those beliefs is frustratingly vague and wholesale. Many people no doubt make some rough, overall judgment about the relative benefits and deficits of religion as one cultural interest among others. The problem is that these impressionistic, anecdotal generalities cancel one another. It proves impossible to assess overall interpretations of life or "visions of reality," especially in terms of their pragmatic utility, for pragmatic consequences—such as human flourishing, orientation in life, peace of mind—may occur, if and when they do occur, independently of or even despite the religious beliefs in question. In the absence of any way to rule out alternative explanations of particular beliefs, pragmatic justifications as typically employed in philosophy of religion do not carry any explanatory power. In the end they overstate the connection between truth and utility. True beliefs are a good basis for action, but why take this to be the nature of truth? True beliefs may foster success, but actions based on false beliefs may produce beneficial consequences also.

Historicist and pragmatist philosophers of religion usually recommend pragmatic adjudication between the sorts of life various religious visions entail, allowing for the ongoing testing and revising of beliefs and practices in the light of the forms of life they make possible. This sort of appeal, however, becomes so latitudinous as to admit everything and to exclude nothing and therefore to become indistinguishable from life itself. The criterion, norm, or standard of evaluation cannot be what "works" or what has "practical effects" for a form of life. Everything works; everything affects a form of life. To be anything at all, a thing (*pragma*) must work, yet this cannot supply us with a criterion of choice among or between religious systems. Further specification of the pragmatic norm in terms of "human flourishing" or "enhancing life rather than dealing death" may introduce some restrictiveness, but only at the price of moving up the metaphilosophical question a notch. What counts as "flourishing"? What counts as "enhancing life"?

In the wake of the culture wars, widespread disagreement in ethics, philosophy, law, and politics, we have no agreement regarding how to define "flourishing," much less "life enhancement" or even "the common good." *Nor should we.* My point is not that everything must conduce toward agreement but that as long as disagreement over these matters is endemic, it will be hard for philosophy of religion to command public and critical acceptance. Its validity is likely to be decided more and more in that private realm to which Richard Rorty relegates religion.

The very idea that practical tests can validate religious beliefs (or theological claims) is itself problematic. Even when religious beliefs are understood as fallible, historically situated, and nonfoundational, requiring or permitting nothing other than pragmatic validation, there is still a need to decide the point at which to call off inquiry and conclude, provisionally and pragmatically, one way or another. How would one know that point? And how would one justify one's claim to such knowledge?

Finally, if religious beliefs are to be judged on the basis of an empirical claim about the pragmatic benefits they produce rather than on the grounds that such propositional attitudes are *true*, they are vulnerable to being outweighed by harmful consequences if the scales happen to tip the other way. Ramakrishna is said to have compared religion to a cow that kicks but gives milk, too. Religious beliefs, theological systems, and spiritual traditions present very mixed and ambiguous historical records. Trying to assess them for their pragmatic benefits is hardly a practical undertaking and, when indulged in by theologians, often amounts to special pleading: the positive and purifying aspects of a religion are selectively considered far more than its paltry and pulverizing side. The ways in which a particular religion may be shown to function in the benign and salutary manner approved by its adherents help to obscure the fact that it may also function to express and reinforce superstition, irrationality, fanaticism, sexism, infantilism, and eschatological abstentions from real moral and political tasks. Among scholars of religion, debates over the functional or dysfunctional place of religion in human culture continue to end in stalemate, with no methodological or theoretical way of determining whether the preponderance of empirical evidence favors Freudian and Marxian reductions, for example, or theological interpretations. The case can be argued either way, with overabundant and inconclusive evidence and counterexamples in support of both. Given this impasse, no assessment of the practical effects of a religion or a theology can ever be conclusive, because the practical effects of any particular religious test case are impossible to correlate in a cause-effect manner. At a more theoretical level, the same difficulty besets the pragmatic justifications of theologies called for by a variety of recent historicist theologians.

At the existential level of analyzing one's own beliefs, it is often tempting to take "pragmatic difference" to mean "personal benefit" or "consequences for an individual." Unlike Peirce and Dewey, William James leaned unfortunately in this direction, giving rise to vulgar interpretations of his pragmatism and risking the conflation of pragmatism with existentialism. The problem with the existentialized version of pragmatic justification is that *any* beliefs whatsoever make some pragmatic difference in the lives of the individuals holding them, but for all we know, this difference is compatible with their being illusory or false. Regarding the pragmatic difference of a belief system or a theology, we want to show the difference its truth value and truth conditions would make in a public way. A recommendation that we test them in the light of the forms of life they make possible does not provide a workable norm either at the existential or the communal level, for the reason that Michel Foucault, a keen observer of human practices, once articulated: "People know what they do; they frequently know why they do what they do; but what they don't know is what what they do does."[18]

Conceptual Scheming and a Common System

If pragmatism is not functionalism, logical empiricism, or existentialism, neither is it relativism. Pursuing the implications of holism further, we can better understand the incoherence involved in relativism concerning the truth of religious beliefs. Davidson's influential paper "On the Very Idea of a Conceptual Scheme" argues against all those conceptual schemers who hold that truth is relative to conceptual schemes of one kind or another, whether they are termed epistemes, paradigms, frameworks, or symbol systems.[19] The notion of conceptual relativism, according to Davidson, depends on a third dogma of empiricism—the dualism of scheme and content, or of organizing system and something waiting to be organized. It is, in fact, this fundamental dichotomy that tempts many philosophers of religion to think of different religious systems as incommensurable worldviews and lends plausibility not only to the idea of the world as a *view* but to the possibility of *alternative* views. If the dualism of scheme and content is purged from its widespread employment in the philosophy of religion, relativism will be eliminated as well. What will remain, as Terry Godlove shows, is diversity of belief, but that is as nonrelativistic as can be.[20]

Contrary to the claims of those who hold that experience, belief, or even reality is relative to conceptual schemes, *Weltanschauungen,* or Wittgensteinian forms of life, all viewed as incommensurable with others of their ilk, holism entails that we can never be in a position to judge that there are systems of beliefs radically different from our own, for the coherence of the idea of a conceptual scheme requires the coherence of the idea of an alternative conceptual scheme, but this idea is incoherent. If an alternative conceptual scheme is translatable into the first conceptual scheme, it is not alternative, and if it is not translatable, nothing intelligible can be said about it to distinguish it from the first conceptual scheme. In the absence of grounds for distinguishing a conceptual scheme from an alternative conceptual scheme, the distinction collapses, and with it the coherence of the very idea of a conceptual scheme, and with that the coherence of most forms of relativism.

The proposal that something might be true in one religious system but false in another parallels the claim that a sentence or proposition p is true in A but false in B. But to suppose this is nonsense. If the meaning of a sentence is given by its truth conditions, then one can suppose that p is true in A and false in B only by assuming that what is false in B is not really a translation of what is true in A—for if there is a difference in truth value, there must be a difference in truth conditions, and a difference in truth conditions is just what we take as evidence of a difference in meaning.

The key notion is that language implies translatability, which should be taken not as a criterion of identity for conceptual schemes but as a condition of language. Failure of translatability (were it possible) would tell us not that members of another culture or religious tradition have a different conceptual scheme but only that they have no language at all. Interpretability, in other words, can be taken as a condition of rational mental life. If it is mistaken to suppose that uninterpretable forms of life express any intentions, beliefs, or desires at all, then conceptual relativism is impossible. There is only *the* conceptual scheme, so to speak, within which mental life exists. But even this is misleading, for the term *scheme* summons up *content*, and it is the very dualism of scheme and content that we need to reject. Rejecting that dualism, we can have a view of mind and world as constitutively interdependent, inextricably engaged with one another. No intermediary such as language or experience is needed between subject and object. Without the distinctness of conceptual scheme and what it organizes, that is, without a formulatable independence of mind and world, truth cannot be relative to conceptual scheme. No duality between scheme and reality can be sustained. Interpretation of tribes and scribes other than our own is possible because of constitutive constraints that provide the background of agreement that makes disagreement about a common subject matter possible. Other humans must share with us various specific beliefs about the world with which we are in causal contact—various specific conceptual contents, standards of formal rationality, and values—if they are to be regarded as rational agents about some of these matters.

The upshot of this argument is the perhaps initially surprising idea that we must consider the bulk of another culture's beliefs as true, or as Davidson says, "we can take it as given that *most* beliefs are correct."[21] The reason for this is that a belief is identified by its location in a holistic pattern of beliefs, and it is this pattern that determines the subject matter of the belief. On Davidson's analysis, before some object in, or aspect of, the world can become part of the subject matter of belief (true or false), there must be endless true beliefs about the subject matter. "False belief," Davidson says, "tends to undermine the identification of the subject matter; to undermine, therefore, the validity of a description of the belief as being about the subject; and so, in turn, false beliefs undermine the claim that a connected belief is false."[22] Interpretation is possible, then, because we can dismiss a priori the chance of massive error. We can rule out as incorrect any theory of interpretation that makes a person assent to many false sentences.

On reflection, the disconcerting quality of this argument gives way to a better recognition of what a system of belief is, an appreciation of the way the truth of a *particular* belief must figure in a whole pattern of true beliefs, and an understanding of the fact that even in the clash between theories or cultures or historical epochs, there is no threat of a massive, global collision of belief systems. This is because the vast majority of common truths go unchallenged and unchanged; they can be treated as context invariant while others are seen to be variable. "Different points of view make sense," Davidson points out, "but only if there is a common coordinate system on which to plot them; yet the existence of a common system belies the claim of dramatic incomparability."[23] Furthermore, "if we cannot find a way to interpret the utterances and other behavior of a creature as revealing a set of beliefs largely consistent and true by our standards, we have no reason to count that creature as rational, as having beliefs, or as saying anything."[24]

Pragmatists will avoid the temptation of thinking that this Davidsonian strategy vindicates our own beliefs and values (whoever "we" are) against others', or the realist conviction that ultimately there will be a single conceptual scheme secure against conceptual relativism. As Davidson cautions, it is "wrong to announce the glorious news that all mankind—all speakers of language, at least—share a common scheme and ontology. For if we cannot intelligibly say that schemes are different, neither can we intelligibly say that they are one."[25] In the clash and clamor of conflicting religious beliefs, relativism will not be rendered implausible by vindicating the view that there is only one rational framework or a single correct religious representation of reality. Not only do those who declare rationality or truth relative employ the scheme-content duality to make plausible the possibility of alternative schemes, but those who think relativism can be defeated only by a defense of objective truth and realism presume the same dualism, since they require that at the end of inquiry we possess the *one true* scheme.

Does this argument suffice against relativism in all forms? Has Davidson provided reasons to reject cases that fall short of asserting complete incommensurability, defined as untranslatability? I think not. In a seldom-noted aside in his essay "The Myth of the Subjective," Davidson comments that we can still have what he terms a "harmless relativism" described as "just the familiar relativism of position in space and time." This is philosophically unexciting, he thinks. "Minds are many; nature is one," he tells us. "Each of us has one's own position in the world, and hence one's own perspective on it. It is easy to slide from this truism to some confused notion of conceptual relativism."[26] One cannot help but notice, however, all that is suppressed in this statement and glossed over in the highly formal terms of the argumentation. *Who* occupies different relative positions in space and time? Not *minds* but human *persons. Embodied* persons who are always and everywhere specified in terms of race, class, and gender. Embodied persons whose distances from each other in space constitute cultural differences and whose distances from each other in time constitute differences in historical consciousness. Reflection on the insistent particularities incorporated in these differences is precisely what has made us postmoderns so hyperconscious and contextualist in our thinking, to the point where Davidsonian reminders of more massive background agreements and taken-for-granted sameness of belief usually seem dwarfed. Were Davidson himself to trace out in a less formal and more particular mode all that is entailed by the "harmless relativism" he himself acknowledges, he could, I suggest, complete the historicist turn that he has been making, traveling the same route as the great historicist philosophers from Hegel to Dewey, all of them challenging the distinction between the sensory content of experience and any constituting scheme. His historicist and pragmatist turn remains incomplete without further explication of the "harmless relativism" that attends positionality in all its aspects.

Further Implications for Philosophy of Religion

Rather than pursue that explication here, I would like to draw several implications from these Davidsonian reflections for the philosophy of religion.

An obvious implication of Davidson's principle of charity, but one frequently overlooked in philosophy of religion, is that the real issues we face concern not overcoming relativism, which offers greatly exaggerated accounts of our cognitive predicament, but adjudicating disagreement. This issue—of disagreement, diversity of conviction, and pluralism of practice—is, of course, not identical to relativism. The interesting feature of cases of evaluative disagreement is that they do not necessarily arise from skepticism about the lack of an independent and neutral standard for judging between theories or beliefs. Indeed, the most critical cases of apparent incommensurability arise not from our inability to make sense of other people's bizarre beliefs but, as David Wong has shown, precisely from those situations in which we *are* able to understand and see how different their beliefs are from our own. We can see, for example, that their beliefs arise in the context of a life that people would want to live, and as Wong concludes, we can understand this because we can relate features of our own traditions to theirs in such a way that we recognize what is gained from that sort of life and what we have lost.[27] A principle of charity is *forced* on us; if we are to maximize the intelligibility of other speakers, we need to assume that most of their beliefs agree our own.

Some will object that agreement, even massive agreement, does not guarantee truth, and disagreement does not by itself spell error. This last observation, however, misses the point. The basic claim is simply that much community of belief is needed to provide a basis for communication or understanding. The extended claim is that objective error can occur only in a setting of largely true belief. Agreement may not make for truth, but much of what is agreed must be true if some of what is agreed is false. Pragmatists can describe the pattern truth must make among sentences but without telling us where the pattern falls.

To other philosophers of religion it may seem that this principle gives us merely a formal context for seeing that communication between language users is possible only if they share massive agreement on many more things than those over which they diverge; they may add, however, that it does nothing to affect the most worrisome cases of intense and interminable *dis*agreement in human culture, cases that are nowhere more evident than in the area of religion. Davidsonian arguments may serve to show that most of our beliefs must be true, but how can we reconcile this reassurance about the limits of disagreement with our knowledge about the many bizarre beliefs and puzzling practices found throughout the world's religions? Does it bring us any closer to determining questions of truth in the worldwide conflict and collision of religious beliefs?

Having disposed, with Terry Godlove, of anything as dramatic as the idea that Methodists and Muslims, Taoists and doubters, live in different worlds, and having dropped any representation of other cultures, religions, or moralities as self-contained, incommensurate, ideological schemes that we can understand only from inside and never judge from outside, we still face the unexceptional fact of human convictional diversity. The diversity of religious outlooks that command our respect or tolerance is plural. Disagreements among them and within them are profound, genuine, and seemingly intractable. Focusing on the fact of disagreement rather than the ruse of relativism helps in formulating a new set of questions not normally raised by philosophers of religion. Why should agreement be valued over disagreement, or sameness over difference? Why suppose that something like consensus and agreement is as important in religion as it is in, for instance, government? Why is the existence of a pluralistic spectrum of religious beliefs across the cultures of the world a cause for philosophical adjudication, as though agreement is the royal road to rationality and alone will shield against irrationalist resentment, hatred, and violence? These assumptions tell us something about the centripetal forces at work in our increasingly global world.

At the same time, however, philosophy of religion has yet to theorize diversity of belief in any way that does not lead either to absolutizing some one convictional set above all others or to relativizing the notion of truth in the light of the mutually conflicting claims of different religions. No one has a good account of this. The most popular approach in world religions textbooks constructs a simplistic narrative according to which all peoples relate to some "ultimate reality" that each group sees partially—the story of the blind men and the elephant is meant to illustrate this. But the elephant begs all the important questions. In addition to criticizing the conservative and protectionist strategies to which this slow-moving animal has been put (epitomized in its use as symbol of the Republican Party in the United States), pragmatists will point out that no one can stand, or even conceive of what it *would* be to stand, at the point where all these perspectives join. And if we *could* imagine the full syncretistic elephant, it would be one in which all the colorful particularities of the living traditions were bleached out.

Relativizing the elephant to different perspectives has become a practice so rampant among philosophers of religion that I doubt this model will be consigned to the Humean flames for its "sophistry and illusion" anytime soon. Nonetheless, on the assumption that Davidson has demolished the scheme-content distinction, I suggest two important methodological points that follow for philosophy of religion. First, religion should not be treated as *a* scheme, alongside science, for example, or in contrast to secular culture. The particularities of religious belief cannot be separated in an exclusivist way from the secular meanings of the culture in general. Claims conflicting with or challenging those espoused by partisan, sectarian, and ecclesial groups are holistically related to those groups simply because they dwell in a larger culture within which discourse inevitably occurs. If the very idea of a conceptual scheme is incoherent, then church or cult cannot form a conceptual scheme utterly incommensurable with culture or society.

Second, if religion (in the singular) should not be treated as one scheme versus science or secular culture as another, neither should diverse religions (in the plural) be thought of as alternative schemes that filter different modes of religious experience. In recent years a growing number of studies of mysticism and religious experience have depicted different religious traditions and their doctrines as though they are epistemological molds into which the raw, unstructured volcanic lava of experience rushes to be shaped, organized, and served up in the distinctive form of a particular tradition. Different religious traditions are treated as different ways of organizing or interpreting either experience or the world. One is asked to notice the impossibility of ever inspecting from the outside a connection or fit between the conceptual scheme and experience (or the world), whether in the case of our own conceptual scheme or of diverse religions. Therefore, it is frequently said, we cannot make any rational choice between profoundly divergent conceptual schemes. Each religious system provides its own incommensurable framework for interpretation according to which it relativizes the world to itself.

The flaw in this model and its use in religious epistemology should now be evident. Not only can we not attach a clear meaning to the notion of neutral or unorganized reality waiting to be organized, so that humans might find orientation and meaning, but any theory of the nature of experience that interposes an ordering mechanism, a mediating category, between the experiencing subject and the environing world will regularly introduce the specter of skepticism by inviting doubt as to whether the schematizing mediation is a distortion rather than a distillation of the so-called content presumed to be out there. Far better to eliminate such dubious intermediaries and do without any device intruding between ourselves as subjects and the world as object.

If philosophers of religion were to agree with Davidson that talk of alternative conceptual frameworks or incommensurable beliefs is incoherent and accept the more radical thesis that the very idea of a conceptual scheme is unintelligible, then we could simply give up the distinction between conceptual scheme and uninterpreted given as this has been employed in the study of religion. And to give *that* up would amount to giving up all transcendental arguments as well as all foundationalist philosophical efforts, exactly the move that pragmatists in a variety of disciplines are currently making. In religious studies pragmatists can cheerfully bypass all the ongoing disputes about the best way to *ground* various basic valuational judgments. We can agree with Rorty that the only thing these foundational efforts accomplish is to take the finished first-level product, jack it up a few levels of abstraction, invent a metaphysical or epistemological or semantical vocabulary into which to translate it, and then announce that it has been *grounded*.[28] As William James said, "These are but names for the facts, taken from the facts, and then treated as previous and explanatory."[29]

Nothing grounds or guarantees convergence to agreement, pragmatists say. In religion as in everything else, the old Socratic virtues are *simply* moral virtues—willingness to talk, to listen to other people, and to weigh the consequences of our actions on other sentient beings. The notion of conversation that Richard Rorty commends as a practical substitute for that of reason is, in the end, ungrounded by appeal to Platonic and Kantian notions of truth as correspondence, knowledge as discovery of essence, and morality as obedience to principle. Can we keep the Socratic virtues without the Platonic defense of them? Can we conduct conversation and inquiry without the conviction that there is something atemporal and binding that lies in the background of all possible conversations? Can we, in short, work without a net and with full awareness of the sheer contingency of our human beliefs and practices? In philosophy of religion this question currently divides the pragmatists from the Platonists.

The Disenchantment of Subjectivity

The most far-reaching implications of holism for method and theory in philosophy of religion involve a new understanding of the public dimension to truth and a critique of the putatively private, subjective dimension to experience. Modernity's long and difficult enchantment with subjectivity, the outgrowth of a misapprehension of the mind's relation to the world, may finally be coming to an end.[30] Platonic capital-T Truth, already in dire trouble before Nietzsche and James, is disappearing in our time, but its replacement by a nonepistemic conception of truth is not widely understood. Disappearing also is the human subject, characterized as an autonomous entity, a rational soul, prior to and independent of history, language, and the body. Here too the final vestiges of Aristotelian notions of substance, essence, and intrinsicality still linger.

The holistic assault on the notion that there are subjective states of mind begins by questioning what the content of such a state would be. Positivism argues that the mind imposes a mental scheme upon the content supplied by the senses. Functionalism argues that a subject, one that is already in possession of a particular need, imposes its given antecedent need for satisfaction or orientation on a cultural or historical context in which it is subsequently satisfied or oriented. Existentialism, like relativism, makes subjectivity the deep touchstone of truth and authenticity ("true for me") and language but a medium, either of representation or of expression.

The problem with these familiar methodological starting points is their common difficulty in establishing that any such scheme could account for the relationship that subjects have to the world. They all assume that the mind itself imposes its schemes on what Davidson calls "an ultimate source of evidence whose character can be wholly satisfied without reference to what it is evidence for."[31] Whenever sensory data, psychological or biological needs, and existential interests and desires have been assumed as the basis of the subject's access to the world and regarded as independent of the schemes imposed on the world, we have had no way of ascertaining the adequacy of the schemes themselves. Haunting doubts have accompanied these efforts. How could I ever be sure that the thoughts and feelings that I expressed in language were faithfully reproduced in the thoughts and feelings of another subject? What about the possibility of systematic misunderstanding? In the end, the evidence cannot be kept uncontaminated from the subject, because the disjunction between scheme and evidence locates the scheme itself within a subjective realm standing apart from all evidence. The subject, detached from the world, defined in the first place as standing outside the world it experiences and as having access to that world only by virtue of an imposition of its own organizing schemes, can hardly answer for the connection of its beliefs with the world it experiences. "Our beliefs purport to represent something objective," Davidson points out, "but the character of their subjectivity prevents us from taking the first step in determining whether they correspond to what they pretend to represent."[32]

The next step in the disenchantment of subjectivity consists in seeing that the received account of the subject simply cannot explain the communication of beliefs. Alternatively, holism understands that such communication is possible only because beliefs themselves have as their objects a world that all speakers of language share. The relation between beliefs and their objects is causal rather than representational or expressive. If beliefs are caused by their objects, no place appears for uninterpreted data on which the subject is presumed to impose itself, and thus there is no coherent account of the realm of the subjective itself. Given the impossibility of using language to describe states of mind presumed to be independent of the public objects that cause them, no such distinction between the subjective and a public world can be established. Any attempt to communicate a realm of subjectivity is obliged to evoke the very world outside of which the subjective is presumed to stand and over which it has been privileged.

What are these states of mind possessed by a subject and known only by their causal relations to the world? According to the holism of the mental, they are the mind's relations to the world, and no distinction can be made between those mental states that have as their object the causal relations among the objects of the world and those mental states that instead display an affective attitude toward objects in the world. Interests or values are no more subjective and no less caused than are other causal relations in the world. Doubts, wishes, beliefs, and desires are identified in part "by the social and historical context in which they are acquired" and are in this respect "like other states that are identified by their causes."[33] The social and historical context defines a public space in relation to which a subject's states of mind are publicly accessible and therefore knowable. No demarcation, dichotomy, or dualism intrudes between publicly available forms of knowledge and the "private" desires, values, or interests on which the received tradition has based its enchantment with subjectivity's special inscrutability, ineffability, and autonomy. From a holist perspective, however, desire, value, and interest are as public, scrutable, effable, and relational as anything else. And that is because relations are constitutive of the mental, not merely the consequence of having a mental state. Thus Davidson can conclude that "the very possibility of thought demands shared standards of truth and objectivity."[34]

Holism requires us to start thinking about religion and the human sciences in quite new ways now that we no longer need to suppose a human subjectivity "inside" us or an objective world "outside," now that the myth of the given has been replaced by the world's causal sway over our entire belief structure, and now that we can see the inwardness or subjectivity once celebrated by religious existentialists such as Kierkegaard and extolled by romantic poets such as Wordsworth to have been a literary effect, produced by prolonged prominence accorded to indexical pronouns. Meaning is social before it is individual.

In the heyday of theology, the conception of subjectivity as a free-standing and self-mastering spiritual entity was transparently only a reflection of the idea of *imago dei*. Holism has spelled the end of this self-image's long fallout in Western philosophy. The disenchantment of subjectivity means that the godlike subject, as an individual center of autonomous consciousness and will, is no longer the source of the world's meaning, its self-identity is no longer a simple given, and its privacy ("only I know exactly what I mean") is no longer self-transparent. In our time, a more edifying and bracing self-image is emerging in which the sharp contrast between subject and object, mind and world, is blurred or erased. Giving a twist to Jesus' admonishment, we might say we have lost our souls but have gained the whole world.

Notes

This article is a revised version of chapter 18 in Nancy K. Frankenberry and Hans H. Penner, eds., *Language, Truth, and Religious Belief* (Atlanta, Ga.: Scholars, 1999), 507–32.

1. Charles Sanders Peirce, "What Pragmatism Is," in *Collected Papers of Charles Sanders Peirce*, vol. 5, ed. Charles Hartshorne and Paul Weiss (Cambridge, Mass.: Harvard University Press, 1934), 276.

2. For the best expressions of Quine's pragmatism, in contrast to positivistic empiricism, see W. V. O. Quine, "The Pragmatists' Place in Empiricism" (1981), in *Pragmatism: Its Sources and Prospects,* ed. Robert J. Mulvaney and Philip M. Zeltner (Columbia: University of South Carolina Press, 1981), 21–39; and W. V. O. Quine, "Two Dogmas of Empiricism" (1951), in *From a Logical Point of View,* 2d. ed., rev. (New York: Harper Torchbooks, 1963), 20–46. For Davidson's critique of scheme-content dualism, see notes 14 and 19. For Rorty's narrative, see Richard Rorty, *Philosophy and the Mirror of Nature* (Princeton, N.J.: Princeton University Press, 1979), chap. 6. On the Davidson-Wittgenstein comparison, see Richard Rorty, "Heidegger, Wittgenstein and the Reification of Language," in *The Cambridge Companion to Heidegger,* ed. Charles B. Guignon (Cambridge: Cambridge University Press, 1993), 337–57.

3. See Richard Rorty, "Pragmatism, Davidson, and Truth," in *Truth and Interpretation: Perspectives on the Philosophy of Donald Davidson,* ed. Ernest LePore (Oxford: Blackwell, 1986), 333–55; and John P. Murphy, *Pragmatism from Peirce to Davidson* (Boulder, Colo.: Westview, 1990). Although he has since wobbled, Davidson could describe himself in 1987 as a "pragmatist" about truth. See Donald Davidson, "Afterthoughts, 1987," in *Reading Rorty,* ed. Alan Malachowski (Oxford: Blackwell, 1990), 134. See also Davidson, "The Structure and Content of Truth," *Journal of Philosophy* 87 (1990): 279–28, where he repudiates correspondence and coherence theories alike. For his regret that he ever called his own theory a coherence theory, see "Afterthoughts, 1987," 136–38. Davidson has been explicit about the relationship of his own views to Rorty's: "Where we differ, if we do, is on whether there remains a question how, given that we cannot 'get outside our beliefs and our language so as to find some test other than coherence,' we nevertheless can have knowledge of, and talk about, an objective public world which is not of our own making. I think this question does remain, while I suspect that Rorty doesn't think so" ("Afterthoughts, 1987," 137).

4. See Davidson, "Structure and Content," 305.

5. Bertrand Russell, *A History of Western Philosophy* (New York: Simon and Schuster, 1967 [1945]), 818; see also Russell, "William James's Conception of Truth" [1908], in *Philosophical Essays* (London: Longmans, Green, 1910), 124.

6. William James, *Pragmatism and the Meaning of Truth* (Cambridge, Mass.: Harvard University Press, 1978), 172.

7. Ibid., 272, 56; see also William James, *The Varieties of Religious Experience* (Cambridge, Mass.: Harvard University Press, 1985), 341–42.

8. A. J. Ayer, *Philosophy in the Twentieth Century* (New York: Random House, 1982), 82; James, *Pragmatism and the Meaning of Truth,* x–xxi.

9. Peirce, *Collected Papers,* 5:407; cf. 384, 494, 553. Peirce's definition can be taken in two strikingly different ways, as saying either (1) that truth cannot be known until the end of time (notoriously long in coming) or (2) that the current best opinion of the communi-

ty of inquirers generates fallible truth claims. In the first, eschatological foundations bolster conjectures. In the second, consensus replaces foundations of any kind. For the sake of simplicity I am taking account only of (1) here.

10. Richard Rorty, "Pragmatism, Relativism, and Irrationalism," *Consequences of Pragmatism* (Minneapolis: University of Minnesota Press, 1982): 160–75.

11. Donald Davidson, *Inquiries into Truth and Interpretation* (Oxford: Clarendon, 1984), 194.

12. Rorty, "Pragmatism, Davidson, and Truth," 334–35.

13. This example is Murphy's in *Pragmatism from Peirce to Davidson*, 112.

14. Davidson, *Inquiries*, 70.

15. Donald Davidson, "The Myth of the Subjective," in *Relativism: Interpretation and Confrontation*, ed. Michael Krausz (Oxford: Oxford University Press, 1989), 159–71.

16. Davidson, *Inquiries*, 194.

17. The definitive critique of the logic of functionalism in the social sciences was made by Carl G. Hempel as early as 1959 in his essay "The Logic of Functional Analysis." See Carl Hempel, *Aspects of Scientific Explanation* (New York: Free Press, 1965). In religious studies Hans H. Penner has provided the most thorough refutation of functionalist theories; see chapter 4 of his *Impasse and Resolution* (New York: Peter Lang, 1989) and "What's Wrong with Functional Explanations," in *Language, Truth, and Religious Belief*, eds. Nancy K. Frankenberry and Hans H. Penner (Atlanta, Ga.: Scholars, 1999), 246–70.

18. In H. Dreyfus and P. Rabinow, *Michel Foucault: Beyond Structuralism and Hermeneutics* (Chicago: University of Chicago Press, 1982), 187.

19. See Davidson, *Inquiries*, 183–98.

20. See Terry F. Godlove Jr., *Religion, Interpretation, and Diversity of Belief: The Framework Model from Kant to Durkheim to Davidson* (Cambridge: Cambridge University Press, 1989; repr., Macon, Ga.: Mercer University Press, 1997).

21. Donald Davidson, "Thought and Talk," in *Mind and Language*, ed. Samuel Guttenplan (Oxford: Clarendon, 1975), 149.

22. Ibid.

23. Davidson, *Inquiries*, 67.

24. Ibid., 137.

25. Ibid., 20.

26. Davidson, "Myth of the Subjective," 159.

27. See David B. Wong, "Three Kinds of Incommensurability," in *Relativism*, ed. Krausz, 140–58.

28. See Rorty, *Consequences of Pragmatism*, 168.

29. James, *Pragmatism and the Meaning of Truth*, 126.

30. For an excellent critical discussion of the disenchantment of subjectivity, recalling Weber's analysis of the disenchantment of the world, see Frank B. Farrell, *Subjectivity, Realism, and Postmodernism—The Recovery of the World* (Cambridge: Cambridge University Press, 1994).

31. Davidson, "Myth of the Subjective," 162.

32. Ibid., 163.

33. Ibid., 170.

34. Ibid., 171.

20. John Dewey's Conception of the Religious Dimension of Experience

CARL G. VAUGHT

When John Dewey wrote his reflections about the religious dimension of experience, he addressed himself to a crisis in American intellectual life. This crisis was generated by a radical opposition between two attitudes about the truth of religion. On the one hand, many people believed in the existence of the supernatural, assuming that a supernatural being is necessary for anything worthy of the name of religion to exist. On the other hand, an increasingly militant group of atheists were opposed to belief in the supernatural because they were convinced that the advance of culture and science had "completely discredited it."[1]

Dewey responded to this conflict by claiming that it depends on a dubious presupposition. Both the defenders and the critics of religion assumed that religion is unintelligible apart from reference to the supernatural, causing the atheist not only to dismiss the truth claims of particular religions but also to turn away from everything of a religious nature (2). In distancing himself from both camps, Dewey claimed that the religious dimension of experience should be freed from the identification of religion with what transcends the natural order. He also urged his readers to embrace "a common faith" that does not commit us to the doctrines of a particular religion but points instead to "the emancipation of elements and outlooks [in experience] that may be called religious" (8).

In urging that this emancipation occur, Dewey was not only attempting to resolve the conflict between two competing views about the truth and value of religion but also trying to affect how his readers felt and what they did about the religious dimension of experience. He was convinced that religious values are deeply ingrained in the texture of ordinary life and was committed to the view that the ethical and the ideal content of religions could be increased if his audience focused their attention on them (8). Yet Dewey also believed that particular religions often prevented "the religious quality of experience from coming to consciousness" (9). As a consequence, he drew a radical distinction between religions, on the one hand, and the religious dimension of experience, on the other (9).

This distinction can be formulated in the following way. A particular religion is committed to "a special body of beliefs and practices" that pertains to the supernatural, and it always has "some kind of institutional organization" (9). By contrast, the religious aspect of experience "denotes attitudes that may be taken toward every object and every proposed end or ideal" (10). Another way to express this point is to say that the difference between *religion* and *religious* is more than the difference between the substantive and adjectival forms of the same root (3). The first case involves an institutional structure and a theological framework that attempt to express and defend a belief in the existence of a supernatural being. The second case involves a positive attitude toward certain values in experience that ought to be enhanced.

One of the principal ways in which Dewey attacked religion as a substantive and turned away from its typically concomitant belief in the supernatural was to focus his attention on the status of religious experience. His primary claim in this connection was that religious experience is not autonomous and does not mark off a separate domain that can be defined in terms of "a special kind of object" (11). Although Dewey was committed to the view that aesthetic, scientific, moral, and political kinds of experience point to realms of their own, he was equally convinced that the religious dimension of experience is a quality that may belong to all these other kinds of experience without having a distinctive kind of object (11).

One of Dewey's principal reasons for insisting that the religious aspect of experience is a second-order phenomenon was to block the inference from the occurrence of religious experiences to the existence of a special kind of object. He did not doubt that transforming experiences often occur, nor was he inclined to doubt their validity. However, he insisted that experiences of this kind cannot be used to prove the existence of a supernatural being. As he formulated the point, "The only thing that can be said to be 'proved' is the existence of some complex of conditions that have operated to effect an adjustment in life, an orientation, that brings with it a sense of security and peace. The particular interpretation given to this complex of conditions is not inherent in the experience itself. It is derived from the culture with which a particular person is imbued" (13). Again, Dewey did not deny the genuineness of religious transformation, nor was he concerned, "save incidentally," to point to "the possibility of a purely naturalistic explanation of the event" (13). Rather, he maintained that the religious quality of experience is the effect and not the cause of the experience in question. As a consequence, he claimed that an experience that has religious force "because of what it does in and to the processes of living and religious experience as a separate kind of thing" must be distinguished (14).

A number of crucial issues emerge from these claims, but the one that needs to be pursued first is whether a dimension of experience can be autonomous without presupposing the existence of a special kind of object with which it is correlated. Dewey took it for granted that the answer is no, leading him to embrace the view that the religious aspect of life is so intertwined with all the others that it cannot constitute a realm of its own. By contrast, my own view is that even though the religious dimension of experience does not presuppose the existence of a supernatural being, this does not imply that it should not be acknowledged as an autonomous domain.

One of the most important results of the phenomenology of religion in the twentieth century has been its success in demonstrating that religious experience is autonomous, not because it marks off a special kind of object, but because it has phenomenological traits that transcend every other domain. For example, in *The Idea of the Holy* Rudolf Otto calls our attention to the *mysterium tremendum,* which is clearly not an object but to which we respond in awe and fascination nonetheless.[2] In *Dynamics of Faith* Paul Tillich identifies faith with ultimate concern, where ultimate concern can be authentic only if the mind, the will, and the emotions are oriented toward what is genuinely ultimate. Yet in this case also, religion can be understood as an autonomous domain without being defined in terms of a special kind of object.[3]

Despite this crucial difference, the relation between Dewey and the phenomenologists of religion is more positive than might at first appear to be the case. On the one hand, they agree that the religious dimension of experience should not be defined in terms of a special kind of object; on the other hand, they agree that religion should not be understood simply as one domain in contrast with others. Dewey expressed this view by claiming that religiousness is "a quality that may belong to all experiences," and Tillich expressed it when he said that religion points to the dimension of ultimacy that manifests itself in all the realms of experience and culture.[4] However, disagreement arises about where to locate the dimension of ultimacy to which religious experience gives us access. Dewey located it in the *attitudes* we adopt toward the "processes of living," while Tillich located it in what *transcends* the opposition between subject and object altogether.[5]

Almost despite himself, Dewey acknowledged the dimension of transcendence in religion by noting that even fundamentalists believe that the "objects of [religious] beliefs are so far beyond finite human capacity that [they] must be couched in . . . metaphoric terms" (40). However, he joined the fundamentalists in failing to appreciate the fact that transcendence of this kind implies that the object of religion is not a being that exists in contrast with others. Rather, the metaphorical language to which we must resort in this case indicates that the ultimate transcends the distinction between essence and existence that reference to a special kind of object presupposes.

The contrast between Dewey and the phenomenologists surfaces most clearly in their contrasting attitudes to the causal factors to which we might appeal in accounting for the occurrence of religious experiences. Having claimed that experiences of this kind "bring about a better, deeper and enduring adjustment in life," Dewey said that they are caused by "all the conditions of nature and human association that support and deepen the sense of values that carry one through periods of darkness and despair" (14). In speaking about the status of mystical experience, he made a similar point by claiming, "As with every empirical phenomenon, the occurrence of the state called mystical is simply an occasion for inquiry into its mode of causation. There is no more reason for converting the experience itself into an immediate knowledge of its cause than in the case of lightning or any other natural occurrence" (37–38). By contrast with this position, it is possible to agree with the phenomenologists of religion that an encounter with the ultimate takes us beyond the confines of ordinary experience, giving as access to what transcends the subject-object opposition and, by implication, to what outstrips the causal nexus in which subjects and objects interact. What Dewey failed to anticipate is that by denying that religious experience is to be defined in terms of a special kind of object, he opened the door for the assertion that experience of this kind transcends the causal nexus in which empirical subjects and objects are implicated.

Despite this difficulty, it is important to notice that Dewey was aware of the special status of the religious aspect of experience as a way of transforming human existence. Contrasting religious experience with aspects of experience that affect "*particular* modes of conduct," that do not pertain to "the entire self," and that are primarily "*passive*," he said that some changes in ourselves "are much more inclusive and deep seated" and "pertain to our being in its entirety" (15–16). Changes of this kind involve a "change *of* will" rather than a "change *in* will," and "because of their scope," the consequent "modification of ourselves is enduring" (17). Against this background Dewey claimed that whenever such a change occurs, the resultant attitude is religious. More precisely, he said, "when it occurs, from whatever cause and by whatever means, there is a religious outlook and function" (17).

The holistic character of this religious outlook and of the existential transformation on which it depends serves to distinguish the religious dimension of experience from all other aspects of life, which pertain to a part rather than the whole. As the phenomenologists have suggested, this points to the possibility that the ultimate transcends the subject-object opposition and transforms our hearts at the place where the mind, the will, and the emotions intersect. However, this possibility places transformations of this kind beyond the reach of scientific explanation. In traditional Kantian terms, the encounter with the ultimate occurs at the noumenal rather than the phenomenal level, where this aspect of the religious dimension of experience makes a naturalistic appraisal of it irrelevant.

* * *

As he developed his concept of a common faith, Dewey took the problem of religious transformation to a deeper level by reflecting on the concept of the self as a whole and on the role of the imagination in giving us access to it within the larger world of which it is a part. With respect to the concept of a whole, he said:

> The idea of a whole, whether of the whole personal being or of the world, is an imaginative, not a literal idea. The limited world of our observation and reflection becomes the world only through imaginative extension. It cannot be apprehended in knowledge or realized in reflection. Neither observation, thought, nor practical activity can attain that complete unification of the self which is called whole. The *whole* self is an ideal, an imaginative projection. Hence the idea of a thoroughgoing and deep seated harmonizing of the self with the Universe (as a name for the totality of conditions with which the self is connected) operates only through imagination—which is one reason why this composing of the self is not voluntary in the sense of an act of special volition or resolution. (25)

Dewey added that a deep-seated adjustment of the self "possesses the will" and is "an influx from sources beyond conscious deliberation and purpose" (19). Indeed, he said that this is one of the most important reasons for the familiar claim that explanations for such phenomena are either supernatural or subconscious.

From a phenomenological point of view, the most serious defect of this analysis of religious transformation is that Dewey failed to appreciate the implications of his own description of the holistic dimension of experience. He

said that "the whole" is an imaginative rather than a literal idea; that it transcends observation and reflection; that observation, thought, and practical
activity cannot produce the unification of the self; that the "whole self" is both
an ideal and an imaginative projection; that the universe with which the self
needs to be harmonized is the totality of conditions with which we are connected; and that the unification of the self does not result from a voluntary
act of will or resolution. In all these ways he placed both the self that needs to
be unified and the totality of conditions to which it needs to be related beyond the empirical domain in which causal explanations are relevant.

In claiming that the idea of a whole is an imaginative projection, Dewey
also overlooked the fact that this projection is meaningless apart from a limit
in terms of which it can be defined. It is this limit to which the phenomenologists call our attention when they claim that the ultimate transcends the
contrasts between subject and object on the one hand and essence and existence on the other. Formulated in a somewhat different way, our experience
of a limit that cannot be transcended is a way of participating in the ultimate
dimension of experience, where the ultimate is the "screen" on which our
imaginative ideas are projected rather than the contents of the projections
themselves.

Dewey seemed to appreciate this point when he claimed that the "unification of the self . . . cannot be attained in terms of itself." Indeed, he even
seemed to embrace it when he said that the "self is always directed toward
something beyond itself and . . . its own unification depends upon the idea
of the integration of the shifting scenes of the world into that imaginative
totality we call the universe" (19). Integration of this kind presupposes that
an "ideal end" that marks the boundary of human experience has conquered
us, and it "signifies acknowledgement of . . . [the] rightful claim [of this ideal]
over our desires and purposes" (20). Dewey's point is ambiguous, however,
because he claimed that the authority that exercises control over us is ideal
rather than actual (21). If he meant that the ideal is not a being that contrasts
with others, he was correct; but if he meant that it is a construction of the
productive imagination rather than an expression of the ultimate dimension
of experience to which the phenomenologists refer, he was not.

It is difficult to know where Dewey stood on this issue. On the one hand,
he acknowledged that the ideal contrasts with us by referring to its intrinsic
nature rather than its bare existence (23). The second way of speaking reduces
an ideal to an object, while the first allows it to stand over against us without
reducing it to one object among others. On the other hand, the claim that
concepts such as the self and the world are imaginative projections suggests
that the framework within which ideals exercise their normative function are

products of human subjectivity. If this proves to be the case, it would be tempting to conclude that the ideals that unify the self with the world are just as subjective as these ideas themselves.

Dewey summarizes his account of the ideals that unify the self with the world by claiming that "the religious is 'morality touched by emotion' . . . [where] the ends of moral conviction arouse emotions that are not only intense but are actuated and supported by ends so inclusive that they unify the self. The inclusiveness of the end in relation to both self and the 'universe' to which an inclusive self is related is indispensable" (23). Dewey claims that the religious attitude generated by responding to ends of this kind is comprehensive and that it is "broader than anything indicated by 'moral' in its usual sense" (23). In addition, he tells us that though these ends unify the self, they are able to do this only if they are sufficiently comprehensive to bind the whole of the self to the whole of the universe (23).

Perhaps the best way to advance the discussion of Dewey's conception of religious faith and to decide whether the brush of subjectivity tarnishes his account of it is to consider the nature of faith in his own case. In expressing his deepest and most passionate religious convictions, Dewey often maintained that he was committed to "the continued [disclosure] of truth through directed . . . human endeavor" and that he trusted scientific inquiry to yield more knowledge and more intelligence as it continued to develop (26). As a consequence, he committed himself to the view that what counts is the scientific method, not particular beliefs (23), and that science's negative attitude to established doctrine, religious or otherwise, "signifies supreme loyalty to the method by which truth is attained" (39).

Dewey claimed that loyalty to such ideals is too infrequent, for energy that might have been devoted to them has been siphoned off into beliefs about the supernatural. As a consequence, he proposed to emancipate the religious dimension of experience from particular religions, so that the religious aspect of life could come to focus in commitment to the scientific method. Dewey claimed that the religious quality of this commitment is bound up not "with any single item of intellectual assent" (32) but with the conviction that the scientific method is "the final arbiter of all questions of fact, existence, and intellectual assent" (31).

It is important to notice that Dewey embraced this point of view, not in the way that he would verify a fact, but by pointing to its value as a way of integrating the self. First, he identified the religious quality of the value in question by asserting that any "activity pursued in behalf of an ideal and against obstacles and in spite of threats of personal loss because of conviction of its general and enduring value is religious in quality" (27). Second, having implied that he had suffered for his faith, he detached the scientific method from any fact that might be discovered by claiming, "Were we to admit that there is but one method for ascertaining fact and truth . . . , no discovery in any branch of knowledge could disturb the faith that is religious" (33). Finally, he placed his faith in the scientific method within the broadest possible context by saying, "I should describe this faith as the unification of the self through allegiance to inclusive ideal ends, which imagination presents to us and to which the human will responds as worthy of controlling our desires and choices" (33).

Dewey's reason for embracing the scientific method was that it leads to the progressive unfolding of truth through cooperative inquiry. However, he claimed that commitment to an enterprise of this kind is religious because it depends on faith rather than sight. Dewey knew that however successful the scientific enterprise has been in the past, there is no guarantee that this will continue to be the case in the future. Thus, he focused on the religious aspect of his attitude toward the scientific method by claiming that if we commit ourselves to it, faith in the value of scientific inquiry will be beyond the reach of criticism. In the final analysis, what counts in Dewey's commitment to "the method of intelligence" is his belief that faith in it will unify the self through its commitment to "ideal ends" that the imagination presents, the will selects, and the intellect regards "as worthy of controlling our desires and choices" (41). In the language of Tillich, what could reflect more clearly the ultimate concern of a religious heart in which the intellect, the will, and the emotions are united?

It is important to notice that the religious faith that animated Dewey is not itself scientific but rather the condition that makes his commitment to the scientific method possible. This condition, in turn, is not grounded in an objective state of affairs but in the imagination that projects it and the will that embraces it. From a transcendental point of view, Dewey's faith rests on a subjective foundation not in the pejorative sense, in which imagination is equated with something fanciful, but in the sense that imagination is the means by which values are projected as controlling ideals. Having begun by attacking the supernatural as an objective domain, it is not surprising that he ends by embracing the domain of transcendental subjectivity. Doing so enabled him to detach religious values from empirical states of affairs and to move beyond objects of experience to holistic concepts, such as the self and the world, that the values to which he committed himself were able to integrate.

This way of formulating the matter is not the way Dewey himself expressed it. He prided himself not only in liberating the religious dimension of experience from particular religions but also in escaping the transcendental philosophy of his idealistic predecessors. Thus, in expressing his views about the relation between ideal values and the imagination, he said, "An ideal is not an illusion because imagination is the organ through which it is apprehended. . . . All possibilities reach us through the imagination" (43). Having claimed repeatedly that the imagination *projects* ideal values that unify the self with the world, he shifted abruptly in this passage from the language of production to the language of apprehension. The question that arises at this juncture, however, is whether the integration of the self with the world arises from the self, the world, or elsewhere. It is Dewey's answer to this crucial question to which I now turn.

* * *

Dewey gave his most "objective" answer to the question before us when he discussed the concept of God. In the course of his remarks, he said that the term designates not "a particular being" but "the unity of all ideal ends arousing us to desire and actions" (42). Then he continued, "The word 'God' means the ideal ends that at a given time and place one acknowledges as having authority over his volition and emotion, the values to which one is supremely devoted, as far as these ends, through imagination, take on unity" (42). Insofar as the ends to which Dewey referred are ideals that measure and regulate conduct, they are not a function of the self but of something outside ourselves to which we are responsible. To the extent that the imagination gives us access to them, the otherness of the values in question are also preserved. In both respects Dewey apparently freed himself from the pervasive problem of subjectivity.

To say this is not to claim that Dewey fell back into a belief in the supernatural but to suggest that the ideals by which we are guided have their own integrity. Dewey formulated the point in the most forceful way possible: "The reality of ideal ends in their authority over us is an undoubted fact" (44). Nevertheless, Dewey reversed his philosophical direction by insisting that an ideal has its roots in the productive imagination's response to natural conditions. In connection with this, he claimed that an ideal "emerges when the imagination idealizes existence by laying hold of possibilities offered to thought and action" (48). Dewey concluded that when the productive imagination does this, it seizes on "precious things" and "projects" them (48).

These passages seem sufficient to show that Dewey moved once more into the domain of transcendental subjectivity, but he confirmed the fact by claiming that the "aims and ideals that move us are generated through imagination " (49). Of course, like the more traditional transcendental philosophers whom he was never able to forget, Dewey was always happy to avail himself of empirical material. Thus he claimed that although ideals are generated by the imagination, "they are made out of the hard stuff of the world" (49). And as if to disavow the transcendental component of his position altogether, he added that the process by which ideals are generated is experimental, continuous, and natural and grows in definiteness and coherence (49–50). Nevertheless, Dewey failed to recognize that the projection that generates ideal ends occurs within a framework that is anything but natural. The act of projection presupposes the concepts of the self, the world, and the connection between them, and it is our transcendental apprehension of these realities that makes natural activity possible.

As the phenomenologists of religion have indicated, the nonempirical concepts that Dewey presupposed point not to supernatural beings that stand over against us but to conditions that transcend the distinction between subject and object and that make the contrast between them possible. He was correct in believing that imagination is essential in giving us access to them, but he was incorrect in suggesting that these ideas are generated by the imagination in its productive capacity. The ideas of the self, the world, and God are religious just to the extent that they ground and transcend the distinctions between subject and object and between essence and existence. As Otto and Tillich have suggested, religion as an orientation toward the ultimate brings us into relation with this transcendent ground, where every transaction is rooted in something that will always lie beyond it.

In my earlier discussion of religious experience, I noted three of its most important characteristics. First, it need not presuppose the existence of a supernatural being that may be regarded as its cause. Second, it transcends the natural order, and the scientific explanation appropriate to it, because it involves the unification of the entire person, where the idea of the whole is a nonempirical concept. Finally, access to this nonempirical order occurs when we respond to the ultimate with the whole of our being, where our intellects, our wills, and our emotions are bound together in a larger unity. Dewey tried to capture the truth of these claims by moving beyond the domain of the supernatural; in doing so, however, he moved back and forth between objective and subjective accounts of the religious dimension of experience. On the one hand, he said that religious transformations of the entire person are beyond our own power to realize; on the other hand, he claimed that they result from projections by the self that make the unity of the person possible. Without a concept of the ultimate dimension of experience that transcends the subject-object distinction, and to which the phenomenologists of religion have called our attention, Dewey's instrumentalism was doomed to vacillate between these two incompatible positions.

It might seem unfair to Dewey to focus so much attention on the idea of religious transformation that often results from an encounter with the ultimate. At one juncture he even said that there is no sudden and complete transmutation of the person and that the belief that there is leads to mistaken individualism (47). Although he gave several examples of radical transformations (11–19), it is true that the burden of Dewey's reflections lies elsewhere. He was not concerned primarily with the problem of individual salvation but with the process in which we can join forces with nature to unify the self with the larger world of which we are parts (47–50).

Dewey said that forces "in nature and society generate and support the ideals" to which we commit ourselves (51). He also claimed that these ideals "are further unified by the action that gives them coherence and solidity" (51). He concluded, "It is this *active* relation between ideal and actual to which I would give the name 'God'" (51). When these points are taken together, they represent a final reversal in Dewey's discussion of the issues before us. Having begun by discussing the religious dimension of experience, he now points to an important task to which he wishes to call our attention.

This stage in his reflections is Dewey's version of what is involved in working out our own salvation with fear and trembling. If we begin with the religious dimension of experience as it expresses itself in comprehensive attitudes toward life as a whole, we can move from there to an acknowledgment of God as "the unity of . . . ideal ends arousing us to desire and actions" (42). God in this sense functions not as an efficient cause but as a *lure,* mobilizing us to action in cooperation with the forces of nature. However, Dewey did not reduce God to a regulative ideal; rather, he placed God between the ideal and the actual. Thus, he claimed that a "working union of ideal and actual seems . . . to be identical with the force that has in fact been attached to the conception of God in all the religions that have a spiritual content" (52). In making this claim, and in saying that *uniting* the ideal with the actual is what matters (52), Dewey turned away from the identification of God with an ideal possibility and suggested that God can be regarded as a demiurge in reverse. According to this way of understanding the concept, God is not an ideal that has been projected by the productive imagination, or an active agent that brings the world into existence, but the *activity* in which the actual is united with the ideal by which it is measured.

This final reversal in Dewey's thinking restores a certain equilibrium to his earlier vacillation between objective and subjective accounts of the issues before us. Having moved back and forth between two accounts of the relation between the self and the world, he ends by placing God in the middle ground between two nonempirical conceptions. In this middle ground, however, Dewey's account of the place of God in human experience tilts toward a telos rather than an arche, giving pride of place to the progressive movement from the actuality of the one to the ideality of the other. This is Dewey's version of what it means to place God beyond the contrast between subject and object, and even if it proves to be one-sided, it tacitly acknowledges the truth of the phenomenological claim that God is neither a subject nor an object but the ultimate dimension of experience that gives significance to them both.

Notes

1. John Dewey, *A Common Faith* (New Haven, Conn.: Yale University Press, 1934), 1. Subsequent references to this book appear parenthetically in the text.

2. Rudolf Otto, *The Idea of the Holy* (New York: Oxford University Press, 1958), 12–30.

3. Paul Tillich, *Dynamics of Faith* (New York: Harper and Row, 1958), 1–4. It is interesting to note that in his recent book *Philosophy and Social Hope* (New York: Penguin Books, 1999), Richard Rorty acknowledges this point and suggests that a "pragmatist philosophy of religion must follow Tillich and others in distinguishing quite sharply between faith and belief" (158). The former brings the person into a relationship with God that is analogous to love for another person, while the second is restricted to propositional attitudes that are not sufficient to spell out the nature of our relationship with God.

4. Paul Tillich, "Religion as a Dimension of Man's Spiritual Life," *Theology of Culture* (New York: Oxford University Press, 1959), 3–9.

5. Paul Tillich, *Systematic Theology,* vol. 1 (Chicago: University of Chicago Press, 1951), 171–74.

21. A Peircean Theory of Religious Interpretation

ROBERT CUMMINGS NEVILLE

For both Judaism and Christianity, the suspicion that central biblical symbols do not refer as they seem to reached a crisis in the nineteenth century. There were problems with biblical symbolism earlier, of course, when the determinism of early modern science threatened the possibility of miracles and early historical criticism undermined the understanding of biblical stories and characters as straightforwardly historical. The crisis came, however, when in addition to these problems the popular European and North American imagination became so formed by modern science as to be overwhelmingly out of touch with the biblical imagination.[1] The cosmos of science is so much bigger and older than the cosmos of the Bible that they are different worlds, and the natural history of the earth is utterly unlike that of a divine kingdom. The biblical and the late-modern worlds cannot be imagined together.

The conflict between the two imaginations is the crisis. One can remain within the biblical world and still try to reconcile apparent miracles with scientific principles. One can form one's life by biblical symbols and stories and still appreciate that many are metaphorical and never were meant literally; after all, who ever thought that geology is the proper discipline for studying the Rock of Salvation? Christian thinkers such as Origen and Augustine in the ancient world, as well as Christians and Jews including Anselm, Bonaventura, Maimonides, the Kabbalists, and Bernard of Clairvaux in the European Middle Ages, had thoroughly worked through interpretative issues of symbolism and allegory. Nonetheless, religion hits a crisis when the fundamental imaginative frame by which we live—the ways we take ourselves to be in space and time and the elementary kinds of things we understand to inhabit our cosmos—cannot be registered within the biblical imagination of those things, and vice versa. The crisis is that biblical symbols cannot make religious contact with the imagination by which we live.

One way to handle the incommensurability of imaginative worlds is to segregate and alternate them: accept the imagination of late modernity for six days a week and switch to the biblical world for the Sabbath. Unfortunately, this solution is impossible in any literal sense. We cannot simply turn off the way we apprehend the world for one day a week and adopt another way. What happens instead is that we pretend to adopt the imaginative world of the Bible all the while assuming that after divine services we can watch television, which is not a talking piece of wood like Moses' burning bush but a device that sorts and displays electrons created in the Big Bang some 13 billion years ago. Pretense is not always a bad thing, but in matters religious it is disastrous. Religious practice shaped by the central symbols of the faith is assumed to have a transformative power for individuals and communities. In every religion, not only the theistic ones, symbolically shaped religious practice is taken to transform souls so that they better apprehend and conform to the ultimate. The segregation of the biblical imagination from the imagination of late-modern life makes religion impotent at the most important level.[2]

That impotence is even worse with the other common ploy for dealing with the incommensurability of biblical and late-modern imaginations. Some people segregate not just their time but their very lives, inhabiting the biblical world for some parts of their lives and the late-modern world for other parts, the former being religious and the latter, secular: think of the fundamentalist engineer who builds space shuttles but also believes that Jesus Christ will return from the sky in clouds of glory. Unfortunately, it is simply impossible to divide spheres of life cleanly according to different fundamental imaginations. As a result the religious passion roused and focused by religious symbols becomes attached to finite projects, such as patriotism and other particular forms of culture, and produces demonic distortions of the religion's intent.

Peirce's pragmatic philosophy of religious symbols allows a way forward from this crisis of imaginations; it allows us to shape our lives by central biblical symbols within the reality of our late-modern imagination. Peirce's account of symbols is a tool that allows us also to criticize biblical symbols from the perspective of what we have learned so that we can appreciate the biblical world and its ways of presenting God without our having to deny what we have learned through modern science or to buy into, say, its approval of slavery, subordination of women, or rejection of homosexuals. Peirce's theory allows us also to criticize the imaginative frame of late modernity so that the prophetic edge of the Bible is not lost: although the twentieth century has produced vastly more knowledge about the cosmos than did the first, it has also been vastly more wicked according to many measures. Peirce's theory does not by itself suggest how we should live with religious symbols, nor does it select symbols for us. It does not engage in criticism of biblical symbols, nor does it provide criticism of our own culture from a biblical standpoint. It does, however, allow for and structure those activities.

In the following I defend this judgment about Peirce in a discussion of four theses: (1) Interpretation is *engagement* with the reality interpreted, which in biblical matters means engagement with the divine, with divine manifestations, and with the ways human life is affected by its relations with the divine. (2) Interpretations, including religious ones, are *true or false;* that is, either they take what is important or valuable from the reality interpreted and carry it over to the interpreters, with the symbols representing those interpreted realities, or they do not. (3) The *carryover* in true symbols involves two aspects: (a) the reality interpreted must be carried over into the imagination of the interpreters, and (b) the carryover affects—indeed, transforms—the interpreters and their imagination. (4) Not all religious interpretations operate at such a level as to employ different basic imaginative structures differentially, although most do. When the religious symbols are biblical, the imaginative structure of the Bible is connected to that of late-modern interpreters insofar as the question of truth is pursued and tested. Thus the imaginations are made commensurate, enabling a determination as to whether the interpretations are valid or true and also whether the imaginative frame that receives them can accommodate them without change.

Interpretation as Engagement

According to Peirce's semiotics, the way people engage the world is through interpretation.[3] According to the more usual semiotic approach, interpretation is the way to engage texts. The connection of semiotics, hermeneutics, and interpretation theory with religion comes historically from the fact that the main text to be interpreted has typically been the Bible. Peirce's paradigm of interpretation, by contrast, is experimental science, epitomized in the laboratory but generalized to mean an engagement with nature.

Roughly put, Peirce viewed an interpretation as a hypothesis about the real relative to the interest of the interpreter that is reinforced, disconfirmed, or corrected when the interpretation is put into play. All human interactions with nature involving any kind of human response are shaped by interpretations, from the most passive perceptions to the most aggressive actions. In his early papers "The Fixation of Belief" and "How to Make Our Ideas Clear,"

Peirce argued that the best way to improve our ideas is to put them in the way of being corrected if they are wrong, as a scientist does.[4]

Peirce was a speculative metaphysician of great originality and power, and he extended his semiotics beyond the usual scale of interpretation theory. For instance, he argued that the human self is not an entity that uses signs or makes interpretations but is itself a living sign whose reality consists in interpreting.[5] Moreover, he argued that all physical and other causal processes can be analyzed according to the developmental structure of interpretation. Material causation he regarded as "frozen mind," and the line between that and "psychical" or "mental" causation is not sharp.[6] He generalized the main categories of his theory of interpretation into phenomenological categories from which he constructed an entire evolutionary cosmology. These are his famous categories of firstness, secondness, and thirdness, related so as to give rise to synechism (continuity), tychism (chance), and agapism (evolutionary love or development).[7] These fascinating parts of Peirce's philosophy are not my direct interest here, but note that they go a long way toward making good on his claim that interpretation is engagement with the world. Peirce included as interpretations not just flights of fantasy and directed intellectual inquiries but also bodily processes metabolizing the world. Dewey adopted Peirce's general claim that interpretation is engagement and exploited it in diverse and fruitful ways, calling it "transaction" or "interaction."[8]

For this claim about engagement, the most pertinent part of Peirce's semiotics is his theory of reference. Reference has three main kinds, according to Peirce. The simplest reference is iconicity, in which a sign or set of signs is taken as an icon of the world;[9] the world is taken to be like the iconic sign. In an icon there is some kind of mirroring or iconic mapping of the object.[10] In religious symbols, for example, an icon might be a crucifix referring to Jesus' crucifixion (Peirce in fact offers this example).

The idea of iconicity has much greater applicability, however. A religious mythic world is taken to be iconic of reality; in mythopoeic times no distinction between myth and reality is recognized. In the religions of the era Jaspers called the "Axial Age," however, this distinction is recognized and problematized. This is not the place to dissect the many levels of myth in human culture. At very deep levels, however, it structures elementary imagination about the size, shape, age, and contents of the cosmos, as well as basic causal patterns. The distinction between biblical and late-modern imaginations made earlier can now be called a distinction between basic myths, and the religious conflict between those two imaginations can be recognized as a clash of mythologies. It does not matter that we late-modern sophisticates know our scientific worldview to be a myth; we have no other myth congruent with the rest of our knowledge with which to image or mirror the world. We know our scientific myth is fallible—indeed, doubtlessly inadequate in ways to be proved sooner rather than later—but we have no practical choice save to take the world to be as the late-modern myth says it is.

The positivist conception of science takes scientific theories to be iconic of their objects. So too do positivist theologies, which suppose that theology must describe religious realities. Conservative theologians who defend propositions about religious realities clearly share this iconic view, as do many theologians who talk in narratives, metaphors, and paradoxes. In a sense the entire modern era as influenced by Descartes has supposed that mental representations are supposed to be iconic of extramental realities, and the problem from the beginning has been how to compare them.

The second kind of reference Peirce called indexical.[11] An index is a sign that refers by some kind of causal connection with its object. In general, indexically referring signs connect interpreters causally with the realities interpreted. Indexical reference, if valid, should align interpreters with the causal processes of their reality insofar as the referring signs interpret those realities in respect to those processes. For religions, indexical reference is important because it is crucial for attunement to ultimate realities. When religions speak of people realizing religious truth, the intent is not so much that people have true icons of religious states of affairs but rather that they become true to those realities. To become a saint, to be more holy, or to actualize religious truth is to interpret reality with those indexes that align people with what is objectively and causally real in their objects. Indexical reference is necessary for engagements with reality that allow interpreters to learn from their experience. Many religious themes put soteriological interests ahead of theological ones, claiming that interpretations that are a bit silly when taken as iconic are true and valuable when taken as indexical. A person indexically related to Jesus such that love of God and neighbor animates the person's life has a true reference, even though the person might be hopelessly naïve and prone to error when ascertaining who the historical Jesus was and whether he really gave the Great Commission.

The third kind of reference Peirce called symbolic; I call it conventional.[12] Conventional signs refer by virtue of the structure of a semiotic system. The semantics and syntax of a language system exemplify the complexities of conventional reference. The semiotic system is structured so as to spell out the meanings of signs in codes, to indicate possible versus impossible references to other signs within the systems, and to shape possible interpretations where an interpretation is a complex sign taking another sign to stand for yet a third sign.

Any sign we consider or mention must be in the semiotic system of some language matrix. Thus iconic and indexical references are abstractions from a richer kind of reference that includes the conventions by which we *speak* of crucifixes, myths, and religious practice. In fact, any religious reference we discuss is at least conventional and likely also to involve indexical and iconic elements. Conventional reference connects simple mirroring or brute causal interaction with other signs, other meaning systems, other mirrorings, and other interactions. Thus religions have very complex symbols. The crucifix is an icon of Jesus' crucifixion, but its meaning is connected with his life and teaching, with the culture of the Messiah, and with his significance for disciples and for the whole of Christian thought and practice. Moreover, the conventionality of religious symbols allows religion to be connected with the rest of life, including morality, politics, art, and domestic living. Conventional reference imbeds religion in larger practice.

Peirce's point that interpretation is engagement with the realities interpreted requires all three kinds of reference. Conventional reference is required because all interpretations take place within the ongoing contexts of living, with a physical and social situatedness, inherited practices and habits, and expectations and purposes. Conventional systems of meaning make the integration of these possible. Moreover, conventions are publicly learned. Whether or not Wittgenstein was right to reject private language as impossible, there certainly is not a lot of it. The evolution of human society depends on communication through shared semiotic systems.

Our interpretations are not solely functions of internal mental fantasy, however. Because of indexical reference, conventional signs connect interpreters causally with the reality around them. Indeed, the elaborate conventional systems of civilized life evolved precisely because the signs that refer conventionally can be used indexically to engage reality. If the conventions did not have some indexical reference, they would be pragmatically and evolutionarily useless. Furthermore, although not all religious interpretations need to be iconic in explicit ways, a great many are, and religious interpretation supposes that its fundamental system of images, its basic imagination, mirrors what is important in reality. For practical purposes, it assumes that its imagination can register what is important to register.

Iconicity is the paradigmatic reference for positivists; indexicality, for thinkers of praxis; and conventionality is the paradigm for postmodern deconstructionists. Peirce himself worried about the view that reduces iconicity and indexicality to convention. He called that view "degenerate" firstness and secondness and suspected Hegel of the fault.[13] In our time deconstructionists have argued that, because any iconic and indexical reference can itself be represented within a conventional semiotic system, and because speech about iconic and indexical reference always proceeds within the signs of a semiotic system, there is no reality outside the system of signs. Everything is a text, and nothing is signified but more signifiers. If everything is internal to the semiotic system, then there is no reality to engage, and human life is only discourse, conversation.

Both indexical and iconic reference involve a dualism of the interpreting sign system and the objective reality to which the signs refer, and this is so even when the objective reality is something in the semiotic system itself. Peirce's theory of reference shows how semiotic systems themselves arise through human evolution as they provide ever more sophisticated ways of interacting with the environment so as to help humans survive, multiply, and flourish. It also explains why semiotic systems have structures that appear to refer to real things outside the systems. Peirce's theory not only saves the appearance but provides a ground for engaging reality more deliberately and for making our interpretations vulnerable to correction.

A deep problem has lurked beneath the surface of this discussion of reference in engagement, showing itself primarily in a tendency to apophatic theology. Most traditions of biblical religion have a point at which they say that God is not an object or thing but instead transcends "thingness." Moreover, all the finite manifestations of God in burning bushes, the leadership of Israel, still, small voices, or even Jesus are not religiously interesting in their finitude alone. We can refer to the finite elements without difficulty or with only the usual difficulties of historical inquiry. What makes them religiously interesting is their connection to a divine ground that in some sense is not finite, that is infinite or otherwise indeterminate. The finite elements must enable reference to the infinite elements by analogy.[14]

Theological traditions affirm the apophatic character of the religious object in different ways. The Aristotelian tradition that fed Aquinas assumed that the syntax of language is iconic of reality, so that reality is made up of substances with properties whose icons are propositions with predicates. Thus St. Thomas affirmed the apophatic character of the religious object by saying that God is not a substance, a genus of substances, or even a genus itself. Theologians with an affinity for indexical reference begin with stories about God's participation in their story, but they end the dialectic of anti-idolatry by embracing mysticism, the practical plunge of the soul into the abyss of love. Theologians with an affinity for conventions, as in the rabbinic tradition, talk as if the talk itself defines God, but their language so intensifies finite reference as to become incommensurate with finite things of life.

If the religious object—God, the Ultimate, the Ground of Being—is beyond reference to finite things, is God beyond reference? If the answer is yes, then God cannot be engaged, and Peirce's theory of interpretation is of no help. If the answer is no, then we have to speak to the issue of nonfinite reference. Peirce's semiotics suggests two responses.

First, there is a distinction between a logical object and the kind of reality that object might have. A logical object is simply something to which we can or do refer. Whether that object is finite, infinite, or a finite-infinite contrast makes a difference only to the signs that are used to interpret it. If the sign is complex enough, as is the case for apophatic theology, it can refer to a logical object that is nonfinite or at least more than finite. The question then is one of meaning, of getting the right signs and theories.

Second, Peirce severely criticized nominalism, which he called the great error of modern philosophy.[15] Only a nominalist expects the objects of reference to be objects in the sense of finite things, especially particular finite things. On the contrary, said Peirce, most of the important things in life are quite general. What is the tendency of the universe? In what does the ideal of the good life consist? What is the spirit of an age? On a more prosaic level, we can enter a room full of people and pick up its mood, its tensions, frustrations, or glee. None of these "objects" is a finite particular, and yet we refer to them in discussion and assume them in life. The reference to them is complex, because we identify them through a great many integrated details. Most of us could not even say what particular things we notice when we pick up on tension in a group. The signs by which we refer to such things are extraordinarily complex, referring in mediating ways to a great many other things but integrating all those other references using what Peirce would call a hypothesis or theory. On the intellectual side of religion, it takes a whole theology to refer to God; that's why theologians are so verbose—the fragment of a theology likely fails its ultimate reference. On the practical side of religion, it takes a vast nest of symbolic networks, supplementing and balancing one another.

With these two observations showing why reference to a transcendent God might not be impossible, we move from a Peircean study of reference to one of meaning or the symbol systems themselves.

The Truth of Religious Symbols

Signs, including religious symbols, have content, and they will be true if that content applies to the reality to which they refer in the respect in which the symbol is taken to represent the reality. Peirce had an extraordinarily original and creative theory of signs, dividing them into trichotomies of trichotomies and ten different classes. His theory of the internal structure of sign systems is not germane here, however.[16] More important is his theory of the structure of religious sign or symbol systems.[17]

Signs (or meanings or symbols) are defined within semiotic systems. What does the *definition* of signs mean in this context? In a classic development of Peircean semiotics, flawed though it is, Charles W. Morris says that the definition of signs has three senses: syntactics, semantics, and pragmatics.[18] Syntatics he defines as the structure of the semiotic system of signs itself; semantics, as the relation of signs to their objects, which Peirce called reference; and pragmatics, as the relation of signs to their interpreter, which Peirce called simply interpretation. For Morris, however, the semantic objects of signs are objects as other signs refer to them and so are within the semiotic system. In addition, the interpreter is not a real interpreter but an interpretive interest and summary interpretation, also within the semiotic system. Thus in Morris's sense, syntactics, semantics, and pragmatics are all parts of what I call the *extension* of a semiotic system. Their study is study of the nature of the system itself—not of its referential relation to realities or of the system's roles in the actual lives of interpreters. We should note, in contrast to the *extension* of signs within a semiotic system, the *intention* of signs in actual interpretation, wherein the signs with their defining system shape interpretive engagements with reality. To engage reality interpretively is to use signs intentionally. Intention involves real reference and real interpretation. But that is not my concern. We should look now at the extension of signs and its role in truth.

Roughly put, the syntax of a semiotic system is its grammar, its underlying structure defining possible relations among kinds of signs. Semantics concerns the way signs are defined in terms of one another. Dictionary definitions are abstractions of semantics. Semantic definitions are often equivocal, with the polysemy playing one meaning off against another, in metaphor and other semantic tropes. Semantic meanings also include shades and resonances of historical or customary use; the metaphor of "rosey fingered dawn," for example, resonates Homer's epic. Pragmatics involves the way signs are defined within their semiotic system by interpreters' interests, purposes, and various interpretive contexts. More formally, interpretive intent defines the fact that a sign refers to its object in a certain respect; this is a formal property of any interpretation—a sign represents its object to an interpreter in a certain respect. In our semiotic system the sign *red* thus represents the barn to the viewer in respect to color; to Senator McCarthy it represents the movie actor in respect of political affiliation; to the auditor it represents the bottom line in respect to financial trouble. Students of semiotic systems, whether verbal languages or visual symbols in European churches, can and should study the syntactics, semantics, and pragmatics of the system's extension. I suspect the distinction between syntactics, semantics, and pragmatics is not as clear-cut as Morris imagined when he took his cue from Peirce's clear distinction between signs as meanings, reference, and interpretation. Surely fundamental levels of imagination, such as distinguish the biblical from the late-modern worlds, lie at the juncture of syntactics, semantics, and pragmatics.

For the case of religious symbols, let us look more closely at the semantics or systems of meanings. Most important religious symbols are semantically defined through networks and nests of symbol systems. By *symbol system* here I mean a relatively tight and unique association of interdefining symbols. For instance, the symbol of Jesus as the Lamb of God is defined within the system that likens him to the first Passover, when the Jews in Egypt slew a lamb or goat and painted its blood over their doors so that the angel set to kill all firstborns would pass over the Jewish homes. In this symbol system Jesus is our Passover lamb. But there is another symbol system defining Jesus as the Lamb of God, namely, the one that associates him with the scapegoat or lamb sent into the wilderness every year in ancient Israel on the Day of Atonement to carry off the sins of the priest and the people. This symbol system says Jesus bears our sins, something not connected at all with the Passover lamb, which is about divine wrath. Those two symbol systems have been employed within Christianity to symbolize the atonement work of Jesus as redeemer. Two other symbol systems have been important for that, too. In one, God is symbolized as contending with Satan over the future of humanity, and Jesus is given to Satan, who has deserved possession of human souls, in order to ransom those souls so that they can return to God; Satan cannot keep Jesus in death, however, and so is cheated while humankind is redeemed. The fourth symbol system for atonement, made popular by Anselm, represents God as having such justice and dignity that human beings should be damned for their sins despite God's love of them; Jesus, God's own son, is sacrificed to balance out the evil of humankind so that God's justice and dignity can be kept while humankind can be restored by God's love.

How do these symbol systems of atonement fit together? Classical theology has attempted to fit them into a network of symbol systems, showing how they all play roles in a larger univocal picture. A theological network is a system of conceptual signs that integrates various components coherently and consistently. Calvin, for instance, developed a theory of Jesus' work under the rubrics of king, priest, and prophet, according to which he was able to integrate a great deal that various biblical symbols say about Jesus. The systems of atonement symbols, however, just do not seem to fit together. Faced with this lack of fit, theologians have three main options. They can adopt one symbol system as the true or dominant one and dismiss the others as false or merely supplementary metaphors. They can back away from the whole problem, attempting to explain how Jesus saves without the problematics of atonement. Or they can say that the several symbol systems, though not consistent in a theological network, function truthfully as a nest of symbol systems. The nest itself is functional in the lives of Christians, so that all the symbol systems apply in the liturgies of the Church, for instance, or in devotional literature.

In religious practice symbol systems are almost always nested rather than networked. Even where a religious community has a large and sophisticated theology that allows theologians to organize the main symbol systems in a coherent network, most people in the community are not theologians and thus apprehend the symbol systems not as organized in a network but as nested in various practices. Consider the symbol systems that are exercised in the Christian eucharist, or Lord's Supper: death and resurrection as the emblem of authentic human existence, the elements as nourishing food for the soul, the celebration of a common meal by Christians, Jesus' inclusive table fellowship embracing the unembraceable, the sacrament as an exercise of solidarity with Christians all over the world and through time, the reference to the historical Jesus by whom contemporary participants define their historical identity, the reference to Jesus as God or the Son of God, the fact that participants both as individuals and as members of a voluntary community are presented to God, the idea that the host is the just king who is imposing his own order, and the cannibal rite of eating Jesus' flesh and blood.[19] These are only some of the symbol systems in the eucharistic rite and do not include those over which the Orthodox, Roman Catholics, and Protestants dispute. The symbol systems here are not congruent but lived with through the liturgical practice of the Eucharist; they come to resonate with, reinforce, and sometimes correct one another. The cannibal rite, for instance, finds its redemption in the system that introduces participants to Christ as the just king and lord of the table.

Religious symbols range from the concrete and particular to the universal, abstract, and theoretical. Stories—for instance, those of the Exodus and Jesus' ministry—are particular, whereas the symbol of God as creator has a kind of universal application and is assumed more than discussed throughout the Bible. The distinction between particular and universal does not cash out to a distinction between vividly gripping and blandly theoretical, however. The story of the Exodus is gripping if you and your group can identify with it, as many African Americans do; but if you identify more with the dispossessed Canaanites or do not identify at all with questions concerning who gets to own a land, then the story has no vividness or gripping quality for you. A symbol such as God as creator, present and presupposed in most other biblical religious symbols, may not be vivid, but it is gripping in the sense of being operative and having effect. For persons of an intellectual bent, even a symbol such as an abstract theory, a comprehensive theology, might be gripping in the sense that it provides the main symbols by which a theologian engages the divine. Just as most of us can perceive tension in a social gathering through signs that integrate the intricacies of a thousand unnoticed subinterpretations, some theologians can find God in the vast hypothetical network symbols of a complex theology.

The difference between gripping and indifferent religious symbols concerns whether those symbols have indexical reference. Gripping symbols put interpreters into a causal nexus with the religious objects in the respects in which the symbols represent those objects. If an interpreter can identify with the Exodus story, that story connects the interpreter with the divine in respect of liberation and divine care, making the interpreter part of the people of God. Without that identification, the person can know the story but remain indifferent. Similarly a nest of symbol systems that cannot be integrated into a network can function in a gripping way. The symbol systems about the atonement are such a nest, and for some people they function so as apparently to effect the work of salvation or justification. Those people can identify with the symbol systems, nested together, in such a way that they are indexically connected with the redeeming history. Other people, of course, do not connect indexically with those symbols at all, especially in this enlightened age. Modern people have little involvement with purification of sin through the blood sacrifice of pigeons or bulls, let alone of humans. Most moderns think it childish and unworthy of God to need horrendous punishment to set the scales of justice in balance and view God's sacrifice of his son as child abuse. Indeed most moderns are embarrassed on an explicit, conscious level by the bloody atonement imagery in all its symbol systems. And yet the liturgies using these symbol systems remain powerful even today to many who disown their apparent content. Perhaps this is so because there is some depth of evil in the human soul, felt but not acknowledged, which can be addressed only by a blood sacrifice or recognized only in a cannibal rite. Perhaps there is a profound human grasp of sinfulness such that in the face of the ultimate, with no excuses or extenuating circumstances or second chances, God must be personified as a judge whose only way to acknowledge humanity is to condemn it. The profound religious symbols engage people indexically with the ultimate even when the iconic reference of the symbols is rejected. In the terms of Peircean semiotics, I suspect that we moderns reject the bloody atonement imagery as having no true iconic reference, while we embrace it as having indexical reference. Iconically, we do not believe that killing somebody else justifies our sins or that God would enjoy that. Indexically, those same stories and symbol systems have healing power and are true for many who disbelieve their iconic reference.

Notice how carefully the argument has sidled up at last to the question of truth, claiming that certain symbols can be true when interpreted with indexical reference even though, iconically, things are not like those symbols say they are.[20]

Now as to truth, I propose the pragmatic hypothesis that truth is the carryover of value or importance from the objects into the interpreters in the respects in which the signs interpret the objects, as qualified by the biology, culture, semiotic systems, and purposes of the interpreters.[21] This formula goes beyond anything Peirce said, but it is a clear extension of his pragmatic correspondence theory. Like Aristotle's, this is a causal theory of truth. For Aristotle, the senses (ultimately touch) causally carry over objects' forms but not their matter, delivering them to the interpreter's mind, which then takes on the same forms. He viewed the purest, most divine knowing to be of those truths that are eternal and have no matter, so that nothing is left behind and the carryover of form carries over the whole reality; Descartes's theory of the light of reason echoes this view. The theory that truth is the carryover of value or importance differs from Aristotle's in respect to what is carried over. If form is what is carried over, then all reference would be iconic only, and we have seen that there are other kinds. Also, it is hard to see how there could be a carryover of form into the mind or brain without supposing a very crude sense of microcosmic duplication of macrocosmic form.

From an evolutionary point of view, organisms need to know what is important in their surroundings for their own security, growth, and flourishing. They evolve sensors and neural responders that register these things. As soon as the brain evolves the capacity to operate causally in terms of semiotic systems, people are able to question what is really important and valuable in their surroundings at a great distance from their immediate survival and flourishing needs. Or rather, given the extraordinary beauty and value of the cosmos, people define their flourishing as being able to ingest the deepest and most important things, becoming transformed in the process into creatures capable of bearing those profoundly wonderful things. Religion, of course, deals at precisely this level of engagement with the ultimately important and glorious and with the human flaws that stand so starkly in contrast.

That truthful carryover is qualified by human biology simply makes the point that the causal processes for mediating what is important have to pass into human biological life. This point fosters inquiry into the scientific understanding of logic as practiced. That truthful carryover is qualified by culture and semiotic systems means that the symbolic forms that embody the valuable and important will be different in different cultures, and people cannot use symbols effectively when they do not have the culture and semiotic systems that define them. That carryover is qualified by the purposes of the interpreters has reference to understanding the act and contexts of interpretation, to which I will return shortly.[22]

The content of a religious symbol is true if, for appropriate interpreters (with the right culture, maturity, state of soul, etc.), it carries over what is important in its object into the interpreter in the respect in which the symbol is interpreted as representing the object. For those who are not appropriate interpreters, the symbol cannot be true. For those interpreters who are not capable of referring with the symbol in the appropriate respect, the symbol cannot be true. When those issues of appropriateness are respected, the question of truth comes down to the question of content: does the content of the symbol, appropriately used to interpret its object, carry over what is important and valuable in the object? It is false if it introduces into the interpreter a value not in the object, or if it fails to introduce the value that is there in the respect in which it interprets the object.

Carryover *defines* truth, I argue, and this is different from determining *whether* an interpretation is true. The latter issue involves criteria of assessing what is carried over. To address this properly, we must turn to interpretation as such, the third of Peirce's topics for semiotics.

Truth in Interpretation

Peirce is famous for his extensive development of the thesis that interpretation is a triadic relation. Whereas much early modern philosophy supposed a dyadic relation of mental picture to real object, and much late-modern Continental semiotics contents itself with the signifier-signified dyad, Peirce argued that a sign relates interpretively to its object only because an interpreter takes it to do so. The interpreter takes the sign to stand for an object in a certain respect, and that "taking" is the interpretation. The expression of the interpretation Peirce called an "interpretant," so that the triad of interpretation consists of sign, object, and interpretant.[23]

I have stressed first the issues of reference and meaning for a Peircean account of religious interpretation because they have usually been subordinated in pragmatic discussions. William James especially, but also John Dewey and George Herbert Mead, focused the concerns for the interpreters and their contexts as the genius of pragmatism. John E. Smith, probably the most astute interpreter of pragmatism in relation to other forms of empiricism and rationalism, named his principal book on pragmatism *Purpose and Thought*, both features of interpreters. Smith's principal topic throughout nearly all his writings is *experience*, which he always develops in terms close to what I have called *engagement*, with direct though mediated connections of interpreters with real objects; yet *experience* names the interpreter's side of the engagement. He is surely right that pragmatism's lever for changing the tradition's approach to correspondence is its attention to the interpreter's purposes, contexts, and community.[24]

The general pragmatic point, begun with Peirce and echoed throughout our tradition, is that the interpreter's purpose determines what there is about the object the interpreter is interested to know. Crudely put, that is *instrumentalism*, the view that people recognize only what reality serves their purposes. Peirce, like Dewey, was far subtler than most views of pragmatism in arguing that what is most important for us to recognize in things are the considerations that help determine what purposes are most worth having. A formal way of stating the point about purpose is to say that objects are interpreted in terms of the respects in which they are of potential interest to the interpreter's purpose. The purpose selects the respect of interpretation.

This point is a very abstract one, however. Only in rare moments do people consciously look for what is relevant to their purposes. In every moment, however, people engage reality with selective interpretations arranged in archaeologically deep layers, starting with the most basic imaginative levels. Individuals may have particular purposes, say, enjoying a song, but this purpose itself rests on larger purposes of leisure and enjoyment of beauty, which in turn rest on a subculture's determinations of what music is beautiful; on the cultural determination of what music is, how life focuses on beauty in sound, and how that fits together with the economic and security purposes of life; and indeed on the fundamental human imagination's determinations of sensations as sounds and other sorts and the ordering of them through temporal experience. Purpose in some sense lies at each of these levels, for there has been some evolutionary reason, if not deliberate choice or the encounter with genius, that shapes individual semiotic systems to consider that reality needs to be interpreted in ways the signs of the cultural system pick up. Indeed, one cannot say that the world's great civilizations have different conventions for picking up on the *same* things. Perhaps their different semiotic systems pick up on reality in somewhat different respects. If so, there are subtle differences among the purposes of different civilizations.

At any rate, the purposes of interpreters are defined within interpretive contexts, and these contexts are nested from earth-boundedness to the particular concerns of the moment in one's neighborhood. Moreover, interpretation is an ongoing affair, with many processes of personal, social, and natural life going on together. The forms of integration of these many processes might well be called a *biopsychic dance*.[25] The integration of organic bodily processes with metabolism is not exclusively an organic matter, because a spirited conversation after dinner can speed digestion and result in a friendship that has powerful social significance for the community. Some parts of the integration take the forms of semiotic systems. While the pragmatists were always careful to keep natural, nonconscious processes at the center of analytical attention, they also drew attention to the fact that the contexts of interpretation are permeated by meaning, shaped by semiotic systems. All human purposes, at every level, reflect the shaping of the deep context by semiotic systems.

Therefore, the carryover of what is important in the object into the interpreter requires the transformation of the object into something that fits into the interpreter's semiotic context. This is the reason for saying that the carryover is qualified by the biology, culture, semiotic systems, and purposes of the interpreter. The deep structure of the semiotic context includes the basic level of imagination.

Because of the function of purpose, either cultural in many layers or communal or personal, it is necessary to clarify what I mean in saying that truth is the carryover of what is valuable or important in the object into the interpreter in the respects interpreted. Supposing form to be what is carried over from the object into the mind will always make it easy to assume that the subjective purposive side entirely determines what is important, as when importance or value is reduced to whatever serves as a means to the purposive end. Precisely because reality is what it is, however, irrespective of what we think about it, what serves or fails to serve a purpose is the character of the object. If one believes, as I do, that all objects have value and that their forms are a function of the values they achieve and exhibit, then what is carried across is the value those objects have insofar as that is relevant to the respects in which they are interpreted, that is, insofar as the objects' values are relevant to the contextualized purpose.[26]

When the primary paradigms of interpretation are propositions, it is easy to assume that what is carried across is information. This occurs when the reference is dominantly iconic, and the value involved is the value the interpreter achieves through being able to respond to the interpreted realities in terms of purposes. When the dominant reference is indexical, however, the carryover involves a value that affects the interpreter's interaction with the interpreted objects. If an interpreter sees something and thinks, "That would be good to eat," and the object is a good food, the interpretive reference is mainly iconic; it goes into the interpreter's repertoire of knowledge and might subsequently be the basis of action. But if the reference is mainly indexical, the interpretation will make a habit of reaching for the food and eating it, and the interpretation will be true if the food nourishes rather than poisons. The indexical causal reference so orients the interpreter in causal ways with the object that its value is carried over into the interpreter, in this instance literally. To see a person iconically as "friendly" is informative but different from seeing the person indexically as friendly by smiling—the smile is the interpretant that embodies the carried-over friendliness in the interpreter's contextualized behavior.

People of course interpret many different things on many levels in a vastly complicated intermixing of interpretive processes, and they have to integrate all the values carried over into their own singular realities.[27] Therefore, the values of interpreted realities are transformed as they are integrated in interpreters to form their personal lives and their interactions with communities and the rest of the world. A person's value is the sum of the harmonies the person makes of interpretive responses to the world, including the ongoing self-reflexive processes of life in community. For the sake of simplicity I have spoken of interpreters in the singular here, but it should be clear that singular interpreters are interdefined in communities when their contextual and purpose realities are semiotic systems.

How does all this apply to religious symbols? In the case of biblical religions, it means that a true interpretation of God carries across something of divine value into the interpreter in the respects in which the symbols interpret God. Remember the complexity of religious symbols, how their meanings themselves are networks and nests of symbolic systems. So the Exodus interprets God's liberating identification of the people of Israel to those in which some divine liberation comes from it. Christians interpret the gospel of Jesus in such ways as God's redemptive action transforms their experience. The complexity of the interpreter's purposive context is even greater than the complexity of symbolic meanings, however.

Consider the context of theologians, for instance. For their purposes, what is carried across needs to be received in terms that are highly communicable, that can be defined with precision within their theological community, and that have a containable and controllable metaphoric reach for which it is possible to minimize apophatic cautions that they don't fully mean what they say. Thus much theological reference is iconic, its meanings are systematic and dull, and its interpretations are intellectual in form and unhelpful as guides to action. Sometimes, however, an abstract theological system can provide a kind of sudden enlightenment, a healing of alienation, and then it functions indexically to reorient the theologian to engagement with God and perhaps fuller participation in a community. I suspect most theologians stay in their profession not primarily because it satisfies intellectual purposes but only because it serves a more direct religious function.

Consider by contrast the context of nonintellectual believers who lead their lives as strongly informed by the symbols. Their interpretations of the symbols are less likely to be found in what they say about their objects than in what we might call practical inferences. But they probably do not make conscious inferences. Their shaping, transformation, or development in practice is simply the way they receive what is carried over. A Jew or an African American might have a richly developed solidarity with the community of Israel, or a surrogate of that, without any "true" verbal interpretation of the Exodus story. A Christian might be richly practiced in love of neighbor and God without much clarity of verbal interpretation. In cases of both kinds, however, verbal interpretation is likely to accompany the practice, words that do speak of the symbols at hand. What is said could not be defended as iconically true from a theological point of view but bears some causal connection with the influenced practice, which itself is the true carryover of divine liberation or love.

To claim that truth is not the replication of form but the carryover of value in interpretive respects is to weaken formal criteria of truth in favor of pragmatic criteria. The pragmatic criteriological question asks whether the value really in the object is carried across into appropriate forms for the interpreter in context. What then are some of the main pragmatic criteria for truth?

The criteria for truth all come from whatever would make a "good case" for the claim at hand within the public that cares about the issue.[28] Therefore criteria are contextualized to the topic at hand and to the particular communities that jointly make up the relevant public. Perhaps the most important singular contribution a Peircean semiotic can make to assessing claims to religious truth is to diagram the question. Before testing a claim with appropriate criteria, at least the following issues need to be identified and distinguished from elements easily confused: What exactly is the interpretive symbol, its symbolic systems, its networks and nests of symbols? (Many hermeneuts stop here.) What exactly is the kind of reference involved, iconic, indexical, conventional, all three in various ways? (Failure to clarify this issue gives rise to inappropriate inferences.) What exactly is the respect in which the symbol interprets the object? (Much confusion comes from the fact the same symbol can interpret a given object in several respects, depending on the interpretive context.) What is the interpretive context, the semiotic system in terms of which the object needs to be interpreted, its purposes, inertial practices of interpretation, its assumptions? Only when all these questions are sorted and clarified is it possible to ask whether the interpretation of the object by means of this symbol carries across what is really important into the interpreter in the respect interpreted. Only when these complex triadic questions have been answered is it possible clearly to ask the dyadic question of truth.

In religious matters, the emphasis on living in the truth, being true, practice, and authentic salvation, enlightenment, or harmony gives great weight to the differences among the kinds of reference symbols might have. So there are, in Peircean fashion, three main kinds of criteria, though we should bear in mind the complexity of prior questions that need to be answered.

Because religious symbols are interpreted with iconic reference, one class of criteria concerns how an icon, theory, symbol system, or religious way of life might be good and in correspondence with what it maps. Whitehead's famous discussion of speculative philosophical theory in the first chapter of *Process and Reality* is the most eloquent statement of this class. He noted that a theory should be formally consistent and coherent. Consistency obtains when the theory contains no contradictions, and coherence obtains when the parts hang together. Where religious symbols can be integrated in networks, these criteria can be applied fairly directly. Where they are nested, and resist formation in a network, the formal criteria of consistency and coherence might have to be translated to aesthetic ones of harmony, resonance, dissonance within greater harmonies, and so forth. The other criteria Whitehead mentioned are applicability and adequacy, which together define iconic mapping. Applicability occurs when all parts of the system have some objective reference, and adequacy occurs when everything in reality has a sign in the system. Because there is no privileged perspective from which to compare reality with iconic theories or symbol systems, applicability and adequacy are high-level criteria and need all sorts of other criteria to be applied themselves. Indeed, they need criteria that are functional with indexical and conventional reference.

The criteria for the truth of interpretations with indexical reference are what Jesus had in mind in saying, "By their fruits you shall know them" (Matt. 7:20). He likely had in mind specifically the hypocrites who profess godliness and act out its contrary. St. Paul generalized the point by listing such marks of the Holy Spirit as "love, joy, peace, patience, kindness, generosity, faithfulness, gentleness, and self-control" (Gal. 5:22–23). These and like virtues are precisely the kinds of criteria we use in judging saintliness, the realized or perfected state of godliness. Nevertheless, it is usually extremely difficult to use such pragmatic "fruits" in judging the comparative truth of particular symbols. In response to this problem, some people dismiss appeals to the fruits of godliness. Could we really expect Orthodox Christians, who believe the Holy Spirit proceeds from the Father alone, to differ in such virtues from Roman Catholics, who believe that it proceeds from the Father and the Son together? Perhaps instead of saying that the criteria are inapplicable, however, we should say that both doctrines, verbally and iconically contradictory, are true in the different contexts of Orthodox and Catholic cultures. Similarly, given the unexplored differences in symbol systems among the world's great religions, and the different respects in which they might interpret ultimate reality, perhaps we should say that, to the extent that they all give rise to sages and saints, they can all be true in their own ways via indexical reference. They all orient people in ways that lead to accommodation to the ultimate. The great weakness of appealing to practical fruits to assess claims about interpretations with mainly indexical reference is that such criteria are not easily tied to verbalizable interpretations. They compare the practices and ways of life resulting from interpretations with what is interpreted but can find no stable verbal way of describing those results as interpretants. Hence it is difficult to make intellectual cases for truths claimed with indexical reference.

Fortunately, the criteria for interpretations with conventional reference involve the breadth and depth of making and testing connections. To call these "coherence" criteria, although tempting, is too rationalistic. Because of the conventional nature of our religious symbols and the rest of our semiotic systems, it is possible to see how religious symbols fit with one another and with the rest of life, with politics, morality, aesthetics, domestic economy, and the rest. It is possible to connect putative religious interpretations with the kinds of analysis and understanding that come from the natural and social sciences. It is possible to compare the symbolic interpretations of one religion with those of other religions. In all these ways conventional reference makes possible a critical dialectic in which ideally every point of view on a religious interpretation can be brought to bear in assessing it. Conventional reference means that there is no fixed limit to the ways by which we can triangulate on signs, their objects, and their interpretations. Conventional criteria offer great breadth.

At the same time, criteria for conventional reference afford depth to religious interpretation in the following sense. Religious symbols—or rather, the concrete habits of thought, feeling, and behavior shaped by religious symbols—stack up in a person in many layers and interweaving connections. By analogy they do the same thing in communities. Most of us are thoroughly confused in the ways we integrate the symbol systems that let us engage reality. Superficially we can line up our symbol systems and the myriad interpretations of reality they give us so as to succeed pragmatically. We get along in society and survive, even flourish. In questions beyond crude social levels of success, however, most people do not clearly sense what is important or how to relate consistently to the ultimate, to "will one thing," as Kierkegaard put it. Spiritual formation, in the biblical religions as in the others, involves lining up the many systems and layers of interpretive life so that they resonate consistently and with mutual reinforcement. Or to switch from musical to visual metaphors, saints see through system after system with translucence so that their engagements with reality seem like spontaneous intuitions. Or to use emotional metaphors, spiritually advanced people can be sincere, so that what they feel in one interpretive system is multiplied through the other systems of their lives. These considerations lie behind the valid claim that the understanding of religion requires considerable participation. Perhaps the faith-seeking-understanding principle begs too many questions at the beginning and seems to be too much about intellectual belief, but it surely describes the depth of critical religious understanding.[29]

Putting together the breadth of a critical public with the depth of spiritual achievement in lining up the interpretive spheres of life, the criteria for interpretations with conventional reference provide maximum vulnerability to correction and maximum internal confirmation. Criteria for truth in conventional reference mark out disciplined ways of integrating various iconic and indexical references with long-range tests of ways of life. We test comprehensive "ways of life"—that is, religions—by living with them, testing their flexibility in changing circumstances, their inspirational power when the ultimate seems absent, and their long-run capacity to stimulate deeper and more subtle engagements with the whole of reality to which they open us.

Before we become giddy over the prospects of the "great conversation" guiding humankind to evolving ever-more-subtle civilized engagements with reality, including the ultimate, we should remember the limitations already mentioned. In the first place, it is rare that much clarity is achieved regarding the meanings of symbol systems, the nature of their reference, the respects in which they interpret reality, and what the interpretation comes to in the interpreting community; hence it is rare even to raise the question of truth in a fair way. In the second place, the breadth of the critical public is never actualized enough for full dialectical engagement; too often the perspectives that might have critical corrections are neglected or deflected, and vulnerability is thwarted. In the third place, the depth of being attuned spiritually in ways that integrate the vast array of interpretations brought into play by the breadth of the critical public is extremely difficult to achieve and, if achieved, to measure; there is a tension, perhaps unresolvable, between the private intensity required to align the shaping images of one's soul and the engagement with enough different spheres of reality to have the right images there in the first place.

All these limitations notwithstanding, this Peircean vision of a community of investigators reveals an extraordinary long-run stability and sophistication for the assessment of the truth of religious interpretations. Politicians check with voters, and physicists include a few other natural sciences and mathematics within their critical public, but the community of inquiry for religion needs to be open to every perspective within creation. Inquiry regarding religious truth defines its depth by being able to line up everything depending on the ultimate with harmony, translucency, sincerity, and the capacity to will one thing. Put these together, and religious inquiry need not be fooled by any limitations to its questioning; it is therefore in the long run more stable and subtle, because more vulnerable, than modes of inquiry that aim at only part of creation with antecedently defined methods.

Commensurability of Imaginations

It is possible to compare the world of the Bible, with its variety of symbols defined in its semiotic system resting on a profound imaginative base, with the world of late modernity, analogously defined. Such a project aims not to assess truth per se but rather to compare two different semiotic systems; it is a study in meanings.

It is also possible, although difficult, to investigate whether the symbols of the ancient world were true for some of those ancient people in the sense that they carried what is important in the ultimate over into the semiotically defined contexts and purposes of that age. Iconic, indexical, and conventional reference must be distinguished for this inquiry to proceed. By itself this inquiry is not religious in the sense of being relevant to what is religiously true for late modernity.

Direct religious inquiry for late-modern people with biblical traditions treats the Bible in its ancient context as part of the contemporary symbol systems by which the ultimate can be engaged in contemporary times. Late-modern people do not themselves understand biblical symbols as they were understood in antiquity, even when contemporary hermeneutics marks out the differences. Late moderns need to integrate biblical symbols with many others that make up the late-modern imagination. The questions of truth, then, concern whether the symbols of the Bible and other symbols can carry over what is important about the ultimate into the interpretive contexts of late modernity. The source of these interpretive symbols is less important than their potential to bring God into late-modern culture and imagination. If they can do this, they can be true and known as such without appeals to authority that pit the first-century world against the late-modern one.

Nevertheless, biblical symbols may have a true message for late modernity that other symbols typical of late modernity lack. In fact, contemporary biblical religions claim to be prophetic precisely because some dominant symbols of late modernity seem to obscure the ultimate, substituting idolatrous concern for power, progress, or passion for a vision of God or weakening any interest or capacity for relating to ultimate things at all.

The approach to religious interpretation derived here from Peirce's semiotic thus offers a way to see how biblical religion, despite its dated imagination, might be true, prophetic, and transformative for late modernity. At the same time, this approach shows how the late-modern critical community can ask whether, with what reference, in what respect, and in what interpretive contexts the symbols of biblical faith might be true or false. This is what was promised at the outset.

Notes

1. This point is by no means new. One of its best recent expressions is a book by W. Mark Richardson and Wesley J. Wildman, eds., *Religion and Science: History, Method, Dialogue* (New York: Routledge, 1996), especially the section on history. Wildman's essay there is particularly acute in arguing that the crisis should not be regarded as "warfare" between science and religion—a rhetorical ploy in serious denial of what has actually happened—but is nevertheless very deep. He attributes the crisis equally to the problems of miracles, historiography, and the scale of cosmology, whereas I emphasize the last. Though only differences of emphasis, and not developed in detail in his essay or here, they reflect different readings of the biblical traditions. Wildman construes both divine agency within the world (miracles) and historical knowledge of the biblical stories (especially of Jesus for Christianity) to be essential to the biblical traditions, such that their compromise compromises those traditions. I, by contrast, construe most if not all references to divine agency within the Bible to be metaphoric tropes even in the ancient world and take the *liturgical* presence of Jesus and the other storied figures to have been from the beginning more important than historical connections (the latter being a theme only in the late-modern world). These are controversial matters of historical interpretation.

2. The crisis of imagination has been worst for Protestantism. Like Reformed and Conservative, if not Orthodox, Jews, Protestants have embraced the culture of European modernity, including its scientific imaginative formation. Unlike any of the other religious movements, however, Protestantism defined itself from the beginning by the doctrine of

sola scriptura, the view that the Bible alone is sufficient for faith and the repository of the only important symbols. Both the Eastern Orthodox and the Roman Catholic traditions had grown since biblical times, introducing trinitarian theology and metaphysical systems that imagined a far vaster cosmos than the biblical one and shaping Christian life by liturgies that pointed to mysteries far beyond biblical Christianity. All these might have been helpful in mediating a scientific understanding. Protestant theology, however, had to retreat to a biblical vocabulary slightly foreign to the wider Christian traditions since the second century. Orthodoxy and Catholicism retreated from acknowledging the scientific imagination until recently. And European Christian theology, paralleled within Reformed and Reconstructionist Judaism, developed a dual track: one was the biblical theology of Protestant confessionalism, and the other was the philosophical tradition of reconceiving God in the light of scientific and other developments, the tradition of Descartes, Leibniz, Kant, Hegel, and Whitehead. Those philosophers all sought to provide reconstructions of religious symbols so as to bring together the modern and late-modern imaginations with the imaginative frame of the Bible. In so doing, however, they relativized the exclusive authority of the Bible. The divergence of these two traditions important for Protestant theology—the confessional, with an insistence on biblical language for theology, and the philosophical, with an insistence on reimagining the biblical symbols before believing them—is one of the major fault lines between conservatives and liberals.

3. In the following notes, references to Peirce are for the *Collected Papers of Charles Sanders Peirce,* vols. 1–6, ed. Charles Hartshorne and Paul Weiss; vols. 7–8, ed. Arthur W. Burks (Cambridge, Mass.: Harvard University Press, 1931–58); references are given by volume and paragraph number; for example, 2.274 indicates the beginning of the discussion of reference in volume 2, paragraph 274. Although discussions of semiotics are spread throughout Peirce's works, the concentrated discussions occur in volume 2 in the section the editors call "speculative grammar." A good general introduction to Peirce that focuses on his semiotics is Robert S. Corrington's *Introduction to C. S. Peirce: Philosopher, Semiotician, and Ecstatic Naturalist* (Lanham, Md.: Rowman and Littlefield, 1993).

4. CP 5.358–410. Peirce's general idea of vulnerability as a virtue for hypotheses has been developed elaborately for religion, from many points of view and by many authors, in the three volumes of the Comparative Religious Ideas Project; see Robert Cummings Neville, ed., *The Human Condition, Ultimate Realities, and Religious Truth* (Albany, N.Y.: SUNY Press, 2000), especially the articles jointly authored by Wildman and Neville.

5. See, for instance, CP 6.238–71, "Man's Glassy Essence." For an excellent study see Vincent M. Colapietro, *Peirce's Approach to the Self: A Semiotic Perspective on Human Subjectivity* (Albany, N.Y.: SUNY Press, 1989).

6. CP 6.66–87, 102–63.

7. CP 1, passim; CP 6.7–87. For good discussions of Peirce's system as arising from semiotics, see Douglas R. Anderson's *Creativity and the Philosophy of C. S. Peirce* (Boston: Nijhoff, 1987) and *Strands of System: The Philosophy of Charles Peirce* (West Lafayette, Ind.: Purdue University Press, 1995).

8. For Dewey on this point, see John E. Smith's discussion in "John Dewey: Experience, Experiment, and the Method of Intelligence," *The Spirit of American Philosophy,* rev. ed. (Albany, N.Y.: SUNY Press, 1983). For an excellent comparison of Dewey with Peirce on the points made here, see Smith's *Purpose and Thought: The Meaning of Pragmatism* (New Haven, Conn.: Yale University Press, 1978), chap. 4.

9. CP 2.274–82.

10. See Ludwig Wittgenstein, *Tractatus Logico-Philosophicus* (London: Routledge and Kegan Paul, 1922), 6.41–7.00.

11. CP 2.283–91.

12. CP 2.292–308. I prefer *conventional* because in religion, nearly all signs are called symbols, and it should be said that there are three kinds of *symbolic* reference: iconic, indexical, and conventional.

13. CP 1.521–44.

14. See my book *The Truth of Broken Symbols* (Albany, N.Y.: SUNY Press, 1996), chapter 1, for an account of the contrast between finite and infinite in any object of religious reference.

15. CP 1.15–42; 6.619–24. This point was so important to Peirce that Hartshorne and Weiss put his strong statements in the first and last paragraphs of their six-volume edition.

16. See Anderson's books cited in note 7 for an exposition of the theory of signs.

17. On Peirce's approach to religion as such, see Michael L. Raposa's *Peirce's Philosophy of Religion* (Bloomington: Indiana University Press, 1989) and Hermann Deuser's *Gott, Geist und Natur: theologische Konsequenzen aus Charles S. Peirce's Religionsphilosophie* (Berlin: Walter de Gruyter, 1993). Peirce's writings on religion have not been collected in English, except for those in the *Collected Papers,* which contains only a small fragment of Peirce's writings. They have, however, been collected by Deuser in *Charles Sanders Peirce: religionsphilosophische Schriften,* trans. with the collaboration of Helmut Maassen, ed. and with an introduction and commentary by Hermann Deuser (Hamburg: Felix Meiner Verlag, 1995).

18. Charles W. Morris, *Foundations of the Theory of Signs* (Chicago: University of Chicago Press, 1938).

19. I analyze this example of nested symbol systems in much greater detail in *The Truth of Broken Symbols,* chapter 3.

20. I have noted several times that the interpreter has to be of the right sort for a symbol to have effective reference. So, for instance, a Chinese Taoist would not have the culture to interpret symbols such as the blood of the lamb unless learned anew. People with no feeling whatsoever for human sinfulness are not likely to be able to refer effectively, whether iconically, indexically, or conventionally, with atonement symbols. Persons abused by their fathers as children are unlikely to be able to refer to God effectively as Father. The way to put this is to say that the objects of reference in the three modes are *primarily* the things to which the interpreter referred, but the *secondary* referents are the types of persons for whom the primary references can be engaging. So reference to God by the symbol Father works only for those secondary referents who have good connotations for father; atonement symbols can refer to God's saving work (the primary referent) only for those with a sense of sin (the secondary referents). Secondary reference is closely connected with the state of the interpreters, a point to which the argument will return shortly.

21. This is the formula I defend at length in *The Truth of Broken Symbols* with regard to religious truth and in *Recovery of the Measure* (Albany, N.Y.: SUNY Press, 1989) with regard to truth in general.

22. See Neville, *Recovery of the Measure,* chap. 4.

23. Peirce's main discussions of this are in CP 2.309–90 but are found in many other places, including CP 8.327–79. The defense of the irreducibility of the triadic relation to

dyadic relations is part of Peirce's overall defense of the categories of firstness, second-ness, and thirdness, for example, in CP 1.417–520.

24. For a very subtle and many-faceted discussion of these issues, see Smith's "Philos-ophy in America: Recovery and Future Development," a reply to many commentators in a festschrift in his honor, Thomas P. Kasulis and Robert Cummings Neville, eds., *The Recovery of Philosophy in America: Essays in Honor of John Edwin Smith* (Albany, N.Y.: SUNY Press, 1997).

25. See Neville, *Recovery of the Measure,* 302–8.

26. That form is a function of value, and not the other way around, as usually thought, is the thesis of my *Reconstruction of Thinking* (Albany, N.Y.: SUNY Press, 1981), pt. 2. That nature can be conceived properly and in line with both science and aesthetic experience as processes of achievement of value is the overall thesis of *Recovery of the Measure,* which also indicates how interpretation is the particular achievement of value in experience through carryover.

27. This is an informal statement of a process anthropology. I provide a formal state-ment in *Recovery of the Measure.*

28. The idea of "making a case" derives from Stephen Toulmin's discussion in *The Uses of Argument* (Cambridge: Cambridge University Press, 1958). It was applied particularly to theological argument by Van A. Harvey in *The Historian and the Believer* (New York: Macmillan, 1966).

29. I have explored this idea of spiritual development as the alignment of various sym-bol systems and the behaviors and feelings they shape in *The Tao and the Daimon* (Alba-ny, N.Y.: SUNY Press, 1982), chap. 11. The issue of participation or antecedent belief is discussed there at length.

22. Faith and Ethics in an Interdependent World

STEVEN C. ROCKEFELLER

In the midst of great cultural diversity, the forces of modernization are creating the structures of a planetary civilization. The local communities and various associations of which we are members continue to be as important as ever, but the local and the global are now linked. Our particular stories are being woven into the larger tapestry of world history. The future will be characterized by increasing worldwide interdependence.

Through television, computers, and cellular phones, we share news and information almost instantaneously throughout the world. Our local economies are now part of global systems of finance and trade. We eat food, give flowers, wear clothes, and drive cars that are produced in distant lands. Financial woes in Southeast Asia send tremors through stock markets in Tokyo, London, and New York. In addition, the long-range effects of a society's patterns of production and consumption are magnified by our ecological interdependence. Different nations and communities affect one another through the planet's atmospheric and hydrological systems. For example, the release of greenhouse gasses in the United States and Europe is causing global warming and rising sea levels that threaten the very existence of island nations in the Pacific Ocean.

However, even though the peoples of the world may be progressively interconnected economically, technologically, and ecologically, we are not united morally and spiritually, and there lies a great danger. We have "globalized only the surface of our lives," states Vaclav Havel, the president of the Czech Republic.[1] Large numbers of people may drink Coca-Cola, watch CNN, and wear blue jeans, but we have not reached agreement on the basic values that should govern our lives together. Having armed itself with weapons of mass destruction, developed industrial systems capable of destroying the ecological health of the planet, and instituted financial systems that perpetuate huge disparities between rich and poor, humanity has arrived at a critical stage in its evolution. Unless we succeed in creating a secure foundation of shared moral values for the emerging planetary civilization and in this way create a real world community, the survival of humanity and civilization is at risk.[2] We need a common moral faith that can inspire people to integrate their economic goals with the quest for security, peace, justice, and ecological well-being.

There are skeptics and critics who contend that global ethics are neither possible nor even desirable in our multicultural world. Some see in the idea of global ethics the danger of new forms of cultural imperialism that could threaten local autonomy, national sovereignty, cultural diversity, and religious freedom. Others fear that the aspirations associated with talk about global ethics can lend support to the kind of utopian fanaticism that inspired Lenin, Mao, and Pol Pot, as well as a host of other zealots who have murdered and maimed in the name of some version of the final truth. These are important concerns that must be addressed.

In what follows, however, I take the position that a planetary ethic is an evolutionary possibility and a social, political, and ecological necessity.[3] I argue that, despite the many cultural differences among groups, a new common moral faith is beginning to take form. Shared ethical values can be developed and exist in an evolving world that respects pluralism, celebrates cultural diversity, and is open to progressive social change.

This essay explores these issues with special reference to the concept of a "common faith" in the philosophical thought of John Dewey and William James. It investigates what the democratic social theory, ethical experimentalism, and religious outlooks of these two American pragmatists have to contribute to an understanding of the nature and development of global ethics. My attention will then turn to the contemporary task of constructing a common moral faith for the twenty-first century, followed by some reflections on global ethics and the world's religions.

Democracy, Experimentalism, and a Common Faith

The idea of universal moral values is not new. It has been a recurring theme in religious and philosophical thought for over twenty-five hundred years. In defending this idea, prophets and philosophers have argued variously that moral values have their source in the will of God, the order of the universe, the rational structure of the human mind, universal moral feelings, or transrational mystical experiences of the Eternal One. Hegel introduced the idea that our rational understanding of the universal moral law is historically conditioned and relative to our time and place in the evolutionary process of world history. Charles Darwin believed that the moral sentiments are fixed in human nature by the evolutionary process of natural selection and reinforced by education. He observed that over time the human sense of community and moral concern has steadily expanded from the family to the tribe, then to the nation, and finally to all humanity. He speculated that one day humanity might develop a "disinterested love for all living creatures."[4] He saw an ethic that embraces all life as an evolutionary potential of the human species.

There are many theories of the origins of morality and the sources of common moral values. There is no agreement on these theoretical matters, and likely there never will be. Nevertheless, each of the approaches mentioned identifies important issues. A sense that our moral values are somehow grounded objectively in the world and that human beings are responsible for respecting these values is fundamental to building an ordered community. A sound approach to morals must respect the role of reason and critical thought. Rational understanding without feeling and passion will not generate action, however; for that, we need an integration of the head and the heart. A mystical sense of unity with the larger totality can only deepen moral feeling. An evolutionary perspective reminds us that our best ideas are the products of history and that fixed or static moral thinking can arrest growth and obstruct justice. Attitudes toward slavery and the rights of women illustrate the need to view moral systems as open to change. It is, of course, not necessary for there to be agreement on the origins of our moral values in order for there to be a consensus on basic moral principles and ideal ends. A common moral faith does not require that we all hold one moral theory.

Dewey and James were influenced by many different currents of thought in moral philosophy. As philosophical pragmatists, however, they developed their own distinctive approaches to the construction of shared moral values. James retained a certain belief in the God of supernaturalism, whereas Dewey was a thoroughgoing naturalist, but they both rejected monism and embraced pluralism and an evolutionary worldview. Their outlook involves three basic convictions especially relevant to the human moral situation: the universe of which we are a part has not made up its mind where it is going; the struggle between good and evil is real; and human choice and decision can make a critical difference in the direction of events. In such a universe ethical guidance is of critical importance. In pursuing moral wisdom, they abandoned the quest for certainty and moral absolutes and developed a middle way between absolutism and complete relativism.

The pragmatism of Dewey and James cannot be understood apart from the American democratic experience and the experimental method employed by the sciences. Pragmatism was developed as a method of critical thought for free men and women engaged in creative democratic living and social reconstruction in an evolving world. This method of critical thought applies the experimental approach to truth to social problems, including the process of making ethical decisions and constructing moral ideals. Dewey and James believed, then, that a common moral faith can best be developed and refined in a social environment pervaded by democratic values and guided by experience and the experimental method. Their approach is an especially promising one.

For Dewey and James, democracy is first and foremost a personal way of life. Dewey, who was especially articulate on this subject, explained that democracy is a great moral ideal that should govern human relations in all spheres and sectors of life—in the home, workplace, and school, as well as in government. Democracy is, then, far more than a political system of free elections linked to an economic system of free markets. Dewey was primarily interested in social or moral democracy, or what can be called spiritual democracy.

The fundamental values of spiritual democracy may seem like commonplace assumptions, but when discussing pragmatism's common faith, it is especially important to be clear about them. The democratic life is founded on respect for the dignity and worth of all persons. It involves a faith in the creative possibilities of human nature when the right conditions of education and opportunity are provided. From the point of view of spiritual democracy, human societies have the twofold purpose of promoting the full realization of the individual and building strong communities. These goals can be achieved only through the development of freedom coupled with social responsibility. Nurturing freedom of mind and conscience is, therefore, a fundamental educational goal. Achieving real freedom requires the full development of the individual's capacity for intelligent moral choice and self-governance. Democracy entails setting people free and empowering them to participate effectively in the decision-making processes that affect them.

Spiritual democracy puts its faith in free and open communication and the sharing of experience across all boundaries of class, position, gender, race, and religion as the best method for promoting individual growth and the building of community. In the relations between groups, fear, hate, prejudice, and intolerance, as well as methods of violent suppression of others, are all antithetical to the democratic spirit. Democracy requires faith in cooperative nonviolent methods of managing conflict and resolving problems. It involves the belief that all persons have a right to express their differences and that the encounter with difference can enrich one's life experience. Dewey once commented that we should "treat those who disagree—even profoundly—with us as those from whom we may learn, and in so far, as friends."[5]

In an effort to free and empower the individual and all groups, especially those who are oppressed or the victims of injustice, Dewey and James developed the method of critical thought known as pragmatism—Dewey preferred the terms *instrumentalism* or *experimentalism*. At the heart of this pragmatism is a faith in experience as the sole authority in matters of knowledge. Dewey and James believed that with the aid of experimental methods of thought, human experience can generate the knowledge, wisdom, and ethical ideals required to meet our needs and direct our desires.

Experience is an inclusive term in the vocabulary of James and Dewey. Experience includes all that human beings suffer and do. It is the product of our interactions with other people and the larger world of nature. Human experience alternates between settled situations and problematic situations that invite effort to reestablish harmony with the world. The mind, according to Dewey and James, developed in the course of evolution as an organ for helping humans overcome practical problems and adjust to their environment. Pragmatists are concerned with methods of thought that can guide action effectively, leading to experiences that are meaningful, inherently valuable, and truly satisfactory with reference to their long-term consequences. Growth in the direction of the richest and most meaningful experience possible is the goal.

From the pragmatist point of view, all ideas, including moral and religious ideas, are to be understood as tools or instruments for assisting human beings in getting around in the world and solving problems. They are guides to action. Accordingly, their truth and value are to be verified and judged by the consequences of acting on them. If, in experience, they are helpful and effective in resolving problems, overcoming conflicts, establishing justice and peace, and promoting growth, and they lead to a progressive improvement in the quality of experience, then they are to be judged true and good. If they are not helpful or lead people into deeper troubles and conflicts, they should be reconstructed. Dewey regarded the task of reconstructing ideas as a sophisticated form of toolmaking or technology.

The critical emphasis in this pragmatist or experimentalist outlook falls on consequences. The truth or moral worth of an idea is to be determined not by where it comes from but by what it leads to. Conservative thinkers commonly look to the past as the authority in moral matters. They find moral authority in ancient divine revelation, revered social custom, or sanctified political tradition. Pragmatists look to the future. They start with inherited ideas, and they have deep respect for this inheritance, but they look to the future and consequences when trying to evaluate it. Dewey and other pragmatists were activists seeking leverage for social reform. Even though they highly valued many American democratic traditions, they saw that much in their society was an inheritance from the past that needed to be changed—for example, oppressive methods of education, great economic disparities, discrimination against women, and racial inequities. The experimentalist approach is an effective instrument of change.

The pragmatists developed a situation ethics that charts a middle way between moral authoritarianism and absolutism on the one hand and moral subjectivism and extreme relativism on the other hand.[6] Authoritarianism appeals to authorities outside the realm of experience, and it suppresses inquiry, critical thought, and debate. Moral subjectivism regards experience to be the sole authority in moral matters, but it precludes any objective grounds for making moral evaluations, which it construes as entirely a matter of personal feeling and private opinion. It denies any basis for a rational discussion about moral values and ideal ends, so that inquiry and debate become pointless. Such moral subjectivism involves an extreme form of moral relativism.

Pursuing a middle way, experimentalism looks to experience for guidance and argues that knowledge of conditions and consequences provides a basis for rational debate, critical evaluation, and objective moral judgments. It rejects both absolutism and subjectivism. It views sound moral judgments as relative to concrete situations. Experimentalism supports a qualified moral relativism that avoids subjectivism.

Dewey believed that the self is in a constant state of becoming and that in and through choice and decision, individuals shape and define their being. Moral decision making is especially important in this regard, because it is directly concerned with the kind of person an individual chooses to be. Dewey believed that the most important moral choice a person and a community can make is the decision of faith.

Dewey used the word *faith* to mean a moral faith in the sense of a trust in and devotion to social and ethical ideals. He understood faith to be primarily a matter of moral conviction rather than intellectual belief regarding matters of fact. "Conviction in the moral sense," he explains, "signifies being conquered, vanquished, in our active nature by an ideal end." The act of faith may be called voluntary, but it does not depend on a particular resolve or volition. It involves "a change *of* will conceived as the organic plenitude of our being, rather than any special change *in* will." A faith in a unified vision of the ideal "possesses the will rather than is its express product."[7]

Reflecting on human nature and the history of cultures with a well-developed moral consciousness, Dewey argues that people have traditionally put faith in those purposes, values, and ideals that they believe will guide their communities toward an ever better quality of experience. This practical faith in moral principles and purposes that promise fulfillment and social well-being is what he had in mind when he wrote about the "common faith" of humanity. The content of this common faith is not static or fixed. It constantly evolves. Devotion to the ongoing cooperative search for fresh wisdom and insight is central to his concept of humanity's common faith. "The discovery of the truth that governs our relations to one another in the shared struggles, sorrows, and joys of life is our common task and winning it, our common reward," writes Dewey.[8]

Dewey points out that we do not originate the ideals and values in which we put our faith. Each generation receives from the past a heritage of values. However, asserts Dewey: "Ours is the responsibility of conserving, transmitting, rectifying and expanding the heritage of values we have received that those who come after us may receive it more solid and secure, more widely accessible and generously shared than we have received it."[9] These words express the fundamental spirit of pragmatism's common faith.

Dewey carefully explained that genuine ideals are real possibilities. The vision of the ideal is developed in and through the power of imaginative vision, but true ideals are not mere dreams. They are potentialities resident in the natural environment, human nature, and social relations that can be actualized with the proper means and by human effort. There is in this sense continuity between the real world and our ideal ends.

As a social, moral, and religious thinker, Dewey was especially interested in constructing an integrated vision of an inclusive or comprehensive ideal. Such a vision would include principles and ideal ends that encompass the self, society, and nature in their interrelations. Fundamental to Dewey's religious and moral faith is, of course, a commitment to democracy and experimentalism as the keys to a free, creative, and meaningful way of living and to pursuing the quest for the ideal in the modern world.

While Dewey did not believe that institutional religion is necessary for the development of humanity's common faith, he did believe that wholehearted faith in an integrated vision of an inclusive ideal can have a religious effect on people's lives, giving their experience what he called a religious quality. He associated a religious effect with the unifying of the self and of the self and the world. In his view, the quality of experience that is distinctively religious involves a deep sense of enduring adjustment with the world, involving inner peace and a sustaining sense of the meaning and value of life. A faith in shared values and ideals can have this kind of unifying, religious effect, and when it does, according to Dewey, it becomes religious in quality. In this way the common moral faith of humanity can become a religious faith. Dewey also believed that the institutional religions can and should contribute to the construction of global ethics.

Defining moral and religious faith along the lines of Dewey's philosophy eliminates any reason for conflict between science and faith. Faith is concerned with ideal possibilities and leaves to science questions about matters of fact. Furthermore, the experimental method of inquiry and evaluation can be used to rectify, refine, and expand our vision of the ideal by providing fresh insights into the possibilities of life and the means required to actualize those possibilities.

Traditionally the concept of faith in Western culture has included some notion that spirit and the divine ultimately rule the world or that on the deepest level of reality the ideal and the real are one. These notions have provided consolation to generations of Christians and Jews in the face of defeat and tragedy. Dewey did profess a sense of cosmic trust and a mystical sense of belonging to the larger whole that deepened his sense of inner peace and helped him to bear tragedy. Nevertheless, he argued that these important religious feelings came not from believing that the ideal is already real in some transcendental realm but from his deep faith in the ideals of democracy, experimentalism, and progressive education and from the deepening of his aesthetic experience. He believed that if people would put their faith in sound ideals, adopt the right attitude, and live well, their spiritual needs would be met. There is much human experience that supports this outlook.

Constructing a Common Faith in a Global Context

The task of building a worldwide consensus around ethical values is complex, and we have no guarantee that it can be achieved, especially considering the persistence of authoritarianism among many religious and political leaders. Nevertheless, the democratic, pluralist, experimentalist thinking of James and Dewey provides a sound and promising general approach.

The objective in this matter is not to create a new religion that will synthesize elements of the existing religions or simply replace them. A common moral faith may acquire religious meaning and value for many people both within and outside the existing religions, but the goal is not a new institutional religion. Nor is the purpose to replace the high ethical demands of the world's great religions with some new ethical minimalism.[10]

Instead, the objective is cooperation among the world's cultures, religions, nations, and peoples in the search for common ground. The process is as important as the final product if the goal is wide acceptance and implementation of shared values. A top-down approach that involves an attempt by one culture, religion, or group of intellectuals to impose their beliefs and values on everyone else will fail. Participation of all concerned parties in a collaborative search for moral truth and liberating ideal ends is a fundamental requirement for creating a common faith and building community, whether it be local, national, regional, or global.

The first step in constructing a common faith is to determine what values people from different cultures and religious traditions already share. Dialogue is the most effective method of exploring what diverse traditions have in common. The objective of dialogue is not to convert the other participants to one's own point of view or to persuade them to adopt some new idea. One enters a cross-cultural or interfaith dialogue to listen and learn from others how they think and view the world and to share with them one's own perspective. The objective is deepened mutual understanding and the clarification of both common values and important differences.

Participation in a cross-cultural dialogue requires the ability to express the ideas and values that form one's own tradition in a language others can understand. It requires that we be bilingual in the sense that we learn a common secondary language beyond our primary languages—beyond, say, the theological and ethical vocabularies of Christianity, Judaism, or Islam. The secondary language we need is one that enables us to explain our own culture and tradition to others whose worlds differ from ours.[11]

The twentieth century was a time of growing cross-cultural and interfaith dialogue, and the United States has been a major center of these exchanges. Through dialogue, groups from different traditions are discovering that their diverse beliefs and practices encompass certain universal moral values. Diverse communities have some shared ideas about what is right and wrong, good and evil, because human beings have certain common capacities, needs, and aspirations.

In discussing this universal morality embedded in diverse cultures, Michael Walzer makes a distinction between a maximal and a minimal morality, which he calls thick and thin, respectively. Each culture, he explains, has its own fully developed (maximal) moral system. Within the thick maximal morality of a culture one can find a core morality of universal values, a thin (minimal) morality. Walzer points out that historically morality does not begin thin and grow to be thick. The minimal is not a freestanding morality. It always exists as part of the maximal and is elaborated differently in diverse cultures. Nevertheless, the minimalist principles are especially important to people, and Walzer contends that they do provide a foundation for a certain limited but significant solidarity.[12]

A good example of an effort to identify the basic moral values shared by the world's major religions is the "Declaration Toward a Global Ethic," which was generated by the Parliament of the World's Religions held in Chicago in 1993. The occasion was the centennial celebration of the historic 1893 World's Parliament of Religions, the first time leaders from the world's major faiths had met together and the beginning of modern worldwide interfaith dialogue. The Christian theologian Hans Küng headed the team that drafted the declaration. Over a two-year period more than two hundred theologians and scholars of religion were consulted in the process of preparing the declaration, and it was signed by over one hundred religious leaders attending the 1993 parliament.[13]

The interfaith dialogues surrounding the drafting of this declaration led to the conclusion that at the heart of humanity's shared moral values lies the Golden Rule, which can be stated negatively or positively. The Jewish and Confucian traditions, for example, tend to prefer the negative formulation: do not to others what you do not want done to you. In the Gospel of Matthew one finds the positive formulation widely used by Christians: "Treat others as you would like them to treat you."[14] Jesus states that this principle summarizes the teaching of "the Law and the Prophets." The Dalai Lama articulated the general idea in both positive and negative formulations when he stated that the whole of Buddhism can be summarized in two principles: "Help others, and if you cannot help them, do not harm them."[15]

The "Declaration Toward a Global Ethic" further points out that all traditions have elaborated the implications of the Golden Rule in at least four common negative injunctions that are prohibitions against killing, stealing, lying, and sexual misconduct. Stated positively, according to the declaration, these injunctions call on people to respect life, deal honestly and fairly, speak and act truthfully, and respect and love one another.[16]

Some may argue that principles such as the Golden Rule and Kant's Categorical Imperative are so abstract and general as to be of little value when trying to decide what to do in concrete moral situations. It is true that they do not provide a sufficient guide, but general moral principles such as the Golden Rule are nevertheless valuable. As Dewey noted, they tell us what to consider when trying to decide what to do. The Golden Rule counsels us to adopt an attitude of wide sympathy, of concern for the interests of all others involved in the situation, of open-mindedness and fairness. Without such attitudes pragmatism's experimental methods of moral evaluation lack orientation and direction. Dewey himself argued that in morals neither emotion nor reason by itself is sufficient. What is needed, he argued, is "intelligent sympathy"—in other words, respect for the Golden Rule coupled with instrumental rationality.[17]

In addition, a global ethic has been nurtured in an especially important way via the post–World War II development of international law. Certain fundamental ethical principles underlie international law. Intergovernmental declarations and treaties often explicitly affirm such principles in carefully crafted language. For example, the Charter of the United Nations, which was adopted by the fifty nations founding the organization in 1945, sets forth a set of shared ethical values. The ideal ends to which these nations committed themselves include the following: living together in peace as good neighbors; ensuring that future generations are saved from the scourge of war; tolerance; respect for the fundamental human rights and freedoms of all men and women and of all nations, large and small, without discrimination on the basis of race or religion; promotion of the economic and social advancement of all peoples; and respect for law, including international law. The experience of two world wars and a pragmatist emphasis on the consequences of failing to establish new levels of international collaboration for peace and justice guided the development of both the United Nations and its charter.

The implementation of the ideals of peace, human rights, and equitable socioeconomic development is an enormously difficult task, and greed, hatred, and self-interest often defeat humanity's noblest efforts. Nonetheless, these considerations should not be used to belittle or reject the consensus reached in 1945. They should only intensify our efforts on behalf of these values.

The development of human-rights law is particularly significant. For most people in the latter half of the twentieth century, the Golden Rule has come to mean first and foremost respect for human rights and fundamental freedoms. The human-rights language used in the Universal Declaration of Human Rights, adopted by the UN General Assembly in 1948, and in the international human-rights conventions that have followed it has become part of our secondary language—part of a universal moral vocabulary. It is used widely throughout the world in national constitutions, legislation, and judicial systems. All educated people know in general what it means.

The Universal Declaration of Human Rights explicitly seeks to articulate a common faith for the whole "human family." Its preamble states that the member nations reaffirm "their faith in fundamental human rights, in the dignity and worth of the human person and in the equal rights of men and women" as "the foundation of freedom, justice and peace in the world." The declaration states that its purpose is to build and promote "a common understanding of" and "universal respect for" these fundamental rights and freedoms. The human-rights code that has been developed over the past fifty years in international law is the most highly developed aspect of the emerging global ethics. Human-rights law is especially significant because in and through the collaborative process of developing it, humanity has been working to define the fundamental social, civil, political, and economic conditions necessary for the development of human personality and the building of community.

The debate concerning these matters is, of course, not over. Some state governments want to revise the Universal Declaration of Human Rights. There are ongoing debates about the relative importance of civil and political rights on the one hand and social, economic, and cultural rights on the other. The rights of women are a matter of ongoing debate in many cultures, and the international understanding of women's rights continues to evolve.

The field of environmental protection and restoration is another area where global ethics are being developed effectively. When the United Nations was founded in the 1940s, there was no mention of ecological security as an essential component of world security. However, this began to change with the Stockholm Conference on the Human Environment in 1972. Over the past three decades the environment has become an increasingly important part of the UN agenda. Furthermore, there has been a growing recognition that the goals of peace, respect for human rights, socioeconomic development, and environmental conservation are interdependent and indivisible. For example, war undermines efforts at environmental protection, and the depletion of resources and environmental degradation can cause violent conflict. Poverty is both a cause and a consequence of environmental degradation. The concern for human rights and the environment overlap, because people have a right to an environment adequate for their health, dignity, and well-being. The protection of people's rights to a healthy environment is called environmental justice.

A survey of forty international declarations, charters, treaties, and related international reports reveals an emerging international consensus around forty-five fundamental principles related to the environment.[18] At the heart of this international movement is a call for a global partnership in support of environmental conservation and sustainable development. The major agreements that lay the foundation for this alliance are found in the declarations and treaties that came out of the Rio Earth Summit in 1992, including the Rio Declaration and Agenda 21, a treaty that sets forth in forty chapters an international agenda for achieving sustainable development in the twenty-first century.[19]

Since the Rio Earth Summit an international effort led by Maurice Strong, the secretary general of the 1992 Earth Summit, and Mikhail Gorbachev, the former president of the Soviet Union, has been focused on drafting and circulating an "Earth Charter" that sets forth fundamental ethical principles for protecting the environment and building a just, sustainable, and peaceful world. An Earth Charter Commission directs this initiative, and its secretariat is located at the United Nations University for Peace, in San José, Costa Rica.

Between 1994 and 2000 consultations on the Earth Charter were conducted throughout the world involving grassroots communities, nongovernmental organizations, international law experts, scientists, religious leaders, business groups, and government representatives. Hundreds of organizations and thousands of individuals participated. A number of draft charters were circulated as the consultations progressed. The project involved the most open and inclusive process ever undertaken in connection with the creation of an international declaration. In March 2000 the Earth Charter Commission approved a final version of the charter, and several months later it was launched by the commission at the Peace Palace in The Hague. The mission of the Earth Charter is to establish a sound ethical foundation for the emerging global society and to help build a sustainable world based on respect for nature, environmental conservation, universal human rights, economic justice, and a culture of peace.[20]

The Earth Charter was drafted in and through a nongovernmental process as a people's treaty, but it is the hope that it will be used and implemented by business and government as well as civil society. It has now been widely circulated throughout the world and translated into twenty-eight languages. Over 8,000 nongovernmental organizations and hundreds of cities in all regions of the world have endorsed the document. UNESCO and some national governments are beginning to use it in educational programs and as a guide to sustainable development. In the United States alone, over 700 nongovernmental organizations spread over forty-eight states have endorsed the Earth Charter, and it is estimated that these organizations have a membership of over forty million citizens. In addition, the document has been endorsed by the U.S. Conference of Mayors and a growing number of individual cities, including Seattle, Wash.; Minneapolis, Minn.; Philadelphia, Pa.; and Burlington, Vt.[21]

The development of a global ethic for environmental protection and sustainable living is a new challenge for humanity. In constructing this ethic, it is possible to draw on a variety of religious and philosophical traditions that have taught respect for nature and reverence for all life, but the message and record of the world's religious and philosophical traditions on this subject is, with few exceptions, mixed. Furthermore, the present challenge requires new forms of long-range, integrated, and global thinking that humanity has only recently begun to explore with the aid of new developments in physics and ecology. Consistent with the method of pragmatism, construction of an ethic that conserves the health and diversity of ecosystems and the integrity of the planetary biosphere must look to science for guidance. Ecology demonstrates that human beings are interdependent members of the larger community of life as well as members of the human community. This suggests the idea of an ecological ethic that, in the words of Aldo Leopold, "changes the role of *Homo Sapiens* from conqueror of the land community to plain member and citizen of it."[22] An ecological ethic means nothing less than an expansion of humanity's moral concerns to embrace not only all peoples and future generations but also the whole community of life. For this we need an inclusive, democratic, ecological vision that integrates compassion with experimental knowledge in new ways.

The Earth Charter attempts to express this new vision. The general idea that pervades the charter is succinctly expressed in a sentence from its preamble: "In the midst of a magnificent diversity of cultures and life forms, we are one human family and one Earth community with a common destiny." The core message found in the principles of the charter is affirmed in two imperatives: respect Earth and all life and accept shared responsibility for the well-being of the human family as a whole, the greater community of life, and future generations. The call for respect involves the notion that Earth in its wholeness, each species, and all living beings possess intrinsic value and warrant moral consideration as ends in themselves, quite apart from whatever utilitarian value they may have for people. We must and may responsibly use nature, but the Earth Charter is based on the assumption that only a radical expansion of humanity's sense of community and moral responsibility to include nature will lead to the changes in human behavior required to protect the environment, secure environmental justice for all people, and ensure the well-being of future generations. The Earth Charter presents an integrated vision that recognizes that peace, social justice, socioeconomic development, and ecological well-being are inextricably linked. Caring for people requires caring for Earth, and caring for Earth requires caring for people. We will go forward into the twenty-first century as one community of life and family of human cultures, or we will bring disaster on ourselves and the other life forms with which we have coevolved on this planet.

The Challenge to the Religions

Without the full cooperation and support of the world's religions, it will not be possible to develop and implement the global ethics that are essential to the building of a world community. Many people throughout the world continue to look to religion for moral guidance and will only embrace an ethic that has the support of their religion. The challenge to the religions is to cooperate in building a genuine world community that is inclusive of all nations, races, religions, species, and ecosystems. This means that they must participate in creating a global ethics and strengthen commitment to the principles of this common faith within their distinctive religious and moral frameworks.

To meet this challenge, the religions must undergo a democratic and ecological reconstruction. They must rethink their theology and ethics in the context of global interdependence in a multicultural world. The democratic reconstruction of the religions has been going on for two hundred years, but resistance remains strong in many quarters. At a minimum, it requires tolerance, acceptance of pluralism, and respect for religious freedom and human rights. The ecological reconstruction is just beginning.[23] Both these creative movements are leading the religions to rethink their visions of community and of the future.

The most difficult and critical task facing the religions is to go beyond tolerance to dialogue and to embrace the ideal of a community of the religions living in harmony with nature that can serve as an inspiring model of global community for the world's nations and peoples. Only if they are able to accomplish this objective will the religions be in a position to provide humanity with the spiritual leadership that it urgently needs at this critical stage in its evolution.

In her recent book *Encountering God: A Spiritual Journey from Bozeman to Benares,* Diana Eck explains that the religions have three basic options regarding the attitudes they can adopt toward one another.[24] The first is a form of exclusivist thinking: one faith and tradition is true, and all others are false. Such exclusivism breeds fear and hatred, however, and often leads to violence. The second option is an inclusivist standpoint: one faith and tradition is both the culmination of humanity's religious development and the supreme religion, but it includes elements of truth found in other religions. The inclusivist view may encourage tolerance, but it also engenders arrogance and justifies cultural imperialism.

A third option is the pluralist view: the truth is not the exclusive possession of any one tradition, and no one tradition has a final inclusive vision of the divine. In other words, no one perspective is absolute. At best each tradition has only a partial understanding of God or the divine. From this perspective, the diversity of religious traditions and visions of God is not an obstacle to be overcome but an opportunity for dialogue and new understanding. This approach leads to the building of a community of the religions.

Dialogue does not mean abandoning one's commitments but rather expanding those commitments to include engagement with others, collaborative inquiry, and loyalty to the whole human family and the Earth community.

If the religions are able to move in these directions, they are in a unique position to encourage and cultivate in humanity a number of universal spiritual attitudes and values that can only deepen humanity's common faith and the bonds of community. These include a sense of wonder and awe before the mystery of being, which can deepen into a sense of the sacredness of all life; a sense of gratitude for the gift of life on Earth; a sense of unconditional responsibility to do what is good; an awareness of the depth and complexity of the problem of evil; a spirit of humility that can curb the excesses of individualism, nationalism, androcentrism, religious pride, and anthropocentrism; and a spirit of forgiveness. All these values are fully consistent with the democratic spirit. They nurture, sustain, and enlarge it. Further, these attitudes and values can be productively integrated with the spirit of experimentalism, but this involves wrestling with complex problems about the nature of revelation.

It is also important to note that the world's great religious traditions include methods of prayer and meditation that are designed to heal the human spirit and promote the growth and transformation of consciousness, nurturing positive spiritual and moral attitudes. Inner healing and transformation are a necessary part of the whole process of social reconstruction and ecological restoration. The religions have a critical role to play in this matter.

Conclusion

In conclusion, as we struggle on the local and national level to sustain and reconstruct our communities, which are often severely stressed, we must now also work to build a global community. In a world where the local and the global are interdependent, the two tasks are related and can be mutually reinforcing. Building a world community can create a secure framework within which our many other communities and associations can flourish. Developing a common moral faith and commitment to it are fundamental to the task of creating world community. The American pragmatist tradition, with its vision of a common faith and its emphasis on spiritual democracy and experimentalism, has much to offer in support of this endeavor. A global ethics adequate to the challenges of the twenty-first century must integrate the ethics of democracy with a new ecological ethics, and the experimental method of moral valuation developed by the pragmatists can be used effectively to advance this endeavor. The support of the world religions is also needed, and their willingness and ability to work together in building a global ethics will grow with the acceptance of pluralism.

Notes

1. Vaclav Havel, "The New Measure of Man," *New York Times*, July 8, 1994.

2. On the urgent need for a global ethics, see Hans Küng, *Global Responsibility: In Search of a New Global Ethic* (New York: Crossroad, 1991), 22; and Samuel P. Huntington, *The Clash of Civilizations and the Remaking of World Order* (New York: Simon and Schuster, 1996), 318–21.

3. See Aldo Leopold, *A Sand County Almanac* (New York: Oxford University Press, 1996), 239. Leopold writes that "the extension of ethics" to the biotic community is "an evolutionary possibility and an ecological necessity."

4. As cited in Roderick Frazier Nash, *The Rights of Nature: A History of Environmental Ethics* (Madison: University of Wisconsin Press, 1989), 44. See Charles Darwin, *The Descent of Man and Selection in Relation to Sex* (New York, 1874), 137–38, 140–41.

5. John Dewey, "Creative Democracy—The Task before Us," in *The Later Works of John Dewey, 1925–1953*, vol. 14, ed. Jo Ann Boydston (Carbondale: Southern Illinois University Press, 1988), 228.

6. For a good overview of Dewey's experimental approach to moral valuation, see John Dewey, *The Quest for Certainty*, in *The Later Works of John Dewey, 1925–1953*, vol. 4, ed. Jo Ann Boydston (Carbondale: Southern Illinois University Press, 1984), 203–28.

7. John Dewey, *A Common Faith*, in *The Later Works of John Dewey, 1925–1953*, vol. 9, ed. Jo Ann Boydston (Carbondale: Southern Illinois University Press, 1986), 13–15. For a more complete discussion of Dewey's thinking on the subject of faith, religion, and religious experience, see Steven C. Rockefeller, "John Dewey's Philosophy of Religious Experience," in *Reading Dewey*, ed. Larry Hickman (Bloomington: Indiana University Press, 1998); and Steven C. Rockefeller, *John Dewey: Religious Faith and Democratic Humanism* (New York: Columbia University Press, 1991), chapters 10 and 11.

8. John Dewey, "Religion and Morality in a Free Society," in *The Later Works of John Dewey, 1925–1953*, vol. 15, ed. Jo Ann Boydston (Carbondale: Southern Illinois University Press, 1986), 183.

9. Dewey, *A Common Faith*, 57–58.

10. Hans Küng and Karl-Josef Kuschel, *A Global Ethic: The Declaration of the Parliament of the World's Religions* (New York: Continuum, 1993), 7.

11. William Vendley, "The Multi-Religious Engagement of Civil Society: The Universal Need for Bilingualism," paper presented at the Symposium on Religion and Global Governance, sponsored by Global Education Associates, Maryknoll, New York, May 3–7, 1997.

12. Michael Walzer, *Thick and Thin: Moral Argument at Home and Abroad* (Notre Dame, Ind.: University of Notre Dame Press, 1994), 1–19.

13. Daniei Gomez-Ibañez, "Moving Towards a Global Ethic," *A SourceBook for Earth's Community of Religions*, ed. Joel D. Beversluis (Grand Rapids, Mich.: CoNexus; New York: Global Education Associates, 1995), 124–30.

14. New English Bible, Matt. 7:12.

15. His Holiness the Dalai Lama, *The Dalai Lama: A Policy of Kindness*, ed. Sidney Piburn (Ithaca, N.Y.: Snow Lion, 1990), 88.

16. "Declaration Toward a Global Ethic," in *Yes to a Global Ethic*, ed. Hans Küng (New York: Continuum, 1996), 9–26.

17. Rockefeller, *John Dewey*, 243, 419.

18. Steven C. Rockefeller, *Principles of Environmental Conservation and Sustainable Development: Summary and Survey*, 1996. Prepared and privately printed for the Earth Council, Costa Rica, and the Earth Charter Project. The text is available on the international Earth Charter Web site: <http://www.earthcharter.org>.

19. *Agenda 21: Programme of Action for Sustainable Development* (New York: United Nations Publications, 1992). See also Nicholas A. Robinson, ed., *Agenda 21: Earth's Action Plan Annotated* (New York: Oceana Publications, 1993).

20. The text of the Earth Charter and information about the Earth Charter Initiative may be found on the Earth Charter international Web site, <http://www.earthcharter.org> and on the Earth Charter USA Web site, <http://www.earthcharterusa.org.>

21. Ibid.

22. Leopold, *Sand County Almanac*, 240.

23. For examples of the way philosophers and theologians are approaching the task of ecological reconstruction, see Steven C. Rockefeller and John Elder, eds., *Spirit and Nature* (Boston: Beacon, 1992); and John E. Carroll, Paul Brockelman, and Mary Westfall, eds., *The Greening of Faith: God, the Environment, and the Good Life* (Hanover, N.H.: University Press of New England, 1997).

24. Diana L. Eck, *Encountering God: A Spiritual Journey from Bozeman to Benares* (Boston: Beacon, 1993), 168.

Index

The University of Illinois Press
is a founding member of the
Association of American University Presses.

Composed in 10.5/13 Minion
with Minion display
by Jim Proefrock
at the University of Illinois Press
Manufactured by Cushing-Malloy, Inc.

University of Illinois Press
1325 South Oak Street
Champaign, IL 61820-6903
www.press.uillinois.edu